WITH

THE GAME PRODUCTION HANDBOOK

HEATHER CHANDLER

CHARLES RIVER MEDIA, INC.
Hingham, Massachusetts

Cover Design: Tyler Creative

CHARLES RIVER MEDIA, INC.
10 Downer Avenue
Hingham, Massachusetts 02043
781-740-0400
781-740-8816 (FAX)
info@charlesriver.com
www.charlesriver.com

This book is printed on acid-free paper.

Heather Chandler. *The Game Production Handbook.*
ISBN: 1-58450-416-1

Library of Congress Cataloging-in-Publication Data
Chandler, Heather Maxwell.
 The game production handbook / Heather Chandler.-- 1st ed.
     p. cm.
 Includes index.
 ISBN 1-58450-416-1 (pbk. : alk. paper)
 1. Computer games--Programming. I. Title.
 QA76.76.C672C446 2005
 794.8'1526--dc22
                         2005032961

Printed in Canada
05 7 6 5 4 3 2 First Edition

CHARLES RIVER MEDIA titles are available for site license or bulk purchase by institutions, user groups, corporations, etc. For additional information, please contact the Special Sales Department at 781-740-0400.

Dedicated to
Mom, Andy, Collier, Rafael, Malcolm, and Panda.
I couldn't have done this again without your help!

Contents

Foreword

The role of producer is often overlooked, not just in the game press but even, sometimes, within the game industry itself. The stars of the video game industry are its lead programmers, lead artists, and lead designers—certainly not its producers. After all, who is the producer but the person who leads and manages the project? And how boring is that?

When a project succeeds, resulting in a highly successful product, it's the team or the star who gets the glory. When a project fails, though, it's the producer who gets the blame.

There is much more to the role of producer than one might think. Producing is not only about managing a schedule or crunching numbers in a budget. The producer usually shares in the vision of the game's design, ever mindful of how that game must appeal to the game-buying public. The producer has to be able to talk the talk with programmers and marketing people, to talk the talk with executives and testers, to talk the talk with artists and salesmen. The producer needs to be conversant with the legalese of contracts and the puffery of ad campaigns. The producer can reduce a huge game design down to a few bullet points or expand a germ of an idea into a lengthy manifesto.

Both good cop and bad cop, both parent and teacher, the producer plays a number of roles donning a number of different hats, throughout the production of a game project. The producer is truly the person in the middle—the focal point for all communication, coordination, and management in the creating of a game.

The producer, at one point or another, will be in touch with all kinds of people in the lifecycle of a game. From the business executive who obtained the IP rights to do a licensed game, to the designer who'll turn it into a game design. From the studio VP who assigns the producer to the project, to the customer support rep who'll field end-user queries about installation problems. From the movie star who lends her voice to the game, to moms and grandmothers who buy games for their kids. From the distributor who wants to know why he should give shelf space to this game instead of that other game, to the junior programmer who's upset that his idea didn't get implemented in the game. From the tester who's found an obscure yet fatal bug, to the freelance artist who wants a sexier credit listing in the game. The producer has to be diplomatic, persuasive, compromising, unyielding, hardnosed, and friendly.

Yet, as important as the producer is to the success of a project, it often happens that the producer receives no training whatsoever for the job. He usually starts by being thrown into the deep end of the pool without formal management training. He is promoted into the role and is expected to learn by doing, to learn by osmosis, or to just know what to do intuitively. Our beloved industry sees the importance of training for its programmers, artists, lawyers, and marketers—but not, so it seems, for its producers.

The widespread lack of producer training has resulted in many project meltdowns. Every year, the halls of the annual Game Developers Conference (GDC) resound with horror stories of projects gone awry. Postmortems are written only about projects that get finished, so the very worst war stories usually go undocumented in the literature.

The industry might not train you. But this book should help. Heather Maxwell Chandler is one of the good ones. She's been there, done that. She knows whereof she speaks. Read this book all the way through and keep it nearby as a handy reference.

Tom Sloper
Game Designer, Producer, Consultant
Sloperama Productions—*www.sloperama.com*

Preface

Twenty years ago, game production was a lot less complicated. Often just one person, in as little as six weeks, would design, write code, generate art assets, and test the functionality of a single game. Back then, a few blocky characters and great gameplay entertained people for hours, which made it easy for one person to perform all the game development tasks. These days, people expect games to deliver more than great gameplay; they want a totally immersive world with living, breathing characters, high-quality sound, compelling storylines, and a game that evokes emotions such as fear, surprise, happiness, and even sadness. For a game to live up to those expectations, many more people must be involved in the game's production.

Managing the production of games in the 21st century is a challenge, especially since there is no standardized process to ensure the successful completion of every game. Games that successfully make it to the shelves often hit many bumps along the way, and the producer and team members may be secretly amazed that the game got finished in spite of these obstacles. The good thing is that developers are getting better at game production, because they are learning from their mistakes and looking to other disciplines for methods to create a more efficient development process.

The purpose of this book is to bring some order to the chaotic world of the game producer. This book won't tell you how to design the next hit game or what cutting-edge technologies must be in the next iteration of the game. Instead, it focuses on the nuts and bolts of managing the development, which includes defining the game's goal, creating a plan to achieve this goal, effectively managing the people who make the game happen, and dealing with all the other bumps along the way.

Game production is not a science; you can't expect each game you work on to present the same challenges and rewards as the last game you worked on. However, common elements exist for every game development team, and improving upon these commonalities and anticipating new challenges is where a producer should focus his efforts.

This book is divided into eight sections, each providing key information about the game production process.

Part I: General Production Overview: This section presents a general overview of the production cycle and roles on the team. It concludes with a discussion of some traditional software development methodologies that are being applied to game production.

Part II: Business Information: This section discusses general legal information any producer must be aware of, as well as the relationship between the publisher and developer.

Part III: Managing People: This section discusses how to hire and retain talent, build teams, and effectively communicate. These skills are a must for any successful producer.

Part IV: Technical Production: This section discusses all the mini-projects that must be managed during production, including voiceover, marketing needs, and motion capture.

Part V: Pre-production: This section discusses all the decisions and planning that occur during pre-production, such as defining the game concept, game requirements, and game plan. A well-organized pre-production phase is a must for a successful production phase.

Part VI: Production: This section discusses all the work that must be managed during the production phase. It includes information on production techniques, the production cycle, age ratings, and localization.

Part VII: Testing: This section discusses how to test and code release games. It includes information on submitting games to Sony, Microsoft, and Nintendo for approval.

Part VIII: Post-Production: This section discusses how to successfully wrap up your project by doing a closing kit and conducting a postmortem with the team.

In addition, several industry insiders were interviewed about their game production experiences, and they have generously offered advice and information that anyone involved in game production will find valuable. You'll find their biographies in Appendix C, "Interviewee Biographies," along with a list of additional resources and books to use for further research in Appendix B, "Resources."

Enjoy the book!

Heather Chandler

heather@mediasunshine.com

Acknowledgments

First, I want to thank Jenifer Niles for working with me on this book. As always, she provided encouragement and helpful advice. Second, I want to thank Tom Sloper for writing the Foreword.

Special thanks to all the people who agreed to be interviewed for this book; the interviews all provide unique looks into the game production process.

A big thank you to my husband for his assistance on this project. He was always there to provide snacks and help whenever it was needed, even in the wee hours of the morning.

Finally, I want to thank my friends and family. This is the second time I've had to spend all my free time writing a book instead of spending time with them. They were very understanding and supportive throughout this process again.

Part

I

General Production Overview

Some people may wonder exactly what a producer's responsibilities are on a game production team. Since they are not usually content creators, they don't contribute assets directly to the game. However, a game without a producer is likely to never see the store shelves.

A producer is the main driving force that guides the game development process to ensure that the work gets done on time and under budget. In addition, the producer leads the team and keeps them motivated during stressful times. The producer also acts a buffer between the development team and all the external forces that are trying to interfere with the team: marketing, the publisher, and licensors.

This section is an introduction to the general game development process and provides basic explanations on what goes on during development and how a development team functions. In addition, information is presented on some software development methodologies that have recently been applied to game development. Topics include the following:

- Game Production Overview
- Roles on the Team
- Formal Production Processes

1 Game Production Overview

INTRODUCTION

If you are a newly minted producer or lead, you probably are wondering what you've gotten yourself into. The burden of responsibility for getting a game created and code released rests squarely on your shoulders. Although you will get a lot of assistance along the way from your boss, your publisher, and your team, you need to understand the game production process and how all the variables fit together. These days, as budgets are rising and teams are getting larger, it is more imperative that the producers and leads responsible for a project have a solid understanding of the game production process and how to modify it to fit the needs of their games.

The production process begins with defining the initial concept and ends with creating a gold master of the final game code, with everything else happening in-between. The game production process differs from project to project, which is one reason why game production can be challenging to manage. One developer has a small team of 15 people working on Web-based games, but another developer has more than 100 people working on a next-generation console game based on a well-known movie license.

Regardless of the size of the team, scope of the game, the budget, or anything else, a basic framework exists for the overall production process. The process can be broken down into four broad phases: pre-production, production, testing, and post-production. Within each of these phases, several goals must be accomplished before moving on to the next phase. Anyone involved in game production must have a general understanding of these phases, since the successful completion of each one directly affects the successful release of the game.

PRODUCTION CYCLE

Figure 1.1 is a diagram of the basic production cycle. The specific game production tasks such as recording voiceover, creating character models, and debugging multiplayer code are not indicated, since these tasks will vary from project to project. The diagram depicts the general goals of each phase and how the success of each

PRE-PRODUCTION CHECKLIST	Y / N	NOTES
CONCEPT		
Is initial game concept defined?		
Are platform and genre specified?		
Is mission statement completed?		
Are basic game play elements defined?		
Is protoype completed?		
Is risk analysis completed?		
Is the concept pitch ready for approval?		
Have all stakeholders approved the concept?		
Is project kick-off scheduled?		
GAME REQUIRMENTS		
Are "must have," "want to have," and "nice to have" features defined?		
Are constraints defined and accounted for in feature sets?		
Are milestones and deliverables defined?		
Has technology been evaluated against the desired feature set?		
Are tools and pipeline defined?		
Is basic design documentation completed?		
Is basic technical documentation completed?		
Is risk analysis completed?		
Have all stakeholder approved the game requirements?		
GAME PLAN		
Is budget completed?		

FIGURE 1.1   Basic game production cycle.

phase builds upon the completion of the previous phase. As you can see, detailing the project plan in pre-production is important as it provides a solid foundation upon which to build the game. A project that does not define a plan in pre-production is likely to encounter several problems that could have been avoided or prepared for in advance.

It is important to note that this diagram outlines a very basic view of the game production cycle and that some games, especially as the stakes get higher, will go through an iterative production process with numerous production cycles. For example, if you plan to create a working proof of concept for your game—a fully polished playable level—you will want to include a few game development cycles in the entire production process, with the first cycle consisting of pre-production, production, and testing of the prototype; the second phase focusing on the core set of features and assets for the game; and a third cycle creating and adding any "glitz" features and assets, such as extra levels. Figure 1.2 is a diagram of multiple production cycles for a single project.

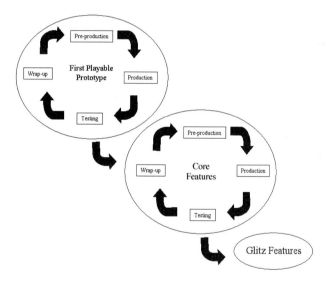

FIGURE 1.2 Multiple production cycles for a single project.

PRE-PRODUCTION

Pre-production is the first phase in the production cycle and is critical to defining what the game is, how long it will take to make, how many people are needed, and how much everything will cost. Pre-production can last anywhere from one week to a year or more, depending on how much time you have to complete the game. One rule of thumb is that pre-production requires about 10–25 percent of the total development time of a game. So if you are working on a six-month project, pre-production will last from a few weeks to about a month. If you are working on a two-year project, pre-production will last anywhere from two to six months. Of course these times will vary, but these estimates provide a good basis for planning the overall project.

The overriding goal of pre-production is to essentially create the game plan, which is basically a roadmap for how to get the game finished and code released. The plan must include information on the game's concept, the features and constraints that affect this concept, the basic technical and design documentation, and finally how much it will cost, how long it will take, and how many people will be needed. Pre-production can be broken down into the following components: concept, game requirements, game plan, and risk assessment.

Game Concept

Jim Lewis, author of numerous books on project management, suggests thinking about the concept as a solution to a problem that must be solved. Therefore, a game concept that starts off as a question presents a problem that can be solved. Would it be fun to play cowboys and Indians in space? What would it be like to race concept cars? After the game's initial concept is determined, usually by studio management or your publisher, it is passed on to the development team as a problem they must solve.

Many concepts start off fuzzy, and the core development team must then flesh them out so that everyone can easily understand what the goals of the product are and what major game play elements are needed to support and strengthen it. For example, if you are working on a realistic tactical military shooter, it would not fit within the game world to use fictitious alien technology. The concept also defines the game genre and hardware platform, as these decisions will shape how the concept grows. When the concept is determined, you have to clearly communicate it to the rest of the team, so they understand it and can get excited about. This can be done by defining a mission statement.

A mission statement gets everyone excited about the game on which they are working. The mission statement answers what is going to be done and for whom it is being done. It is ideal to get the team members involved in defining the mission statement, because everyone can give their feedback and help shape the mission, which gives everyone a stake in the project. This sense of ownership is imperative to building a strong team. Keep in mind that the mission statement doesn't need to state "how" these things are going to be done, as the "how" is going to be addressed when the project plan is put together.

After determining the initial concept, start adding the basic game play elements to it. This includes initial thoughts on the game play mechanics, the control scheme, the genre, the story, the characters, and other hooks that will set the game apart from the competition. Prototyping the elements helps to further define the game experience. Prototypes can start off on paper, and as the ideas develop further, playable prototypes are created. If possible, try to create a polished prototype that will be representative of the final game play experience.

As these concepts are further detailed, conduct a risk analysis to determine what the game production's biggest risks are. At this point, several unknowns exist, so it will be difficult to determine specific risks. However, if a few constants are already defined, like the team size or technology, they can be used as the basis for an initial risk analysis. Risk analyses will be done throughout the project in every major phase of development. If you don't take time to define the development risks, you are likely to encounter unexpected problems on the project that could have been minimized if they were identified as risks earlier on.

After the concept is fully defined and a prototype is created, you pitch it to studio management and the publisher. This is their chance to see how the team has created a solid game from the initial concept. They will likely have feedback on the pitch, which needs to be incorporated by the team. If they like what they hear, they will approve the game for further pre-production. When this happens, the producer will organize an official project kick-off to present the fully approved concept to the team. Chapter 13, "Concept," discusses the concept phase in more detail. After the concept is defined, the next step is to figure out what the game's requirements are.

Game Requirements

The game requirements include the basic art, design, and engineering features that must be supported, any constraints on the project, and basic technical and design documentation. The features must all fit within the established concept and mission statement. It is important to involve the team in determining the core feature set and prioritizing the other features so they can develop a sense of ownership of the game. The feature set should include some unique elements that set it apart from other games. One way to do this is by having everyone list their "must have," "want to have," and "would be nice to have" features, discuss them, and then create a final prioritized feature set. Chapter 14, "Game Requirements," presents one method for doing this.

Constraints should be factored in when determining the feature set priorities. For example, everyone can agree that building a new graphics engine is a must-have feature, but if there is not ample time to do this, this feature will be dropped down to a "would be nice" feature and the team must figure out other ways to achieve the graphics goals for the game.

Basic project constraints are time and resources. If the game started development in January and must be ready to ship by Christmas, the time limitation for the project is about 9 months. On top of that, if only 15 people can be assigned to the team, a resource constraint is now created. The constraints are what make game development challenging.

After the feature set is defined and fit within the constraints, the milestones and deliverables for each milestone are defined. Some projects are scheduled around monthly milestones, and other projects are scheduled around first playable, alpha, and beta milestones. Either method will work, as long as what deliverables are expected at each milestone are clearly defined and published to the team. Deliverables refer to elements in the game, such as art assets, technical features, and level scripting, that demonstrate game play and the look and feel of the game universe.

While the feature set is being defined, technology is researched to figure out what works best for the proposed game. This includes looking at the hardware constraints, exploring middleware solutions, and evaluating any suitable internal technologies. In addition, thought must be given to what tools are needed to create the game assets and the best way to establish a production pipeline.

As all of these elements are more defined, the team must create some basic technical and design documentation focusing on the core aspects of the game. As illustrated in Figure 1.2, games can be comprised of several production cycles, so this documentation must focus on fleshing out the current production cycle. The documentation details are added to the core features as pre-production continues, so that by the time production begins, everyone has the information they need to begin their work. Finally, conduct a risk analysis at this stage to determine what the game's biggest risks are so far.

When the game requirements are determined, all the decision-makers in the process should review and sign off on them. This includes studio management, the publisher, and even marketing. Along with the development team, these groups also have a stake in the project and want to make sure that their best interests are considered during the requirements phase. As people review the documentation, they will have feedback that will likely affect the constraints. It is a good idea to centralize all the feedback, determine what can be incorporated, and then send the revised plan for everyone to review again.

It may be difficult to get everyone on board with the requirements, especially if the groups are at different geographical locations. In cases like this, the producer will want to schedule a time and place where everyone can meet together (either in person or via conference call) to come to a consensus and finalize the requirements. Please refer to Chapter 14, "Game Requirements," for more information.

Game Plan

The game plan is where all of the information is pulled together to show how everything will be accomplished. The producer spearheads the effort to prepare the budget, schedule, and staffing needs for the game, but he must work with the team to determine them. If the producer does not consult with the core development team, especially when it comes to schedule and staffing, it will be hard to get the team members to buy into the game plan. This is especially true if the schedule is extremely aggressive and the producer is counting on everyone to work at their highest level of productivity. Refer to Chapter 15, "Game Plan," for details on creating budgets, schedules, and staffing plans.

When the budget, schedule, and staffing plan are assembled, the team reviews them to make sure they can achieve the desired game requirements. If not, the plan or the game requirements might need to be amended. In fact, the game requirements and game plan are both updated whenever something changes on the project. Don't forget to conduct another risk analysis and have all the stakeholders review the plan as well.

Pre-Production Checklist

Figure 1.3 is a pre-production checklist you can use to track your progress during this phase.

PRE-PRODUCTION CHECKLIST	Y/N	NOTES
CONCEPT		
Is initial game concept defined?		
Are platform and genre specified?		
Is mission statement completed?		
Are basic game play elements defined?		
Is protoype completed?		
Is risk analysis completed?		
Is the concept pitch ready for approval?		
Have all stakeholders approved the concept?		
Is project kick-off scheduled?		
GAME REQUIREMENTS		
Are "must have," "want to have," and "nice to have" features defined?		
Are constraints defined and accounted for in feature sets?		
Are milestones and deliverables defined?		
Has technology been evaluated against the desired feature set?		
Are tools and pipeline defined?		
Is basic design documentation completed?		
Is basic technical documentation completed?		
Is risk analysis completed?		
Have all stakeholders approved the game requirements?		
GAME PLAN		
Is budget completed?		
Is initial schedule completed?		
Is initial staffing plan completed?		
Have core team members approved the schedule and staffing plan?		

FIGURE 1.3   Pre-production checklist.

PRODUCTION

The production phase is when the team can actually begin producing assets and code for the game. In most cases, the line between pre-production and production is fuzzy, as you will be able to start production on some features while some features will still be in pre-production. This start of the production phase is also affected by any checks and balances that the publisher or studio management has in place. For example, the team might be unable to begin full production until a playable prototype has been created and approved.

If everything is planned for during pre-production, the production phase should have no surprises; of course, this is rarely the case. After your team has started full production, there is a high chance that some feature or asset will need to be added, changed, or removed. However, if you have a tiered implementation strategy that focuses on getting the core features and assets completed first, it is easier to plan for unexpected changes.

The production phase is focused on content and code creation, tracking progress, and completing tasks. In addition, risk assessment is ongoing during production, so you are prepared for any unexpected events that negatively impact the game's production cycle. Production is loosely categorized into the following phases: plan implementation, tracking progress, and task completion.

Plan Implementation

Plan implementation requires the producer to communicate the final plan to the team and provide them all the tools and resources needed to implement it. Make the plan publicly available to the team in a format that is easily accessible, such as a team Web site or designated area on the network. Include all the documents created in the pre-production phase, with the schedule and milestones in a clearly visible place. It is also helpful to post hard copies of key deadlines throughout the team rooms.

When the plan is communicated to the team, you, as the producer, must be vigilant about keeping everything in the plan up to date. If a feature design, milestone deadline, or asset list changes, it must be accurately noted in the game plan and communicated to the team, studio management, and possibly the publisher. Making these changes in a timely manner is important, because everyone is using the project plan as the main point of reference. If the plan is not updated throughout the production process, it is likely that features will be overlooked, or the wrong features will be implemented.

Feature creep, the inevitable problem of new features being added to the project during the actual production phase, usually happens because things are changing on a regular basis. Someone will think of a great idea for the game and will want to add it to the feature set without thinking of the impact this will have on the game's schedule or resources. Feature creep is not good for the project as a whole, because every time a new feature is added, more resources must be allocated to design, implement, create assets for, and test the new feature. This means that the resources already in use will be stretched to the limit and adding extra features might cause the game to miss an all-important code release deadline. If feature creep is not controlled during production, the game will quickly run out of time and resources. Of course, this can be avoided if you keep a tight control on feature creep. Chapter 17, "Production Techniques," has more information on how to control feature creep.

After the game plan is implemented, art, design, engineering, and testing are even more dependent on each other for completing tasks. If the artists are waiting on design for the details of a specific level design, they may be in a holding pattern if this documentation is not ready. If the cinematics team is waiting for final voiceover files from the sound engineer, it will delay their work and put the final deadline for the cinematics at risk. As the producer, you are responsible for working with your leads to quickly resolve any task dependencies. In some situations, the cinematics team might be able to do other work while waiting for the voiceover files, and so on. Tracking progress helps the producer, and leads can identify bottlenecks in the production process.

Tracking Progress

Tracking progress against the game plan is critical to knowing where the game is at any given time in production. If you don't have a plan to track against, your game will quickly get out of control, and you will find yourself in an unpleasant situation. If you don't know how much longer it takes to complete a feature, or how much of the feature is already completed, how can you know whether the game team is on track to meet their deadlines?

Progress tracking does not have to be complicated. In fact, the more complicated it is, the more unlikely people will do it. For example, you might decide to track the progress in Microsoft Project, and if you are an expert in using this software, it will be very easy for you. However, if you don't know how to use the tracking features in Microsoft Project, you might avoid tracking the progress altogether. In any case, you must implement a method that will work for you and the team, as they also need to be aware of what progress has been made. One simple way to do this is to create checklists or to track tasks in Microsoft Excel. Chapter 15, "Game Plan," has more details on how to track tasks during production.

Task Completion

Task completion in most areas of game development is fairly straightforward, especially when the work results in a tangible asset, as with art and design assets.

Determining when engineering tasks are completed is difficult, since there are no hard indicators regarding when a piece of code is complete, especially when bug fixes can always be made to the code.

Defining exit criteria is a good way for a producer or lead to more accurately determine when a task is complete. Exit criteria are conditions that must be met before a task is deemed finished. For example, a design document is complete after it is written and approved; a character model is complete after the artist adds the final texture to it.

The exit criteria must be easily understood by everyone, especially the person who is actually doing the task. For a task that is difficult to define criteria for, the producer can meet with the appropriate team member to determine what the exit criteria are. If you are an independent developer working for a publisher, the exit criteria for the major milestone deliverables must be clearly spelled out in the publisher-developer agreement.

Production Checklist

Figure 1.4 is a production checklist you can use to track your progress through the production phase.

PRODUCTION CHECKLIST	Y/N	NOTES
PLAN IMPLEMENTATION		
Is game plan clearly communicated to team?		
Is game plan in publicly accessible place?		
Can plan be easily updated with changes by producer?		
Does everyone on team have the necessary resources to do their work?		
Is process in place for controlling feature creep?		
Is risk assessment happening on a regular basis throughout production?		
Is process in place for managing task dependencies?		
PROGRESS TRACKING		
Is there a game plan to track progress against?		
Is process in place for producer to track all task progress?		
Is progress posted in visible areas in the team rooms?		
TASK COMPLETION		
Does each task have clearly defined exit criteria?		
Are these exit criteria publicly available to the team?		
Are all stakeholders in agreement on what the exit criteria are?		

FIGURE 1.4 Production checklist.

TESTING

Testing is a critical phase in game development. This is when the game gets checked to ensure that everything works correctly and that there are no crash bugs. Testing is ongoing during the production process, as the Quality Assurance (QA) department will check milestone builds, new functionality, and new assets as they become available in the game. After beta, when all the game assets and features are fully implemented, the main focus of the development team will be fixing bugs and creating new builds for QA to test. The testing phase can be considered as two parts: plan validation and code release. Chapter 21, "Testing," contains more detailed information on the testing process.

Plan Validation

The QA department's main responsibility is to write the test plan for the game and validate the game against this plan. The test plan is based on what assets and functionality are outlined in the game plan. If the game plan is not updated, QA cannot create the appropriate test plans. The producer and leads work closely with the QA department to make all the necessary information available to write accurate test plans. In addition, the QA department works with the development team to educate them on the testing process and how to use the bug-tracking software.

The game must be validated in all areas, and, depending on the size of the game, this can require a lot of testing time. For example, if working on a PC game that is localized into two languages, the QA testers need to check several PC configurations, with different operating systems, sound cards, and video cards. In addition, they must check each of the localized versions on these configurations.

The QA department is not only responsible for finding bugs, they are also responsible for regressing bugs that the development team has fixed. Usually a bug is not considered closed until the QA department has rechecked the bug in the game and verified that it is fixed.

Code Release

After a game has been thoroughly tested, the QA department will start the code release process. The code release process is different from normal QA testing, in that they are looking at code release candidates (CRC)—builds that the development teams considers ready to ship. At this point in production, all of the major bugs are fixed; the functionality is working as designed; and all the game assets are finalized. The game just needs one last set of checks to confirm that it is ready to be shipped to the manufacturer.

The producer must make time in the schedule for the code release process so that QA has ample time to make the final checks on a game. The time for this will differ, depending on the size of the game and the size of the QA department. Ideally, there is enough time for QA to run through the entire test plan on the CRC, which could take as little as a day or as long as a week. If they can complete the entire test plan and are confident everything checks out against the plan, the game is considered code released, and the disc can be shipped to the manufacturer for replication. Please refer to Chapter 22, "Code Releasing," for more details on this process.

If you are working on a console title, you will also need to submit the game to the console manufacturer for approval. They have their own checks and balances for each game, and if they do not approve a game, it is not manufactured until the problems are corrected and the game is resubmitted for approval. There is a chance that even if the developer's QA department code releases a game, it may not be approved by the console manufacturer. However, developers are usually given an opportunity to resubmit builds for approval until they get the final sign-off.

Testing Checklist

Figure 1.5 is a checklist to be used for the testing phase of a game.

TESTING CHECKLIST	Y/N	NOTES
VALIDATE PLAN		
Is test plan written?		
Is game plan updated for QA?		
Has test plan been updated with any changes to the game plan?		
Are testing milestones accounted for in the schedule?		
Is bug-tracking software available for the testers and development team?		
Are all areas of the game tested?		
Are all bugs regressed and closed?		
CODE RELEASE		
Has development team submitted a final code release candidate?		
Is there ample time in the schedule for QA to complete the test plan on the code release candidate?		
Has QA approved the product for code release?		
CONSOLE ONLY: Has code released game been submitted to console manufacturer for approval?		
CONSOLE ONLY: Has console manufacturer approved game for final replication?		

FIGURE 1.5   Testing checklist.

POST-PRODUCTION

After the game is code released and approved for manufacturing, the game development process needs to be wrapped up before it is officially completed. Many times, this step is forgotten or ignored, which is unfortunate. This is when the team can relax, prepare a closing kit for future projects, and review the pros and cons of their recent game development experience. The post-production phase consists of two things: learning from experience and archiving the plan.

Learn from Experience

Learning from experience is the best way to improve the game development process for future projects. One way to do this is by conducting a postmortem at the end of a project. A postmortem is a chance for everyone to review the good and bad on a project and to propose solutions based on these experiences for future projects.

As a producer, you plan to conduct "mini" postmortems at key points during development, such as alpha and beta. It is never too late to learn something about improving the process, even mid-project. Chapter 23, "Postmortems," provides details on how to conduct and publish a postmortem.

Archive Plan

After the game is code released, it is archived for use on future projects. This is done by creating a closing kit. This kit contains all the design documentation, source code, source art, final game assets, final music files, and everything else that was used to create the game.

Closing kits are necessary because the publisher may want to create a special version of the game to be bundled with a piece of hardware, or the development team might want to re-use the code or assets for another project. Closing kits are especially useful if your team works on a franchise and wants to base the next iteration of the franchise on the previous game's source code. Chapter 24, "Closing Kits," has more details on how to create and archive these kits.

Post-Production Checklist

Figure 1.6 is a post-production checklist for tracking your progress.

WRAP-UP CHECKLIST	Y/N	NOTES
ARCHIVE PLAN		
Is closing kit completed?		
LEARN FROM EXPERIENCE		
Is postmortem completed?		
Is postmortem published to the entire development studio?		

FIGURE 1.6   Post-production checklist.

SUMMARY

The game production process can be challenging for a producer to manage, but if it is approached methodically, these challenges can be minimized. This chapter presented an overview of the general game production process from the producer's point of view. General information was given about pre-production, production, testing, and post-production on a project. These areas are presented in more detail in subsequent chapters in this book. The next chapter provides a general overview of the roles on a production team, which should be viewed in the context of the general game production process.

2 Roles on the Team

In This Chapter

- Production
- Art
- Engineering
- Design
- Quality Assurance Testing
- Team Organization
- Corporate

INTRODUCTION

In order to better understand the production cycle, it is important to know what types of roles are normally found on a game development team. Obviously, the roles vary from team to team, depending on the project needs, the company size, and the scope of a project. For example, if you're working on a cell phone game, your team might be four people who all fulfill multiple roles on the project. But if you're working on a next-generation console game, your team might have more than 80 people, with each person assigned a specific role on the project.

This chapter discusses the general roles available on a development team and how the teams are organized. In addition, nonproduction roles such as sales and marketing are discussed. For more in-depth information on roles and job descriptions, please refer to *Get in the Game!* by Marc Mencher.

Wade Tinney and Coray Seifert, Large Animal Games

If you are working in game production, you need to have a deep understanding of games and why people play them. It's amazing to us how many people, who don't play games, apply for jobs at a game company. Would you apply for a job at a film studio if you didn't watch movies on a regular basis? One must not only play games, but also think critically about them. If you don't understand interactivity and how a given set of choices affects a player's game experience, it's unlikely that you'll be able to effectively contribute to the development team. This ability to think critically about gameplay is especially important for producers and designers.

Aspiring game developers must also be able to interact constructively with other members of a creative team. Gone are the days when a commercial game could be created by a single person. It is now imperative for developers to understand the importance of teamwork in creating a successful product. Even team experience from other creative industries is a good start; if you have experience working collaboratively on a film project, for example, or even on a school project, that experience can help prepare you for the game industry.

In addition, you must have the discipline to complete your tasks within tight deadlines, without handholding, and in many cases, with fewer resources then you would really like. Frequently, smaller development teams depend on each member to wear many different hats and do whatever it takes to get the game done. This can include designing parts of the game, making decisions on budgets and schedules, or even creating art assets. If you are able to quickly adapt to situations like these, you will be right at home making games.

PRODUCTION

Production roles run the gamut from production coordinator to executive producer. People involved in game production are focused on managing and tracking the game's development and are the main intermediary between the development team and anyone external to the team, even studio management. Those in production roles should try their best to keep the team happy, motivated, and productive. The production people aren't usually responsible for actually creating game assets; their main responsibility is to efficiently manage the people creating the content. This keeps the team's time focused on actually completing game tasks instead of tracking schedules, dealing with personnel issues, managing external vendors, negotiating contracts, proofreading marketing copy, and anything else external to creating game content.

Three basic production roles exist, although the names may vary from company to company:

■ Executive Producer
■ Producer
■ Associate Producer

Not all of these roles are necessary for a development team, so the responsibilities can shift for each role, depending on what the project requires.

Executive Producer

A executive producer (EP) is usually a producer with five to ten years of production experience. EPs most often oversee multiple projects, and their main function is to ensure that all the games in development are running smoothly and efficiently. They are focused on broader production tasks—researching hardware and middleware needs, establishing employee training programs, negotiating contracts, evaluating external vendors, and other things that will benefit future and current projects.

They normally report to the studio vice president or chief executive officer (CEO). They manage multiple producers and work with them individually to evaluate and implement solutions for potential problems on the projects. EPs are not involved with the day-to-day operations of the development team and do not communicate with the project leads on a regular basis, as that is the producer's responsibility.

Producer

The producer is typically a developer with three to five years of production experience and who has worked as an associate producer on several titles. The producer is usually in charge of a single game and the entire development team. The producer is one of the most visible people on the project, and is the team's representative to anyone outside the team. Their primary responsibility is to make sure that the game is delivered on time, on budget, with all the expected features, and at the highest quality possible, while keeping the team enthusiastically focused on their work. Although a producer is heavily involved with the project leads in making creative decisions, their main focus is on facilitating the development process, not on dictating the creative content and game features.

The producer reports to an executive producer or studio vice president and works closely with marketing, sales, operations, public relations (PR), studio management, creative services, legal, third-party console manufacturers, and external vendors. The producer also manages the game development plan, communicates it to the team, tracks it, and neutralizes any risks to the plan. Basically, a producer steers the development team toward completion.

Producers can focus on different areas, depending on the needs of the project and how the development team is structured. The most noticeable division in production roles can be seen when comparing a "publisher" producer with a "developer" producer.

A developer producer (DP) directly manages an internal development team. He or she works closely with the art, engineering, design, and quality assurance leads on the project. As a core team, the DP and leads work together to create the development plan and update it as necessary; the DP is also involved in the day-to-day production of the game. If working for an external publisher, the DP will communicate on a regular basis with the publisher producer. Figure 2.1 is a diagram of a DP's main points of contact.

FIGURE 2.1 Developer producer's main project contacts.

A publisher producer (PP) represents the publisher's interests and usually works with external developers. Rarely do they manage the actual development team, but instead, oversee other departments that are not directly involved in the internal game development cycle, such as sales, marketing, quality assurance, and localization. A PP can manage multiple projects, especially if they are not all scheduled to be released at the same time. Figure 2.2 is a diagram of the PP's main points of contact.

NOTE

An article in Secrets of the Game Business, Second Edition, *entitled "Producer, Friend or Foe" gives more details on the types of producers one may encounter on a project, such as a creative producer or a project manager.*

FIGURE 2.2   Publisher producer's main project contacts.

Associate Producer

An associate producer (AP) typically has one to three years of experience and may have started out in an entry-level development position, such as a quality assurance tester or production coordinator. The AP's primary responsibility is assisting the producer with any production-related tasks. A more experienced AP can also be in charge of producing a major aspect of the game, such as localizations, music and voiceover, cinematics, or open beta tests.

The associate producer reports directly to the producer and may be one of several on a project. They interact with the team on a day-to-day basis and may also be tasked to help the art, design, and engineering leads when necessary.

Background and Training

Because producers have a variety of backgrounds—some started out in game development and worked their way up, and others worked in a different industry and transferred to game development—there are no set guidelines for what skills a producer must possess. Some producers are more technical than others and work most effectively when focusing on ways to push the technology during game development, while others may be more effective at guiding the design features of the game. However, anyone working in a production position must have the following characteristics:

Strong leadership skills: These include abilities such as motivating teams and individuals, negotiating conflicts, building consensus, and providing the guiding vision of the game from beginning to end.

Effective communication skills: All written, verbal, and nonverbal communication must be clear, diplomatic, and timely. This includes the ability to deliver bad news in a sensitive fashion, giving constructive feedback, and answering any questions in a forthright manner. (It is fine to say, "I don't know; let me find out and get back to you.")

Highly developed organizational skills: These include creating schedules, delegating tasks, and tracking all the small details of the project. Knowledge of project management principles is extremely useful.

Desire to work with (and for) others: Overall, a producer is there to serve the team and not the other way around. The team is actually creating the content for the game, and the producer must create a working environment that allows them to be their most productive. This means the producer must always be available to listen to complaints, suggestions, and questions from the team and deal with them in a positive and open-minded fashion. If you don't enjoy working with people, then production is probably not the best fit for you.

There is no set training or academic program geared exclusively for producers at this time. But there are several areas a producer can concentrate on to build up his skills:

Knowledge of the game industry: Keep up to date with the latest industry technology and trends, talk with other developers, and play games.

Project management training: Take some classes in project management, or better yet, become a certified project manager. The Project Management Institute (*www.pmi.org*) regulates a well-known certification process. Chapter 3, "Formal Production Processes," Part V, "Pre-Pproduction," and Part VI, "Production," in this book provide further information on project management.

People management training: Learn how to effectively manage and motivate people. Several books and classes provide valuable information on how to manage a diverse group of people. Part III of this book, "Managing People," discusses management in more detail.

Public speaking experience: Become more confident when speaking at team meetings by taking some public speaking classes. Also, Toastmasters (*www. toastmasters.org*) is a club where people meet to work on public speaking and leadership skills.

INTERVIEW

Stephanie O'Malley Deming, Producer, Xloc

A producer must be a good diplomat and have the ability to communicate with people on all different levels, from a texture artist to the vice president of the studio. A producer must figure out what motivates each person on the team and use this knowledge to get people excited about their tasks. Good organizational skills and the ability to multitask are musts.

Someone who wants to be a producer should start at the bottom, either as a production coordinator, assistant designer, or QA tester, and work your way up. Gain as much hands-on experience as you can, because experience counts for an incredible amount. Being in the trenches helps you understand how and why decisions are made and allows you to foresee potential issues in the production schedule. It also gives you the ability to knowledgeably converse with and lead the developers on your team and ensure that the best decisions are made for the design, engineering, and art aspects of the game. After you become a producer, you have many different experiences to pull from and can understand which processes will work best.

ART

Artists are responsible for creating all the graphical assets for the game—characters, cinematics, vehicles, buildings, and levels—and as technology becomes better, the quality of the assets must match the advancement. This is especially true for the next generation of hardware. There is more memory, processing power, and storage space, which gives the artists the ability to create highly detailed objects, realistic-looking terrain and water, and special effects for explosions and weather that are comparable to the real world.

Artists work closely with the designers on what objects, worlds, and cinematics are needed and also work with engineering to determine how to utilize the technology most effectively in the art production pipeline. If a large number of art assets need to be created, artists are likely to outnumber other team members by two to one. Each team will have different titles for the art positions on a development team. The basic art positions are as follows:

- Art Director
- Lead Artist
- Concept Artist
- World Builder or Level Designer
- Asset Artist

- Animator
- Technical Artist
- Marketing Artist

Art Director

The art director's main function is communicating the artistic vision to the team. This person is skilled in all aspects of creating digital art and is responsible for ensuring that all the artistic assets relate to each other within the game. An art director is a very skilled and respected artist who has five to ten years of work experience. Not all projects will have an art director on the team.

Lead Artist

The lead artist works closely with the art director to ensure that the artistic vision is maintained throughout the development process. The lead manages the quality of the art assets and the day-to-day tasks of the team and is a go-between for the art director and the art team. This allows the art director to focus on the creative aspects of the game, instead of managing personnel. If there is not an art director on the team, the lead artist assumes the responsibility for defining the artistic vision. The lead artist is an experienced and respected artist with at least three to five years of game development experience.

Concept Artist

Concept artists are visionaries. They are responsible for creating concepts of all of the art assets before they are produced. They are skilled in 2D art, traditional drawing and painting methods, and sometimes in 3D art. They work directly with the art director in creating and documenting the artistic vision of the game.

World Builder or Level Designer

The world builder or level designer is responsible for building the geometry and creating the textures for the game world. They are skilled in 2D and 3D art, and it is helpful if they have an understanding of level design. In some companies, this position is considered to be a design position, since the way the game world is mapped out has a huge impact on gameplay.

Asset Artist

The asset artist also has 2D and 3D art skills but is responsible for creating the assets that appear in the game world. This includes such things such as characters, weapons, vehicles, props, user interface (UI) screens, and any other necessary game assets. Some asset artists will specialize in a particular type of asset, such as vehicles.

Animator

Animators are responsible for creating all the in-game and cinematic animations. They need to be skilled in traditional 2D and 3D animation. However, 3D animation is more desirable for game development, especially to take advantage of next-generation technology.

Technical Artist

The technical artist manages the technical side of asset creation, such as creating collision volumes, making sure that objects are exported correctly, and applying Havok physic attributes to an object. They will work closely with engineering on the art tools and art pipeline, and therefore need to have enough technical knowledge to communicate with engineers.

Marketing Artist

A marketing artist creates all the marketing assets for game. This includes taking game screenshots, creating high-resolution art, packaging, and anything else that marketing needs to promote the game. This person is usually skilled in 2D art and has some knowledge of 3D art.

Background and Training

The background and training required for a game artist is pretty well-defined. In general, an artist must posses artistic skill and be able to express this skill in traditional artistic mediums such as painting, drawing, and sculpting. Another critical component is how to use 2D or 3D software to create assets. Most universities or art schools will offer classes on how to use the software, so this is not a huge hurdle to overcome.

Knowledge of the game industry is also beneficial for artists, as technology is always changing, affecting how art can be used in the game. If artists keep up with these changes, they can bring this knowledge to the games they work on and continue to improve the graphics as the technology gets better.

Finally, artists should have strong communication skills because they will be communicating with designers, engineers, and production personnel on a team. Effective communication makes everyone's job easier on the project.

ENGINEERING

Engineers are involved in every single aspect of the game—graphics, animation, scripting tools, physics, UI, sound, and more—and they are responsible for creating all the code that makes the game work. They have to take design documents, define the necessary functionality, write code that creates the functionality, and then revise the functionality based on feedback. They also work closely with art to determine the technical art needs for the game.

Game programming is much different from programming business software, especially in regard to the high priority placed on creating an *entertaining* software package. Game programmers usually have a passion for games and understand the unique skills required for this position. Game engineers must be able to work well with creative types, managers, and other engineers on a project so they can realize the vision of the game as a team. The basic engineering roles on each game project are as follows:

- Technical Director
- Lead Engineer
- Engineer

Technical Director

The technical director, a counterpart to the art director. The technical director must be knowledgeable of the latest technology and determine how it can best be used in the game code. They focus some of their time on research and development and are ultimately responsible for setting the coding standards, determining which technologies are used in the game, coding and maintaining libraries, and so on. Not all projects have a technical director. A technical director must be a skilled programmer with at least five to ten years of experience.

Lead Engineer

The lead engineer is responsible for managing the day-to-day tasks of the team. The lead also works closely with the technical director to determine what technologies are needed for the game. The lead may or may not have a chance to actually create code for the game, as it depends on how busy he is managing the engineers. If no technical director is part of the team, the lead engineer is responsible for setting the technical standards of the game. A lead has three to five years of experience, general knowledge of all areas of game technology, and good communication skills.

Engineer

Engineer is a general title for a role that can have many variations within a development team. Many game engineers are well-versed in several areas of programming but will probably choose to focus on one or two specialties. However, it is important that engineers are flexible enough to move out of their specialized areas to work on other things if needed.

Some basic areas of engineering that are found on a development team are as follows:

Networking Engineer: This position is responsible for creating multiplayer code. This engineer works closely with the multiplayer designer to ensure that all the necessary gameplay functionality is supported.

Sound Engineer: This position focuses on creating the sound engine for the game. This engineer works closely with the sound designer to make sure that the sound engine can support the desired sound features for the game.

Graphics Engineer: This position is responsible for creating the graphics code. This person will work closely with the technical artist on the art tools and art production pipeline.

Tools Engineer: This person is responsible for creating all the proprietary tools used during game development. This includes scripting tools, lighting tools, exporters, localization tools, and any other tools that can be coded to streamline the game production pipeline. This person will work with many different people on the team to get an understanding of what tools are needed.

AI Engineer: This position focuses on the artificial intelligence (AI) behaviors in the game. The engineer works closely with design on what behaviors and functionality are needed for the characters in the game.

Background and Training

Many game engineers have a degree in computer science, although a fair number of game engineers are self-taught. Whatever path is taken, game engineers require knowledge in programming languages, operating systems, compilers, debuggers, and application programming interfaces (APIs). After being educated in these basic areas, engineers must continually educate themselves in the latest technology and understand how this impacts their work. Game technology is constantly changing, and new gaming platforms are guaranteed to emerge every three to four years.

As with artists and production personnel, engineers should also have knowledge of the game industry and a desire to make games. Additionally, they need to have strong communication skills, the ability to work in a team-based environment, and get along with a variety of personalities.

INTERVIEW

Tobi Saulnier, President, 1st Playable

Game software is becoming more complicated and sophisticated in terms of lines of code and complexity of math. This means that engineers must have a broader and deeper understanding of it than typically feasible for someone who is purely self-taught. Two of the most basic areas that game engineers work on are the core game engine and the game code that runs on top of the core features provided by the engine.

An engineer working on the core game engine for a console game needs to be a good assembly coder and comfortable working with hardware and compliers. The areas they might work on include rendering, effects, physics, and lighting. The focus is on getting the code to run more quickly and getting more graphics piped through memory, on some very idiosyncratic systems. This person should also have an understanding of CPU and memory usage—specifically for game engines—and be comfortable crossing the boundary between software and hardware. An engineer in this position will need to have a high threshold for frustration, because if working with new hardware (which is often the case in game development), the compilers and

→

other tools will be buggy and not mature. And by the time the compilers *are* mature, the hardware will change.

An engineer working on game-specific code must understand and be able to implement game state management, character-handling algorithms, AI, and other behaviors into the game. This area is becoming quite complex as well, especially with the next-generation platforms with so much processing horsepower available. An engineer in this position must be able to work with changing specs, because many of the behaviors they are implementing will be tuned throughout the production process. These changes often are identified only after enough of the game is playable that some play testing can be done and the designers realize that the behaviors are not creating a fun experience.

Large games will have niche areas, such as networking and sound programming, that become big enough that an engineer can work just on one of these specific areas for the entire project. Other engineers are needed to work closely with design and art, as writers for AI scripts, shaders for artists, or to create tools that speed up production bottlenecks. These engineers have a technical background but work largely with the nonsoftware creative people on the team so it is useful if they have some art or design experience themselves.

Basically, a company is looking for an engineer who is very adaptable with a strong engineering background as a foundation. It is important that an engineer be a quick learner to be able to change what he is focused on, either to adapt to what a particular game needs or to be able to help with an area that becomes the critical path for a particular project. Depending on the team size, for example, the engineer may be coding UI for one project and then move on to coding the animation system on another project. In addition, engineers must be able to work with other people's code and, of course, write code that other people can also work on. Games require modified code from project to project, which means that different engineers will be working on the code base. With the newest systems, it would be quite unusual to be able to have the luxury of building the game from ground up.

DESIGN

Designers have a broad range of responsibilities on a development team, such as designing the game's control scheme, creating the characters' backgrounds and personalities, and designing the combat system. Ultimately, they are responsible for creating a compelling and immersive gameplay experience. In order to accomplish this goal, designers must work closely with artists and engineers to determine how to utilize art and technology to best bring the game to life.

Designers are involved in the game production process from start to finish. In pre-production, they are brainstorming and prototyping potential gameplay ideas and then documenting the ones that will work best within the game's limitations. During production, they are implementing the game design, which includes scripting missions, writing dialogue, and play testing. Their duties also include incorporating feedback and redesigning certain aspects of the game when necessary. In addition, designers must work cooperatively with the other team members throughout the development process. Their basic design positions on a development team are as follows:

- Creative Director
- Lead Designer
- Designer
- Writer

Creative Director

Each development team will interpret the role and responsibility of a creative director differently. Normally the creative director is responsible for communicating the overall creative vision to the team and ensuring that this vision is carried through to every aspect of the game.

In order to be successful at this position, the creative director must interact with many different team members. Figure 2.3 is a diagram of the types of interactions a creative director might have on a project. As you can see, the interactions revolve around the members who are directly responsible for generating creative assets. The creative director makes sure that the environments, characters, music, dialogue, and gameplay all work together to form a cohesive whole. It is important to note that the creative director does not assume the role of the art director, but rather works closely with the art director in determining the look and feel of the game. Also, not all projects have creative directors. Someone in this position usually has five to ten years of work experience and lead design experience on several shipped titles.

Lead Designer

The lead designer is responsible for managing the day-to-day tasks of the design team and acting as a go-between for the creative director and designers. The lead designer directs the design team in documenting the design concepts, prototyping gameplay, implementing design features, balancing gameplay, and redesigning features as needed. If no creative director is on the team, the lead designer is responsible for communicating the creative vision. A lead designer usually has at least three to five years of design experience.

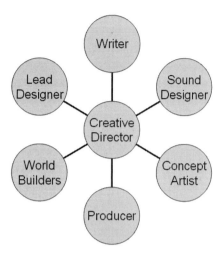

FIGURE 2.3   Creative director's main project contacts.

Designer

Designer is a general title for a role that has different functions on a team. The designer is responsible for creating, prototyping, implementing, and balancing different areas of the game, depending on his expertise. A few types of designers on a team are as follows:

Systems Designer: This person designs the system components within the gameplay. Examples include the scoring system, the combat model, the controller scheme, and the character creation system.

UI Designer: This person designs the game's User Interface (UI). This includes how the UI screens will function and fit together in the game.

Level Designer: Also known as a world builder, this person creates the level layouts for the game. Some developers consider this to be an art position instead of a design one. In some instances, the designer creates the level designs on paper, and then an artist builds the levels.

Scripter: This person places the interactive objects and enemies in the levels. Essentially, they control how many enemies a player will face, where the gameplay challenges appear in a level, and how nonplayer characters will interact with the player's character, and so on.

Writer

The writer is responsible for creating the story elements, characters, and dialogue for the game. They interact closely with the lead designer and/or creative director to ensure that these elements are in keeping with the game's creative vision. The writer also writes marketing and PR copy, Web site content, the manual, and anything else that needs to be written. Writers must have some experience in writing for interactive media and definitely be experienced in creative writing.

Background and Training

As with producers, no clearly defined guidelines exist regarding the skills a designer must posses. Designers come from a variety of backgrounds with no standard job path. Designers need strong communication skills, both written and verbal, because they must clearly communicate abstract creative concepts to an entire team of people and guide these people in making these ideas concrete. Designers are familiar with a variety of game theories and play a lot of games. Ultimately, they must be open-minded and have a sense of what the player finds fun and entertaining.

INTERVIEW _____

Clint Hocking, Creative Director, Ubisoft

Game design is such a new field that there isn't really a specific path toward it. You need to be able to see both the system design aspect and the experience design aspect of a job. As far as I know there is no really effective way to receive training in both of these things.

The best advice I can give to anyone who wants to be a game designer is to get a broad education. Go to a good liberal arts school or a good engineering school where interdisciplinary study is emphasized. Get a degree in computer science with a minor in fine art or the inverse. While you're studying, work on games and play games. Design pen and paper role-playing games, board games, card games, Web-based games or text adventures; make an independent film to learn how to work in desperate situations with small teams of people with diverse artistic and technical talents; anything you can do to get a broad range of experience working with both technical and creative people is going to be useful.

After doing a little bit of work in the mod community and releasing a level for an Unreal mod called *Strike Force*, I got my start in the game industry as a level designer on the first *Splinter Cell*. My level ended up being selected to go to E3, where we received a lot of recognition, and my other level ended up being the OXM demo level for the game.

$\rightarrow$

During *Splinter Cell's* development, the game designer left the project at the alpha deadline, and I was asked to take over for him. The writer also left the project, and because I have a master's degree in creative writing and had been working quite closely with the writer, I was asked to take over that job, too. When we started working on *Splinter Cell: Chaos Theory*, I took on the dual role of lead level designer and scriptwriter. About halfway through, I also took on the role of creative director. It's been quite a roller coaster, and I've been very lucky to be in the right place at the right time.

On development teams, the roles of the various designers depend upon and are defined by the designers' specific talents. I, myself, have been a level designer, a lead level designer, a game designer, a writer/designer, a creative director. . . . I have worked with designers who are very methodical and process oriented, designers who are very creative, and some who are very technical.

Currently I am in pre-production as a creative director. I work directly with the lead programmer, the producer, and the marketing manager. Underneath me are the creative leads, the game designer, art director, lead level designer, writer, etc. So at the high level, the creative director has a lot of influence over the game concept, and at the next tier, the game designer has as much influence as the other creative leads. In smaller projects, the game designer might be equivalent to the creative director.

A level designer is responsible for delivering a level; a scripter is responsible for delivering working code; a writer/designer is responsible for delivering script. *Pure* game designers might be responsible for working with focus tests to deliver focus-test reports, then communicating with level design about what the reports mean, and then delivering documentation that illustrates the follow-up plan to the producer or creative director. Certain designers, like a creative director, lead level designer, or a game designer will be responsible for playing the game constantly and delivering regular evaluations of the content, comments, and criticism and tasks to the level designers so they can improve their levels.

Usually, the most senior creative person on the project will have a lot of influence in the early stages. In the beginning there is a lot of freedom to be creative, but the further you move along, the less freedom you have and the more constraints you adopt. Toward the end of the project, the creative lead has almost no say, and in the last days before shipping, the lead programmer is the one who runs everything. In a sense, influence migrates from creative to technical over time at a pace dictated by the producer.

As a general rule, the best designers—whether leads or not—all have one thing in common. They are all able to see the systems, content, and experience (or whatever aspect of the design they are focused on) from the perspective of the player. The best designers are able to let go of the specific direction they have for the experience and design in such a way as to facilitate the player's ability to express *himself* in the interactive space. Unlike other creative fields where the creator has a lot of authorial control over their creation, game designers do not create *specific experiences*, they are *enablers* who create the possibility for people to engage in a meaningful set of experiences. It's difficult to understand this and let go of your authorial control, but it's critical to being a good designer.

QUALITY ASSURANCE TESTING

Quality assurance (QA) testers are a vital part of the game development process and are involved in play testing and finding defects in the game. Testers usually begin their work in the production phase, after playable game builds are available. They are involved in the development process until the end and are often the last people to finish working on the game. Testers work closely with all members of the development team and are a good resource for testing prototypes and new features. The basic testing roles include the following:

- Lead QA Tester
- QA Tester

Lead QA Tester

The lead QA tester works closely with the producer and other leads on a project to evaluate the game's features from a testing point of view. For example, if the game is going to feature 50 variables for creating a character, the lead QA tester will estimate how long these variables will take to test and then most likely suggest that the number be greatly reduced to save on testing time. This is because testing combinations of different variables can quickly eat up valuable time, which is needed for testing other areas of the game. The lead QA tester also determines, along with the producer and leads, when the game is ready to be code released.

The lead QA tester is responsible for writing the game's test plan. In order to do this, he must know exactly how every part of the game functions, so these details can be included in the test plan. Finally, the lead QA tester manages all the testers and assigns them specific areas of the test plan to check. A lead QA tester has two to three years of experience as a QA tester.

QA Tester

A QA tester is responsible for checking the game's functionality against the test plan, testing new features and prototypes and finding defects in the game software. In addition, they check that the game meets all of the console manufacturer's technical requirements. They spend a majority of their work day actually playing the game and, therefore, have informed opinions on the overall *fun factor*.

Background and Training

There is no formal training for a testing position. In general, testers are people who enjoy playing games and have the ability to analyze problems and determine their cause. Testers should have good written and oral communication skills so they can clearly describe a bug to a developer. Lead testers should also have good organizational and communication skills since they are responsible for managing a team of people.

The testing department is a good entry into the field of game development since testers are exposed to all aspects of game development. They also communicate directly with the developers on a daily basis.

TEAM ORGANIZATION

The team hierarchy can be organized in several ways, depending on the team size and the roles to be filled. Small companies might have a single person fulfilling multiple roles on a project, such as producer-lead designer, and large companies might have a person with a single, clearly defined role, such as UI artist or AI engineer. Whatever the team size, it is important to establish a clear hierarchy so people know whom they need to talk with to get information.

Figure 2.4 depicts a general organization chart for a typical small team with a producer/lead structure. The producer manages the art, engineering, design, and QA leads, and the leads manage the rest of the development team. With the team organized in this fashion, it is still possible for a single person to fulfill multiple roles, even though it may cause some conflict. For example, Wade Tinney is a producer/lead designer at Large Animal Games. He sometimes finds his producer side disagreeing with his designer side, especially if it means adding more time or money to the project.

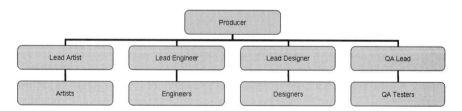

FIGURE 2.4 Small team with producer/lead structure.

Figure 2.5 is an organizational chart for a larger team. It still follows the producer/lead structure, but now specialized areas are evident in each discipline. In a structure like this, a network engineer reporting to the lead may be in charge of several other network engineers. Also, an associate producer is included on this team to assist the producer with the day-to-day management of the production tasks.

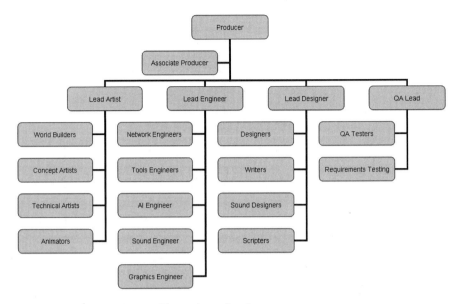

FIGURE 2.5 Large team with producer/lead structure.

Figure 2.6 shows an organizational chart for a team headed up by an executive producer and directors in each discipline. This structure is likely to be more common as development teams continue to get larger. With this particular structure, both the producer and creative director report directly to the executive producer. The producer is in charge of managing all the team personnel, and the creative director is in charge of managing the creative vision of the game. This reporting structure is different for each development team.

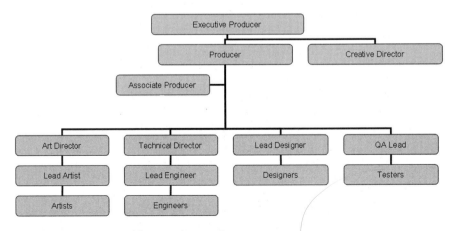

FIGURE 2.6 Team with executive producer structure.

This structure also indicates that the leads are the intermediaries between the directors and the rest of the team. In addition, a production coordinator is added to assist the associate producer with day-to-day tasks. This is especially helpful if the associate producer is managing several areas of the game, such as localizations and the voiceover recordings.

CORPORATE

Any full list of game credits includes recognition for all the corporate people who are integral to creating and launching a successful game. People in these roles are responsible for creating the packaging, marketing campaign, sales plan, and anything else that supplements the actual game. These people normally communicate with the producer and are treated as external members of the development team. These departments include the following:

- Marketing and Public Relations
- Creative Services
- Sales

Marketing and Public Relations

The main responsibility of the marketing department is to market the game to the target consumer. Their challenge is building a compelling marketing campaign around the game's features, story, and gameplay experience that entices players to buy the game. In order to be most effective, marketing should be involved with the game during pre-production. This gives them the opportunity to suggest features and other ways to make the game more marketable. For example, they might suggest using licensed music from a popular band, casting celebrity voices, or adding some unique new gameplay features.

Public relations is responsible for generating publicity for the game through Web sites, magazines, and television spots. This includes setting up interviews with the development team and organizing press tours for the game. In addition, they create unique publicity events to get players asking questions about the game. For example, Ubisoft has organized several special appearances in public places by Sam Fisher, the main character from the *Splinter Cell* franchise. Marketing and public relations work together closely to ensure that they are both presenting a unified vision of the game to the target audience. Please refer to Chapter 12, "Marketing and Public Relations," for more information.

Creative Services

Creative services works closely with the marketing department to create the packaging and manual for the game. After the look and feel of the packaging is decided, creative services generates the necessary assets, creates the final layout, and coordinates the printing of all the materials.

Because the producer is more familiar with the game than someone in the creative services department, the producer is expected to provide the manual text, screenshots, and other game assets for the printed materials. See Chapter 12, "Marketing and Public Relations," for more information on the process for creating the packaging and manual.

Sales

The sales department is responsible for selling the game to retail stores, such as Wal-Mart, EB Games, and Best Buy. They also determine whether special editions of the game can be created to increase sales. For example, a special edition of *Half Life 2* was released by Sierra that included a T-shirt, strategy guide, and a remastered version of the original *Half Life*.

SUMMARY

With so many people involved in creating games and growing teams, it is essential for the producer to understand everyone's roles and responsibilities on the team. This chapter presented general overviews of the production, art, engineering, design, testing, and corporate roles on a team and briefly discussed the background and training necessary for these roles.

With a clear understanding of team roles, the producer can decide on the appropriate team structure and production process to use when developing a game. The next chapter discusses some formal production processes that can be effectively used on development teams, including the Personal Software Process and agile methodologies.

3 Formal Production Processes

In This Chapter

- Pros and Cons
- Personal Software Process (PSP)
- Scrum
- Project Management Institute (PMI)

INTRODUCTION

Game developers tend to shy away from using a formal software engineering process (perhaps because they are afraid of stifling the creative energy on the team) and instead jump right into production without making a clear decision on how to manage the development cycle. This worked fine 25 years ago when the teams were small and everyone clearly understood their development responsibilities. The games were also much simpler to create—fewer assets, fewer lines of code, and fewer features. Today, teams are larger, games are more complex, and games are simultaneously released on multiple platforms and in multiple languages. Developers are now realizing they must find better ways to manage the development cycle, and to do this, they are looking at how software engineering processes are managed in other industries and finding ways to adapt these to game development.

Personal Software Process (PSP) and an agile methodology known as scrum are two software development processes that have been successfully used by game developers in recent years. Other software processes can also be adapted to game development; which one you choose depends on the type of game, the constraints, and the available resources. There are pros and cons of using any type of process, so take this into account when researching which one will be best for your development team.

Formal production processes are a large topic and to discuss them in detail is beyond the scope of this book. However, this chapter presents general information about the pros and cons of using a formal process, how two studios successfully implemented PSP and Scrum, and the benefits of the Project Management Institute (PMI).

PROS AND CONS

Because many game developers are not trained in project management processes, no common terminology or method is used from project to project. This makes it difficult for teams to understand how their tasks fit into the development process and impact the work of others. For example, a designer can't script a level until the artist has built it, or an artist can't add lighting to a level until the lighting tool is coded. It is important for the team to be aware of these dependencies, so they can schedule their work accordingly. When the work is not properly scheduled, the critical path becomes overloaded, and bottlenecks develop in the workflow, putting the project at risk. Using a formal software engineering process can alleviate some of these issues.

Many software engineering processes, such as PSP and scrum, require the team to be involved in determining what tasks need to be done, estimating how long the tasks will take, and tracking the progress of these tasks. This level of team involvement gives people more ownership of their work. Morale increases because people directly control their tasks, which means they can have a direct effect on the success (or failure) of the project.

When people see that the game production is under control, they are more confident in the game's success. A formal process allows the team to see tangible progress, which motivates them to move forward in their work. For example, Scrum uses *burn-down* charts to show the progress the team is making. These charts allow teams to see when they are ahead of schedule, behind schedule, and right on schedule. If they are behind schedule, they can see this sooner rather than later and correct the timing before it becomes a problem that puts the project at risk.

Another benefit of using formal software engineering processes is that project metrics can be generated on how long it takes to do a task, and this information can be used when estimating similar tasks on future projects. Overall, this allows the producer and the team to generate more accurate task estimates. The more accurate these estimates are, the easier it is for a team to plan the production cycle, decide which features and assets can be implemented, and determine more confidently when the game will be finished. For example, if an artist accurately tracks how long it takes to create a 200 m × 200 m level, this information can be recorded and then used to estimate this same task on another project.

The producer and leads greatly benefit from using a formal process. When a standard process is in place, it is easier to bring in new team members and get them quickly up to speed on the game's development progress. New people joining the team can get to work right away, instead of having to spend a few days figuring out what they are supposed to be doing. Additionally, the producer and leads can spend their time actually managing the game development process, instead of putting out fires. Because you know exactly where the project is at any given time, no huge surprises should sneak up on you. That's not to say it won't happen, but the likelihood of it happening will decrease.

There are some cons to using a formal software engineering process, but many of these can be overcome with time, especially when people start to use, understand, and be comfortable with the process. One issue with using processes like Scrum or PSP for game development is that these processes are really more suited to engineering tasks and less to design and art tasks. The processes were originally developed for software engineering because there is often uncertainty in how long it takes to code a feature, how long bug fixing takes, and the scope of the work. By establishing these processes, the engineering tasks are more controlled, and exit criteria can be established to determine when code is completed.

People may be reluctant to try a formal process for a variety of reasons. For some, their unfamiliarity with the process will be a deterrent, as they may be unwilling to try something with which they have little experience. Others might perceive this as something rigid that will stifle creativity and innovation; they also might feel they are less involved in project decisions, rather than more involved. For people who are worried that creativity will suffer, explain that there is more time to prototype and polish the game, since the majority of their time is now spent on implementing project features, rather than on putting out fires. Finally, people might be concerned that the company culture will become more corporate and less fun. Explain that this is a process to help the team, rather than control them.

Other things to consider when using one of these processes is the cost to train and implement. For example, with PSP everyone needs to take a two-week training course; this is not only expensive, but having people unavailable for two weeks impacts the project. If you are planning to spend the money to train people, make sure that the company and the people are committed to making the process work. Any time or money investment made in these areas will be worth the increased efficiency and decreased project risk.

PERSONAL SOFTWARE PROCESS (PSP)

Personal Software Process, established by the Software Engineering Institute at Carnegie Mellon, teaches engineers to understand and improve their own process of coding. The emphasis is on how to teach engineers to manage the quality of their code, make commitments they can actually fulfill, improve their estimating and planning, and reduce bugs in their code. A large part of this involves conducting code reviews at every stage in the software development cycle.

PSP is a big commitment, as engineers must go through a two-week training course and complete 10 homework assignments. Also, in order for PSP to be most effective, all the engineers on the team must be trained and use this process together on a project, which can be expensive. The training costs are recouped by having more certainty and stability in a given code deliverable. For more information, refer to Appendix B, "Resources," for the official PSP Web site.

Team Software Process (TSP) is another component of PSP. TSP is when everyone on the team, including designers and artists, applies the principles of PSP to their work. The goal is to build self-directed teams who establish the project goals, formulate a plan to meet these goals, and then track their progress toward these goals. If TSP is integrated effectively into the production process, the team is more motivated and is able to successfully complete more aggressive project schedules—mainly because they were involved in creating the plan, fully understand everything that must be accomplished during development, and can quickly see where the project is getting off track much sooner than before.

INTERVIEW

PSP and TSP, Tobi Salunier, President, 1st Playable

Personal Software Process™ (PSP) is a professional training program for software engineers that is designed to help an individual learn more about their own software engineering process and ways to improve it. In particular the training focuses on how to plan tasks and catch bugs earlier, which both result in more accurate schedule estimates. We had just finished a big project at Vicarious Visions, with a long crunch time, and one of the priorities of the postmortem was to find ways to improve our game development process. I had heard about this process in my previous R&D position with General Electric, through my involvement with the quality initiative there. Since the complexity of software is one of the biggest factors in long projects, it seemed that trying PSP at Vicarious Visions could be part of the solution. But it was going to be a challenge to convince game developers that a structured process as taught by PSP would have value for them. Like any kind of process improvement, software process is not something you can force people to do and like; people don't want you to tell them that something is good for them—instead, they want to judge for themselves.

$\rightarrow$

The great thing about PSP is that the training program is designed for people to get firsthand experience in the process and then determine if it something they want to use on a game development project. The training comprises two one-week classroom training sessions, separated by a couple of months. This staging approach lets people adopt new habits and collect their own data to validate which techniques work for them. The training focuses on the individual, so that each person has a chance to identify and improve weak areas and tailor the material to what was most useful for each.

We decided to send all the engineers for the training program in order to get the most benefit possible. As in any major training program, if you don't train everyone, the process will not be as effective; people come back from training enthusiastic to try something new but won't be able to keep up the momentum if they are in the minority. One big downside is the cost; in addition to the time allotted to it, the course fees are also fairly expensive (for a game developer). In addition all project managers had to schedule around the training time. However, we felt the investment would be worth it in the long run. As a company, we were only going to work on bigger and more complex projects and even a couple of weeks delay in one of these big projects would cost far more. Therefore, even if people did not have buy-in for PSP before training, I was hoping they would see the value of it after training and be willing to utilize at least some part of it.

Team software process (TSP) is an additional component of this professional training. TSP involves the entire team and provides a structure to make sure that the team has the support they need for the individuals to apply all that great process they learned about for PSP. The great side benefit of TSP is that it provides a structure for your basic project planning process that ensures that the team all understand and are working toward the same goals. Basically, TSP requires the team to meet together for four solid days and create the project plan and task list in a concentrated amount of time. This is different than the more *ad hoc* planning approach, which might use similar steps but perhaps involve fewer team members for each and that is staged over a period of a few weeks. Although it can be painful to have the whole team committed to that week of planning (since many may still be wrapping up their prior projects), involving the team with all the planning up-front is more efficient in the long-term, and the team is less likely to forget tasks that should be included in the plan.

External coaches can come into a company and help launch this process. Most people in development are doers, not planners, so it takes a lot of discipline to get that up-front time into planning. A coach can help keep people on track during the planning phase.

When we trained people in PSP at Vicarious Vision, we did not know whether a team would be interested in also using TSP. We did not want to assume teams wanted to use TSP, but we certainly would support any that did. After PSP training there were quite a few people who were interested to taking that next step with TSP, and many of them were put on a project together to develop *Spiderman DS*. If this

$\rightarrow$

team could successfully use TSP, their peers would be more apt to see TSP as something that would be successful for their projects.

There were several benefits to using TSP for *Spiderman*. First, we could not have successfully completed this project within the tight deadlines of a launch title without a watertight process for planning and communication. Beyond just the short development cycle, a launch title on the *DS* brings a unique set of development issues—such as working on a platform that is not final and having to wait for certain components to be available for testing. TSP allowed us to maintain a much tighter feedback loop so that everyone would see sooner when our assumptions weren't working out and we needed to replan.

One advantage of TSP is that the team is tracking their own progress and is the first to see when they are getting off the plan. In most cases they can also fix the issue themselves. Because the TSP task list and plan is visible and available to everyone, the team could also ask for help in a more data-focused way. For example, they could request resources to help with a specific and clearly defined set of tasks, instead of just asking for more people. Also, if they wanted to add a new feature to the game, they could look at the plan and constructively cite what the impact would be—more time would be needed; another feature would need to be reduced or cut; or another resource would be needed for the project.

There are some cons about using TSP as well, but I think the benefits far outweigh them. For one thing, the training for PSP and TSP is expensive and requires a time commitment. The company has to be willing to spend the money and time to follow through completely on the training, or they will not be able to successfully implement it.

Additionally, qualified coaches and trainers are hard to find. and they really are necessary when initially implementing TSP into your production process. They can make the transition much easier and are an invaluable resources for answering any questions about the process.

Finally, TSP requires a large amount of data collection—people have to track how much time each task took and update their task list on a daily basis. The team may be reluctant to track this information as well, especially if they think the information will be used to judge people. For example, if a programmer constantly takes longer to complete a task than the initial estimate, he may feel vulnerable if management is reviewing his tasks. This could result in overall inflating of tasks, or inaccurate data to be collected, which then will cause management to start to discount the team's plans. At that point TSP will lose any advantage it might have for planning more accurately and will ultimately lose the buy-in of both the team and management. If there is a basic culture of trust between management and the team, this issue can be avoided.

SCRUM

Agile development is a set of methodologies that are focused on realizing true product value through iteration and feedback. Agile development does not encourage the team to build several discrete components of a game, put them together at the end, and then hope everything works as planned. Instead, agile development emphasizes building an initial iteration of the game that contains very basic functionality and then building on this functionality throughout product iterations until the game is completed. There are several agile methodologies to choose from, including scrum. For more information on Agile development, please refer to *Integrating Agile Development in the Real World*, written by Peter Schuh.

Scrum is a management-focused methodology that is flexible enough to be used in a wide variety of game development environments. It is relatively easy to implement as it requires no formal training, only a commitment by the team to use the process. The basics of scrum involve creating subsets of self-directed teams within the larger project team, which are headed up by a "scrum master," who is empowered to remove any impediments that affect the team's working progress. The teams are cross-functional (artists, designers, and engineers), small (normally 5 to 10 people), and work together to complete a set of tasks that will result in a tangible deliverable at the end of a set period of time. These set periods of time are called *sprints* and are usually one month in duration. The sprint is the building block for the game's progress, because at the end of every sprint, there is a tangible and playable game deliverable. The next sprint builds upon the previous sprint in an iterative process. For more details on Scrum, please refer to the book *Agile Software Development with SCRUM*, by Ken Schwaber and Mike Beedle.

INTERVIEW

Scrum, Clinton Keith, Chief Technical Officer, High Moon Studios

My background is in the defense industry. A lot of the same project management issues this industry encountered in the 1960s and 70s are the same ones that we are now running into with game development. For example, in the 1970s the defense industry started using the waterfall approach (phased implementation of design, coding, integration then testing), in the hopes of reducing their failure rate for projects with large teams. However, what they found was that the failure rate increased with this approach; instead of a 30–40 percent failure rate, they were now experiencing a failure rate of 60–70 percent. By studying the reasons for this, they realized that projects should be completed in iterative steps, rather than one big step of multiple phases. With the introduction of the first formal iterative development process, the failure rates were reduced.

I got involved with game development in the mid-90s and discovered that the industry was adopting many of the same waterfall practices as their team sizes grew. Delays were growing as a result. I knew I needed to find a way to reduce failure and was studying how Japanese developers handled their software development processes. In general, some of the more successful Japanese developers are very iterative and are more interested in seeing product iterations instead of planning documents, yet their projects

→

were still often late due to a lack of process. I started experimenting with methodologies that combined more planning with iterative development and began to apply this while I was the Director of Product Development at Angel Studios.

When I took over the role of CTO at Sammy Studios I read a book called *Agile and Iterative Development* written by Craig Larman, which discussed the fundamentals of agile development. To sum up, agile development is focused on discovering true product value through iteration and feedback in the fastest possible way (through increments) using well-defined, yet simple processes. The key to this methodology is to design, implement, integrate, debug, and tune vertical slices as you go, instead of dividing the project into phases for each. Fewer assumptions and hidden work build up as a result.

After reading about the four areas of agile development, it seemed like scrum would fit in well with the development processes I was already using. Scrum is more of a management process that is simple to understand and start doing effectively; I could get this process up and running in a single month and see an immediate improvement.

Scrum was a fairly easy sell to the team since it was very close the methodology we were already shifting to. The biggest change was to adapt the scrum method of 30-day milestones (Sprints) and posting the burn-down charts on the wall. Burn-down charts track the daily progress of the team and show the remaining time that is needed to complete the prioritized goals of the Sprint. If the team misses some of the lowest priority goals at end of the 30 days, those goals are moved to the following month's Sprint.

I find scrum works well with game development because it forces the team to make monthly builds of the game early in the project. Since the process is iterative, the most important aspects of the game are being completed earlier in production and can continue to be polished are added to as time allows. The team can react to emerging gameplay while there is time. It can cancel features that are turning out not to be fun or viable and emphasize and expand upon features that are better than we'd hoped for. So instead of spending the bulk of pre-production time creating a 500-page design document that describes the game, we can actually build a working prototype that showcases the major gameplay features. Another way to visualize it is by thinking of a cake; every month, the team is taking complete slices out of a seven-layer cake. Conversely, with traditional processes (such as waterfall), the team works to create the infrastructure of a cake, and at the end of alpha, they are stuck with a cake that has no frosting.

Scrum development can be attractive to publishers because they can get a better idea of what the game will be like and are more comfortable risking five or six million dollars on the project. They can track the monthly progress of the game through the builds and don't have to wait six months to see whether they are wasting money. If the publisher is more involved in the development process, they can also look at

→

the burn-down charts and have a clear understanding of the game's progress and when features will be implemented.

Publishers may be reluctant to buy into this development process as first, since they need to be educated that writing huge design documents and creating a Microsoft Project schedule only give the illusion of control. Scrum actually gives more control to the process since a tangible deliverable must be ready every 30 days, which gives a more accurate picture of the progress. Eventually, I hope to get publishers involved in the planning process for each monthly Sprint.

There are many pros to using scrum. The biggest improvement is the overall morale of the team. People are more enthusiastic and productive because they can take ownership of their tasks and have direct control of what they are doing. People are more likely to attack impediments to their work if they feel a sense of ownership, and scrum gives them this. Because a big part of scrum involves self-organized teams, the team will work together to attack problems instead of waiting for management to solve them. This means management spends less time putting out fires and more time managing the process and ensuring that all departments are operating at maximum efficiency. Also, the producer does not have to spend 20 hours each week trying to figure out what's going on with the game, because with scrum, all the information is at their fingertips (posted on the wall of our war-room).

Scrum also prevents team burnout. Since we are tracking the tasks so closely and can measure the progress of the game, we now have evidence that after a certain period of time (usually two weeks), overtime ceases to be effective. After a few weeks of working overtime, people are actually less efficient than if they were working normal hours for the week. With this information, we can schedule overtime in small doses (a few days) if we really need to push to hit a deadline. The team is happier, and we are getting better quality work from them. Also, by focusing on the removal of impediments raised in daily 15-minute meetings, we find an amazing increase in productivity. It's a great example of working smarter rather than harder.

One con of scrum is that we are still trying to figure out how to effectively include art and design in this process. Since these areas are more subjective, it is harder to fit them into a quantifiable process. Right now, we have small teams comprised of a few programmers, some artists, and maybe a designer. They can all work together to design and implement a feature. This gives design more control, since they don't have to wait months for their design documents to become functional features in the game.

We're still learning how to adapt scrum to game development. Scrum is best suited to projects with uncertainty and emerging value. However, when creating content that doesn't have uncertainty (such as an expansion pack, downloadable content, or even just the production of levels for the game), more traditional processes can be used. These include documents, Gantt charts, and detailed Microsoft Project schedules. As long as there is certainty with what you are making, you can create the master plan that shows your publisher you are going to hit that Christmas ship date.

PROJECT MANAGEMENT INSTITUTE (PMI)

Project Management Institute (PMI) is a professional organization focused on the principles of effective project management. They administer a globally accepted certification exam, Project Management Professional (PMP), and maintain the Project Management Body of Knowledge (PMBOK). Their Web site, *www.pmi.org*, has a lot of information on project management best practices and provides information on how to become a certified PMP. If you want to learn more about the basics of project management, this is a good general resource with which to begin.

> **RECOMMENDED READING**
>
> *Rapid Development,* by Steve McConnell, outlines several different software development methodologies and discusses how to use them effectively. The author is a recognized expert in his field and is an evangelist for improving software practices in all industries.
>
> *Project Planning Scheduling and Control,* by Jim Lewis, presents very practical and easy-to-understand information on basic project management principles. The book includes several forms that can be easily integrated into your team's production process.

SUMMARY

Managing people and projects can be challenging, but several tools and resources are available and in use in other industries, which can make the process much easier. Game developers are just now starting to realize these ideas can also be adapted to game development and have had success with implementing s crum and PSP. This chapter presented some basic information on formal production processes and how these can be helpful to producers and leads. It concluded with a list of recommended reading helpful to any producer responsible for managing game development.

This concludes the first section of the book, which presented general information about the game development process, team roles, and project management processes. The next section discusses the business side of game development, including legal issues and working with your publisher.

Part

II

Business Information

Even though the primary focus of game development is creating an entertainment product, a producer needs to be aware of some business information in order to be successful. An understanding of basic legal concepts is necessary for dealing with licenses, intellectual property rights, and external vendors.

Also, if a producer is trying to pitch an independently developed game to a publisher, an understanding of how publishers operate is useful. This section focuses on basic business information that is beneficial to a producer. Topics include the following:

- Intellectual Property Rights
- Developer Agreements
- Pitching a Game to a Publisher
- Developer and Publisher Relationships

4 Legal Information

INTRODUCTION

As a producer, there may be instances when you will have to communicate with an attorney or a publisher's legal department on certain matters. For instance, a developer producer participates in negotiating development milestones in the publishing agreement, or a publisher producer might work with potential licensees to define the details of a licensing agreement. In each instance, the producer works with qualified attorneys to ensure that all the legalities are properly handled, but it is not necessary for a producer to have a law degree. However, it does help if the producer is knowledgeable about some general legal issues they might encounter during game development.

Tom Buscaglia, a well-known attorney specializing in games, was interviewed by the author for some general information about what legal issues a producer should be aware of. He has also written a series of articles on basic legal information that developers, especially independent ones, should know. The article information is listed in Appendix B, "Resources." The information gleaned from the interview is paraphrased throughout the chapter.

INTERVIEW

Tom Buscaglia, The Game Attorney

After the assets are secured and the initial deal is done, a producer will not be dealing with legal issues on a day-to-day basis, if things are running smoothly. However, in some instances a lawyer needs to be consulted, especially when an independent producer is creating a game for a third-party publisher. Some examples are as follows: the actual project is starting to deviate and exceed the original scope of work that was detailed in the publishing agreement; minor modifications are made to a deliverable agreement; the funding source changes; or anything else affects the quality and timing of the agreed-upon deliverables. In cases like these, the publishing agreement must be amended to compensate for the additional time and expenditures the developer incurs. This is necessary to keep the developer as a viable economic entity.

Publishing contracts, like any other contract, are organic—not static—and when necessary should be amended and reviewed throughout the entire development process, either by the producer or the producer in conjunction with an attorney. Additionally, if the game sell-through warrants it, an attorney's assistance may be necessary for a post-release audit of the game sales to make sure that the publisher is paying out the royalties accurately.

The producer and his attorney should review all of the game assets from day one to make sure that all of the game assets (art, 3D models, music and sound, program code, and, of course, any third-party trademarks) are unimpaired and owned by the developer. After all, you can't sell what you don't own. So, making sure that the developer owns exclusive rights to all of the content in the game is the essential first step to selling any game.

INTELLECTUAL PROPERTY RIGHTS

Creative ideas are a commodity in the game industry; every day, developers are creating new characters, new storylines, new code, and new game designs, in the hopes that these ideas will come together and create an entertaining gameplaying experience. All of these elements are considered Intellectual Property (IP). IP rights legally protect inventions, symbols, and creative expression and can be bought, sold, traded, given away, licensed, and so on, in the same way as tangible property (like real estate). However, since an IP is an idea and, therefore, intangible, it must be expressed in some discernable way to make it tangible and protected by law.

Several basic types of IP are legally valid: copyrights, trademarks, trade secrets, and patents. The differences depend on how the idea is expressed. Producers should be familiar with the differences between these, especially independent producers working with a publisher. If the publisher is interested in your game and is ready to sign a deal, they will most likely demand that the copyright in the game be conveyed to them so they can create derivative products and reproduce the product free and clear. However, if you are a well-known developer such as Peter Molyneaux or Wil Wright, you are in a better position to negotiate with the publisher and are likely to retain the copyrights to your work.

Additionally, development teams must be careful that they do not include assets in the game that are trademarked or copyrighted—unless the legal rights are obtained to do so. For example, Coca-Cola® vending machines and Crayola® crayons cannot be used in games without contacting the companies who own these properties and finalizing a contract to use these rights. In some instances, product placement deals can be negotiated with these companies that will benefit both parties.

Copyrights

Copyrights protect an individual's or group of individual's original expression of an idea into a tangible medium. Examples include literary works, musical works, and sculpture. However, copyrights do not protect the *actual* idea or concept, regardless of the form in which it is expressed. Only the actual expression of the idea can be copyrighted. For example, you cannot copyright your idea for a game, unless it is expressed in a tangible form, like computer code.

The good thing is that copyright protection is immediately in effect from the moment the expression of the idea is made tangible; you don't need to specifically register the work with the copyright office in order to be protected. However, by registering your copyright, you have access to all the legal benefits to enforce the copyright in a court of law. Copyrights are governed by federal law.

If you are an independent developer working with a group of people to create a game that you will then pitch to a publisher, you need to have everyone on the team assign the copyright to you or a common company, as the developer. The publisher will take your company and game pitch more seriously if they know you have already secured the copyrights and have the authority to turn these rights over to the publisher.

Trademarks

Trade and service marks, both called *trademarks*, are identifying symbols, words, or devices used to distinguish the trademarked good from other similar goods. For example, the Ubisoft logo is a trademark that distinguishes the games it publishes from other games and the shape of a Coca-Cola bottle is a trademark that distinguishes it from other colas. Trademarks are governed by federal laws.

Trademark rights prevent other people from using a similar mark, but the rights do not prevent others from making similar goods and selling them under a different trademark. Thus, at the grocery store, there is a wide variety of orange juice from which to choose, but it is all identified by different trademarks.

Trademarks must be distinctive so that they are truly capable of distinguishing themselves from other similar goods. Some trademarks are stronger than others and, therefore, more enforceable. The strengths of a trademark are judged by a range of terms from weakest to strongest: generic, descriptive, suggestive, arbitrary, and fanciful. Generic marks are weak and nondistinctive because they use a common term that describes the actual item, such as "Coffee" or "Game." Generic marks are not protectable as trademarks.

Descriptive marks describe the function or intended purpose of the good, such as "low fat" for foods that are low in fat. Again, these marks are not protected by trademark law, unless through extensive sales and marketing the marks become closely identified with a particular good or service and acquire a secondary meaning, such as "Holiday Inn."

Suggestive marks do not describe the good directly, but rather require some thought as to how the term applies to the good. Suggestive marks are considered distinguishing and are protected as marks: for example, "Primsacolor™" colored pencils and "Memorex®" tape recorders. The trademarks suggest the function of the good without describing the actual good.

Arbitrary marks are common words, symbols, and devices that have no relation to the good they are distinguishing. Apple™ computers is a well-known example. These marks are inherently distinctive and do not need to acquire a secondary meaning when used as an arbitrary mark.

Fanciful marks are created solely for the purpose of acting as a trademark. These are the strongest type of trademark and easily enforceable; examples include "Kodak®" and "Xerox®."

Trademarks must be registered with the United States Patent and Trademark Office (USPTO). Before registering, you may want to hire a company to do a full trademark search to make sure that the mark is available. After you have submitted the application, the office will determine whether the mark is unique and register it if so.

Trade Secrets

Trade secrets are information that a company keeps secret and which give them a competitive edge. Trade secrets cost money to develop and bring economic value to the company that owns them. Trade secrets are governed by state laws, and protection exists only when the information is kept confidential and cannot be lawfully or independently obtained by other people. Examples of trade secrets are methods, techniques, and formulas, with a well-known example being the secret formula for Coca-Cola.

Trade secrets also apply to commercially viable ideas, such as games ideas, but in order to maintain the idea as a trade secret, it must be kept confidential. This is where nondisclosure agreements (NDAs) are handy. If you want to share your game idea with someone and still have it considered to be confidential, you will have someone sign an NDA before sharing the information with them. See "Non-Disclosure Agreements (NDA)" later in this chapter for more information.

Patents

Patents apply to inventions. Patents prevent others from making, using, or selling the invention for a fixed period of time, which is currently 20 years. In order to obtain a patent, the inventor must fully disclose how the invention works, including diagrams and descriptions. An idea cannot be patented. The invention must also be new, involve an inventive step, and have a useful application. For example, software patents can involve such things as operating systems, compilers, graphics systems, and file systems.

Patents must be registered with the USPTO and are expensive to obtain. Also, when the 20-year term has expired, the patent becomes public domain, and anyone can make, use, or sell the invention.

LEGAL AGREEMENTS

Legal agreements are contracts between two or more parties that outline what the responsibilities and duties of each party to the other are. As a producer, you might be involved in negotiating the terms of legal agreements for external vendors, publishers, and licensees. For example, you might determine the milestone schedule and deliverable lists for an external development contract. This section will give a general overview of some common legal agreements in which you may be involved: employee/consultant agreements, work for hire, non-disclosure agreements (NDA), publisher agreements, and end user license agreements (EULA).

Employee/Consultant Agreements

Employee/consultant agreements are used by independent developers to ensure that everything the development team works on is wholly owned by the company. Essentially, each person on the team signs over their IP rights to the company. This means the company has the authority to sell the IP rights to a publisher, which will make your company more attractive to prospective publishers.

Although the agreements will be tailored to a specific company, they cover several main points. This first is to define specific IP ownership issues, such as which IPs belong to the company and which IPs belong to the employee, and the second is to collectively transfer all ownership of the designated IPs to the company. In addition, guidelines can be set for employees who leave before the project is completed, such as having to fully document their work or agreeing not to poach other employees from the company. The language can be as restrictive as the company deems necessary. This type of agreement should be drafted by an attorney.

Work for Hire

When an external vendor creates something for use in the game, such as music, art assets, or code, he owns the created assets and is protected by one of the intellectual property rights discussed earlier in this chapter. This means you do not have any legal rights to use them in a game, unless you expressively obtain permission from the vendor to do so. However, this does not mean the vendor is obligated to grant you exclusive rights; he may want to license these assets to other game companies as well.

This problem can be avoided if a work for hire agreement is put in place before any assets are created. This agreement transfers all the rights to the person hiring the vendor, and for all intents and legal purposes, the hiring party is considered the creator of the work. For example, if you hire a composer under a work for hire agreement to create music, after the work is completed, you own all the music rights free and clear. This means you can use the music in other products you create, or you can license it for use to other parties.

It is important to note that there are only two situations in which a work for hire can exist. The first situation is where an external vendor is commissioned to create a completely new work and signs a work for hire agreement before the starting anything. In addition, the work must fall within one of nine categories of commissioned work detailed in the Copyright Act: a translation, an instructional text, a test, answers for a test, an atlas, a contribution to a collective work, a compilation, supplementary material, or a contribution to a movie or other audiovisual work. For example, a magazine article could be a work for hire as it is a contribution to a collective work, but a novel could not be a work for hire, because it does not fall into any of the previously mentioned categories.

The second work for hire situation involves any work created by employees that is within their scope of employment. For example, all the code written by a programmer who is an employee on your development team is work for hire. He does not own the rights to the work, as the rights are held by the employer. Of course, this situation can get complicated if working with part-time employees, and in that case, a lawyer might need to be consulted. For more information on work for hire agreements, please consult the U.S. Copyright's Office circular entitled, "Works Made for Hire Under the 1976 Copyright Act," which is listed in Appendix B.

Non-Disclosure Agreements (NDA)

As discussed in the section on IPs, game concepts and ideas are not protected by copyrights and trademarks. This means the developer must protect them as trade secrets, and a non-disclosure agreement helps do this. Basically, an NDA states that what you are discussing with another party is to remain a secret, thus enabling the concepts to be considered trade secrets. If you discuss your concept with someone who hasn't signed an NDA, the concept loses its trade secret status and becomes public domain. So if you want to protect your ideas, don't discuss them with anyone without having an NDA signed.

The two common types of NDAs are unilateral and mutual. A unilateral NDA is used when you are discussing your game concept with someone who is outside of the game industry, such as an independent investor. This protects any ideas you discuss with them, because they don't have secrets—you do. A mutual NDA is used when people in the industry are discussing ideas with each other, such as when a publisher discusses game concepts with an independent developer. This protects the information revealed by both parties. In instances like this, the publisher is likely to provide the NDA.

The catch is, most publishers are reluctant to sign any type of NDA with external developers. This is because publishers review hundreds of games a year; there is a risk they might have a game similar to the one being pitched already in production or the concept stages. You can always ask them, but chances are they will not sign one. Of course, this creates a dilemma for any developer pitching an idea, but in all likelihood, if a publisher is not interested in your game, they will tell you and won't be interested in copying it.

Development Contracts

Development contracts between a publisher and external developer outline what responsibilities each party has to the other. These contracts cover all the issues involved in the developer/publisher relationship, including the financial terms, elements of the project, asset deliverable and advance payment milestone schedules, IP ownership, marketing plans, distribution plans, and obligations of each party.

The financial terms will define exactly what the payment schedule and royalty structure will be. The developer's advances are usually divided into a series of payments that are tied to milestone deliverables. The specific milestone content and deadlines will be detailed in the developer's obligations section of the contract. In addition, specific submission and approval guidelines are set forth for each deliverable.

One of the most important items covered in the contract is the transfer of IP rights from the developer to the publisher. This means the developer relinquishes all rights to the game's code, characters, textures, story, concepts, and anything else that goes into creating the game. It might also cover any proprietary tools the developer creates to streamline the game development process, such as scripting tools, texture editors, or software plug-ins. If the game is based on an existing license, such as a movie, detailed guidelines of how the developer can utilize the license are included.

Development contracts also discuss other contingencies, such as who is responsible for QA testing, localization, publicity, and ancillary rights (such as movie and television deals). Also, as with employee/consultant agreements, information is also included on how disputes between the parties will be arbitrated. The publisher is responsible for finalizing the publishing contract, although the developer will need an attorney to review it before signing.

End User License Agreements (EULA)

End user license agreements protect the publisher and establish a license agreement between the owner of the IP and the end user. The basic purpose of the EULA is to eliminate the resale and rental of the game. However, because of the way console games were originally classified for IP rights, they can be resold and traded; so that is why you are able to rent console games or buy used copies at the local game store. With PC games, the EULA can be written in such as way to make resale illegal. The publisher usually provides a standard EULA for eligible games.

LICENSES

INTERVIEW

Stuart Roch, Executive Producer, Treyarch

When thinking of schedule concerns in particular, ample consideration must be taken on the producer's part to send approval packs off much sooner than they would normally feel necessary. When dealing with a movie licensed game, a producer needs to factor in the longer turnaround time that is a result of active film production schedules, especially when the directors are integral to the creative process.

On *Enter the Matrix,* Warner Brothers approved many of our assets, but in most cases they did so for legal reasons rather than creative ones. Since the Wachowski brothers were so involved with the creation of the game, Warner Brothers allowed them responsibility for the majority of the creative approvals, leaving Warner Brothers the time to help us more with the business side of the game production.

$\rightarrow$

Enter the Matrix was even more unique than other licensed games because the Wachowski brothers were so supportive of the game from the start, thus, giving us a near all-access pass to the film production. By having a nontraditional and completely complementary relationship with the Wachowski Brothers, they opened doors for us that we wouldn't have even been able to approach otherwise. Whether it was working with the primary talent, the costume designer, the visual effects team, or even just bouncing ideas off the brothers themselves, the personal Wachowski touch meant we had a closer collaboration with the film production than I believe was ever attempted up to that time.

Games based on licenses, such as Spider-Man™, James Bond™, or the National Football League™ are becoming more common each year. The allure for publishers to secure well-known licenses is the ability to build upon an audience who is already familiar with the brand, which generates higher awareness for the game and translates into higher sales. For example, it is easier to market an adventure game based on Harry Potter™ than to market one featuring an unknown character and universe. A Harry Potter game immediately means the game will feature Harry and his friends, wizards, amazing adventures, mythical creatures, and a host of other magical characters. An unknown character does not have any immediate associations, so players must be educated about what elements are.

A producer is not normally involved in the actual processing of securing the interactive rights to a license; instead, the producer is usually assigned a project with a specific license already attached. This means the producer must plan for the impact this has on production, particularly on the design, schedule, and asset creation.

Depending on how the licensing deal is structured, the licensor may be minimally involved in the actual game production or be extremely involved in determining the game design, assets, and features. At a minimum, it is likely the licensor has approval rights over the general game concept and key assets, since their main concern is to protect the integrity of the license. For example, if making a game based on a Disney® cartoon, it is unlikely that the developer would be allowed to create content that would get an M rating, as these titles are geared toward children; so a game will never involve Mickey Mouse going on a shooting rampage. These approvals need to be clearly spelled out in the licensing agreement, and the producer must account for these approvals in the schedule. You don't want to hold up production on a title because you forget to schedule two weeks to receive final approval from the licensor on the game concept.

In addition, there may be a bible that clearly spells out what can and cannot be done with characters and settings based on a license. It might detail what types of clothing the character wears, what actions he can perform in the game, what other characters from the universe can appear in the game, and so on. The producer needs to get this information during pre-production so it can all be accounted for and integrated properly into the game. Overall, the producer must be proactive about working with licenses, so establishing a good relationship with your licensing contact is the first step to ensure that approvals, concepts, and assets are approved in a timely fashion.

Create a schedule for the licensor that shows when assets and builds will be sent for approval and indicates the deadline for receiving approval so that the licensor has a better idea of how these approval cycles impact the game's schedule. If you can be proactive about getting the licensor everything they need, you are more likely to have a positive working relationship with them.

INTERVIEW

Jamie Fristrom, Creative Director, Treyarch

When working with a licensor, time must be added to the production schedule for receiving approval on all these materials, and the licensors usually will take as much time as they can. You can have clauses in the contracts that limit how much time they have to approve something; if you don't hear something from them by the deadline, it is "deemed approved," and you can move on with production.

Sometimes you'll find yourself working with two licensors: for example, a movie based on a book or comic. The approval rights will be divvied up between the licensors, or you'll have to submit everything to both parties.

Your licensor probably will leave actual gameplay mechanics or design documentation up to you, but they'll still want to see regular builds of the game so they can see how things are progressing. There are probably many things you just can't do with their character. For example, he might not be allowed to kill anyone, which affects the game design. This can be challenging, but it sometimes helps us to be creative and do things that haven't been done before in games.

SUMMARY

Although producers are not expected to be knowledgeable about all the legal issues involved with developing a game, they should have general knowledge of some of these issues, particularly intellectual property rights, developer agreements, and licenses. This chapter presented a brief overview of these issues and provided examples, so that you, as a producer, will be better prepared to discuss these issues.

The next chapter discusses developer and publisher relationships, information on how to pitch a game to a publisher, and how to manage the developer-publisher relationship. These elements are important for any producer managing an independent developer who is looking for a publishing partner.

5 Developer and Publisher Relationships

In This Chapter

- Pitching a Game to a Publisher
- Managing the Developer-Publisher Relationship
- Third-Party Manufacturers

INTRODUCTION

Developers must have open communication with their publisher, as the publisher is ultimately responsible for creating the final packaged product and marketing it to potential buyers. Publishers must work well with developers, because without the developers, there are no products to sell. These relationships can get very complex, especially if an independent developer and publisher are working together. More complexity is added if they are working on a console or cell phone title that is submitted to a third-party console manufacturer for approval. This chapter discusses the major aspects of the developer-publisher relationship, from pitching a game to a publisher to managing such a relationship.

PITCHING A GAME TO A PUBLISHER

As games get more expensive to make and require larger teams, publishers are very selective about which developers they work with. Wholly owned developers usually have direct access to the people making decisions about which games to develop and, thus, are not under as much pressure to create and pitch a game idea. If a wholly owned developer does not have an idea for a game, it is likely that the publisher will have a game in mind for the developer.

Independent developers, on the other hand, must find a publishing partner to help them get the game finished and on the store shelves. The developer might have a great game idea and already be in pre-production on it, but unless they can find a publisher, it is unlikely the game will be released or turn a profit. In order to find a partner, the developers must pitch their games to potential publishers.

Pitching games is not an easy task, as the developer must be able to successfully communicate the full game experience for the player, even though the game is still not completed—in fact, the game might only be in the concept phase and have no tangible assets. The publisher must get a clear understanding from the pitch on whether the game will deliver on this proposed experience and be profitable.

Because publishers are pitched several hundred games a year, most of them have some type of pitch process in place which allows them to quickly understand the game's potential. It helps them to decide which games are not suitable for their needs and which games warrant more attention and possibly some initial financial support. The pitch process itself will vary based on such things as the type of game being pitched, to whom it is being pitched, how far along the game is in development, and what type of partnership is needed.

Some developers who pitch games do not convey the appropriate information the publisher needs to make an initial decision about the game's value. Since publishers are reviewing several hundred games a year, it is imperative that the developer has an understanding of what information and materials are needed for the pitch. The best way to learn how to pitch a game successfully is to talk to other developers and to someone in the publisher's acquisitions department. Lee Jacobson, the Vice President of Business Development and Acquisitions for Midway Entertainment, has some concrete advice on what is needed to prepare a game pitch that will get noticed.

INTERVIEW

Lee Jacobson, VP of Business Development and Acquisitions, Midway Entertainment

Ten to fifteen years ago, games used to be all about the novelty of the gameplay mechanics. Now that games have evolved into more mainstream entertainment, it's really about telling stories and how the stories are executed. Also, as games are getting more expensive, publishers have more departments, such as publishing, marketing, sales, and product development, that are weighing in on game decisions. Because so many people are involved, an independent developer who is pitching an original game must be able to communicate the idea in a very limited amount of time. When I get pitches from developers, there are three assets that I find invaluable for judging the game's publishing potential.

The first item is a very brief treatment of the game. This is a one to two page executive summary of the game that explains the essence of the game, how it can be positioned in the marketplace, and how it can be communicated to the customer or retailer. If you have to go through a long dissertation explaining the merits of your game, it is likely the mass market consumer will not immediately understand the game's appeal.

Don't spend time creating a detailed design document. At the pitch stage, this is not important. For one thing, publishers don't have time to read them. Also, after a publisher starts working with a developer, the publisher's feedback will affect the game's design. Unfortunately, most developers spend a lot of time of writing a document that details all the gameplay mechanics and all the wonderful features of their game, but are unable to describe their game in one or two sentences that show why people will want to buy the game.

The second item, and it really is becoming the norm, is a playable prototype or vertical slice of game. It doesn't need to be long, but it must show how the final game will look and play—no apologies for visual quality, animation quality, production values, camera cuts, lighting, and so on. I always tell developers I would much rather see a two-minute slice of gameplay where the environment looks amazing, rather then a huge world where you can wander for two hours but it looks horrible.

A highly-polished demo is more likely to get the developer to the next step in the publisher's pitch process. It lets the publisher know that the developer not only understands what the game is about but also knows what the consumer needs to see. This is important; a lot of developers lose sight of this and don't realize it's not about what they think is cool, but what the consumers think is cool.

The third thing is a game trailer. It only needs to be 30 seconds to one minute long, but from the moment it starts, everything—including the mood music, the animation, the setup, and the camera angles—must work together to convey the emotional experience of the game. It has to be edited right, narrated correctly, and interlaced with game footage in order to give the publisher an understanding of how cool the game is.

→

The high production values of the trailer will reinforce the idea that not only does the developer understand how to make a game, but they also understand how to turn it into an entertainment vehicle. These game trailers can easily be disseminated around the publisher's organization and allow anyone to immediately get a feel for whether the game works or doesn't. Game trailers also are handy since everyone can pop in the video and easily view the highlights of the game.

There is other supporting material developers can prepare to demonstrate that they understand the game's market and what they want the game to do; for example, a very brief overview of the game's competitive titles and how the game's features make it different from what is already out there. Don't make the mistake of listing technical features as game features, such as better real-time normal mapping. Instead, focus on what distinguishes the game and how the publisher can sell it to a mass audience. Other information to include is a summary of other games created by the developer and the review scores. Information of this nature helps the publisher determine how risky a particular developer may be. Finally, include a top line assessment of the schedule and approximate budget; this information will get more detailed as the game makes it further in the process.

The typical deal is the standard publisher-developer model in which the publisher funds 100 percent of the game's development as an advance against future royalties and sales of the game. In this deal, the publisher typically provides the third-party commercial software, the tools, and the development kits. The developer is required to fulfill monthly milestones that are evaluated on a regular basis by the publisher. Various royalty structures can be brought to bear on this. As the risk profile changes from the publisher to the developer, the deal can change.

There are also co-publishing deals. In this instance, the game is usually fully funded by the development studio, and they are looking for a publisher who can package the game and distribute it to retailers. The publisher will get a distribution fee, which is usually a percentage of the game's sales. The fee depends on what the publisher brings to the table, which can range from packaging and distributing the game to funding the marketing campaign.

MANAGING THE DEVELOPER-PUBLISHER RELATIONSHIP

After a developer and publisher have committed to a relationship, the relationship must be maintained, regardless of whether the developer is independent or owned by the publisher. The basics of maintaining the relationships are similar in each case—the publisher needs to be informed of the game's progress, and the developer needs resources and support from the publisher.

Ignoring this relationship can be detrimental to the development process. If the developer does not communicate with the publisher on a regular basis about the progress of the game, the publisher might become frustrated at the perceived lack of progress. This frustration may cause the publisher to allocate needed resources to another project, assign the project to another developer, or cancel the project. If the publisher does not give feedback to the developer throughout the production process, the developer might fulfill all the milestone requirements, but the finished product may not be what the publisher thought he was getting. In cases like this, the publisher might ask for additional changes after the fact, which means additional costs and resources for both the developer and publisher.

This relationship is made more complex because both the developer and publisher have a high stake in the game's success and will do whatever they can to ensure this success. Additional complexity is added because there are people on both sides who have a say in how certain things will be in the game. For example, publishers often assign their own producer to work with the developer, in concert with the developer's producer. This situation of having two producers on the project might create some confusion if the two producers' responsibilities aren't clearly defined.

The Publisher Producer (PP) is the publishing company's representative and will make sure that all sales, marketing, operations, and testing efforts are in sync with the game's production schedule. He is usually responsible for reviewing the developer's milestone deliveries and authorizing payment. Additional responsibilities might include coordinating the marketing and localization tasks on the game.

If the developer is owned by the publisher, they still submit builds for approval but have an advantage because they are on the publisher's payroll already. The developer's payment is not tied to completing the milestone deliveries. This does not absolve the developer from delivering completed milestones on time, but it does provide them more flexibility regarding when these milestones are reviewed.

The PP is not responsible for the day-to-day management of the development team. This responsibility is the Developer's Producer (DP). The DP is responsible for creating the game development plan and making sure that this plan is completed during the production cycle. The DP is deals with any HR issues within the team, equipment requests, and anything else that directly affects people on the development team.

INTERVIEW

Tobi Saulnier, President, 1st Playable Productions

The role differences of a producer in an independent and publisher-owned studio are very different. In some respects they are the same; however, in other aspects the whole relationship with the customer is fundamentally changed.

→

For example, when working as an independent studio, each contract offers a substantial business risk if any delays or other issues are encountered. You might lose a lot of money and endanger your business; you might lose that customer and endanger your business; and so on. Additionally, since your customers probably each have their own unique processes and systems, for each project you will need to translate between whatever set of processes and systems your customers are using and the internal systems being used by your development team—bug databases, forms, approval processes, and so on.

As a publisher-owned studio, you might incur the wrath of your boss if you go late or over budget, but the consequences are much lower in that your studio is unlikely to be closed (unless that is the only project you are doing, and you have repeated performance failures). Also, there's a lot more conformity within an internal studio with respect to processes and systems. Because you only have the one customer, all your processes with the publisher are consistent and can be streamlined. However, your customer now has greatly increased visibility into the project and has a lot more direct control of everything from features to the development approach. For instance, instead of debating the price for a project and providing a service that will cause them to choose you over other developers, you need to be able to justify your budget and negotiate a feasible scope and schedule with your marketing department. So, as an internal studio, the customer management aspect of the producer role is fundamentally different; it becomes more management of organization hierarchy versus management of customers.

INTERVIEW

Jeff Matsushita, Greenlight Czar, Activision

Most companies have a formal method of overseeing the progress of titles in production. In my current role at Activision, it is my job to use this kind of a process to ensure that the development cycle is on track, that the product is meeting our expectations, and that everyone involved with the title is on the same page. Through this and my previous experiences, I have had the privilege to work with many developers, both internal and external, and gain some interesting insights into the way developers and publishers work together in our industry.

Many factors affect the relationship between the developer and the publisher, such as the terms of the deal, whether the developer is internal or external, and the developer's track record for shipping high-quality titles on time and on budget.

Another factor that influences this relationship is who brings the Intellectual Property (IP) to the table. For instance, the publisher will feel more strongly about a project when they provide the IP. In this case, the publisher will likely have more feedback in

$\rightarrow$

the development process, since they want their license to be represented appropriately. In essence, the publisher becomes the developer's customer. On the other hand, if a developer brings an IP to the table, the publisher will focus on working with the developer to ensure that there is a strong marketing effort to support the developer's vision of the game. These instances are rare as the developer must bring a strong, established franchise and have a history of executing on it, or they must have a high-quality game that is very close to completion.

Because of the increasingly larger budgets necessary to develop and market AAA games, publishers are more cautious with unproven properties and with unproven developers. In most cases, publishers will go only to proven developers with established IPs. Additionally, publishers will prefer to work with an internal developer on a new IP so they can have better visibility into the project and better assess risk.

In a broad sense, I like to differentiate between the *project* and *product*. I see the *project* as the results of the developer's hard work—the program, the art, the sound, and so on. The *product* is the final package that is advertised to the media, shipped to the distributors, and purchased by consumers. In short, the publisher is responsible for taking the developer's *project* and making it into a *product*. The publisher takes the project, tests it, submits it for approval, creates a marketing campaign, designs the packaging, puts it into the box, and handles sales and distribution of the product. When the IP starts with the publisher, they may also fund the development and provide the initial key creative elements. The key thing is that the publisher takes the efforts of the developer and converts it into something that produces revenue for everyone. In the most basic terms, it can be said that the publisher is in the business of selling games, while the developer has the job of making games.

To facilitate this process, a publisher will assign a producer to work on the title. This publisher-side producer is responsible for tracking the overall risk associated with the development of the project, which includes making sure that the developer is providing everything promised in a timely manner and is managing the development team effectively. In addition, the producer works with the developer to help them make the best game possible. The producer will deploy publisher resources for focus-testing features and providing feedback to the developer. Finally, the producer also continually herds all of the processes of production to make sure that the development, marketing, testing, and localization efforts remain in sync.

The developer, on the other hand, is responsible for completing the project. Unless there are specific IP-related assets brought to the table by the publisher, this includes everything required to develop the software and is usually provided to the publisher in the form of deliverables predetermined in the early stages of the engagement. The decision on how to manage the project team is the developer's choice. The publisher does not necessarily have a say in how the deliverables are completed so long as they are delivered on time. If, however, the deliverables slip, are of marginal quality, or the developer is showing clear signs that they are suffering from other problems, the publisher will likely show greater interest in how the project is being

→

completed. This does not mean the publisher wants to step in and take over, but they might demand greater visibility into the project to make sure that the game is going well and that their investment is not at risk.

In order to minimize these kinds of things from happening, the developer must provide as much information as possible when delivering milestones to publishers so as to shape expectations properly. For instance, a game rarely shows well early in development. A prototype that has only basic scenes, basic controls, basic visual effects, and so on will not likely impress too many people who have no context in which to place it. When a developer provides these kinds of builds, it is essential they spend the time to set up the deliverables carefully so that everyone understands why the materials are successful and how they show that the development is proceeding with a minimum level of risk to quality, schedule, and even sometimes, budget. The publisher wants to understand how such a limited portion of the overall game fits into the development plan and how it will evolve into a AAA title.

Another aspect of establishing context is for the developer to be clear about what "done" means. If not explicitly defined, "done" can mean anything from being viewable on a development kit with placeholder art, basic features playable in-game, or bug-free and ready to ship. Naturally, if the publisher is expecting final quality and the developer only meant to provide first pass, people will end up arguing about the value of the build and inevitably begin questioning the progress of development as a whole. But if there are details on what is included in the deliverable, for example, 10 percent of all animations are finished, polished, and viewable in-game along with the list of animations completed, the publisher can gain a much better understanding of what is included in the deliverable. Accordingly, the publisher can better assess the state of the game. If the publisher is looking at a deliverable that the developer says is done, and it is obvious that it is not done, the publisher will lose trust in the developer, and the developer is not likely to understand why.

In order to help mitigate this, most publishers prefer that the developer spell out the specifics of the milestones. In these cases, the publisher will not dictate what the content for each deliverable is, but they may have milestone definitions of what is expected at alpha, beta, first playable, and so on that map appropriately with the state of development. The developer is responsible for telling the publisher when the game engine, animations, art, AI, and so on will be completed and then managing the project to deliver on these milestones. The only time the publisher gets involved in the development process is if they don't think things are getting finished and their development is at risk.

In every situation, having a strong publisher-developer relationship with open communication is important. The publisher and developer each have obligations to fulfill in this relationship in order for the title to be successful. The most important is to spend as much time as possible spelling out the specifics of deliverables. As the only ultimate criterion for a successful development is whether or not a game is fun— an abstract concept at best—it is important that in all other ways, communication is in the most concrete terms possible.

Independent Developer

Independent developers rely heavily on the publisher to provide the finances for completing a game. After a publisher has signed on a developer, they negotiate a delivery and payment schedule for the project milestones. This schedule is affected by factors such as the hardware platform, the scope of the game, terms of the contract, any licensed intellectual properties (IPs), and other project variables. No delivery and payment schedule will be exactly the same, although the same types of deliverables will be expected throughout the process.

During the initial pre-production phase, the publisher will expect to get detailed design and technical documentation, a full budget, schedule, and staffing plan, and a gameplay proof of concept. In some instances, these materials have already been created and presented to the publisher in the initial pitch.

At this stage, the publisher may want further information on what production processes will be used to track the progress of the game. This is a valid concern since the publisher is making an investment in the game and wants to realize a profit on this venture. If the PP is not confident in the DP's ability to manage the production process, the PP may become very involved in the day-to-day production tasks being performed by the team. This is not an ideal situation, as the publisher is not interested in running a development team—that's why the project was assigned to an external vendor in the first place. However, the publisher will do whatever is necessary to protect the investment.

After full production has started on the title, the publisher expects to see regular builds of the game. While reviewing the build, the PP will provide feedback and will request changes to the game. This is expected to happen within a reasonable scope, and the additional feedback will likely improve the overall quality of the game. For example, the PP might ask for a level to be rescripted or for the game controls to be adjusted.

In some cases, the publisher will request a major feature change or for a new feature to be added. When the DP receives these requests, he needs to evaluate the request to see whether it fits within the agreed upon scope of the game, as outlined in the documentation and milestone schedule. In some instances, the request replaces a planned feature and, thus, might not impact the scope or schedule negatively.

In other instances, the feature request will impact the schedule and resources, meaning additional production costs are incurred by both parties. When this happens, the DP must immediately make the publisher aware of the impact: the schedule may need an extension; the developer may need to hire more people; or other features must be cut in order to accommodate the request. If any of these changes happen, the DP and PP must renegotiate the milestones and payments.

A developer dealing with additional feature requests and feedback from the publisher may get frustrated, but if a solid working relationship is established with the PP, this frustration can be minimized. The PP is there to help the developer, and a good PP will work with the developer to deal with any unexpected issues on the project.

INTERVIEW

Wade Tinney and Coray Seifert, Large Animal Games

We are a small independent developer who makes games for the casual, downloadable games market. In the past we would usually have six or so projects in development concurrently, varying in production time from six weeks to six months. This model was successful for us, but now that our catalog of original titles is earning royalties, we are in the position of not having to do as many small projects. Our focus now is on larger projects, with a six- to eight-month development cycle. We have both internally funded projects, like *Rocketbowl*, as well as third-party publisher funded projects, such as *Saints & Sinners Bingo*, from which we also receive a share of the back end.

Publishers are a relatively new phenomenon in the downloadable game space. There are only a few companies who are actively funding third-party development at the moment.

Although we are not a traditional PC or console game developer, the relationship we have with our publisher is similar. We work with them to create a development plan at the beginning of the project, which defines the core features, the milestones, and the payment schedule. However, the publisher we work with is smaller, which means we have to deal with less corporate overhead, and there is greater flexibility in general.

Over the course of a six–eight month project, we usually have about eight key milestones, which include such deliverables as design complete, core feature complete, and content complete. The publisher works with us during the development process to ensure these milestones are delivered complete and on time. The publisher provides some QA resources, produces marketing materials, and secures deals with distribution partners.

We have a good relationship with our publisher. We speak with the publisher about once a week, depending on where we are in the project. When issues arise, we may speak with them several times a day. Overall, if things are going well during the development cycle, the publisher is not actively involved. But if the publisher has some concerns, they are brought to our attention and we will address them. The publisher gives good feedback, and it never feels like it is mandated; they trust us to deliver a quality game experience.

For a small developer working in the downloadable games market, having a publisher-backed product can have significant advantages. A publisher can really help push your game to the top and secure a better deal and better promotions with an online game distributor.

Publisher-Owned Developer

As stated earlier, the big benefit of being a wholly owned developer is that the finances are guaranteed, which means the team can concentrate on making the game, instead of worrying about getting their milestone payments in a timely fashion.

In this type of relationship, the publisher is also more intimately involved with the team during the development process, which means they can offer more resources to the team. For example, the publisher can temporarily lend the team experts from other internal projects, making it possible for the team to complete a critical task on time. It is also easier for the publisher to make feature requests and grant schedule extensions to ensure that a requested feature gets into the game.

Some publishers will still assign a PP to work with a wholly owned developer. The PP will work with the DP to coordinate the testing, marketing, and other tasks for the game. The PP is not likely to run the day-to-day activities of the development team but may be more involved in what production processes are used, especially if there are company-wide processes that must be adhered to.

Jamie Fristrom, a creative director at Treyarch, has this say about the developer-publisher relationship: "Being owned changes your outlook on staffing. When you are independent, you try not to hire people until you are sure you need them. When you are in-house, you try to get people as soon as possible, even if you are not sure you need them. Since your publisher or owner is trying to place people at several different studios, and they are not focused just on your studio, more time is needed to get the right people. When they come along, we want to get them before they are assigned to another developer."

INTERVIEW

Tobi Saulnier, President, 1st Playable

Before Vicarious Visions was owned by Activision, it was an independent developer who worked with many publishers. Having this variety of customers and unique contracts has a major impact on the management of product development.

Vicarious Visions' approach was to assign an internal producer to each title, who was called a project manager (PM) to distinguish that role from the publisher producer (PP). The PM is involved very early in the initial project assessment of feasibility. The PM is multidisciplinary and must be able to communicate with art, design, engineering, and the publisher. In addition, the PM must be able to understand the marketing and sales limitations of the project. They work directly with the PP who provides the channel for all marketing plans, financial backing, license requirements, ship dates, and so on.

→

Although the management at Vicarious Visions provided a lot of support, especially early in the development process, during most of the development, the PM was the main point of contact for the PP. This helps streamline the communication between the developer and publisher. After a project is ready to begin, the PM is provided a project charter that documents the internal goals and assumptions of the game that were developed during the sales process, and this is used to prevent loss of information during the hand-off to the development team.

As the project begins, the PM works closely with the PP on what the constraints are for the IP. For example, specific guidelines are defined on what characters and story elements can be used, what new content can be created, and what themes can be used. As pre-production progresses, the PM works with their development team to make sure that they understand the constraints and that open questions are resolved.

During pre-production, the PM works with the designer and leads to create the game design and technical design documents, style guide, and development schedule, which defines the details of the remaining milestones.

After the game design document is completed and the title goes into production, the project requires much less marketing interaction and is entirely in the hands of the PM as the team proceeds toward the agreed-upon features and schedule. The PM is responsible for making sure that everyone has what is needed to be productive, presenting the in-progress assets to the PP for review, filling out licensor approval forms, and other things.

The PM role can change depending on how overworked or experienced the PP is. Sometimes, the assigned PP has only one project and, thus, can provide more support to the PM. In other cases, the PP will have 10 projects and cannot provide a lot of support to the PM. This means the PM must be prepared to step up to handle such diverse tasks as licensor approval paperwork, localization, early testing coordination, and preparation of materials for marketing and PR, even if the PP is ultimately responsible for them.

Ultimately, the PM must do whatever is necessary to keep the project organized and running smoothly. This includes attention to the game, reviewing features and play-testing, monitoring progress through resource allocation, and tracking schedules.

The PM must also write build notes and obtain milestone approvals from the PP. Finally, as soon as the project runs into issues, the PM works with the project leads to find solutions. It helps if the PM has some area of expertise in art, design, or engineering so they can understand the hands-on details of how the game is put together. Between all of these roles, the PM is also the team's lead cheerleader and attends to the care and feeding of the team, ensures that milestones are celebrated, and everyone manages to have some fun between the deadlines.

THIRD-PARTY MANUFACTURERS

Games published for proprietary hardware platforms, such as consoles or cell phones, must be submitted to the appropriate third-party manufacturer for approval, such as Sony®, Microsoft®, or Nintendo®. In most cases, the developer needs to get the game concept approved by the third-party manufacturer before production begins on the game. For example, both Sony and Microsoft require a product proposal before development begins on a title. If the developer skips this step in the process, he might find that the fully developed title is rejected outright by the manufacturer before it is even submitted for formal approval and manufacturing.

These manufacturers also have a standard set of requirements that each product must meet in order to be approved for release, so the developer must plan for these requirements in the pre-production and production phases. Usually the manufacturers will assign an account manager as the main point of contact to help the developer navigate the submission process. If you are working on a highly anticipated title, the manufacturer might have feedback on how to improve the game to best show off the specific features of the gaming platform. Refer to Chapter 22, "Code Releasing," for more information on the console submission process.

SUMMARY

Independent developers have a different publishing relationship than developers who are wholly owned by their publishers. These relationships are reflected in how the producer interacts with the publisher. In each case, the producer is still responsible for guiding the team through the development process but may take on different sets of responsibilities based on the publisher-developer relationship. This chapter discussed these relationships and some ways for producers to effectively manage it. It also gave information on some best practices for putting together a game pitch.

This chapter concludes the "Business Information" part of the book. The next part of the book focuses on how to effectively manage people on the development team. The first chapter in the section discusses how to hire and retain quality talent.

Part III

Managing People

Because people are the most valuable resource on any development team, an understanding of how to effectively manage people is critical for any producer. Even when the game is dangerously off-schedule, if the team is well managed and motivated, they will have a better chance of delivering a successful project.

People skills don't come naturally to everyone, but don't worry if you are not a people person. If you are serious about being an effective leader for your team, you can improve your management skills.

This section of the book focuses on what skills are necessary for successfully managing the people side of projects. Information is presented on how to motivate a team, how to provide feedback, how to identify talent, and how to improve communication between yourself and the team. Topics include the following:

- Hiring and Retaining Talent
- Project Leadership
- Building Teams
- Motivating People
- Effective Communication

6 Hiring and Retaining Talent

In This Chapter

- Hiring Talent
- Retaining Talent
- Training

INTRODUCTION

Having the right mix of talent and personalities who are passionate about games goes a long way toward making the game a success. A group of people may work together on a single game for four years or more, and if they don't get along or complement each other's talents, the game's quality and chances of success will diminish because more time will be spent managing personalities than making the game. For instance, the producer or lead should not spend an excessive amount of time with a difficult personality in the hopes that he will improve, as this takes the producer's attention away from other critical areas of the game.

As a producer, you may not have hiring or firing privileges, but you are involved in the interview process and have some influence on who is hired and added to the team. The hiring process allows you to be selective about which people eventually become employees. As a producer, you want to be selective about who is hired, because you will be responsible for dealing with any personnel issues, such as tardiness, low-quality work, missed deadlines, and so on. This chapter presents some general information on hiring, retaining, and training talent from the producer's point of view.

HIRING TALENT

Finding talent can be difficult, especially if you are not located in one of the game development hubs in California, New York, or Texas. However, people with a talent and passion for making games are more than willing to relocate for the right opportunity. You have several available resources for finding talent—working with recruiters, posting job openings on the company Web site, and recruiting people at game development conferences and trade shows. Also, keep in mind that the right person for the job might find you, as there are numerous people interested in making games for a living. They may not be experienced for some of the more senior positions, but they might be excellent entry-level talent.

You may have an on-site Human Resources (HR) department that handles the hiring process, or you may be able to use your publisher's HR department. In either case, the HR department is usually the initial point of contact for all potential candidates and handles the logistics of creating and posting job descriptions, collecting resumes, coordinating phone interviews, making travel arrangements for in-person interviews, negotiating salaries, and extending final offers.

The producer is responsible for informing the HR department of what the hiring needs are, providing details for the job description, and interviewing prospective candidates. The producer may also determine who else on the team needs to interview the candidates.

The interview process begins by looking over submitted resumes and selecting a list of prospective candidates for an initial phone interview. The producer or lead usually conducts this interview and makes a recommendation on whether this person is brought in for an interview. If someone is brought in for an on-site interview, as many people as possible should have the opportunity to interview him. Ideally, everyone on the team can be involved, but this may not be possible if there are more than 10 people on the team. In cases like this, the main people interfacing with this person on a regular basis are involved in the interviewing process.

After the candidate is interviewed, the producer and other people involved in the process provide feedback on the candidate's strengths and weaknesses. This information is used to determine whether an offer is extended. If this is for a senior position on the development team, such as a lead, studio management is also involved in the hiring process and likely has final say on who gets hired. This is especially true if it is a large studio with multiple projects, as it is assumed the candidate will roll on to other projects as necessary.

INTERVIEW

Wade Tinney and Coray Seifert, Large Animal Games

We have set up a reliable and controlled process for screening potential Large Animal employees, which cuts down on the time spent interviewing developers and brings the best candidates to the top of the list. When we are looking to fill a new position, we post the job description on our Web site along with an online questionnaire that each applicant must answer before uploading their resume. We include questions such as, "Have you worked on a game project?" to "What are the last three games you played?", and "What's the best job you've had, and why did you like it?" This questionnaire serves as a good filter, giving us a more accurate sense of an applicant's personality, communication skills, and professionalism than a resume can provide.

We had more than 150 responses to an ad we posted recently for an artist—an overwhelming response for a small company like ours. By using a questionnaire, we were able to narrow down the list to 10 candidates that we targeted for phone interviews. For example, many people on the list were quickly eliminated because of their unprofessional responses to the questions, which often included typos and poor grammar. These responses indicated that the person was not that serious or passionate about the position and had a low attention to detail. When we had a short list of ten candidates, we asked them for references and followed up with at least two of those people for each candidate. Then we did short 10-minute phone interviews, and finally, had in-person interviews with 6 applicants.

Like most companies, retaining people is an issue for us, but no one who has worked there for longer than six months has ever left. Quite simply, we want Large Animal to be the best job that our employees will ever have. We want an atmosphere that is both fun and challenging, and for our employees to have a quality of life that is better than they'd have at larger game companies that can afford to pay higher salaries. All of us have worked for large companies in the past, and we've made a conscious choice to remain small so we can preserve the strong sense of camaraderie and creative involvement. Since casual, downloadable games are much smaller than a typical retail title, employees at Large Animal have the opportunity to work on a much greater variety of projects than they would at a traditional PC or console developer.

Screening Resumes

Screening resumes and reviewing portfolios is the first step in narrowing down a pool of potential candidates. When looking at resumes, make note of whether the candidate's work history has any major gaps—this could indicate that he was fired, and it took a while for him to find another position, or that he took time off to go back to school, was laid off, or needed time to attend to personal matters. You will want to ask the candidate about any gaps in employment during the initial phone interview.

If the candidate has a history of hopping between jobs—six months at one company, one year at another company—this is a red flag. It may indicate that he is not very dedicated to his job and is more interested in salary increases or that he has a hard time staying employed. On the other hand, he could have a had a run of bad luck with lay-offs at several companies in a row.

If a candidate lists shipped title credits on the resume, don't feel guilty about double-checking them. It is not unheard of for people to exaggerate (or even outright lie) about their contribution to a game. Moby Games (*www.mobygames.com*) is a Web site that lists game credits and is a good place to double-check this information. Moby Games is not a comprehensive list by any means, but it is a good starting point to do a quick reference check.

Additionally, you might want to check out what type of reviews the candidate's titles received, especially if you are looking to fill a lead position, and this person has a lead credit on other titles. If the games consistently have poor reviews, you might want to ask about this if you choose to interview him. GameRankings.com (*www.gamerankings.com*) and Metacritic (*www.metacritic.com*) are both useful online databases with game reviews.

Pay attention to how the candidate describes his job responsibilities at previous jobs. If the descriptions seem to have a lot of words, but little or repetitive information, he might be padding what his actual duties were on the game. Be especially wary of any outrageous claims that don't seem to fit with the job title, such as a scripter stating, "completely redesigned the single-player aspects of the game during production." You will definitely want to get more information on things like this during the phone interview.

Finally, pay attention to how much industry experience the candidate has. It is unlikely you are interested in hiring someone with absolutely no experience for a intermediate position on a team. If you are looking to hire someone entry-level, you might be open to looking at someone with no industry experience, but try to determine whether their previous work experience prepares them for an entry-level position. Also, does this person play games? Although this may not be a huge factor for certain positions, you do want someone who enjoys having fun and has a general understanding of games.

INTERVIEW

Melanie Cambron, Game Recruiter

The interviewing process really begins with the resume. When screening resumes, I look for a career that has made a logical progression. The game industry is volatile, and layoffs are very common, so a history of rapid job changes does not always spell

→

trouble, as it might in other industries. Nevertheless, you need to exercise caution because you don't want a new employee who jumps ship in 30 days. For me, a solid candidate is someone with an education who has worked in the industry for a while, has shown good stability and growth at each prior company, and has successfully shipped well-received titles. Furthermore, I look for people whose salary and job expectations match up with their experience and sought position.

Next, for those candidates who make it past the resume screen and into the interview, it is important to remember that not only is the company evaluating the candidate, but the candidate is also evaluating the company. It is crucial that all key team members interview the candidate, particularly those who will be interfacing with this person on a regular basis, and it is also important that those same team members check their egos at the door. Often, younger team members take the interview opportunity to flex their power in a less than favorable fashion. Although it's vital to really get to the meat and potatoes of a candidate, it's just as vital to do so without arrogance. To get the key talent you want, the company needs to be perceived as welcoming.

The company must also be perceived as "smart," so prepare the team to properly interview. Make sure that everyone has an understanding of the basic questions to ask during the interview to elicit details on the candidate's skill set and how he has interacted with people and teams in the past. Go over these questions with team members before the interview.

When the interviewing is completed, it's time to analyze the results. If you have multiple people interviewing a candidate, you will rarely get a 100 percent consensus on whether to hire a candidate, so you must weigh the opinions based on several factors including the interviewer's position on the team, the working relationship the interviewer would have to the potential employee, and how much you trust the interviewer's ability to judge character and skills. Investigate why those who said "no" did so. Are their objections reasonable? If possible, it is an excellent idea to gather the interviewers together and discuss the prospective candidate in a round-table forum. This helps elicit a more well-rounded perspective, and you might discover the candidate gave different information to different people.

Interviewing Talent

After the resumes are screened and potential candidates are selected, most companies do an initial phone interview before bringing the candidate in for an on-site interview. The phone interview allows you to get an initial idea about what the candidate is looking for. If he has unreasonable or different expectations about salary, responsibilities, working conditions, and so on, the phone interview is a good way to find out before spending additional time and money pursuing this candidate.

Ask basic questions in the phone interview and try to get a feel for the person's personality, passion, and talent. Some interview questions include the following:

- What type of position are you looking for?
- What do you think the job responsibilities are for the position you're applying for? Why are you suited for this position?
- Why are you interested in leaving your current position?
- What skills do you bring to our company? What skills will you develop by working for us?
- What are your strengths? What are your weaknesses?
- What types of games do you play?
- Have you played [Insert name of game developed by your company]? What did you like about it? What would you change?

If the position requires relocation, ask the potential candidate whether this is a problem, and what the timeframe is for his relocation if an offer is extended.

If the candidate is selected for an on-site interview, schedule multiple interviews on the same day so the candidate can meet with as many potential team members as possible. Make sure that the team understands how to properly interview people. If they don't understand how to interview someone, good candidates will be less than impressed by questions such as "Who's your favorite G.I. Joe character?" and "Who would win, Darth Vader or Sauron?" Additionally, questions like this don't give any information about the candidate's skills, background, or how he can apply his experience to your development team. So although team members who ask questions like this might really like the person and encourage you to hire him, you have to question the validity of their judgment, since they don't have any information to make an educated guess on how well the candidate will actually perform his duties on the team.

Appropriate interview questions revolve around the applicant's skills, previous experiences, job expectations, and future career plans. The on-site interview is where you and the team can get firsthand information about his philosophies on game development, how well he works with teams, and how well his skills fit the position. Questions include many of the same ones asked during the phone screening, plus more specific questions as necessary. For example, if you are hiring a 3D modeler, the art lead needs to get specifics about the candidate's skill using 3D graphics software. An engineering candidate needs to be grilled by the lead engineer on his coding skills and what programming languages he knows.

Don't shy away from asking the candidate to demonstrate his skills. For instance, if you are hiring a scripter, ask potential candidates to bring some scripting samples to the job interview. Also, consider setting aside some time during the interview to give him a mini-tutorial on the scripting tool used for your game and see whether he can put together something simple in 30 minutes. Artists should bring their portfolios, and engineers may be able to bring code samples, as long as the samples are not confidential.

Providing Feedback

After the candidate is interviewed, the team provides feedback on whether this person is a good fit for the position. As discussed earlier, it is rare for the producer to have the final say on who to hire for a position; this decision is normally made by studio management, who will give careful consideration to the producer and team's feedback. If multiple candidates are interviewed, finding someone suitable is more likely. However, you may have only one or two qualified candidates at a time for a position, so feedback needs to be considered carefully before HR extends an employment offer.

The key thing to remember when providing feedback is to be specific about what you liked and didn't like. Saying someone is a "solid candidate" does not give any information as to why this person should be hired. Specifics like "gave intelligent answers to questions," "was able to come up with creative solutions for some common issues we face on the team," and "identified areas of improvement in our development process," provide more definition on what a person's strengths are. Also, remember to be objective in your appraisal of a candidate—really consider the talents and skills he brings to the position, not whether he is a Star Trek fan, has a strange haircut, or went to your rival university.

If you don't think a candidate is suitable for a given position, don't hesitate to explain why. Again, provide specifics. You will need to tell others your reasons—especially if they have a positive impression. If there are some red flags about the candidate, but otherwise you think he is a possible fit, discuss these red flags with others involved in the interviewing process to find out whether they had these same reservations as well. Overall, it is good to get everyone together to discuss their feedback on the candidate so the assessment is more well-rounded.

INTERVIEW

Working with Recruiters, Melanie Cambron, Game Recruiter

Recruiters are most effective when you are looking for top-caliber talent, especially if this talent works for the competition. This prevents you from having to approach this person directly, which can be bad form.

The first step for working with a recruiter is to prepare a very detailed job description. The more information you can give the recruiter about the job and the team, the better. Work environment? Team chemistry? Team dynamic? Shortcomings of other candidates? Type of personality that would fit well? Type that wouldn't? The more specifics, the fewer candidates you will need to interview, and the faster the recruiting process.

$\rightarrow$

Armed with this information, the recruiter approaches possible candidates and assesses their potential. The recruiter addresses all of the client's and potential candidate's questions and expectations at the beginning of the process to reduce any surprises on either side. This puts the review process positively underway with both parties feeling confident that the basics, such as relocation allowances, salary, benefits, and immigration concerns, are already covered to everyone's satisfaction. The recruiter then coordinates the phone screening and face-to-face interviews and checks references if necessary.

After a candidate is selected, the recruiter will facilitate the hiring process by coordinating the offer, the relocation, and any visa issues. Finally, when the candidate is settled into his new position, the recruiter will follow up with both the candidate and the client to make sure they are satisfied.

RETAINING TALENT

Retaining good talent is a challenge for many companies, as people are always looking for a better opportunity or work situation, especially if they are not happy in their current position. If you have talented people on your team you want to keep, do what you can to fulfill their expectations and keep them happy. This doesn't mean you have to cater to their every whim, but it does mean you need to give them the necessary resources to do their jobs; that you listen to their complaints, suggestions, and ideas; and that you provide them an opportunity to grow with the company.

Surprisingly, money is not the primary motivator for most people; trust and respect are. If given the choice, most people will choose to make less money and work at a company where they are respected by their peers, listened to by management, and trusted to make choices about their contributions, rather than make more money in an environment where they are treated disrespectfully, ignored, and given no choices about their contributions. Money certainly helps retain talented people, but if they don't have the other things, they will start looking for a company that can provide them, even if it means a pay cut.

People also want to be rewarded for commitment, loyalty, and high-quality work. Again, this does not necessarily translate into a monetary reward—although bonuses are certainly appreciated—but instead is given in the form of more responsibility, increased respect within the company (especially from management), and higher profile assignments. If someone feels like his contributions are not properly recognized, he will be become frustrated and eventually leave the company. It is critical that you know which employees are surpassing expectations and really working hard to make the game the best it can be, so you can give them the recognition they deserve. These people are the ones who will be your most loyal team members and will serve as positive examples for how other people on the team can expect to be treated if they demonstrate the same traits.

In addition to these intangible benefits, there are also some tangible benefits that contribute to a more employee-friendly working environment:

Good benefits (full medical, dental, eye care, vacation, paternity leave): A good benefits package goes a long way to show employees that the company values them.

Health club membership: Encourage employees to be fit; this contributes to better health and less sick time away from work.

Flexible working hours: Flexible work hours allow people to tailor their work time so they can put in their best work—some people work better early in the morning; others prefer working late into the night. In order to foster collaboration among all team members, set core hours when people are required to be in the office.

Up-to-date, functional hardware: People become frustrated if they are expected to perform their tasks on hardware that is not suited to their tasks. Out-of-date hardware will cut into the production schedule because it will take people longer to complete their work on slower machines. When you are talking about compiling code or rendering characters, inadequate hardware can add days to the schedule.

Free sodas and snacks: Everyone enjoys small treats like this, and this is something inexpensive the company can provide. Don't forget to provide healthy snacks and fruit juice.

Downtime to play competitors' games: Set aside some time around 5 P.M. for the team to check out the competition. This is a great team-building activity.

Creative and appealing work environment: You can't expect creative employees to do their best work in the middle of a cubicle farm. Provide them something interesting to look at and some toys to play with.

Of course, there are many other things that show employees they are valued. Please see Chapter 7, "Teams," for more examples.

TRAINING

Making people successful in their position requires additional training. After all, people can't be expected to know everything. Although there is an implied assumption that people have the ability to perform well on their assigned tasks, this does not mean they always have the necessary tools to do so. For example, if someone is asked to step in to a lead position in the middle of development, he might not be prepared to switch gears from content creation mode to management mode. Although he may have the ability to do this, he might need some coaching or training in basic people management skills such as conflict negotiation or motivation.

Additionally, he will have to think about the game as a sum of its parts, instead of just worrying about one aspect. An art lead, for example, needs to lead the artists who are creating all the art content for the game—textures, models, levels, cinematics, and so on. So it is important to take time out for training, as this will save money in the long run.

Some people are highly motivated self-developers and will find a way to get the training and information they desire. They will tell you what classes and books they need; they will ask questions; and they will ask others for performance feedback. Some people will need more guidance in determining their needs, but it is important to find out what the needs are and to fulfill them.

Key areas where an employee might need further training are leadership, communication, and technical skills. Anyone in a lead position will benefit from training in all three of these areas, especially if they are new to the position. It might be difficult to find training programs for improving leadership and communication skills, but the local university may offer continuing education classes in these areas. Technical training can be handled internally, if necessary, by technically proficient people on the team. Books and online classes also are good training resources. In addition, several organizations, conferences, and Web sites provide information, and even classes, on improving game development skills.

INTERVIEW

Tracy Fullerton, Assistant Professor, University of Southern California

The University of Southern California (USC) School of Cinema-Television is very good at training people to work collaboratively on creative projects. Collaboration is a cornerstone of their filmmaking program and is deeply ingrained in the production process they teach. In the Interactive Media Division of that program, we have built on that tradition. The idea is not to make a huge project your first time out, but rather you work on several small projects and prototypes that revolve around different types of games. It is challenging, but the participants become very limber in understanding how games work. In the intermediate classes, students work on larger projects that are team-based. On the advanced projects, the teams are even larger, and each person works in a specialized area.

This process has a reality to it, in that as students get to the advanced projects, they really have to start selling themselves to the person who is the producer or director on the project in order to be chosen for the position. This methodology also has a practical base, because when students get out in the real world, they need some skills in pitching and speaking with others who may not be knowledgeable in the specific language of game development. That's one of the things we emphasize in the interactive program—this sense that students can work together and function collaboratively so they don't just walk out with a game they made all by themselves, but rather walk out with a game made in collaboration with a number of other people.

RECOMMENDED RESOURCES

There are several valuable game development Web sites, organizations, and conferences that provide a wealth of information. The professional organizations are a great place to meet like-minded game developers, and conferences and trade shows are always a great place to network.

$\rightarrow$

Organizations

International Game Developers Association (IGDA)—*www.igda.org*:   This is an association dedicated to the game development community. They are also one of the sponsors of the annual Game Developers Conference.

Academy of Interactive Arts and Sciences (AIAS)—*www.interactive.org*:   This is an academy that promotes common interests in interactive entertainment.

SIGGRAPH—*www.siggraph.org*:   This is an association that focuses on graphics in interactive entertainment. They host an annual conference every year for digital content creators.

Conferences and Trade Shows

Consumer Electronics Show (CES)—*www.cesweb.org*:   This is an annual trade-show that showcases the latest consumer technologies.

Electronic Entertainment Expo—*www.e3expo.com*:   This is a three-day conference held each May in which the publishers demo their upcoming games to buyers and journalists.

Game Developers Conference—*www.gdconf.com*:   This week-long conference held each March features lecture, tutorials, and round tables presented by working members of the game development community. It also features a job fair and vendor expo.

D.I.C.E. Summit—*www.interactive.org*:   D.I.C.E. is an annual summit focused on the creative challenges of game development.

General Game Industry Information

Blues News—*www.bluesnews.com*:   This is a Web site that presents the latest industry news, game reviews, and other information about games.

Develop—*www.developmag.com*:   This is a game development magazine published in Europe.

The Escapist—*www.escapistmagazine.com*:   This is an weekly online magazine that covers gamers and gaming culture.

Gamasutra—*www.gamasutra.com*:   This is a Web site with all kinds of game development resources such as job postings, industry news, and articles about game development.

GameDev.net—*www.gamedev.net*:   This is a another Web site containing technical articles about game development, book reviews, forums, job postings, and other useful information.

Game Development Search Engine—*www.gdse.com*:   A great resource for game development job postings and potential candidates.

$\rightarrow$

***Game Developer Magazine**—www.gdmag.com*:   This is a magazine published in the United States that features articles on game development. It also includes job postings.

Game Rankings—*www.gamerankings.com*:   A useful Web site that posts all the reviews of a given game and determines an overall average based on these reviews.

Metacritic—*www.metacritic.com*:   Another Web site that posts and averages all the reviews of a game.

Moby Games—*www.mobygames.com*:   A Web site that collects and posts information on game credits and other news about the game industry.

SUMMARY

Because people are the most valuable and most expensive resource on a game development team, finding and retaining good talent is important. This gets more difficult as the game industry gets larger, so companies are working hard to become the employer of choice for the best talent in the industry. This chapter discussed how to hire, retain, and train talent and included information on how to screen resumes, what questions to ask during an interview, and how to keep talent happy and productive. The next chapter discusses how to take all these talented individuals and build them into a productive development team.

7 Teams

In This Chapter

- Project Leadership
- Picking Leads
- Team Building
- Team Buy-in and Motivation
- Quality of Life

INTRODUCTION

Game development is a young industry—both in the length of time it has been around and in the age of the people. This is reflected in the sense of immaturity that is prevalent in development teams. Some people have the misconception that working at a game company is all fun and games. Although making games is fun, people are still expected to show up for work on time and be accountable for their work on the project. As a producer you must manage this young talent and ensure that each person makes a useful contribution to the game.

In order to be a strong and effective producer, you must develop your leadership skills so you can maintain the team's morale, take care of the team's needs, and keep everyone motivated throughout the game's development. This is a challenge since it requires managing many different personalities, helping people discover their strengths, and neutralizing any risks to team morale, such as shortened schedules, difficult personalities, and so on. The producer must take this responsibility seriously;

otherwise, people will stop collaborating with each other, and the quality of the game will suffer.

If the producer is committed to building and maintaining a strong team, many of the other risks on a project will be minimized, mainly because the lines of communication are open, and people are aware of these risks much sooner in the process. Because of this, the risks have less chance of snowballing into more serious problems. This chapter discusses some ways to build strong teams and maintain project momentum, even during stressful times.

INTERVIEW

Tracy Fullerton, Assistant Professor, University of Southern California

When I am a producer, I think of my role as being quite a bit about social engineering—making sure there is an environment where people can do their best work, feel like they are contributing their best efforts, and have the necessary resources to do the work. Some other people will tell you that the producer's job is to get the project in on time and under budget. This is also very important, but I am more focused on making sure the team and the processes are running smoothly. This involves a lot of walking around and talking to people, so you can see what people are working on and help facilitate their collaboration with others on the team.

The best possible way to manage the team is to make sure that every single person on the team, including the executives, feels a sense of authorship. Sometimes, not everyone wants everyone else to feel that sense of authorship; they want to make decisions on their own and dictate to everyone else, and that's where you can get into hairy situations. But if you can keep people communicating and create a good atmosphere in which the executives feel like their input is important, and the artists, technologists, and designers feel like their opinions have an impact on the game, then that's the best possible situation.

RECOMMENDED READING

The Essential Drucker

Peter F. Drucker is considered one of the foremost experts on management and has written on the subject of management for several decades. He is a firm believer that people must be managed to their strengths and given opportunities to develop themselves in the workplace. *The Essential Drucker* is a concise reference of his management philosophy and is recommended reading for anyone who wants to become a better producer or lead. Topics discussed in this book include effective decision making, picking good people, knowing your own strengths and weaknesses, and many others that focus on being an effective people manager. Complete information on this title can be found in Appendix B, "Resources."

PROJECT LEADERSHIP

The producer is viewed as the team leader and is usually the official representative of the team to marketing, management, and anyone else external to the team. Additionally, the producer is directly responsible for the well-being of the project and everyone on the team, so it is important for him to be an effective and positive leader. If the team is headed up by an ineffective or negative leader, then the team and the game are going to suffer. If you don't think you possess natural leadership qualities, don't worry. More than likely if you are already a producer, it means you exhibited enough leadership qualities to be entrusted with a team and a game. If you are hoping to become a producer, you can develop any existing leadership qualities you already have. In order to do this, however you need to take an active part in developing your skills, as it is rare that a company has a training program in place for this.

So what is a leader? A leader is someone who presents himself with confidence and has a strong vision, values, and an appreciation for the people with whom he is working. He is able to pull together a group of people to achieve a shared vision and hold people accountable for their work. He is constantly projecting passion, enthusiasm, and a positive attitude about his work. Most importantly, a leader has the courage and initiative to take risks, make unpopular decisions, and do whatever is necessary to achieve the project goals.

A leader is defined more by what he does, than by his assigned position on the team, which means that someone else besides the producer can be a leader for the team. It might be hard to pick out the leaders in your company, but if you think about it, someone will come to mind—like the well-respected artist who is always driving people to create the highest quality art.

The good news is that you can become a better leader if you work at it. The key is to have a good understanding of your personality and temperament so you can develop your natural leadership abilities. There are a few basic leadership archetypes—someone charismatic who inspires people to do the impossible, the strong silent type who leads by example, and a person who personally works with each member of the team to bring out their best qualities. Become familiar with them and figure out which style or styles best fit you; you will find that different leadership styles work better for different situations. If you don't work to improve your leadership skills, you might find yourself in charge of a team that is demoralized, unhappy, and nonproductive.

RECOMMENDED READING

Leadership

Project Leadership by James P. Lewis provides practical advice for someone in a leadership position on a project team. Several techniques are presented for improving your leadership skills.

The Leadership Challenge, by James M. Kouzes and Barry Z. Posner, is a research study of all types of leaders in different organizations. The findings are distilled into fundamental leadership practices.

On Becoming a Leader by Warren Bennis is considered to be a leadership primer with in-depth information on leadership characteristics and what you can do to develop these characteristics for yourself.

The 7 Habits of Highly Effective People by Stephen R. Covey is a respected resource for self-improvement. It presents seven main areas of growth that will have a positive impact on your interpersonal relationships.

PICKING LEADS

As discussed in Chapter 2, "Roles on the Team," people in lead art, design, engineering, and quality assurance positions are not normally content creators; instead they manage the content creators and provide leadership and guidance for the project. The most effective leads have expertise in their fields and strong people skills, which means they can advise people, such as the producer or junior team members, on what techniques and processes are needed to get the desired result. For example, an art lead who is knowledgeable of the technical limitations of console hardware can converse intelligently with both art and engineering about what tools are needed to create realistic terrain. In addition, the art lead helps the art team to successfully complete their project tasks by managing the schedule, providing useful feedback, answering questions, arranging for tutorials in new techniques, defining the art production pipeline, and other things. A lead engineer and lead designer provide the same types of services to the engineering and design teams, respectively.

Strong leads are an invaluable asset for any producer. If the producer can depend on the leads to manage the day-to-day art, engineering, and design tasks, he can concentrate on the other aspects of the project, such as localizations, managing external vendors, dealing with the marketing and legal departments, updating senior management on the project status, and providing the leads and team with the necessary resources to do their jobs. If a lead is not as strong in one area as another, the producer must provide training for the lead to improve in that area, in order to avoid problems down the line. For example, a lead designer who is a talented designer but not easily approachable, cannot manage the design team effectively. The other designers might be reluctant to come to him with concerns for fear of being yelled at or rudely dismissed. If a lead designer continues acting this way, even with proper coaching and training, the producer may consider replacing him with someone who may not be as talented a designer but has much better people skills.

When choosing leads, there is a tendency to appoint someone who is talented and has successfully shipped a few games. The benefit of doing this is that an expert is readily available to offer technical or artistic guidance to team members. However, this person might not have any formal management training and is suddenly expected to manage other people's tasks and schedules, effectively communicate expectations to the team, and communicate with management on high-level issues. These are tasks they might not even be interested in taking on. They might want to focus on strictly creating assets for the game.

In fact, a lead should not be the most artistically talented or technically gifted person on the team. You want to keep these talents doing what they do best—creating high-quality assets for the game. If you move these high-quality content creators to lead positions, they don't have time to create content, and the quality of the game will be less than it can be. In reality, the best managers should be leads on project—these are people who are organized, work well with others on the team, have strong communication skills, are knowledgeable in their field, and are respected by their peers. It is easier to help someone improve their knowledge of artistic and technical techniques, than it is to train someone to be a better people person, so keep this in mind when picking leads on the project.

Ineffective leads who do not improve upon their weakness can put a project at risk. How many times have you heard someone on the development team complain about how ineffective or useless their lead is? If this is a common complaint and is not dealt with immediately, the people under this lead will stop asking questions, pointing out risks, and making progress on the game. Instead they will quickly lose interest in their contribution to the game and watch things on the project slowly erode as communication breaks down between the team members.

In some cases, a producer might not have the authority to replace an ineffective lead who did not respond to coaching. In instances like this, a liability is created that the producer has to work around. The producer might decide to take on part of the lead's role and provide the management or technical skills the lead is lacking, or may unofficially grant lead status to a junior member of the team who shows a lot of promise as a future lead. If you are stuck with a lead who becomes a liability, try to deal with the situation without further alienating any of the team members who are under this lead.

INTERVIEW

Jamie Fristrom, Creative Director, Treyarch

An effective lead can't just be an expert in his field; he also has to possess strong people skills and the ability to be a leader. People skills determine how effective his management style is for getting people to do what they've been asked to do. It is common for people to get promoted to a lead position based on their talent alone, but they often don't have the leadership skills for the position. If a lead cannot correctly manage the people under him, these people will not progress in their skills or careers and will become frustrated, which contributes to low morale and puts the project at risk. If someone is not working out as a lead, it is fine to put them back in their old role. We have done this a few times at Treyarch without any big problems.

In my personal experience, it is better to promote people who exhibit natural leadership skills instead of assuming it is something that can be learned. I have seen situations where someone is promoted to a lead position, and it is evident within six months that this person is not suited for the job. At this point, it is probably too late to train him to be a lead, so your choices are to replace him with someone else, appoint a co-lead, or hope that he can finish the job without putting the project at substantial risk.

TEAM BUILDING

Team building is a critical part of the game development process and often one of the most neglected. There is a common misconception that assigning a group of people to work together creates a team, which is definitely not the case. A *group* is comprised of individuals whose work is directed by someone who is head of the group. A *team* consists of a group of people who are working together toward a common goal and are holding each other mutually accountable for the outcome, which is a big difference from a group. In order to have strong teams, they must be built and supported throughout the project.

As the project leader, one of the producer's main responsibilities is to build a strong team by any means necessary. This is not something for the faint of heart or for those who are easily embarrassed. For one thing, you must be able to deal effectively with all different types of personalities and get them all working in harmony with each other. You need to deal with your team as both individuals and a team by creating the best working environment you can for the individual, while still doing what is best for the team.

Also, a producer takes some risk in getting people to participate in "team-building" activities, especially because such activities can best be described as corny or cheesy.

However, if the producer makes no attempt to build a team, he will never have a team, just a group of people doing work as directed by their lead or producer—meaning no sharing of ideas, no collaboration, no sense of ownership or pride in the project, and no passion—which can lead to less then stellar games that register on the consumers' radar. This section discusses some simple team-building techniques that have proved to be effective in a game development environment.

INTERVIEW

Melanie Cambron, Game Recruiter

Intelligence, combined with creativity and quirkiness, is common in the game industry and also makes this business unique relative to other industries. The industry often attracts (or breeds) people who are brilliant at their jobs but have difficulties socializing and meshing with others. With these types of personalities, I educate both the client and the employee on the situation and try to find a way that this person can fit. Because game development is collaborative and socially oriented, it is a rare instance when an arrangement can be made so the person can just sit at his desk and complete his tasks without interacting with anyone. When you are looking to add talent to your project, be certain their personality blends well with the team.

Similarly, it is vital that the team be led well. Egotistical, verbally abusive leads have destroyed teams, creating working environments so bad that talented people leave the company just to get away from this person. Management needs to continuously monitor team dynamics and create a working environment that allows open expression so they can be made aware of situations like this and nip them in the bud.

In sum, social chemistry is critical to a strong team, and whether brilliant junior programmer or veteran lead designer, the social stuff does matter.

Getting to Know Each Other

How well do you really know your teammates? Even though you might have worked on one or two projects with them, do you know exactly what they contribute to the project, or better yet, do you even know their first and last names? Small development teams of 10 people or less may know this information, mainly because everyone on the team fulfills multiple roles and is dependent on the work of several others on the team.

However, as development teams get larger, it is not uncommon for someone not to know everyone's full names or even who is on his team. This basic information is important for people to know. This might seem elementary, but there are instances every day of someone asking their friend in a loud whisper, "Hey, who's that guy? Is he on my project? What does he do?" Providing answers to these simple questions can go a long way in building a strong team.

One of the first things to do when a new team is assembled is to have everyone introduce themselves and briefly describe what they will be doing on the project. They only need to spend a minute or less doing this; it is likely that most people will not remember everyone's names after this initial meeting anyway, but this starts the "getting-to-know-you process."

If anyone new is added to the team, send an introductory email to the team a few days before the person starts working there, and then on his first day make personal introductions to everyone on the team. There is nothing more awkward than for someone to come into the office on Monday morning and see a stranger sitting at a nearby desk. This is made even more awkward if the new person and his teammate are never introduced to each other, especially if neither party can overcome shyness and make their own introductions; they could end up working side by side for weeks and still have no idea who the other is.

If there is money in the budget, consider having a project kick-off event at a local bowling alley or restaurant to give people the time to socialize with each other in a nonwork environment. People might feel more comfortable interacting with each other in this casual setting, and it allows them to get a better feel for what the other people's personalities are like.

In addition, create nameplates with the person's name and department; for example, "John Doe, Character Artist." These are displayed on people's desks and provide a nonintrusive way to reinforce everyone's name and what they do on the team. As people put faces to names and see who is responsible for which cool features in the game, they might start talking with people they've never interacted with on a personal level. This is what team-building is all about. Nameplates also makes it easier for a new person to become familiar with his teammates and their job roles.

Set aside a few minutes at each weekly team meeting for one or two people to give a five-minute presentation on their game development background, favorite development techniques, hobbies, or anything else they want to tell the team about. People on the team might find that John Doe shares their same interest in hang-gliding, *World of Warcraft*, or big band music, which goes far in creating more rapport among team members. In addition, these presentations are something fun and interesting that the team can look forward to in the weekly meetings.

INTERVIEW

Wade Tinney and Coray Seifert, Large Animal Games

At Large Animal, we are committed to building a strong team that works well together. Although it may be easier for our 12-person company than it is for larger companies with hundreds of employees, team building can be effective at a company of any size if there is a commitment to do it.

We want everyone working at Large Animal to feel a strong sense of creative ownership of the games we make. The fact is, everyone on the team has a deep impact on the game, and the finished product is a reflection of our collective effort. Great ideas can come from anyone, and we want everyone on the team to feel comfortable sharing their thoughts with the rest of us. Also, we find that people enjoy themselves the most and do their best work when they are excited about the material, and we like to do lots of research to get to know the content we're working with. For example, when we worked on *Rocketbowl* we took the whole team bowling so they could figure out other gameplay mechanics that would work well with bowling. These sorts of "field trips" are not only a great way to stimulate new ideas about the game you're working on, but they also give people a chance to establish rapport with each other outside of the office—another important aspect of building strong teams.

Effective team communication is important even when it's not directly about the games they are building together. At Large Animal, we all eat lunch together almost every day and discuss the latest movies, games we've been playing at home, and other outside interests. We also play board or card games, which is a great excuse to interact with each other in situations that don't solely revolve around work. Not only do these analog games often give us ideas and insights into the digital ones we make, but it's amazing how much you can learn about your fellow team members and their individual strengths by sitting across the game table from them. Otherwise, we might never have known that our lead programmer, Yossi Horowitz, has such an incredible poker face. Seriously though, we believe that the most efficient team communication is built on a rich shared vocabulary of jokes, references, and memories. Conversations about work are just much more fun to have with someone with whom you enjoy having *non*work conversations.

We want everyone to have an understanding of how the individual tasks they are working on fit into the big picture of that game. One thing we do to encourage this is start each morning with a short team meeting. We spend about 25 minutes talking about what everyone did the day before, what people are working on today, and whether there are any roadblocks that will prevent that work from being completed. We learn a great deal about each other's work patterns from hearing everyone talk about their tasks. Occasionally, someone won't realize there is a problem they can help with until they hear about it in the meeting.

Role Definition

People on the development team have a strong desire to contribute and want to know exactly what their role is on the team. Conflict is generated if roles are not clearly defined. For example, if there are two lead artists on a large development team, and they have not defined what areas each of them is overseeing, confusion results. Artists on the team won't know which lead to go to with questions or problems, and the leads themselves won't know how to definitively allocate any new art responsibilities, which might result in features and assets being unfinished when the game ships. The artists and the leads will become increasingly frustrated with this situation, leading to less efficient and lower quality work and possibly conflict between the leads and the artists.

This frustration can also occur if a junior programmer does not specifically understand what his tasks are on the project. If the lead engineer tells a junior programmer to work on the user interface but never states exactly what the expectations are, the junior programmer won't know whether he is supposed to be leading a task force to get the UI designed, prototyped, and implemented, or whether he is supposed to merely implement the tasks he is given (but at the same time he might not know who is responsible for assigning him tasks).

These situations can be remedied by clarifying people's roles. Jim Lewis, author of *Team Based Project Management*, has developed a simple role clarification exercise that can be done at the beginning of the project, and should be done during the project whenever new people are added or there seems to be role ambiguity. This is also a good exercise for the producer and leads to do during pre-production, so that everyone is clear on who is responsible for which aspects of the project.

The exercise begins with each person answering the following four questions:

- How does the company see your role on the team?
- How do you see your role on this team?
- What resources do you need in order to effectively carry out your role?
- What do you need to know about other people's roles in order to do your job better?

Each person writes answers to these questions and comes prepared to discuss them in a meeting. Each person begins by presenting his answers, and then everyone discusses them and comes to an agreement on how that person's role is best defined. Ten to twenty minutes should be allocated to each person. If you do this for a large team, it's probably best to schedule a few separate meetings instead of trying to have a single meeting that lasts for hours. At the end of the meeting, role definitions can be typed up for each person and posted on the team Web site and displayed in the team rooms. Figure 7.1 is an example of a spreadsheet that can be used to organize this information after the exercise is completed.

Role	Organization Expectations	Role on Project	What do I need from others?	What do I need to know about others?
Producer	—get project done on schedule —meet quality standards of project —lead and motivate the team —carry vision of project to management, marketing, and external people	—lead the team in getting the project done on time —schedule and track progress —interface with management on behalf of the team —hold the vision of the project and communicate to team —motivate the team —deal with personnel issues —order the necessary resources for the team —set up production processes —work with marketing and PR —work with leads on management and communication skills —coordinate localizations —work with external vendors —be knowledgeable about what everyone is doing on project and the progress they are making —keep team informed of progress and up-to-date on any project changes —set up and maintain team Web site —indentify risks, red flags, and solutions	—notification of any risks or red flags —information on how each person is doing on the project and how they are performing in their role —information on what resources you need to get your job finished —assistance with communicating information to the rest of the team	—what each person's special skills are on the project —what each person needs on the project to get their work done —understanding of engineering, art, and design limitations

FIGURE 7.1 Example of a role definition spreadsheet.

Cross Training

Cross-training is the practice of training people in disciplines they haven't worked in before. For example, have an engineer shadow an artist for the day and learn how to create textures. Or send an artist to work in the QA department for the day and learn how to find bugs and enter them in the database. After people walk a mile in someone else's shoes, they gain a greater appreciation for that person's contribution to the project.

This might even lead to improvements in the process. For example, if an artist walks an engineer through the process of importing a level into the game and then has the engineer do it, the engineer might realize there is a way to improve the current set of tools to make this easier for the artist. A designer with some basic training in how to create 3D levels will gain a greater understanding of how to document his level designs on paper so they are more easily translated into 3D spaces by an artist.

Cross-training is also a good way to integrate new people into the team. On their first week, they can spend part of each day shadowing an artist, engineer, or designer. This helps them to more quickly become part of the team and learn what people's roles and responsibilities are on the project.

RECOMMENDED READING

Management

The Tao of Coaching by Max Landsberg offers several solid coaching exercises accompanied by fun-to-read and easy-to-understand examples.

The Mythical Man-Month by Frederick P. Brooks is a well-respected book that contains a lot of important insights about the human cost of software development. This book is highly recommended for anyone working in software development.

Marcus Buckingham and Curt Coffman, authors of *First Break All the Rules: What the World's Greatest Managers Do Differently,* researched managers at several companies to determine what qualities great managers possess.

Peopleware by Tom DeMarco and Timothy Lister. This book is geared toward team leads and managers who head up software development teams. It offers a lot of practical advice for building teams, picking the right leads, and increasing productivity.

Seating Arrangements

Seating arrangements can impact the strength of the team. If you have all the engineers, designers, and artists sitting in separate groups, getting communication to flow between the groups is difficult. If like disciplines are sitting together, they will have a tendency to focus on only what assets they are creating for the game, instead of taking into consideration what the other disciplines are contributing as well. This leads to situations where artists complain about engineers, engineers complain about designers, designers complain about artists, and so on. This is very bad for team morale, because it creates a "us" versus "them" mentality within the team.

While artists, engineers, and designers might prefer to group themselves by discipline, with the reasoning that this is more conducive to consulting with your peers on a technical or artistic issue, this does nothing to build the team. A better seating arrangement is one in which people working on similar features are grouped together, so they can be in immediate contact with other people working on similar functionality for the game. For example, grouping level artists, graphics engineers, and scripters together creates a cross-functional team within the team that handles all aspects of creating a playable level in the game. Even though those people are in different disciplines, they are dependent on each other's work to successfully get something up and running in the game. You can also seat the animators and the engineers working on the animation system together, which helps streamline the feedback process.

In addition, think about the personality types that are sitting near each other. If possible, make sure that positive and enthusiastic people are seated throughout the team rooms. These people bring a natural positive energy to the team and really get people excited about what they are working on. They also help mitigate the negative energy from people who have a tendency to complain.

The team might object to switching around the sitting arrangements, especially if this is something they are not used to. In addition, they may be concerned about the increased noise level in an environment where people are encouraged to talk with each other. In order to keep the working environment productive, inform people that any meetings lasting more than a few minutes and/or consisting of three or more people must be conducted in areas outside the team room so as not to disturb others. You can also invest in noise-canceling headphones for everyone on the team. This way, people can feel more comfortable in the more open environment.

Team Meetings

Team meetings are also a good opportunity to enhance team building. As discussed earlier in this chapter, team meetings are a great way to introduce new team members and become more familiar with who existing team members are. Team meetings are primarily a venue for discussing the progress of the game and to provide a forum for team members to raise questions and concerns. As development teams get larger, this regular forum will be more important to team members who are not privy to the day-to-day happenings with everything on the project.

Provide a complete project update in each meeting. Discuss what progress has been made in the overall game plan, what marketing and PR events are being planned, how things are progressing with getting approvals on licenses, the current status of any hardware requests, and anything else that happened in the past week on the project. This information helps people to gain an understanding of the game as a whole and see how their work fits into the big picture. It is also a real morale boost for the team to hear how much work was accomplished in the past week.

Team meetings are also a good opportunity to discuss any rumors circulating about the project or the company. If there is no truth to the rumors, make this clear in the team meeting. If there is some truth to the rumor, set the team straight on exactly what the situation is. Doing this is much better than for people to start basing decisions on rumors that have gotten out of control. Also discuss any upcoming milestones and potential schedule changes. If people are reminded a few weeks in advance of an impending milestone, they may start working more efficiently to avoid crunch time before the milestone is due. If the schedule changes for any reason—the deadlines are shortened or extended—inform the team about it and explain the reasons why. The team has a vested interest in the game and has a right to know when there are any changes to the plan.

Establish a regular meeting time so that the team meeting becomes a fixture in the team's mind. This way you can jot down notes during the week of what items to discuss in the next team meeting, and people will come to rely on the team meeting as a resource for useful information. It also doesn't hurt to occasionally provide some cookies or donuts during the meeting.

Team Web Site

A well-maintained team Web site functions as the central source of information about the project and is a great team-building resource. The Web site is a living repository for design documents, prototypes, task lists, pictures of team members, and any other project-related materials. The Web site should be well organized so that people can easily find the information they need. Types of information to include on the Web site are as follows:

- Design documents
- Technical documents
- Meeting schedules
- Meeting minutes
- Weekly status reports
- Marketing updates
- Process guidelines
- Vacations and absences
- Key milestone deadlines
- Milestone deliverable descriptions
- QA testing plans
- Contact information (phone numbers and personal email addresses)
- Forms (expense reports, change requests, and so on)
- Names and tasks for each team member
- Prototypes
- Development schedules
- Play testing guidelines
- Important announcements (new team members, schedule changes, and so on)

Storing this information in a publicly accessible place allows the team members to be as informed as they choose to be about the project. Some people will rarely visit the team Web site; others will make it their home page and check it on a daily basis. The team Web site is also a great tool for educating new people about the project or for directing management to the most current set of design documents.

In order to make the team Web site an effective tool, always keep it up-to-date. This way the team can rely on the Web site for the most current project information. This also ensures that everyone on the team has equal access to all the information—not just the few people who constantly check in with the leads on the status of the project. The minute the team realizes the Web site does not contain the latest information, they stop using it as a development tool and instead rely heavily on the producer and leads to directly supply them with the necessary information.

TEAM BUY-IN AND MOTIVATION

Team buy-in and motivation are important elements of a strong team. If the team feels ownership or has buy-in, they are more effective and produce higher quality work. People who are highly motivated and passionate about the game will also not mind putting in the extra work when necessary to make the project the best it can be. This does mean you can take advantage of their passion and implement mandatory crunch times for an extended period—that's one of the fastest ways to demotivate the team and will likely result in lower quality of work and a lot of unhappy people.

Team buy-in results when people believe their feedback, opinions, and concerns are being considered when making decisions about the project. It also results when people can clearly picture the project's success in their minds, which means the game ships on time to great reviews, and it is a number one best-seller for months. If people can visualize and share this success, they are more than willing to work on a project for six months or two years in order to make this success a reality.

If people on the team are not motivated or don't have buy-in, this is a serious problem. If one or two unhappy people are on the team, this number will increase quickly if these people are visibly unmotivated or vocal about their dissatisfaction with the project. When this happens, the producer must deal with the situation as soon as possible in order to prevent damage to the overall morale of the team.

Warning Signs

Employees give numerous signals to indicate their discontent with the work environment. If you notice any of them in your workplace, try to amend the negative situation before losing a valuable team member. Some of these warning signs include the following:

Absence: Do they come to work on time? Do they leave early? Do they frequently miss work? Although excessive absences could be related to personal issues at home and might not mean they are unhappy, it can indicate that the person is searching for employment elsewhere. It could also mean they don't feel their contributions to the projects are valued and are, therefore, bitter about coming to work.

Lack of Effort: Are they productive? Do they miss deadlines or not care if they do? Do they use their time efficiently? Or do they spend a lot of time away from their desks, chatting with other employees, or playing games and calling it "research?" Note that this can also indicate that employees are overwhelmed by their tasks and are afraid to discuss this with management. Rather than tackling the issue head-on, they just waste time hoping the problem will go away.

Complaints: Do they frequently complain about management or other team members? For example, "I could do his job better. Why did they hire this guy? He doesn't know anything about. . ." The more proactive complainers will look for other jobs. The less proactive complainers will stay on, but their complaining will create an unpleasant work environment for other employees, which can potentially lead to more dissenters.

Commitment: Are they reluctant to commit to long-term assignments? Anyone who is thinking about leaving a job will be reluctant to commit to a long-term assignment because they might feel guilty if they end up leaving before the assignment is completed.

Apathy: Are they actively involved in the project, or do they just come to work and put in their eight hours without any comment? If people are not excited about the project they are working on or the role they have the project, they will become apathetic and less effective employees. Additionally, if people have been extremely involved in the past but suddenly become apathetic, you can bet that some specific incident has triggered this. Apathy can quickly spread throughout the team if it is not addressed.

Unfulfilled Requests: If an employee has requested something, like a new computer, and has yet to have his or her needs addressed without a good explanation, the perceived lack of caring can have long-lasting consequences.

By the time these warning signs manifest themselves, it can be too late to salvage the situation and turn it into something positive. A producer who is constantly gauging the mental health of the individuals on the team might catch some of these warning signs sooner, before the situation gets too out of control. This is why it is important for the producer to know the employees and their work habits. For example, some people who are constantly late might just be really bad about getting up on time.

INTERVIEW

Stuart Roch, Executive Producer, Treyarch

If your development team is demoralized, you're certainly going to know it. Productivity can sag; team members will seem less jovial than you remember them being; sick and personal time might increase; and you'll hear about the water cooler grumbling through underground channels. The trick of the proactive producer is to make sure that the team doesn't get demoralized to begin with. Managing a project correctly from the start and being organized with a regular schedule and feature reviews can mean the difference.

When a team is demoralized, there is often very little you can do to lift them out of that. Offering financial bonuses has little effect, as do pep talks in the regular team meetings. The thing that gets a team demoralized, more often than not, is a project that is significantly behind schedule, causing a death march, or a product that just isn't fun, causing a general malaise rather than passion from the core team. When the project is behind, producers will have to deal with the demoralized team in many different ways, depending on the situation, with the understanding that at that point, there might be little that can be done to get the team fully energized again.

Addressing the Warning Signs

The first thing to do after spotting one of these warning signs is to talk to the employee about it. If you see any of the aforementioned signs, it is your job as a manager to find out what is going on. Obviously, you deal with someone who has personal issues differently than with someone who has work-related issues, but you must uncover the issues first. Use questions such as: What do you think about this project? Is there anything you would like to have done differently? How would you handle this situation (a good question to ask in instances when there are known problems with the project)? The answers to these questions can reveal a considerable amount of information about why the person is unhappy and what can be done to improve the situation.

Open communication is the key to spotting and addressing these signs. Is someone coming to you repeatedly about the same problem, even if you have addressed the problem? This probably means that you have not provided an acceptable solution for this person. You need to be open with this person and find out why they are dissatisfied. You cannot be all things to all people, and some people will never be happy with what you do; however, some might have specific, fixable, and reasonable requests. If you can fulfill these requests, you come closer to having a happier employee and creating a better environment.

INTERVIEW

Melanie Cambron, Game Recruiter

If a producer has a team that is falling apart, he needs to make it a priority to get them motivated. A locker room half-time type pep talk can have a hugely positive impact. If teams aren't being informed of what is going on with the game as a whole, they have a tendency to spiral outward, instead of inward and together. Even though they are only working on a small part of the game, they need to know what is going on at the company level. Make the team feel like they are truly a unified group, working together toward a common goal.

Showing Appreciation

Another way to improve morale and to create a more pleasant working environment is by showing your appreciation to the team on a regular basis. This lets them know you view them as people, not just resources in your project schedule, and are aware of the sacrifices they are making to create a great game. Even though some of these gestures seem small and silly, they do not go unnoticed, even if no one on the team comments on them. Some examples of simple gestures that mean a lot are as follows:

Provide food during crunch time: If the people are working late, buy them a healthy dinner. If working on the weekend, have lunch catered. Also, go to Sam's Club® and stock up on candy, pretzels, and other snacks (healthy ones, too), so there is something for people to nibble on during the day. The team appreciates the free meal, and there is less downtime if food is available at the office.

Celebrate monthly birthdays: Once a month during team meetings, bring in a cake or ice cream to celebrate birthdays for that month. People always find this fun and like knowing who is celebrating a birthday with them.

Celebrate project milestones: The development team works hard to hit milestones on time, so show your appreciation by bringing in a cake to celebrate or by providing free movie tickets to the team. Better yet, give the team a few hours off during the day so you can all go see the movie together.

Launch/ship parties: When a project is complete, organize a final celebration to celebrate the project's success. If there is enough money in the budget, arrange to take the entire team out for a nice dinner.

Say thank you: Remember to tell your team "thank you" for a job well done. This can be done in the team meeting, via email, or both. This simple gesture lets the team know their work is appreciated.

Sharing Vision

If the team collectively understands the vision of the game, they will have a better idea of how their work contributes to the game as a whole. Therefore, it is important to keep the team informed of the game's vision, especially when this vision changes. A shared vision means the team understands the overall goals of the game, what the game's major features are, how the storyline and characters fit, and who the target audience is. In order for the team to best understand these things, the producer needs to inform the team when critical decisions are made and the reasoning behind these decisions. Knowing this information helps them to adjust their work so that it fits within the new vision of the game.

Strong, clear, and open communication is key to establishing a shared vision with the team. A simple way to do this during pre-production is to post the initial game concept and vision on the Web site. Continue building on this concept with design documents and prototypes so the team can participate in the game's evolution from concept to gold master.

During production, set aside time during the weekly team meetings to demo the latest version of the game. Point out what new elements were added to the game since last week and call out who contributed these elements to the game. As the game gets more stable, set aside times for the team to play test the game and participate in multiplayer sessions. Additionally, publicly post key information about the game in the team rooms. This includes concept art, mission summaries, control schemes, and anything else that helps communicate what the game is.

Team Survey

If the development team seems to be suffering from low morale, it's the producer's job to find out why and remedy the situation as quickly as possible. However, if the whole team seems to be unmotivated, discovering the cause of it is more difficult as you must figure out why a group of people is dissatisfied, instead of just an individual.

One way to do this is to conduct an anonymous team survey. The survey asks questions about how well people understand the project's goals, how well they understand their deadlines, and how confident they are in the project's success. Also, ask questions about how to improve communication, what issues are of concern, and what elements of the game are most exciting to them. It is useful if you set up a numerical rating system for the answers, as this makes it easier to collate the information and prioritize what areas people are most dissatisfied with. On free-form questions, ask things like "What are the top three things that excite you about this game?" or "What are the three things you are most concerned about on this game?" so that people can provide specifics on each answer. This allows you to collate the responses and see what specifics are mentioned most frequently.

An anonymous survey is effective in uncovering unidentified problems. People are more honest with their opinions if they don't have to worry about getting in trouble for them. Don't be surprised if you hear complaints about things you didn't even know about or if people complain about what a bad job the producer is doing.

When the surveys are returned, collate the information and write up a summary report. Share this report with the team and schedule a team meeting to discuss all areas of concern, what steps are being taken to address these concerns, and who is in charge of following up with these solutions. The attack plan is the most important aspect of the team survey, because it shows the team that their concerns are valid, and actions are being taken to improve the situation. If you don't let the team know what action is being taken, it is likely they will chalk up the survey to another useless management exercise and become further demoralized.

When the big issues are addressed, and the team seems to be on an upswing, you might want to have them take the survey a few months later. Doing this is helpful to see whether the team's attitude is more positive and whether they are still worried about the same things. If the same concerns are on this second survey, it is likely that the action plan was not as effective as it should be. In cases like this, continue getting feedback from the team on what solutions they think will fix the problems and then follow through on them. If the survey shows the overall morale is higher and there are less problems, the action plan can be considered effective. The second survey will also reveal the next set of issues that need solutions.

INTERVIEW

Heather Chandler, Media Sunshine, Inc.

With any development team, one has to keep a close watch on the team morale. If the team does not have high morale, the quality and efficiency of their work will suffer. Every member of the development team has something important to contribute to the team and needs to be told their work is appreciated.

While I was working on the Xbox® version of *Ghost Recon 2*, I came up with the idea of the "Hero" speech. At the time, we were working hard to get our demo ready for E3. We were also in the process of finalizing the name and image of the game's hero character. During our regular team meeting, I handed out sealed envelopes to everyone on the team and told them that they contained the final name and image of the "hero character." Everyone opened their envelopes and saw there was a small mirror inside. When they saw these mirrors, I started talking about how they were the heroes of the game. Without them, the game would not be very strong, and we had to count on each other to get the work done. Admittedly, this seemed like a fairly corny idea on paper, but several team members told me afterward that they really appreciated what I said, and that they felt better and more enthusiastic about their contributions to the game.

QUALITY OF LIFE

INTERVIEW

Melanie Cambron, Game Recruiter

Quality of life means different things to different people. For some it's an affordable house, good schools, and being home for dinner with the family. For others, however, it's all about the work and making a great game. Work is their hobby. It's this group you need to watch. Although you don't need to chase them out of the building every night at 6 P.M., you should make the point that you want them fresh and rested. Remind them that they are more productive when they are refreshed and can approach the game with clear eyes.

Some of these late workers might be there because they've relocated for the job and don't know anyone or any place to go for entertainment. Take the time to introduce them around and invite them to something fun. Team barbeques can be great releases and possibly uncover common interests beyond work.

Above all, keep in mind that development teams work really hard, and they should, but not at the expense of their marriages, personal relationships, and health. Care about their happiness and mental health, and they'll care even more about the project.

In recent years, the quality of life for developers has come under scrutiny by the game development community, mainly because people are more vocal in expressing their concerns about the detrements of working long hours at the expense of family, friends, and health. Ask any developer about this, and they will undoubtedly recount a time when they worked insane amounts of overtime for several weeks in a row. In the games industry, working these hours is referred to as "crunch time" or a "death march" and is pretty much an expected and accepted part of game development, but at what cost? These same developers who put in this overtime will also tell you that family and personal relationships suffered; their health started declining; or both. Does working these extra hours really make the game better? Is it worth it to the developer to live, eat, and breathe work? How can the working hours and quality of life be improved?

The International Game Developers Association (IGDA) is actively working on this issue and has created a special interest group dedicated to improving the quality of life for game developers. The information they've compiled is accessible on their Web site: *www.igda.org/qol*. In 2004, the committee authored a white paper on the current state of the industry's working conditions, which included discussions on the challenges of achieving a healthy work-life balance as a game developer, the negative impact of crunch time, job instability, and weakness in how development teams are organized and managed. This paper presented compelling reasons for improving the quality of life, such as studies showing that extended crunch time actually decreases productivity, and that as developers get older and start families, they are planning to leave the industry for jobs that allow them to spend more time with their families.

Unfortunately, because producers are leading the project and are in charge of the schedule, they are often blamed for these poor working conditions. If the game is not properly and realistically scheduled by the producer, the team might find themselves working massive overtime to get the core features of the game implemented. Additionally, many producers do not have any type of formal training in managing projects, especially software developments projects, which makes it more difficult for them to properly determine the scope, time, and resources for any given project.

One of the ways to improve the quality of life is by studying formal project management techniques and researching how companies outside of game development are able to run projects without burning out their employees or making them unhealthy—government contractors, business software developers, and other corporations running large-scale projects. This is an area that the IGDA is looking at for solutions, and they have posted a lot of information about best practices for software development on the Quality of Life Web site.

The reason quality of life is an important issue is because the current crop of talent is getting burned out, unhealthy, and missing out on spending time with family and friends. This decreases the overall morale, efficiency, and quality of work on a team. Developers are beginning to understand that solving these issues won't happen overnight, but they are also looking for improvements that will improve the situation now, such as the following:

> **Planning limited crunch time in the schedule:**   If one to two weeks of crunch time are scheduled ahead of time around key milestones, people can plan the impact this will have on their personal lives. Additionally, if it is known when crunch time is going to happen, people can focus on working more efficiently during the time leading up to crunch time so they can minimize the amount of overtime they actually work. Studies have shown that working extended crunch time decreases productivity, so don't schedule more than two weeks of overtime in a row.

> **Awarding comp time at the end of a project:**   Comp time is additional time off to compensate for overtime hours worked. When a project is completed, give employees comp time so they can relax, recharge their batteries, and come back to work refreshed.

Management training for producers and leads: Strong project and people management skills are critical in solving the issues of crunch time and work-life balance. Good people managers know how to keep teams motivated and boost morale. Good project managers can control the schedule, which results in less overtime, better quality work, and a stronger team.

INTERVIEW

Stuart Roch, Creative Director, Treyarch

More so than anyone else on the team, producers have the greatest responsibility to their team and the greatest control over quality of life. As the team leader, continuous project mismanagement all but guarantees crunch time and poor quality of life, just as proper project scheduling and control from the beginning can nearly eliminate the need to crunch for all but focused, task-based milestone mini-crunches.

Although a company culture may be such that crunch time is regarded as part of the job, it is the producer's responsibility to limit the scope of the project design to what is sensible—given their schedule constraints—and make proper course adjustments as needed to keep the team working to reasonable goals, if the project starts getting off track. In a properly managed project, crunch time should be kept to a minimum and when called for and be based on task-based goals for short bursts, rather then being called as a team-wide crunch with no definite end goal. Minimizing crunch time on the project and handling it correctly when needed is one of the best things a producer can do to keep a team healthy.

When crunches are needed, it's important to remember the families your developers have at home. I've found that doing small things like sending flowers to a spouse on a team member's anniversary or rewarding a team member's job well done with a gift certificate to a nice restaurant, so the spouse can share in the reward, go a long way toward recognizing the family sacrifices at home. Of course, these small gestures cannot fully remedy any negative feelings from a team member's family, so producers must be mindful of the fact that crunch time doesn't impact the team members alone.

SUMMARY

Teams come in many shapes and sizes, but it is important to remember that individual people make up the teams, so producers must have the ability to deal with the individuals and with the team as a whole. If people on the team are not happy and productive, the team won't be either. So you, as producer, must focus a good portion of your efforts on building and maintaining strong morale and high motivation on the team. This is done by picking strong leads, engaging in team-building exercises, and quickly addressing any warning signs of disgruntled employees. To do this, you must have strong people and project management skills and be a good communicator. The next chapter details some ways to foster good communication on a project and explains how to use communication as a tool to improve interactions on the team.

8 ■ Effective Communication

In This Chapter

- ■ Written Communication
- ■ Verbal Communication
- ■ Nonverbal Communication
- ■ Establishing Communication Norms
- ■ Communication Challenges

INTRODUCTION

In the numerous postmortems published by *Game Developer Magazine*, communication is often cited as something that needs to improve during the game development process. But what exactly does it mean to improve communication? How do people know whether communication is bad in the first place? What is good communication? These are hard questions to answer, because everyone has a different way they prefer to receive information, which means different forms of communication are more effective for some people than others. People might think they're communicating something clearly, only to later find that there was a miscommunication with the other person.

As a producer, it is your responsibility to foster good communication on the team and ensure that everyone is receiving the correct and necessary information in a format they understand. Types of communication happening on a daily basis during any project are written (email and meeting notes), verbal (meetings), and non-verbal (body language). This chapter discusses some general ways to improve in these areas of communication and some simple ways to deal with communication challenges.

WRITTEN COMMUNICATION

During game development, written communication is usually the producer's primary form of conveying information. How many emails do you send and receive in a single day? For most producers and leads, it can be upwards of 100 or more—which is a lot of information to read and digest in a single day. This means that each email interaction must be clear and concise, so that you don't spend all day at the computer handling your email, instead of interacting with the team on a more immediate level. Here are a few guidelines for writing clear and effective emails:

- Use informative subject headings.
- Put the most important information at the beginning.
- Keep the wording concise.
- Include specifics, especially for deadlines and other important information.
- Set up mailing lists to reduce internal spam.
- Use the high priority label sparingly, or else people will ignore its importance.
- Use correct grammar and write in coherent sentences.
- Use bulleted lists to quickly convey major points.
- Use a font that is large and easy to read.

When writing other types of documentation, such as meeting notes or status reports, a lot of the preceding guidelines apply. In addition, create a standardized format so that people can better understand the information being presented. In some instances of written communication, especially if the information is critical, you need to follow up with people in person to confirm they got the email, notes, or report and are interpreting the information correctly. This only takes a few minutes to do, and if the information is vital, the time spent is worth the investment.

VERBAL COMMUNICATION

Face-to-face communication is the preferred and most effective form of communication, especially if you are delivering bad news or need to get people motivated to meet deadlines. Face-to-face is more personal: people can read your body language;

you are instantly available for questions; and people are interacting with you instead of reacting. However, it can also be unreliable, since verbal communication is open to interpretation, and some people are guilty of "selective hearing," and only take away the information they choose to.

Meetings, be it formal or informal, are one of the main forms of verbal communication for a producer. So it is important to make the most of all of your meetings. From a process standpoint, this means setting an agenda, taking notes, and writing down action items for each meeting (Chapter 17, "Production Techniques," has more information on running useful meetings).

For meetings to be effective, you have to think ahead of time about what needs to be said and how it can best be communicated. For example, if you are discussing some major gameplay changes with the team that just got handed down from management, don't start off the meeting by complaining about management and how ridiculous these changes are. Instead, focus on the positive aspects of the changes and present the reasons these changes were made to the team diplomatically. This doesn't mean you have to sugar-coat the reasons, it just means you have to be sensitive to how this information is presented so you don't rile people up unnecessarily—and people are likely to respond better to positive rather than negative communication.

Also, make sure that you understand what people are telling you. Communication is a two-way street, and if you misunderstand one of your team members, this can reflect poorly on you. Active listening is a technique that ensures you have a better understanding of what you are being told. This technique is not easy to do effectively the first time, but you will become better with practice. Active listening means you are actively engaged in what the person is telling you and show this by occasionally rephrasing what the person said to you. You don't need to rephrase everything they tell you; this becomes an annoyance to the person trying to talk, and they might feel you are just parroting back their words, instead of listening to them. Instead, focus on rephrasing the key points of what they are telling you. For example, if someone is complaining about a co-worker, you can say something like, "so, let me make sure I understand this, Joe is giving you a hard time because he thinks you are behind on your tasks, when in reality, Sam is behind, which is affecting your work." If you are correct, the person will show agreement and continue with his conversation. If you are incorrect, the person will tell you the information again, possibly in another way, until you rephrase back to him what he needs to hear.

This can work in the reverse as well. If you are presenting information to someone, such as changes to the production schedule, wrap up the conversation by asking what the changes are and how these will impact the person's schedule. It's not difficult to get someone to rephrase what was said back to you, and if they are incorrect, tell them the information in a different way until you are satisfied they understand. In most cases, you should also follow up conversations and decisions with key information in an email. This way, a written record is always available for reference.

When you are verbally communicating with someone, keep in mind these basics:

- Don't mumble; be clear in your enunciation.
- Don't talk in a low voice, especially during meetings.
- Don't use swear words as this comes across as unprofessional.
- Don't talk over people; have conversations with people.
- Pause every once in a while, so that people have a chance to say something.

NONVERBAL COMMUNICATION

What you communicate nonverbally has just as must impact as what you say. For example, how many times have you gone to ask someone a question, and they act like you have disturbed them from something important (even if they were surfing the Web at the time)? You feel like you are intruding, even when you have a valid, work-related question to ask, and you are apt not to approach that person again until absolutely necessary. Also, how often have you caught someone in a bad mood, for whatever reason, and they take it out on you just because you happen to be around? What about people who don't take you seriously; they turn everything into a joke and act like you don't know anything? Incidents like this are not pleasant, are often annoying, and can impact how you perceive people at work.

As a producer, you must be especially aware of how your nonverbal cues come across to the team. As their leader, you must always be accessible for any question (no matter how small), be able to turn a negative into a positive (and not the other way around), and act in a decisive manner (even when asking people for help). You don't have the luxury of being moody, disinterested, or fake to anyone—behaving like this will quickly diminish any respect or authority you have with the team.

For example, if you are in an office, don't keep your door shut all the time. If you are in a cubicle, don't constantly have your head phones on. Both of these things indicate that you are unavailable and don't want to be disturbed by anyone. This can be off-putting to team members who feel more secure in knowing you are always available to them. Remember that one of your main responsibilities as the producer is to serve your team, not the other way around.

If someone approaches you to talk and you find them annoying, don't roll your eyes or sigh; instead, act like you are ready to talk to them and fix whatever problem they are having. A friendly "hello" goes a long way, so when you walk through the team rooms, smile, stop by people's desks, and look at what they are working on. When you show genuine interest in what the team is doing, they appreciate the recognition.

Because nonverbal cues are so important and people each have a preferred method of giving and receiving information, it is useful to read some books on psychology to understand people better. In addition, there is a lot of information about different personality types and how they interact with each other, which is useful to understand when managing large groups of people with diverse personalities. For example, the book *Type Talk at Work* discusses how the 16 Meyers-Briggs personality types are likely to function in a work environment. The author discusses effective ways to communicate, set goals, build teams, and so on with each personality type. Keep in mind that personality types are stereotypes, so don't expect everyone to fit neatly into a single category.

ESTABLISHING COMMUNICATION NORMS

Communication norms are guidelines that everyone subconsciously or consciously adheres to when interacting with each other. These norms are formulated in several ways: they can emerge naturally over time; they can be defined up front; or they can be triggered by a problem that needs a solution. For example, if you make it a habit to stop by your boss's office first thing each morning to give a brief update on what you plan to accomplish for the day, an unspoken norm is established between you and your boss. If you miss a morning of chatting with your boss, you both might feel that something is off but you can't quite put your finger on it. In another situation, your boss requires you to stop by his office at 9 AM each morning and update him on what you plan to do throughout the day; if you don't do this, the boss will want to know why you missed your appointment with him—this is an established norm. And, finally, if there is an issue on your project that puts the ship date at risk, your boss might institute a policy in which you have to submit a task list to him each morning—this is a norm established as an answer to a problem.

Establishing communication norms for your team can help foster good communication among them. Also, involving the team in defining a set of norms is a great team-building activity—everyone has a say in what the norms are and everyone agrees on the final list. After a set of norms is established, other norms will be naturally evolve that will improve the overall communication between team members, leads, the producer, and studio management.

Conducting a meeting to establish some communication norms is simple. Get the whole team in the room, ask people to discuss some of the communication issues they are having on the project, and establish what areas need improvements. When people define the communication issues, they can more easily formulate a set of norms. After the problems are defined, explain to the team what norms are and ask them to brainstorm on what guidelines will work for them. When they have thrown out all their ideas, have everyone participate in narrowing down the ideas and defining the norms. Here is an example of some team communication norms:

- Know who the point of contact is for your questions.
- Be considerate of other people's time.
- Don't mumble or be a low speaker.
- Don't yell or raise your voice.
- Be constructive with criticism, don't complain.
- Act professionally toward your peers.

INTERVIEW

Jamie Fristrom, Creative Director, Treyarch

I had read several books on producing movies and television shows, since these resources offer advice that is applicable to game production. What I find interesting is that film and television are mature industries, and because of this, they've developed a shorthand that allows them to effectively schedule and hit their dates. It is a simple matter of what shots are needed and what characters are in these shots. They don't need a really heavy scheduling system with Gantt charts or MS Project, because they already have a system in place that makes production easy for them.

I think we will eventually get to this point in game development, where we will have a similar shorthand, with the production of characters, levels, and other assets following a standardized process, no matter what the game. We would still need to block out the production plan, but if we had shorthand and common practices, it would be much easier to accurately estimate when a game will be finished.

COMMUNICATION CHALLENGES

Communication challenges are to be expected in any situation, even if everyone is clearly communicating with each other. But clear communication will certainly decrease many challenges. Some basic areas where extra care must be taken with communication are resolving conflict, delivering bad news, and giving effective performance feedback.

Resolving Conflict

Conflict happens on any project, so don't be surprised when it happens on your project. Some basic causes of conflict are personality differences, miscommunication, disagreement on how things should be done, and differences in what things should be done. As a producer, you will be involved in conflict and will need to mediate conflicts between other team members. Don't be afraid of confrontations, because if conflict is not dealt with in a timely and assertive manner, it will not escalate.

One of the main points to keep in mind when there is conflict is don't attempt to resolve the conflict when emotions are running high. You or the other person might say something that is regretted later, and the conflict becomes worse. For example, if a feature is cut from the game for schedule reasons, and you find out a few days later that your lead designer has instructed the designers to continue working on it, don't confront him about this while you are still visibly angry. Give yourself some time to cool down, and then deal with the situation. The same goes when you are mediating a conflict between other people—they should only discuss the situation after each of them has cooled off.

Before discussing the conflict with the other party, take some time to figure out exactly what the conflict is. With the example given previously, the conflict could stem from the designer misunderstanding that the feature was cut from the game, that the designer did not agree with this decision, or that the designer does not respect your authority and is trying to undermine it. Whatever it is, make sure that you fully understand what it is and formulate ways to deal with it.

When you finally meet with the other person to resolve the conflict, start by stating the facts of the conflict. When doing this, follow these guidelines:

- Don't generalize the situation by saying words like "always," "never," and "constantly." Stick to the facts and don't interpret or embellish.
- Don't assume you know what the person's motivations are for doing something. There are many reasons why people act they way they do, and you won't know why until you ask the person.
- Don't confuse issues and personalities. For example, if someone misunderstands what you said, don't assume it is because the person is stupid.
- Don't resolve conflicts publicly. If someone acts improperly during a meeting, don't reprimand them there, instead deal with the situation privately after the meeting.

After you have laid out the facts, describe the tangible impact this situation has on the project, so the person has a better understanding of the cause and effect. Give the person a chance to respond and then let the person know what needs to be done to remedy the situation. When you do this, show them how an improved situation will be a benefit to them and the project. Using the preceding example, the conversation might go like this:

"The team agreed to cut the feature from the game because there was not enough time to implement it. This decision was communicated to the team in the team meeting and via email. On Wednesday, I found out from another designer that you instructed the designers to continue working on it. This has caused them to get behind on their design documentation for the UI, and now UI engineering is hold until the documentation is complete. [Give the person a chance to respond.

He may apologize, state why he wants to keep the feature in, or have an emotional reaction. No matter what he does, be prepared to assertively state your solution to the problem. However, you will want to tailor your response appropriately to the situation.] The designers need to get the UI design documentation finished, so please have them work on that until it is completed. If you feel strongly about this feature, we will schedule a meeting to discuss it again with the leads—maybe we can put in a scaled-down version or replace another feature."

Of course, every situation is different, but this format presents a good guide for keeping the conversation focused on resolving the conflict. If the person has an emotional reaction during this meeting, tell him you can't continue the discussion and will set up another time to talk with him.

Delivering Bad News

There may come a point during game development when bad news must be delivered to the team. Things such as project cancellations, layoffs, and key people leaving the company might fall into this category. Although it seems daunting to be the one responsible for telling people the project got cancelled, or the ship date pulled in, or that someone was fired, it's not so bad if you do it with honesty and compassion. First and foremost, be honest about why something is happening. You don't have to get into the nitty-gritty details, but do provide the context of the decision and answer any and all questions as honestly as you can.

Second, be sensitive about how the news is delivered. Even though something bad might be happening—such as layoffs—don't overemphasize the negative aspects. People will feel bad enough already for their friends who may be let go. Instead, discuss the reasoning behind the layoffs, what steps were taken to minimize the impact, and what is being done to take care of the employees who have to find new jobs.

Finally, deliver bad news in a timely fashion. People have a natural instinct for when things aren't quite right, and they will start jumping to their own conclusions about what is going on. In cases like this, the rumors are sometimes much worse than what is actually happening, and by the time you actually address the problem, morale could be at an all-time low. If you see groups of people whispering in the hallway or by the coffee machine, it probably means there is concern among the team that something bad is going on at the studio. As a producer, it is your responsibility to address these concerns quickly and confirm what the problem is. If there is not a problem, and rumors have started circulating about something, call a team meeting and ask the team what their major concerns are. Discuss the issues and make sure that the team is satisfied with the results of the discussion by following up with people afterward.

INTERVIEW

Stuart Roch, Executive Producer, Treyarch

As long as you have an existing relationship with the team of talking to them straight and being honest with them, delivering bad news might not be as scary as it seems. Although no one on the team likes to hear bad news, such as their project being delayed, they look to the producers to be there to deliver such news and answer any questions in good times and in bad. Keeping the team informed at all times by communicating all types of project news might be difficult, but this communication is a necessary part of the job and should be handled in an honest and straightforward fashion.

Giving Effective Feedback

Most companies give annual performance reviews to let employees know which areas they excelled in and which areas could use some improvements. These performance reviews are an excellent learning tool for the employees, especially if the they are working toward a promotion or want to improve their skill sets. Providing feedback to employees at other times during the year is also important (even when it is not a formal review), because it is not really fair to assess the employee only once a year. If they are provided with regular feedback, you will create stronger and more skilled employees. Also, regular feedback is critical if the employee is having problems with his work habits or quality of work.

In order to fairly assess each employee, the producer and the appropriate lead must be involved in the feedback process, as well as anyone else the employee reports to directly. This way the employee gets a well-rounded assessment of his project contributions and more constructive feedback. Most employees look forward to receiving feedback on their work because they want to make sure they are doing a good job or improving in areas of weakness.

Here are some general guidelines for giving effective feedback:

- Base feedback on personal observations, not on what people tell you about someone. It is not fair to the employee.
- Give feedback often and in a timely fashion. If you see that an employee is under-performing, don't wait until the annual performance review; talk with him as soon as possible.
- Be specific with feedback. Don't just tell an employee he needs to improve his work habits, cite specific examples of his bad work habits and then offer suggestions on how to improve them.

■ Focus feedback on behaviors and not on individuals. For example, instead of telling someone he is difficult to approach with comments, tell him that because he constantly interrupts and cuts people off, he makes it difficult for people to talk to him.

■ Be constructive with feedback, not destructive. You don't want the employee to feel badly about what he did in the past; you want the employee to understand what he must work on for the future.

Keep in mind that even negative feedback can be delivered in a constructive way. You don't want the person to come away from the meeting feeling like they've been picked on. But they should come away with a clear understanding of what things they need to improve.

SUMMARY

Communication is a huge part of any team effort, and good communication helps build a stronger team. Because communication comes in several forms—written, verbal, and nonverbal—it is important to understand how to use each of these forms effectively. This chapter presented an overview of how to do that, along with some practical types to enhance communication. The chapter concluded with some guidelines on how to handle specific communication challenges.

The next chapter begins the section on technical production. In this section, information is presented on how to schedule subprojects within the production, such as voiceover shoots, motion capture shoots, and the creation of marketing assets. These elements have a direct impact on the production process as a whole and must be added to the production schedule.

Part IV

Technical Production

Technical production refers to game elements that are usually managed as subprojects within the production cycle. This elements include voice, music, and motion capture.

Voiceover and music contribute a large part to the sound and feel of a game. A good voiceover performance can make a good game great, and a bad one can make a good game not so great. The same goes for music and motion capture. On large development projects, these are several elements that are likely to be outsourced, and producers must understand how to schedule for these within the production phase.

Marketing is also an important part of production, as the marketing needs directly impact the production process. For instance, if marketing is planning the launch of a Christmas title, they need marketing art, developer interviews, and playable builds of the game well in advance. If the producer cannot accommodate the marketing needs, the sales of the game are negatively impacted.

This section of the book discusses these subprojects within a game development cycle and provides several details on effectively dealing with these unique needs. Topics include the following:

- Planning for Voiceovers
- Contracting and Licensing Music
- Setting Up a Motion Capture Shoot
- Working with Marketing

9 Voiceover

In This Chapter

- Planning for Voiceover
- Choosing a Sound Studio
- Casting Actors
- Recording Voiceover
- Voiceover Checklist

INTRODUCTION

Quality voiceover in a game is becoming a player expectation. Players want to be immersed in a game world, and that means the characters must be believable and speak in a way that fits the game world. Great voiceover work adds to a game's appeal and makes a good game better. Conversely, poor voiceover work detracts from the game experience and makes a good game seem below average.

Because of this desire to fully immerse the player in the game world, voiceover work is also becoming more complex and, thus, more challenging to manage. There are more characters, more lines of dialogue, and more diverse uses of dialogue within the game. For example, *Tom Clancy's Ghost Recon* had about 600 lines of dialogue and about 5 unique voices, but *Tom Clancy's Ghost Recon 2* had more than 2500 lines of dialogue and more than 15 unique voices. The voiceover in *Ghost*

127

Recon was limited to generic battle cries, yells, and other things that just gave the player feedback on what was happening in the game but did not develop or shape the characters. *Ghost Recon 2* used the voiceover to bring the characters to life by having them banter back and forth with each other, give the player important tips for completing missions, and weave together a story that connected all the missions in the game. Other games, such as *Grand Theft Auto: San Andreas* have even more complex and challenging voiceovers to manage.

If your game has thousands of lines of dialogue with numerous characters, work must start months in advance to write the script, secure a recording studio, audition actors, and record and process the voiceover files. As with all the other aspects of game development, if these tasks are carefully planned for, you will have more success during the voiceover process.

PLANNING FOR VOICEOVER

Initial planning for game voiceover needs to happen in the pre-production phase. In this phase, the goals of the voiceover design can be defined, and any technical considerations for reaching these goals can be explored. If voiceover is an afterthought in the development process, it is more difficult, time consuming, and costly to implement.

One thing to keep in mind when planning for voiceover is that you want to wait as long as possible before actually recording the final voiceover. This is because voiceover dialogue will change a lot during the course of development. For example, during play-testing, the designer might decide that adding a line of dialogue is necessary to make it clearer to the player what the mission objective is. This can be done more easily and cheaply if the final dialogue has not been recorded. So even though you will not need to record the final voiceover until well after alpha, you must have the basic plan outlined in order to accommodate any last-minute voiceover changes or additions.

Voiceover Design

Voiceover is a key way to communicate the personality of the game characters and the story to the player. For example, the player can tell whether the character is male or female, human or otherworldly, and serious or happy-go-lucky. This is also a good way to communicate important information about a given situation to the player. Is the character scared, confident, angry, or in danger? Is the voiceover coming over a radio broadcast or from another location? Voiceover can also tell the player the character's nationality, or whether the character speaks another language or has an accent. All of these factors have to be accounted for when creating the voiceover design.

Additionally, the voiceover design is the biggest determining factor of how much it will cost to get the desired voiceover effects. The design details how voiceover will be used in the game, how many lines of dialogue are needed, how many characters will have spoken parts, and which dialogue will have additional processing and effects. Usually the game designer and sound designer work together on the voiceover design to make sure that it is fully thought out and works for the game.

For example, if working on a massively multiplayer online game, the designers might decide that every single nonplayer character must have several hundred spoken responses to different situations. If there are 100 characters in the game, the amount of dialogue can be well over 10,000 lines, which creates a huge amount of sound assets to record and track. After looking at the initial design and realizing there is not enough time or money to record this amount of dialogue, the designers can go back and revise the voiceover design accordingly.

The voiceover design will differ for each game, with the game genre being a major influence on some of the differences. For example, role-playing and adventure games usually have conversations going on between characters and, therefore, tend to have a large cast of characters and extensive dialogue. Games that are not story driven, such as racing games and some action games, usually have fewer speaking parts and use the dialogue to direct the player through the gameplay space or to create atmosphere.

Technical Considerations

In addition to creative decisions about voiceover, technical decisions must be made as well. The technical factors, such as file formats, will differ based on the game engine being used, but there are a few general technical considerations to keep in mind when planning for voiceover in the game.

Avoid Concatenation

Concatenation is a method where separate lines of dialogue are spliced together in the game engine and played in the game. For example, "Hello, my name is [Character Name]" would be created in-game by splicing together the recorded line "Hello my name is" and another recorded line with the character's name. Programmers might want to use concatenation to cut down on the amount of memory needed to find the appropriate sound asset and to reduce the amount of game assets to track. However, concatenation is a problem for localizations, since different languages have different grammatical rules. Additionally, concatenated dialogue is difficult to record, because it is hard to match the voice inflections and pitch for each line of dialogue. When the full line is played in-game, what the player is likely to notice is that two files are spliced together, instead of there being one continuous file.

Managing Assets

Whether the game includes 100 or 10,000 audio files, thought must be given to how these assets will be tracked and managed during the development process. The more audio files there are, the more important an audio asset management system is. At a minimum, establish a single location in the source control database for storing all the source audio assets, the voiceover script, and character descriptions. This way, any changes that are made to the assets, scripts, or character notes are tracked, and it ensures that everyone is working from the most current version. If multiple versions of the script are available, you might accidentally record from the wrong one during the final recording session. This can be a costly mistake, since it is likely you would need to re-record the correct dialogue at a later date.

Additionally, an asset management system makes it easier to determine whether the recording studio has delivered all the necessary assets. Ideally, one of the engineers can set up an automated process to validate the audio asset filenames against the filenames listed in the voiceover script. If the files delivered by the recording studio are not validated and accounted for right away, you might find yourself missing key audio files. If these missing files are not noticed until later in the project, more costs could be incurred if you have to go back to the recording studio for them.

If there are a lot of speaking parts with numerous lines for each part, you might want to consider setting up a database to track all the voiceover assets. A database can be useful since you can sort by many different variables. For example, if you have 10,000 lines of dialogue to record, it is likely this will take several months to do. A database can allow you to sort by the characters you want to record in a given week or by which dialogue has been recorded and which has not.

Filenaming Convention

Decide the filenaming convention before recording any voiceover, even placeholder files, for the game. If a convention is not established at the beginning, a lot of confusion will result if the game designer, sound designer, and recording studio are all using different ways to refer to the files. It will be impossible to determine what has been recorded and what hasn't. If the placeholder voiceover files are named the same as the final voiceover files, you can simply swap in the final files and easily replace the placeholder files.

Choose a convention that will allow someone to look at the filename and know exactly who said it and where it is located in the game. In Figure 9.1, a filenaming convention has been chosen that indicates the mission number, the character name, and the chronological number of that character's lines in that section of the game.

Name	Dialogue	Filename
Bad Guy #11	We're in the van, commander. We're going to lose the police on the interstate.	01_bg_01.wav
Bulletpoint	Sensei, they're heading for the highway! I'm going up!	01_bp_01.wav
Sensei	I will meet them on the ground.	01_ss_01.wav
Civilian #4	Oh my god! Somebody, help me!	01_c4_01.wav
Sensei	Be at peace. I will summon medical personnel now.	01_ss_02.wav

FIGURE 9.1   Example of filenaming convention.

File Formats

The source formats for audio files are usually some type of .wav or .aiff file, which is something a recording studio can easily provide to a developer. When the source files are delivered, an engineer can covert the audio files for use in the game. The sound engineer creating the source audio files needs to know all the specifications so he can deliver files with the correct bit depth, sample rate, format, and target platform. Figure 9.2 lists some common sound specifications and formats used in games.

Bit Depth	8 bits	16 bits	24 bits
Sample Rate	22 Khz	44Khz	96Khz
Type	Mono	Stereo	Stereo
Format	WAV	AIFF	WMA
Platform	PC	Mac	PC

FIGURE 9.2   Sound file specifications.

Bit depth, also referred to as *resolution*, is how many bits a sound file uses in a set interval of time. Higher bit depths mean higher sound quality because more bits are used when playing the sound.

Sample rate is how many times per second a sound wave is converted to a digital format. Higher sample rates equal higher sound quality. Bit depth and sample rates work together, with common pairs being 8 bit/22 kHz (used for low end audio), 16 bit/44 kHz (CD quality audio), and 24 bit/96 kHz (DVD quality audio).

Type refers to mono, stereo, or another type of playback. Mono indicates that the sound file plays on a single channel, and stereo indicates the sound file plays on multiple channels.

Format refers to the format of the sound file. PC sound files are commonly in WAV or WMA formats, and Macintosh sound files are usually in AIFF format. Platform refers to either PC, Macintosh, or proprietary console platforms.

The source files should be delivered uncompressed for the highest sound quality, especially if they are going to be converted to another format for use in the game. Uncompressed files can also be useful for sound mixes, experimenting with different special effects, and for correcting any corrupted sound files. However, if the source files need to be compressed, the proper compression scheme must be used.

Voiceover Script

A voiceover script is the main document that details all the dialogue to record for the game. A script that is well-organized and contains all the necessary information for the actors, sound engineers, and development team goes a long way in making sure the voiceover process is problem free. The script should be the central location for any and all information about the dialogue, including filenames, audio effects, context, and inflection. If these elements are located in separate documents, there are more assets to track, and it is likely that any updates to dialogue would not be carried over to every single document, which means mistakes are more likely to be made.

A spreadsheet is the best format for organizing the voiceover script, because all the information can be clearly presented and organized in a logical fashion. Another benefit of converting the voiceover script into a spreadsheet is the ability to use filters to sort the information in different ways. An actor or casting director will sort it by "character name." A sound engineer will want to sort it by "effects" to quickly see which files get effects. For these filters to work properly, all the information must be consistently labeled. Figure 9.3 is an example of how the voiceover information can be organized into a spreadsheet. Note that all the dialogue is listed in chronological order to show how the conversation flows between all the characters.

The first column lists the line number. This is useful to have during the recording session so you can quickly reference any of the lines with an actor, which is especially true if you need to re-record a line, or a "pick-up" line. Just tell the actor which line numbers will have pick-up recordings. The second column lists the name of the character speaking the line. The third column lists the dialogue. The fourth column lists the mission or area where this dialogue will be heard. The fifth column lists the type of information that is being conveyed—for example, is this banter between characters, information directing the player to a specific objective, or dialogue for the cinematics? This information is useful to note so you can quickly sort the voiceover script by dialogue type.

Line #	Name	English Dialogue	Mission	Type	Effects	Context	Inflection
1	Bad Guy #11	We're in the van, commander. We're going to lose the police on the interstate.	1	Mission Open	Radio	The bad guys have just stolen the plans for the Omega Device, and plan to outrun the police.	Serious
2	Bulletpoint	Sensei, they're heading for the highway! I'm going up!	1	Objective		Bulletpoint's been monitoring the bad guys' radio chatter, and now knows their plans.	Loud, serious
3	Sensei	I will meet them on the ground.	1	Objective		Sensei's just received an update from Bulletpoint, and plans to intercept the bad guys on the highway.	Calm
4	Civilian #4	Oh my god! Somebody, help me!	1	Non-Player Character		The bad guys have just run his car off the road, and he's crawling from the wreckage, wounded.	Yelling, terrified
5	Sensei	Be at peace. I will summon medical personnel now.	1	Cinematic	Echo	Sensei is using his mystical healing powers on the wounded civilian.	Calm

FIGURE 9.3 Voiceover spreadsheet.

The sixth column lists any special effects that need to be added during post-processing, such as radio effects. The sound engineer will need this information in order to ensure that all the dialogue is processed with the correct effects. The seventh column provides context for the dialogue. The eighth column provides information on the character's inflection of the line. These two columns are important for the actor. Even though the actors will have someone directing them at the shoot, these columns provide some basic information about what is needed and can help them prepare. Additionally, when this script is sent to be localized for any international versions, this information is necessary for the translators and localized voiceover actors. The ninth column lists the correct filename that will be used by the game.

If any of this information is missing or located in another file, there is a bigger chance that something will be forgotten, and mistakes will be made. The most expensive problem that may occur is not getting all the necessary dialogue recorded at the voiceover shoot. It is time-consuming and expensive to book voiceover actors for each recording session, so if the voiceover script does not detail every line to record, some dialogue might be missed during the recording session, which means the actors would need to be called back at a later date to pick up any missed dialogue.

A traditional cinematic script format can also be useful, especially for actors recording dialogue for cut scenes, but this should not be the primary format for the script. This might also be the format the writer originally uses to write all the in-game dialogue and cinematic cut scenes, as it is a more familiar format and more readable during the writing process. This format is also useful for reviewing the dialogue, because a group of people can easily get together, assign parts to each other, and read the lines aloud to check for pacing, content, mistakes, and so on. However, any dialogue written in a traditional script format must be converted to the master voiceover spreadsheet during the process, so the spreadsheet remains the main dialogue source document for the project.

Placeholder Voiceover

If there is time in the development cycle, recording placeholder dialogue and integrating it into the game is a great way to hear how the dialogue sounds in the game. When listening to the placeholder dialogue, the designer and writer get a better idea whether critical information is being clearly conveyed to the player. Also, they can hear how the dialogue sounds, understand the pacing, and figure out whether any additional dialogue must be written before the final voiceover recording.

Many members of the development team will be happy to be voiceover actors for a few hours, and the producer and writer can get some experience communicating with actors on what types of performances are needed. Placeholder dialogue should be done several weeks in advance of the final recording session in order to get the most benefit and make any adjustments to what is needed at the final recording session.

The other benefit of placeholder dialogue is working out any issues with the audio asset pipeline. Checks can be made on asset and memory usage, the filenaming convention, the file format of the in-game audio assets, and other things that affect the technical aspects of the audio. The placeholder files should have the same filename as the final voiceover files. This way, the placeholder voiceover files can simply be replaced by the final voiceover files when they are ready. This also allows the sound programmer and sound designer to make sure that they both understand how to work together to get the voiceover up and running in the game.

Schedule and Staffing

An initial voiceover schedule needs to be created early in pre-production so there is time to find a sound studio and schedule the recording session. As mentioned earlier in this chapter, it is better if the actual recording session takes place as late as possible during production, as the dialogue needs will change over the course of the project. Also, if dialogue is recorded too early in development, retakes might be needed down the line. This can be costly, especially if the original actor is not available and all the dialogue needs to be re-recorded with a new actor in order to match the voice for the retakes.

If thousands of lines of dialogue need to be recorded, you probably will want to schedule multiple voiceover sessions in order to accommodate the needs of the project. This will allow you time for any pick-ups on dialogue recorded in earlier sessions.

The general rule of thumb is that 50 lines of dialogue can be recorded an hour. A line of dialogue is usually considered to be one sentence or about 8–10 words.

In some instances, the cinematics team might need to get the final recorded dialogue earlier in development, so they have time to animate the characters to the dialogue and work on lip-syncing. In this case, you might want to schedule a session earlier in development just for recording voiceover used in the cinematics. You will need to work closely with the cinematics team to determine the best time for the cinematic voiceover recordings. If these recordings are done too late in the schedule, the cinematics team might not have enough time to finish their work. Scheduling this correctly is even more critical when working with an external cinematics vendor, because there is less control over their schedule.

Figure 9.4 is a general overview of the main tasks to schedule for the voiceover recordings. These timeframes are based on recording 3,000 lines of in-game dialogue with 8–10 actors. The lead times should be made longer if the game contains more dialogue and more actors.

Task	Resource	Deadline
Initial Dialogue Written	Writer	~3–4 months before beta
Placeholder VO Recorded	Sound Designer	~3–4 months before beta
Send Bid Packages to Sound Studios	Producer	~3–4 months before beta
Book time for VO Recording Session	Producer	as soon as you have decided on a sound studio
Updated Dialogue Written	Writer	~6–8 weeks before sound shoot
Additional Placeholder VO Recorded	Sound Designer	~6–8 weeks before sound shoot
Audition Actors	Sound Studio	~4–6 weeks before sound shoot (more time if casting a large amount of actors)
Cast Actors	Writer/Producer/ Sound Designer	~4–6 weeks before sound shoot (more time if casting a large amount of actors)
Final Dialogue Written	Writer	~2 weeks before scheduled sound shoot
Dialogue Recorded	Writer/Producer/ Sound Designer	~3–4 weeks before beta (more time if a large amount of dialogue is to be recorded)
Dialogue Processed and Ready for Development Team	Sound Designer	~1 week before beta

FIGURE 9.4 Overview of voiceover schedule.

Many variables can affect the schedule, and these should be taken into account when creating the schedule. Some of these variables include the following:

How many lines of dialogue: More dialogue means more time is needed in the schedule.

The project's production schedule: If working on a six-month project, the voiceover process must be accelerated to get everything completed.

How much voiceover is needed for the cinematics: Voiceover used in cinematics might need to be recorded sooner so the artists have time to animate to the dialogue.

Actor availability: Every actor might not be available when you want them; they could be already booked or on vacation.

Recording studio availability: The recording studio might be booked well in advance with other projects, so it is best to tentatively block out time with a studio a few months before your projected recording date.

Adding extra time into the schedule will help accommodate some of these unexpected items.

Because organizing and running a voiceover shoot is time consuming, designate one person to be in charge of this task. If there is not a huge amount of voiceover to record, this person will not be on this task full time. However, if there are 10,000 or more lines to record, or celebrity actors are being used, or multiple sound shoots need to be scheduled, this could well be a full-time task for one person to coordinate over the course of a few months.

This person would be responsible for communicating with the writer, sound designer, recording studio, and anyone else involved in the voiceover process to ensure that all the tasks and deliverables are taken care of in a timely fashion. Usually, an associate producer or a sound designer can handle the management of this task. In some instances, when working with a large publisher, the publisher will take on the responsibility of coordinating these tasks. The key thing is that a single person is in charge and acting as the main point of contact.

CHOOSING A SOUND STUDIO

Finding a sound studio that is easy to work with and provides high-quality assets will make the voiceover work go more smoothly. A good sound studio will work closely with the development team to ensure that the final recordings are correct for the game. They will provide invaluable assistance in auditioning and casting actors, running the actual recording sessions, and delivering the audio assets in a timely manner. They may also provide additional services on request, such as voiceover direction, tracking, paying the union actors on the project, and special effects processing.

When choosing a sound studio, have a clear idea of what your needs are for the project. If you need to record only a few hundred lines of dialogue with a single actor, you might want to think about using a smaller studio and non-union actors. If you are recording a large amount of dialogue with a number of actors, and the dialogue is for a high-profile title, you might want to use a larger studio that has a lot of experience running sound shoots.

It is a good idea to talk with other people who have recorded dialogue for other games; they often will have a sound studio to recommend, and you can get first-hand knowledge of the pros and cons of a certain studio. A few questions to keep in mind when researching sound studios are as follows:

Do they have experience recording videogame dialogue? Experience with videogame voiceover will help them better understand what the voiceover needs are. Not having game-specific experience is not a major concern, as long as they are experienced in recording voiceover.

Are they a union signatory? Union signatories are authorized to pay union actors. If a studio is not a union signatory, you will have to hire a union payroll service or set your game company or publisher up as a signatory.

What types of recording equipment are available? Is the equipment, such as the microphones and mixing board, adequate to meet the quality expectations?

What software is used for editing? For example, if the game's sound designer is using Pro Tools to edit the audio, he might want to use a studio that records with Pro Tools.

What size is the studio? If there is a need to record multiple actors at once, can the studio's recording booth accommodate this? If several people are present at the recording session—writer, producer, sound designer—is the studio large enough for all of them?

Are they set up for phone patch-ins? If it is important for someone to participate in the recording session, but they are unable to physically be at the studio, can they be patched into the session via the phone? This is especially useful if you are working with a studio in another city.

What is the turnaround time for audio deliverables? How quickly can they turn around the audio after the recording session? This estimate must be included in the schedule. If the project is on an accelerated schedule, it might be necessary to make this a deciding factor when choosing a studio.

What options are available for receiving audio deliverables? Will the audio assets need to be burned to a CD and mailed to you, or can they be posted on an FTP site? Can the files be delivered in different file formats and with different compression schemes? Is the studio willing to use proprietary software to convert the files to the preferred file format for the game?

What are the rates? Studios usually charge hourly or daily rates for the actual time that actors will be recording in the studio. They also charge rates for processing the files after the recording session. In addition, rates are charged for the actors' time, and these rates will differ for each actor.

What additional costs are incurred? Examples of services that incur additional costs are auditioning and casting actors, directing actors, writing dialogue, and so on. Extra costs may also be incurred for discs, meals, postage, and so on.

How much advance is needed to book studio time? A studio might be booked several months in advance or might need to be booked only a week in advance. It is also good to know what the chances are for booking any last-minute, pick-up sessions.

Bid Packages

Sending bid packages to several sound studios gives you an opportunity to compare prices and services, enabling you to choose the best studio for your project. This is also a good way to learn how much time they will need to record the voiceover and how responsive they are with questions.

Studios might have a preferred format for receiving bids, so check with them first to see whether they have specific bid forms you must use. If they don't have a specific form, check with them on what information is needed and create a form that will clearly present the key information the studio will need to calculate the bid. At a minimum, they will need to know how many lines of dialogue will be recorded, how many unique game characters will have dialogue, and how many actors will be used to record this dialogue.

Sending an exact line count estimate is very important when creating a bid package. This is the basis of a lot of the studio's time and cost estimates. First, each studio might have a different method for determining line count, but generally count each sentence (about 8–10 words) as one line. Don't make the mistake of basing the actual line count off of how many rows are used in the voiceover spreadsheet (see Figure 9.3), as this might give an inaccurate count if an actor has a paragraph of dialogue listed in a single cell on the spreadsheet. A miscalculation in the line count makes it very difficult for them to accurately schedule the actors and determine costs.

For example, actors are booked for a maximum of four hours for a single recording session. If they exceed this four-hour period because the line count was much larger then planned for, they will need to be rescheduled for an additional recording session, which incurs extra time and cost. Also, they might be unable to reschedule during the time you have already booked with the studio, which means the actor and studio both have to find another time to finish the session. This delay could put the game project's schedule at risk.

Other important information to include in the bid is how many unique voices are being recorded and how many actors are needed to record them. According to the rules of the Screen Actors Guild (SAG), a SAG actor is allowed to record up to three unique voices in a single recording session for a flat fee. If they do any additional voices, they must receive extra compensation. If you carefully manage the expectations for the character voices in the game, you can cast actors to do multiple voices, and thereby save money. For example, if you had a skilled voiceover actor do three minor roles in the game, you need to cast and pay for only one actor.

If casting for a major voice that will be heard throughout the game, you probably want to have the actor chosen for that role do only that voice. This way the actor can focus on bringing the main character to life, and the voice will stand out as unique in the game. Additionally, the amount of dialogue for a major character in the game might require several recording sessions, which means there would not time for the actor to record additional voices in a session.

Another thing to keep in mind, as far as costs go, is that actors get paid for a four-hour minimum. So if the actor is only needed in the recording studio for one hour, he will still get paid for four hours of work. Because you have to pay for the actor's time anyway, it is good to record as much dialogue as you can during the session—alternate line reads and additional generic lines that can be used in the game (such as greetings, screams, and anything else that might prove to be useful later in development).

Other things to include in the bid are as follows:

File processing: Indicate whether you want the sound studio to fully process all the files and remove pops, clicks, and other sound artifacts from the final audio files. Also indicate whether you will need any special effects processing for the files, such as radio fuzz.

Unique actor needs: For example, if you are looking for an actor who can do a certain accent or speak a specific language, include this in the bid. Although this will not affect the studio recording fee, it might affect the actor fee.

Union or non-union: If the project requires union actors, additional union fees are added to the bid for the actors' time.

File delivery formats: Indicate what format the files are to be delivered in. For example, you would need to specify uncompressed .wav files at 24 bit/96 kHz. If you want additional file formats, such as compressed 16 bit/44 kHz indicate that as well. Also, detail how you want these files delivered—burned to a disc, uploaded to an FTP site, and so on.

Tentative schedule: Let the vendor know what type of schedule you want to work on. Indicate when you will be able to deliver the final line count and final voiceover script and when you need to receive the final audio files. This will help the vendor manage his time. The vendor might have to speed up the turn-around time for the final audio deliverables in order to accommodate the game's audio schedule. If the vendor does not have the time or resources to take on a project with certain schedule constraints, he can let you know during the bid process.

CASTING ACTORS

Casting the correct actor for a role is one of the most important aspects of the voiceover process. If the correct actor is cast, he can go beyond recording lines of dialogue and instead add something extra to the character and really bring it to life. Casting actors has many elements to consider in order to get the right person for the job.

Union Versus Non-Union

One of the first things to consider is whether you will hire union or non-union actors. Your choice depends on the project's budget, the scope, and the schedule. Non-union actors are cheaper, since there are no additional charges for union fees. However, it is difficult to find talented non-union actors. When using non-union actors, even though you are saving money up front, you could end up spending more if it takes a long time to find suitable actors, or if the actors need numerous chances to record each line correctly. If the project's voiceover needs are minimal, around a few hundred lines, it is probably not a huge risk to go with non-union actors.

In the United States, union actors are members of the Screen Actors Guild (SAG), the American Federation of Television and Radio Artists (AFTRA), or sometimes both. Union actors are more readily available because they can be contacted through databases maintained by SAG and AFTRA. Costs for using union actors include the actor's normal fee, plus an additional percentage that goes directly to the union for the actor's pension and health benefits.

Additionally, union actors have very strict work guidelines and must be paid according to a fee schedule set by the union. For example, all union actors must be paid for a minimum of four hours of work, regardless of how long the session actually took. Also, union actors are limited to no more then three unique voices or characters per recording session. Any extra voices cost additional money.

Union actors are more expensive to hire, but this cost can be justified since they are certified professionals. If you are working on a large project and need to hire several actors, you might want to consider hiring union actors.

Celebrity Voices

In the last few years, using celebrity voiceovers has become very popular. Using celebrities lends a cinematic quality to the game and is useful for marketing and public relations (PR) purposes. However, additional time will be added to the schedule, because contracts need to be signed, and approval might be required for the final voiceover files that appear in the game. Additionally, there might be restrictions on the actor's availability and how many hours of recording he can do. If using celebrity voiceovers, start pre-production for the voiceover process earlier so there is time to deal with any unexpected issues.

If you are using an internationally well-known celebrity, check with his agent to see how the celebrity's voiceover for the localized versions should be handled. The publisher might be contractually obligated to use a specific voiceover actor who has been approved by the celebrity to dub his lines into other languages. This was the case with Bruce Willis, who voiced the lead character in *Apocalypse*, a Playstation® game published by Activision®. He recorded the character's lines in the English version, and specific actors whom he already had approved recorded the lines in the localized versions.

INTERVIEW

Stuart Roch, Executive Producer, Treyarch

We were fortunate that we worked as closely with the Matrix production team as we did. Getting AAA Hollywood talent into the recording studio for dialogue recording can be a real trick, but with the help of the film production, we were able to schedule time with the Matrix talent on days where they had a light shooting schedule or on days between their primary film commitments. Through the cooperation of the Wachowski brothers and the Matrix production team, the scheduling of time with the primary talent for things like voiceover, motion capture, or digital photography went off without any problems. Whenever possible, I'd recommend working with the film production office as closely as possible to ensure that the time you need to spend with the talent is organized, therefore, making it as painless as possible for both the game development team and the actors themselves.

Preparing Character Descriptions

Character descriptions give a clear idea of who the character is and how he might sound. These notes are useful for actors auditioning for a particular role, as they don't have to guess who the character is and can focus on creating a voice that defines the character. The descriptions also help a casting directing further narrow the field on the type of actor needed for the role.

Figure 9.5 is one example of a character description template. A picture is invaluable to as it gives a clear idea of the type of actor needed for the role. Other key information such as gender, age, and ethnicity is described to further narrow the field. A brief description of the voice tone and speech patterns is helpful. The actor voicing the lines can use this information to determine how the character will sound. The last part presents information on where the character appears and his major role in the game. Generally, this type of description is useful for a game in which there is some freedom in how the lines are read.

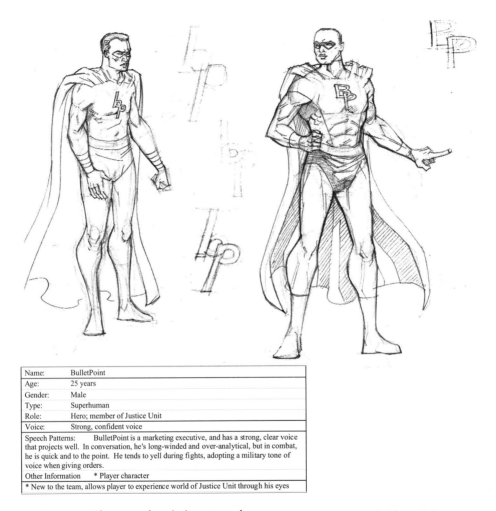

Name:	BulletPoint
Age:	25 years
Gender:	Male
Type:	Superhuman
Role:	Hero; member of Justice Unit
Voice:	Strong, confident voice
Speech Patterns:	BulletPoint is a marketing executive, and has a strong, clear voice that projects well. In conversation, he's long-winded and over-analytical, but in combat, he is quick and to the point. He tends to yell during fights, adopting a military tone of voice when giving orders.
Other Information	* Player character
* New to the team, allows player to experience world of Justice Unit through his eyes	

FIGURE 9.5 Character description example.©2005 Richard Case. Reprinted with permission.

Figure 9.6 is another example of a character description. This one takes a different approach in that detailed information is presented about the character's background and personality. This background information might not even appear in the game, but it presents a more fully fleshed-out character.

A voice description presents the character's tone of voice, speech patterns, and accents. The references section includes references to famous actors who have a

voice similar to what the character should sound like in the game. This is very helpful for the casting director and for actors.

Name	**Ice Queen (real name Melanie Cole)**
Background	Born in 1979, Melanie grew up in Virginia Beach, VA. Her father was an architect and her mother worked as a receptionist. An average student, Melanie studied at Tidewater Community College for two years before transferring to Old Dominion University, where she graduated with a degree in History in 2002. Melanie's parents died in 2004, when her Sentience manifested itself. The freezing blast leveled three homes, killing a total of seven people. Horrified, Melanie fled, but was later apprehended by police. Later that day, her Sentience erupted again, destroying the police station and killing several officers. Bulletpoint and The Sensei were called in, and were able to incapacitate Melanie. She was taken to Masada, where the Justice Division were able to train her in the use of her powers. Since then, Melanie has learned to control her Sentience, and has proven herself a capable member of the Justice Division.
Personality	Melanie is extremely distant, and has difficulty forming lasting relationships with people. Though she has fought beside the other members of the Justice Division for two years, she still refers to them by their code names, and refuses to socialize outside of work. Members of the Division have joked that her most powerful offensive weapon is the Cold Shoulder. She still grieves for her family, and feels a profound sense of remorse for the lives that she ended, even though she's aware that the deaths were accidental. Despite hundreds of hours of training, Melanie fears that she may lose control of her Sentience, resulting in more innocent deaths.
Voice	Melanie's voice is low and firm. She only raises her voice when chastising or disagreeing with someone. She often sounds arch or condescending, particularly when explaining things to others, and can come across as callous when delivering bad news. She speaks unaccented English.
References	Gillian Anderson (The X-Files)
Sample Dialog	"That's really too bad, but that's not our problem. We're here to apprehend Zomborg, and that's all I'm really interested in talking about."

FIGURE 9.6 Another character description example. ©2005 Richard Case. Reprinted
with permission.

The sample dialogue section lists actual dialogue the character will be speaking in the game. This is useful because it gives some samples the actors can use when creating audition tapes. A better judgment can be made on how an actor will sound for the role if he is auditioning with dialogue that will actually be used in the game.

This type of character description works well for major characters that need to be more defined. This also works well for characters that have appeared in previous incarnations of the game and have developed their personalities and backgrounds within the game universe.

Auditions

Auditions give you an opportunity to hear several different actors read for each character. Depending on how the auditions are set up, it also gives you an opportunity to see how well the actors take direction, how wide their ranges are, and whether they are capable of doing multiple voices. The recording studio will handle the auditions or recommend a casting agency who does them.

If there is no time or money to set up a separate audition, the actor selections can be made by listening to an actor's voiceover reel. This is not recommended, as it does not allow you to hear exactly how the actor is going to interpret your game's character. You will have to trust that the actor is right for the part based on nongame-specific information.

The basic audition process involves scheduling time for the actors to come to the studio to record some sample dialogue from the game. When they arrive at the studio, they are presented with character descriptions and a voiceover script. The voiceover director, if one is hired, will take them through the script and prep them for the audition. The actor will record the sample dialogue, and these lines will be processed and made available for the developer. The developer then will make final actor selections based on the audition tapes.

To successfully pick the right actor during the audition process, keep several things in mind. First, someone from the development team should be present either on the phone or in person at the auditions. Having someone from the team participate in the auditioning process is key, since they will be able to advise the voiceover director on what specific characteristics they are looking for from the actor. For example, if the character has a Russian accent, the developer can clarify whether this accent should be heavy, light, exaggerated, or more realistic. This way, when the developer is reviewing the auditions, he does not have to wonder whether the actor who used a light Russian accent is capable of doing a heavier, more realistic accent.

The other benefit of having someone from the team at the audition is that he will have firsthand experience of what it will be like to work with a particular actor. For example, the actor might need a lot of detailed direction, might be difficult to work with, or might not have a broad enough acting range for a pivotal character. All of this information is useful when making the final actor selections.

If someone from the team is not available to attend the audition, get feedback from the recording studio on the actors. Recording studios tend to work with the same group of actors over and over and will be able to give valuable feedback on an actor's ability to deliver what is being asked for. They will also have feedback on how well the actor takes direction.

Second, make sure that the sample dialogue for the audition reflects the type of dialogue that actually will be in the final version of the game. If working on a realistic military game, include sample dialogue that reflects how soldiers speak. Also, the dialogue should include a wide range of emotions, volumes, and lengths for the actor to record. For example, include dialogue that is conversational, angry, shouted, whispered, happy, and so on. Also include dialogue that is a short in-game comment—"area secured"—and longer dialogue made of several sentences that might appear in a cinematic. This wide variety of sample dialogue will give you a better idea of how well the actor fits the character.

Third, don't be afraid to request that additional actors are called in for auditions. If there is no one suitable for the character you are trying to cast in the first round of auditions, it is better to call in another group of actors to audition. Recording voiceover is very expensive, and it is better to find the right person for the role instead of having to recast the part later.

Auditions should be done well in advance of the actual recording session so there is time to choose the actors and book their time. Please refer to Figure 9.4 for a general time table for the auditions.

Selecting and Booking Actors

After the audition tapes are complete and handed off to you for review, the final actor selections must be made. If several people have a stake in which actor is chosen for a particular role, you will want to listen to the tapes together and determine who to cast. This can be a frustrating and laborious process, especially if everyone has different opinions as to what they are looking for in the character. This is where the character descriptions become useful: if the descriptions are detailed enough, everyone should have a similar understanding of how the character will sound. If your team is not even in agreement on the basic character description, you may find it difficult to agree on an actor.

Although your main focus is to get the right actor for the character, several other vocal qualities besides acting ability must be considered when evaluating the audition tapes:

> **Enunciation:**   The words must be clearly articulated and free of any mouth noises, such as pops, clicks, swallows, and lip-smacking. Also listen to how the sibilants sound; some actors pronounce words with an "S" or "P" that is too

hard or soft. These types of speech patterns might be difficult to minimize in the recording session.

Breathing patterns: Listen to how the actor breathes when speaking. If he takes loud gulps of air when reading sentences, this will be audible in the recordings. A good sound editor can minimize some of the breaths if they are taken during logical breaks in the dialogue.

Pitch: Determine whether the actor's pitch is a good match for game. If the pitch is too high and squeaky or too low and gravelly, it will be difficult for players to understand key information. If the actor has a wide range, it should not be a problem for them to pitch their voice appropriately. However, if their range is not very broad, it will be difficult for them to change the natural pitch of their voice.

Cadence: Listen to the rhythm of the actor's speech. Does it sound natural or like a sing-song voice? If the character has an unusual cadence to his voice, this is not a problem. However, if the actor naturally has an unusual cadence, this can be problematic.

When a final decision has been made on all the actors, communicate your choices to the sound studio. They will take this list and schedule the actors for the session. If you are scheduling the actors yourself, first put the actors on "avail" and then do the final booking after the recording schedule is confirmed with the sound studio. *Avail* means the actor is available for the recording session but is not fully committed; it is equivalent to penciling something in on a schedule. No money is owed to actors on avail. *Book* means the actor is fully committed to the session and will receive a payment, even if the session is cancelled or rescheduled; essentially the actor has committed his time to the project and can't book any other jobs during this time period.

RECORDING VOICEOVER

After the actors are booked and the studio time is scheduled, you are almost ready to record the actual voiceover. Recording voiceover can be a stressful process since there are many elements to prepare and finalize before the actual session. This stress is minimized if the voiceover spreadsheet is final and ready to go, all the actors are cast and scheduled, and the development team has prepared for the session.

Preparing for Recording Session

Because the actors are scheduled for a maximum of four hours at a time, it is important that their time is used efficiently in the session. To maximize the actor's time, you must prepare several items before the recording session.

First, decide who will be directing the actors and what additional people will attend the session. Having multiple people at the recording session is fine, as long as there is only one person working directly with the actor. If you are working with celebrity talent, the publisher may want to have someone at the session as well, especially if they want to film the session for PR use. The development team might want to have several people present as well, such as the producer, a designer, a sound designer, and so on. It is a good idea for the actual writer of the dialogue to attend the session, as he will be the best person to advise the voice director on the context and delivery of the lines. If the writer has experience directing voice actors, he might be able to direct the session.

Make sure the voiceover script (see Figure 9.3) is final and ready to go. This script must be sent to the recording studio in advance so they can prepare the scripts for the actors. The studio will break out the scripts by character. Bring the electronic version of this script to the recording session as well. If any dialogue changes are made, the script can be quickly updated with these changes. Additionally, if there are extra takes selected or additional lines added, the spreadsheet can be updated to reflect this.

The files from the actors' original auditions should be available for them to hear at the recording session. This will quickly remind the actor of the voice that was created for the character and give the voiceover director a good starting point for discussing any voice changes with the actor. If several shoots occur at different times in the schedule, audio files from previous recording sessions must be made available to the actors so they can match the dialogue they have already recorded. The sound studio will have access to these files and can prepare them for the sessions.

Bring the latest version of the character descriptions. These notes will refresh the actor's memory of the character and give the voice director concrete information on how to communicate the character to the actor.

Gameplay footage or a game trailer are also useful tools to show the actors what the game is about and how their voices will be used in the game. It is not necessary to bring a playable demo of the game; time spent setting up the demo and playing it can be spent actually recording dialogue. If gameplay footage is not available, be prepared to describe the general gameplay experience to the actor so he will have a better understanding of how his dialogue will be used.

Put together a pronunciation guide for key words that must be pronounced consistently. This is especially necessary for words that have been specifically created for the game, such as unusual character names and fictitious location names.

Real-life words should also be included, such as foreign language phrases, international names and locations, and words that are commonly mispronounced. The pronunciation guide should include a phonetic spelling of the word. If there is time, audio files can be recorded of the correct pronunciation and played for the actor during the session.

Finally, have the most up-to-date schedule for each day of the recording session. This will help you track the actors' coming and going and will make it easier for you to reschedule actors if necessary. For example, an actor might be booked for a four-hour session, but complete everything in two hours. The schedule can be consulted to see whether any other actors can be scheduled at an earlier time, in order to maximize the time in the recording booth.

Directing Actors

Professional voice directors can be hired to run the actual recording session. The advantage of using a professional is that they are well-versed in working with actors to get the desired performance. The drawback is the expense. However, this can be a good investment if recording thousands dialogue lines with numerous actors, because you are likely to get the needed performance the first time around and will not need to re-record dialogue at a later date. Most sound studios can help you locate a professional director for your session.

If someone from the development team is going to handle the voice direction, make sure this person is an effective verbal communicator. It will be this person's responsibility to make the actor feel comfortable and clearly communicate feedback to the actor. This person must be sensitive about giving the actor critiques and direction, so the actor does not get frustrated during the session. Most importantly, this person must remain positive and focused, even during a difficult session in which the actor is not responding to the directions given. Instead of getting frustrated, this person must devise different ways to direct the actor to the proper performance.

Some general guidelines for voiceover direction are as follows:

Let the actor warm up: Have the actor do a few dry runs of some of the dialogue to get him warmed up and ready to go. Sometimes the actor might not be really warmed up and relaxed until he is well into the recording session. In cases like this, check the dialogue that was recorded at the beginning of the session and have the actor re-do it if necessary.

Save all yelling until the end of the session: If there is a lot of yelling or loud talking, inform the actor about this beforehand. Yelling tires out an actor's vocal cords, and he will want to schedule enough time in between voiceover sessions to rest them. All yelling and screaming should be done at the end of a session, so the vocal cords are not worn out at the beginning of the session.

Provide specific feedback to the actors: If you are requesting a re-take or a pick-up, provide specific information to the actor about what needs to change. If the actor does not have specifics, he is likely to deliver exactly the same performance he gave the first time around. For example, he might not be enunciating clearly, or the delivery might not match up with the intended emotion. Make this feedback clear to the actor so he can deliver the performance for which you are looking.

Don't stop the actor after each line reading; keep the flow going: Most actors can quickly run through an entire page of dialogue and do two to three takes of each line of dialogue. For example, if the script has 20 lines of dialogue, the actor can read the first line with three different deliveries or inflections, go to the next line, and repeat the process until he has read all the lines on the page. This is much easier for the actor to sustain the character he has created—stopping after each line breaks the actor's concentration and will take too much time during the recording session. Two to three line readings should provide enough choices for the final take, especially if the actor really brings the character to life.

INTERVIEW

Wil Wheaton, Voiceover Actor

I have done voiceover work for *Ghost Recon 2, Rainbow Six: Lockdown, Grand Theft Auto: San Andreas,* and *Everquest 2.* I play a lot of games so I have a good idea of how the developers expect the voiceover to sound in the game. This can save time in the voiceover session because I can quickly communicate with the developers in a shorthand that they understand.

Doing voiceover is not easy because the actor has to rely solely on his voice to convey character and emotions. Doing voiceovers for games adds an extra level of complexity because the context of the in-game dialogue is not usually presented in a scripted format. Often we are reading lines from a spreadsheet, and these lines willbe used and re-used in many different ways in the game. Recording dialogue for cut

scenes is much easier for an actor, since the lines are usually presented in a straightforward format, similar to a movie script.

For an actor to give a good performance, he needs to understand what's happening in the game. It is important to explain what archetypes and themes are in the game so the actor can fully understand it. If he doesn't understand the game's context, it will be difficult for him to perform in a way that fits the character and the game.

Using movie references is a good way to describe to the actor what the tone or theme of the game is. The developer can say something like "this game feels like. . ." and then insert an appropriate movie title. For example, the game *Grand*

Theft Auto: Vice City is a combination of *Scarface* and *Miami Vice*, while *Grand Theft Auto: San Andreas* is more like *Boyz n the Hood*. For some actors, it is very useful to have a picture of a character. There are differences between describing something as a Cold War game, which a broad description, and describing a game as a modern-day noir, which is more specific. The more information they get, the more specific they can make the characters.

In order to communicate with actors, you need to understand how to talk to them. Actors speak in a special language, and the techniques used to communicate with them are different. Actors are emotional people and need to be handled in a sensitive fashion. For example, don't unnecessarily criticize a performance; instead provide specific feedback on what you liked and didn't like about a performance. This makes it much easier for an actor to adjust his performance to achieve the desired result.

Taking an acting class is helpful in learning how to work with actors. It helps you learn the language of acting—for example, "give it more energy" has many different interpretations, whereas "be more desperate" is a clear direction. An acting class also helps you understand the psychology of an actor.

If you are directing an actor, make bold, clear, specific choices. Don't say, "I don't know, just try something." Statements like this make actors feel insecure. On the other hand, don't dictate to an actor exactly how they should deliver the line. If you wanted it delivered a specific way, you don't need to hire an actor, you can do it yourself. If you do need a certain performance, explain to the actors why, don't just have the actor mimic the desired performance.

Multiple directors on a voiceover shoot are bad. Actors do not know who to respect and will get conflicting directions from each of the directors. This creates a situation that is very confusing, frustrating, and a waste of time for all involved. If multiple people are going to be at the sound shoot, designate the person with the best communication skills as the director. Everyone will give this person feedback on the actor's performance, and this person will synthesize this feedback and give it to the actor.

Let actors play with the character a bit; in some instances they will bring something to the character that wasn't there before, especially since every actor brings his own experiences to the character. Remember that actors make their living playing make-believe; they will get inspired and might create something magical. Above all, cast the right people and work together to find the character.

Selecting Takes

During the voiceover session, actors do multiple readings, or takes, of each line, and the final take is selected from these choices. Accurately noting this information is important because the sound engineer and the sound editor are usually two different people. The sound engineer is responsible for recording the session and handing this session off to the sound editor for processing. In order for the sound editor to know which take is the final, he needs script notes that track how many takes were recorded for each line and what was chosen for the final take. Each sound studio might have a slightly different way of doing this, so discuss their process of recording and selecting takes before the recording session starts. For example, some studios might label multiple takes for a single line as "1A," "1B," and "1C" with the number corresponding to the line number. Pick-ups recorded for this same line at a different time in the session would continue the pattern.

Alternative takes can be chosen for a single line, and these should also be noted in the script notes as alternatives. You will also want to designate a way to distinguish alternate takes in the filenaming convention. This way, the final take and the alternative take are easily differentiated. Keep in mind that studios charge for how many lines of dialogue they process and deliver, so if you end up adding a lot of alternative takes, the cost might increase.

Audio Deliverables

After the dialogue is recorded and the takes are selected, the files are sent to the sound editor for processing. He will be responsible for preparing the final audio deliverables in the correct format and filename. As discussed earlier, define ahead of time which formats are needed, what special effects are needed, and what the filenames are. This will save a lot of confusion when the development team receives the files and starts integrating them into the game. Some studios will provide the raw data of the entire recording session upon request. This data can be useful if the sound designer needs to edit some of the files or if another take needs to be used.

VOICEOVER CHECKLIST

Creating a checklist of what tasks must be completed for the voiceover session can be helpful. Figure 9.7 is an example that can be used.

VOICEOVER CHECKLIST	Y/N	NOTES
PRE-PRODUCTION		
Is initial voiceover design completed?		
Are intial character descriptions written?		
Is initial voiceover schedule completed?		
Is initial voiceover budget completed?		
Is file naming convention established?		
Is file management system established?		
Are file delivery formats defined?		
Are casting notes written with sample dialogue?		
Have bid packages been sent to sound studios?		
PRODUCTION		
Is sound studio selected?		
Has final decision been made on using union or non-union actors?		
Have recording dates been tentatively booked with the sound studio?		
Is initial voiceover script written?		
Is placeholder dialogue recorded and implemented in the game?		
Are auditions scheduled?		
Are celebrity voices being used? Are they available for the tentative dates?		
Are final actor selections completed? Are they available for the tentative dates?		
RECORDING SESSION		
Are dates finalized and booked with the actors?		
Is the voiceover script final?		
Are audition files available for the actors to listen to?		
Is pronunciation guide final?		
Is game footage available to show the actors?		
Is voice director booked for the session?		
Are all final takes selected?		
POST-PRODUCTION		
Has sound studio edited the final takes of audio files?		
Are files delivered in correct format? Are uncompressed versions available?		
Has the raw data from the recording session been delivered?		
Has voiceover script been updated with any dialogue changes and alternate lines?		

FIGURE 9.7   Voiceover checklist.

SUMMARY

Because voiceover is a noticeable part of the game, recording quality voiceovers is important. As games get larger, voiceover becomes even more important and complex to include. Gone are games with just a few hundred lines of dialogue recorded by developers; instead, thousands of lines of dialogue spoken by professional voiceover actors is now the norm. In order to make the most of the game dialogue, find a good sound vendor who will work with you on recording quality voiceover. This chapter discusses some of the key tasks that must be completed when managing game voiceovers. Information is presented on how to find a vendor, how to cast and direct actors, how to format the voiceover script, and how to select the work for the game.

10 Music

INTRODUCTION

Music is an effective tool for setting the tone of a game and makes the game world more immersive. The *Silent Hill* series uses music and sound to great effect to enhance the creepiness of a world inhabited with demonic creatures. In some cases, music is the one of the last things considered on a project, and the producer starts looking for a composer well after the game has started production. In other cases, music is an integral part of the entire game and planned for during pre-production. For example, the *Tony Hawk* series of games is known for licensing music from well-known bands. Licensing music on this scale requires a lot of planning and legal negotiations. If the licenses are not secured before the game is code released, the music track will likely be removed from the game.

Things to keep in mind for game music include technical considerations, budgets, schedule, and how music will be used in the game. In addition, you might want to license music instead of having original music composed. This chapter will give a general overview of how to plan for and use music in your game.

PLANNING FOR MUSIC

As with any other elements in the game, music needs must be discussed during pre-production. You don't necessarily have to finalize the entire music plan at this point, but it is advisable to determine how much money you want to spend, decide whether you are going to license music, compose original, or both, and tentatively put together a schedule for getting the music assets finalized and integrated into the game. Also, if you expect the music score to evoke a certain atmosphere, discuss this in pre-production to ensure that the music meshes well with the art and design elements.

Music Design

The sound designer will work with a lead designer or creative director to determine the music needs for the game. For example, if the game is an action-adventure game where the player spends a lot of time exploring the world and part of the time fighting the enemy, one type of in-game music can be used while the player is exploring, and another type of music can be used when the player is fighting.

When determining the music needs, consider which major areas of the game will need music:

- In-game
- User Interface (UI) shell
- Cinematics

This can then be broken down within each category. For example, if using in-game music, is the music coming from an ambient source within the game world (such as a car radio), or is it constantly playing in the background? The UI shell might have one piece of music that continuously loops or consists of several songs that cycle while the player is in the UI. The cinematics might be scored directly to the image, or several generic music loops can be composed and placed in the soundtrack by the cinematic artist.

After you have an idea of where music is going to be used in the game, estimate how many minutes of music are needed. Most composers charge by the minute when creating original music, and the rates can vary from $300 a minute to upward of $1500 a minute. The rate depends on who the composer is, whether the music is recorded with live musicians, or whether the music is created digitally. Additionally, if live musicians are used, you might also need to compensate the musicians; your composer can work out the details with you and the musicians.

The amount of music varies for each game and might be budget dependent. For example, if you need 30 minutes of original music and can spend only $10,000 on music, you will need to find a composer who can do the job for around $300 a minute. On the other hand, you can reduce the amount of music needed for the game and spend money on a composer who charges more per minute. If you find a composer with whom you want to work, and they also want to work with you, more than likely, you both can agree on fair terms.

Technical Considerations

During pre-production, the sound designer and sound programmer will need to discuss any technical constraints that affect how the music is implemented in the game. These technical constraints might create some challenges but will also be opportunities to figure out creative solutions to overcome them. Some of the technical things to consider are as follows:

Memory limitations: Consoles and cell phones have memory limitations to consider when designing the sound for games. The code will need to limit how much music is stored in memory, as this memory must be shared with other assets, such art and scripting. Cell phone games are limited by this, even more so than console titles.

Streaming audio: Streaming audio consists of sound files that stream directly off the disc and play in real time. Streaming audio does not have to be stored in memory, which means that memory limitations can be mitigated if this is used as one way to deliver audio in the game. The sound designer will want to specify which audio files to stream and which to load in memory, so there are no performance issues. For example, using streaming audio for an AI response might slow things down since the code will have to search on the disc for the appropriate file and then play it. If AI responses are loaded into memory, the appropriate response will play immediately.

Disc space limitations: Another limitation to consider is how much space you will have on the disc to store sounds. If you have several gigs of space available for the entire game, it is likely this will not be an issue. However, if you are planning to include multiple languages on a single disc, there must be enough room on the disk to store every set of localized voiceovers.

Compression: As with cinematics, music files will need to be compressed for the final version of the game. Compression allows for more music and sound effects to be included in the game, because the file sizes are reduced. The sound designer will want to determine which compression scheme gives the most beneficial result, both in terms of sound quality and space needed on the disc. If the files are compressed too much, the sound quality is very poor; many nuances will not be heard.

Custom soundtracks: If your game supports functionality for custom soundtracks, it means that the players import their own soundtracks into the game, either by using a CD or MP3 files. So if someone wants to listen to classical music instead of heavy metal while racing cars, the option is available. If your game includes this feature, you might choose not to spend as much money licensing popular music since it is likely many players will personalize the game experience with their own music selections.

Audio formats: Which music formats will your game support? There are several formats to choose from, each with different pros and cons. In general, the sound designer and audio programmer will want to support the format that gives the best quality sound and stays within the memory limitations. For example, MIDI files are used for cell phone games; the sound is not the best quality, but it does not take a lot of space to store several minutes of MIDI music. Other digital audio formats available with higher sound quality include WAV, ADPCM, Redbook Audio, and MP3.

Schedule and Staffing

Whether you plan to license music tracks or hire a composer, you need to determine the music needs well before your game reaches beta. By beta, it is usually too late to commission a composer for original music, because you will not be able to find someone who works on such short notice. If you do, it is unlikely the quality of the work will be as high as it can be, due to the limited time. It will also be too late to start negotiating with music publishers on which tracks you are interested in licensing.

Alpha is a good time to start approaching music publishers for licensed tracks or for sending out bid packages to potential composers. If you hire an external composer, make sure the contract specifies that the work he is doing is a "work for hire." This means that your company owns the IP rights to the music, not the composer. Please refer to Chapter 4, "Legal Information," for more information about work for hire.

If you have an in-house composer available to do work on your project, it can be tempting to manage this person without a formal deliverable schedule, since you can go speak to him any time you want. However, this is not recommended. As with any team member, the composer needs to specifically know what his deadlines are so he can plan accordingly. If he needs to deliver the final music mixes by beta, he must have scheduled milestones between pre-production and beta so he can hit his deadlines on time. The nice thing about having an internal composer is that they are readily available for any emergency music needs that arise on a project. Also, any work done by an in-house composer is fully owned by his employer.

As with voiceover, it is helpful to implement placeholder music during production to get a better idea of the final music needs and how things sound in the game. Just don't forget to remove any placeholder music before the game ships, especially if you are temporarily using licensed music to which you don't have the rights. Also, make sure that no early marketing footage of the game features any licensed music you don't have the rights to, as this can turn into a legal issue if the musician or his publisher find out.

When putting together your music schedule, include deadlines for any music needed for marketing purposes. For example, marketing may need 1–2 minutes of music for an E3 game trailer. If the game is at an alpha stage, the final music might not be ready, or the final tracks might not be legally licensed. In this instance, you want some placeholder music that marketing can use free and clear and that evokes what the final game music will sound like. If the final game is using an orchestral soundtrack, placeholder orchestral music can be used for the trailer. If you have already hired a composer or have an in-house composer, he can probably compose some music for this one-time marketing deliverable in 1–2 days.

After you have decided on a composer or finalized which tracks you are going to use, you need to determine the deadline for getting all the final music assets for the game. The composer should plan to deliver the final music mixes about one month before beta. If it is in the contract, the final music deliverable should also include the *stems*. Stems are the individual instrument tracks that exist within the final music mix. The stems can be used to compose variations for commercials, game trailers, or future games.

Plan to have all the music rights finalized and contracts signed about one month before beta. This ensures that everything is ready to go in time for the game's ship date. If you can't get a music track secured by beta, think about replacing or removing that track from the game.

Figure 10.1 is a general overview of the music deliverable schedule for a game. When the composer starts delivering music for you to listen to, you will want to schedule the specific deadlines for sending him feedback and getting the revised music tracks back for review.

Task	Resource	Deadline
Music design determined	Sound Designer/Sound Engineer	Before production starts
Initial music deliverables defined	Sound Designer	By Alpha
Add placeholder music in the game	Sound Designer	By Alpha
Send bid packages to composers (if working with external composer)	Producer	By Alpha
Start negotiating for music rights (if licensing music)	Producer	By Alpha
First set of compositions delivered by the composer	Composer	~2–3 months before Beta
Composer delivers final music mixes	Composer	~1 month before Beta
Secure all final music rights	Producer	~1 month before Beta
Implement all final music in the game	Sound Designer	By Beta

FIGURE 10.1   General overview of music deliverable schedule.

SCHEDULING FOR CINEMATICS

If you have pre-rendered cinematics in the game and are using original or licensed music, you must consider the cinematic deadlines when creating the music schedule. For example, a composer who is creating original music for a set of cinematics needs to see a rough version of these cinematics before he can begin his work, so he has a clear idea of how much music is needed and what events in the movie will be emphasized by the music.

Usually, composers want to compose to picture so the music can be timed appropriately to key events in the cinematic. In order for this to happen, the composer needs to get a final and correctly timed cinematic, with voiceover and sound effects tracks, a few weeks before his final music deliverables are due. This allows him to tweak the final timing of the music track for the cinematics and correctly mix it to blend with the voiceover and sound effects.

If any edits are made in the cinematic after the final music is delivered, you have to send it back to the composer for the music to be retimed. Depending on how extensive the edits are, this can take some time, because the composer rearranges and removes parts of the music to fit within the new timing. If possible, avoid editing the cinematics after the final music, voiceover, and sound effects are completed, as this adds more time to schedule and can put the project at risk.

If the composer is just delivering music loops that play as background music in the cinematic and is not relying on the music to punctuate key images in the game, the timing is not as critical. If any edits are made, the music will continue looping as necessary until the cinematic ends.

Bid Packages

Send bid packages to several composers during pre-production so you can get an idea of prices, how responsive they are, their music style, and how long it will take them to compose music for your game. Composers might have a preferred format for receiving bids, so check with them first for any necessary forms. In general, the bid packages must include as much information about the game's music needs as possible. Things to include are as follows:

- Grand total for how many minutes of music are needed
- How many different pieces of music are needed
- How long each piece of music must be
- Specifics on where each piece of music will be located in the game (UI, in-game, cinematics)
- Any sound, voiceover, and music mixes that are needed
- Format for music deliverables
- Final deadline for receiving all final deliverables

Figure 10.2 is an example of what information to include in a bid package. This is a fairly straightforward way of organizing what music cues are needed and the deadlines.

Music Cue	Length	Mixing Details	Location	Format	Notes	Deadline
Main Theme	120 secs	Full Dolby 5.1 mix	UI	.wav	Main theme for the game, will be heard whenever players are in the UI shell screens. Must match the look and feel outlined in enclosed "Music Vision" document.	April 30, 2007
Loop 1	30 secs	Stereo	In-game	.wav	Heard in game as a looping piece of background music. Must match the look and feel outlined in enclosed "Music Vision" document.	May 30, 2007
Loop 2	30 secs	Stereo	In-game	.wav	Heard in game as a looping piece of background music. Must match the look and feel outlined in enclosed "Music Vision" document.	May 30, 2007
Intro Cinematic	180 secs	Stereo, music + voiceover + sound effects, music must be timed to picture.	Cinematic	.wav	Deliver final music, vo, and sound effects mixes on separate tracks.	June 30, 2007
Midtro Cinematic	60 secs	Stereo, music only, background music, no timing.	Cinematic	.wav	Deliver final music, vo, and sound effects mixes on separate tracks.	June 30, 2007
Outro Cinematic	90 secs	Stereo, music + voiceover + sound effects, music must be timed to picture.	Cinematic	.wav	Deliver final music, vo, and sound effects mixes on separate tracks.	June 30, 2007

FIGURE 10.2 Example of music bid.

In addition, you will need to provide some documentation and samples on what you want the music to sound like. The music vision document should provide general information on the music genre, game play themes, and any other special considerations (such as regional flavor). It should also include samples of music from other games, soundtracks, bands, composers, or any other audio that can closely convey the sound and feel you want for the game. After you send out the bids, follow up with each composer and make your final selection.

WORKING WITH A COMPOSER

Most likely, your sound designer will be working directly with the composer. The producer is usually involved as a sounding board for opinions and might have final approval on the final music tracks for the game. The producer is definitely required to approve the deliverables and make payment to the vendor.

Before the composer can begin working on the music, he will need to get a much better idea of what the game is about. So send him a build of the game or a game trailer if a build is not available to play. In addition, concept art, character descriptions, and the storyline can also be helpful to convey the look and feel of the game. The composer can review these elements, along with the music vision document, to determine the themes and inspiration for the music.

After the composer has these elements, he can begin roughing out the music tracks. Plan on several rounds of feedback between the composer and sound designer before the final music is ready. The composer will provide a rough audio mix of the initial music that can be reviewed by the sound designer to ensure that it is on the right track. This is where the feedback process begins.

The feedback process needs to be well defined beforehand so that time is used wisely and the composer is not waiting weeks (or months) for feedback. It is important that all feedback is communicated in writing to all appropriate parties. If verbal feedback is provided via a conference call, write up the notes from the conversation and email them to make sure there is a written record.

Establish deadlines for when feedback will be provided and when it will be implemented. For example, when the composer delivers samples for review, he should expect to hear feedback within three days. If no feedback is given, he can assume that everything is fine and proceed with the next phase. After the sound designer has given feedback, the composer needs to determine when the next set of samples with the feedback incorporated will be ready for review. This deadline is communicated in writing to the sound designer.

Finally, when anyone is giving feedback, make sure that it is useful and constructive. It's not enough to say "eh, I really don't like this, but I can't put my finger on why," because that gives the composer nothing to work with. He won't know what to change in order to get it the way you want. Instead, be specific about what you don't like, even if you think it sounds silly. For example, "I really don't like the screeching at the end of the song, it is too shrill and may annoy the player. Maybe it can be toned down or replaced with something else." This type of feedback is much easier to work with. If possible, provide specific time codes on the areas of the music you are critiquing.

It is a good idea to gently remind composers of upcoming deadlines, so they can be sure to deliver on time. They might get so caught up in doing the work that they forget their final deadline is in three days. This way, you can be sure that you have everything you need when you need it.

LICENSING MUSIC

If you are licensing music, determine which bands you are interested in and start contacting their publishers. The publishers usually handle all negotiations for music rights. If it is a popular band, these negotiations can take some time, so start the process as soon as you can. Keep in mind that if you are licensing music, it is likely you will not be able to alter it in any way.

The contract might limit how many minutes can be used, how much additional mixing can be done on the track, or what other bands can appear in the game. The rights may cost a flat fee or may entail an advance against royalties on each copy of the game sold. You might also be able to get the band to record a special version of the song or even record an original song for use in the game.

The game publisher will likely have their legal department involved in the process as well. This way the publisher can be sure that all the appropriate rights are accounted for in the agreement. The agreement should clearly define how the music can be used in the game, how the music can be used in marketing materials, and whether the music can be used on demos or game trailers. It should also detail whether the track can appear on a game soundtrack, which is something that is becoming more common.

INTERVIEW

Raymond Herrera, 3volution Productions

I have been playing games since I was 10 years old and have always wanted to blend music and games together. I started 3volution Productions along with my business partner, Laddie Ervin, to make this happen. We are involved in all aspects of audio and games: composing original music, licensing music, voiceover, and sound effects.

→

Our gaming background makes it easier for us to work with developers in determining the music needs for the game. In some instances, the developer will know exactly what is required—15 songs for X amount of money. Other times, the developer is looking for some guidance on what music to include in the game—original music, licensed music, and so on.

The biggest factor in determining the music options for a game is how much money is available and how much music is wanted. If a lot of music is needed and the budget is limited, the developer can remix songs. Remixed songs are beneficial to the game and the band. The band now owns a remix and has worked with people they never thought they'd work with, and the game gets a custom track and the ability to use the band's name, without a high sticker price. When doing remixes, actual sounds and voiceovers from the game can be used to really tie it into the game. For example, we used the team call-outs and the ammo sounds the player hears in the game for the *Rainbow Six: Lock Down* theme.

We believe that videogames can benefit from using music the same way that movies currently do—select a hit song that can be used as an anchor and then remix it or license the original and feature it in the marketing campaign. This song can then be the feature on a game soundtrack album, along with other music that is inspired by the game.

Another way to get quality music without spending a ton of money is by putting together a *super group* of musicians who work for a few days on creating and recording a song that exists only for the game. For example, for the WWE game we worked on, there was a super group that consisted of me on drums, Shavo from System of a Down on bass, Wes from Limp Bizkit on guitar, B-Real from Cypress Hill on vocals, and DJ Lethal as the DJ. In some cases, marketing will pay to have a music video made for this song and played on MTV.

In order for us to make the most impact with music, we like to be involved with the game at the pre-production phase. This way, we can find creative ways for developers to make the most of their budgets. For example, if we put together a super group to record a song, marketing can be persuaded to have the money for this come out of their budget. This means the developers don't have to invest a lot of money in the music, but still get a unique and high-quality song for their game. Also, if we are involved early on, we can make sure the music, voiceover, and sound effects are tightly integrated.

When first starting to work on a game, we talk with the developers to find out what they need and what the attitude of the game is and then talk to the marketing people. When talking with the marketing people, we get them excited about all the cross-promotion opportunities—game sound tracks, iTunes™, bands going on tour and showing clips from the game, and music videos.

The process begins with a conference call between 3volution and all interested parties. When the initial meetings are completed, we create a guideline based on these discussions of what type of music will be created, the file formats, and any

→

other notable details of the deliverable. This is sent to each and every person involved in the process—the publisher, the developer, marketing, and so on. This guide is useful because it holds everyone accountable to what was said and agreed upon. After that, all feedback is handled via email. Everyone is copied on the email chain so everyone has a chance to give their opinion. In addition, milestone deadlines are set up and scheduled with the developer. More time means better quality.

Music is the last thing that is worked on in the games. We are hoping this will change because music can be integral part of making a game more effective and fun to play.

SUMMARY

Using music effectively in games is not difficult to do. If you are able to define your music needs up front, you can determine whether you need to hire a composer to do original music or whether you can license music from a popular (or not so popular) musician. This chapter discussed things to consider when defining your music needs, how to prepare bid packages for composers, how to work with composers, and some basics on licensing music. These are the major areas a producer must be aware of when including music in the game.

11 Motion Capture

In This Chapter

- Planning for Motion Capture
- Working with a Motion Capture Studio
- Preparing for a Motion Capture Shoot
- Motion Capture Checklist

INTRODUCTION

If you are working on a game where the character motions are highly visible to the player and important to the overall look and feel of the game, you might want to consider using motion capture as part of the character animation process. With motion capture, actual motions from humans, animals, or even objects can be recorded and implemented in the game for a more realistic and natural effect. Also, as technology advances, players expect to see game characters moving and behaving in a realistic fashion.

Motion capture must be planned for well in advance so that the animators have time to clean up the motion capture data and get the animations working correctly in the game. Based on the amount of motions captured and the number of animators working on the project, this can be several months of work, but well worth the effort

167

for the end result. If you are planning to use motion capture, determine the needs in pre-production. As with any other project, planning and organization are the keys to success. This chapter presents a general overview, from the producer's point of view, of how to plan a motion capture shoot. For more detailed information on this topic, please refer to *The Animator's Motion Capture Guide* by Matt Liverman.

PLANNING FOR MOTION CAPTURE

The lead artist and animator are heavily involved in the motion capture (mocap) process, as they are the ones who know what the animation needs are and are responsible for getting the animations implemented in the game. The producer will work with them to find a vendor and plan the session.

To begin with, the animator will need to make a master list of all the animations required for the game. This include how the characters walk, run, pick up items, hold items, crouch, lay down, spin around, and any other movements seen in the game. The animator then decides which animations he can create from scratch and which animations will be based on motion capture. The advantage of animating something by hand is that an unusual movement can be created that a real person wouldn't actually be able to do. Also, it might be faster to create a good-looking animation from scratch than to edit motion capture data to get the same effect. The disadvantages of animating something from scratch is that movements might not seem very natural or realistic, especially if the character is engaging in a common activity such as walking.

One of the biggest advantages of using motion capture is to create these realistic motions. If an actual person is recorded walking from one end of the room to the other, several small characteristics such as gait, arm movement, and head movement are difficult to include in an animation created from scratch. Of course, one of the disadvantages to motion capture is cost. It can be expensive to capture motions for the game, especially if thousands are needed.

INTERVIEW

Stuart Roch, Executive Producer, Treyarch

When preparing for mocap, the most important thing a producer can do is get started on the organization early. You will need to contact and visit a couple of mocap studios to not only find the best possible deal, but also make sure that the technology suits your project's particular needs, that the mocap team personality fits with that of

→

your team, and that you find a studio that stands a good chance of being in business in the long term. In my experience, the mocap business is a tough one, and the last thing you want is to sign up with a company that goes out of business mid-way through your project, leaving you holding the bag.

When looking at competitive bids, it's important to not only look at the direct costs such as the stage time, expendable media, or the cost of mocap markers but to also pay attention to what can sometimes be hidden costs. A cost that can bite you later if not negotiated and spelled out carefully, for instance, is the cost of mocap processing. If the mocap processing costs are specified to be charged by the second, you can run into nasty circumstances where you end up paying $30 or $100 a second for precious seconds when the actor is in a t-pose or when the animation is starting and ending. If you can negotiate a deal to get charged by the motion, you can save the mocap studio and your animators a lot of overhead in analyzing each second of a motion caputure take to be purchased and save yourself the headache of keeping an eye to the bottom line on each second of animation later.

Regardless of which way the contract is spelled out, you'll need to have detailed descriptions of what makes an easy, medium, or complex move. An easy shot might cost you $15 a second, but a complex multi-person shot might cost you $100 a second, so you don't want to be having arguments with your vendor later about why a walk cycle has been classified as complex simply because your contract wasn't detailed enough.

With regard to scheduling, the timing of the mocap session can be flexible depending on the schedule of your animation team. Be aware of the fact that when working with a movie and sharing talent or stage time, a Hollywood production might want to do mocap earlier or later than you might be comfortable with, putting additional pressure on your animation team to either prepare for the shoot very early in their schedule or do mocap late, forcing them to crank to get all the animation in the game.

Motion Capture Requirements

If the lead artist and animator decide that motion capture is necessary, they will need to determine the following:

How to manage assets: Motion capture data generates a lot of assets, so the animator needs to have a process in place for managing the motion capture data and converting it to an animation asset to be used in the game.

Filenaming convention: A filenaming convention is necessary so that the animator can look at the filename and understand what the motion is without having to open the file. The filenaming convention must be established months in advance so the information can be communicated to the motion capture vendor.

File formats: Although the game might use a proprietary file format for animations, a decision must be made on what file format is needed for the motion capture data that is being recorded.

Motion Capture Shot List

After the animator determines the motion capture requirements and has a list of which movements should be mocapped, he will organize the movements into a master shot list. Figure 11.1 is an example of a basic mocap spreadsheet. More information can be added as necessary.

ID #	Base Position	Motion Description	Length	Character	File Name
1	Upright	Walking (default movement)	3 secs	Bulletpoint	bp_up_walk_1
2	Upright	Walking (default movement)	3 secs	Montezuma	mz_up_walk_1
3	Crouched	Crouched walk, when sneaking around	3 secs	Bulletpoint	bp_cr_walk_1
4	Crouched	Crouched walk, when sneaking around	3 secs	Montezuma	mz_cr_walk_1

FIGURE 11.1 Basic mocap spreadsheet.

The first column lists an identification number for the shot, which will be important to refer to during the actual mocap recording session. The second column lists the base position the character starts and finishes in. A base position is necessary so the animator can blend between different animations without the motions popping during the transitions. The third column describes the motion to be recorded. The fourth column lists how long the motion is. The motion capture studio might also base their rates on the length of each motion, so this information is important to include. The fifth column lists which game character is doing this motion. This is important to note so that the correct actor is recording motions for the character. The sixth column is the filename.

This shot list is the master sheet for all the motions to be captured for the game. Keeping this spreadsheet under version control is recommended so there are not multiple versions. You don't want to go to the motion capture shoot with the incorrect list.

Schedule

As stated earlier, motion capture sessions need to happen early enough in the project so the animator has time to clean up the data and implement the animation into the game. Figure 11.2 is a general overview of the main tasks to schedule for the motion capture. These timeframes are based on a two-year development cycle for a game with 500 motions done by 1–2 actors. This also assumes that the motion capture studio will be able to capture 100 useable motions per day during the recording session. The lead times are longer if the game contains more motions and more actors.

Task	Resource	Deadline
Initial motion capture list completed	Animator	~6–8 months before beta
Send bid packages to motion capture studio	Producer	~12–14 months before beta
Book time for motion capture shoot	Producer	as soon as you have decided on a studio
Audition actors	Motion Capture Studio	~4–6 weeks before motion capture shoot (more time if casting a large amount of actors)
Cast actors	Animator/Producer	~4–6 weeks before motion capture shoot (more time if casting a large amount of actors)
Final motion capture shot list completed.	Animator	~2 weeks before scheduled motion capture shoot
Motion capture recorded	Animator/Producer	~6–8 months before beta (more time if a large amount of motions or complex motions are to be recorded)
Motions processed and implemented in game	Animator	~1 week before beta

FIGURE 11.2   General tasks to schedule for a motion capture shoot.

WORKING WITH A MOTION CAPTURE STUDIO

When choosing a motion capture studio, it is important ask the following questions:

What is the turnaround time for animation deliverables?   You need to find a studio with a quick turnaround time, in order to make the most of your production schedule. If their turnaround time is longer than anticipated, but you still want to use them, include ample time in the schedule to allow for this.

How many hours are in a shooting day?   Many motion capture studios plan for an eight-hour shooting day and will charge for overtime if the session extends past that.

What is the process for auditioning and casting actors?   The motion capture studio should be able to help you find actors for your project. Motion capture is strenuous work, so you want to be sure the actors are used to it.

What are the rates?   Some studios charge by the second, and some studios charge by the motion. Simple motions involving one person are much cheaper then complex motions requiring multiple actors.

What additional costs are incurred?   Are there any other costs for catering, props, or special setups?

How much advance notice is needed to book studio time?   Can you book the studio months in advance before you have the shot list finalized? Also, find out whether penalties are incurred for canceling a previously booked session. If you cancel far enough in advance, you might not get charged.

Bid Packages

Sending a bid package to different vendors allows you to compare costs and schedules. Although one vendor may be slightly more expensive, they might also re-target the animations for you on the character models. It all depends on what services you need and how much money you can spend. Include the following items in a bid package:

- How many actors are required
- How many motions require a single actor and how many require multiple actors
- How many motions will be captured
- Length of time for each motion
- How many motions need editing
- How many motions are looped
- What props are required (if any)
- Delivery deadlines
- Delivery format

PREPARING FOR A MOTION CAPTURE SHOOT

After you have picked a vendor, cast actors, and booked studio time, start preparing for the motion capture shoot. If you are planning to do 500 motions, the motion capture shoot will last about five days if you are well organized. Before the shoot, prepare the following:

Final motion capture shot list: Sort this list by character and then motion type. For example, you will do all the upright walking animations for Bulletpoint first, followed by crouching animations, and then the running animations. A motion capture actor should work no more than six hours a day, especially if he is being used for more than one day. Anything longer than six hours will wear out the actor, and the motions on the subsequent days will not be as crisp.

Daily schedules: Create a schedule of when actors are needed each day and which motions are being recorded. Circulate this schedule to everyone involved in the shoot so everyone is on the same page about what the goals are for that day.

When you are ready for the actual motion capture shoot, you will need to have the lead animator, the producer (or associate producer), and the motion capture director. The animator and motion capture director will work closely with the actors to get the desired motions. The producer is there to keep things moving, so the session stays on schedule.

If the actors are not familiar with a move, they will need some time to rehearse it. Make sure that the animator can provide clear directions on what he is looking for; he should also be prepared to demonstrate the move when necessary. The animator should think of movement examples beforehand, so time is not wasted during the shoot while he thinks of the way to describe the motion to the actor.

If necessary, multiple takes can be done for a motion. The motion capture studio does not usually charge for multiple takes; they only charge for the final motions they deliver to you. Therefore, at the end of each shooting day, the studio asks the animator to go through all the day's takes and select the ones he wants. The studio might have the animator select takes throughout the day, so their editors can start cleaning up the data.

INTERVIEW

Stuart Roch, Executive Producer, Treyarch

When looking for mocap talent, you can work off referrals or simply find talent through traditional Hollywood channels. In many cases, the mocap studio you work with will have a roster of talent from which you can pull, so use the vendor as a resource if you are unsure how to proceed. After you identify mocap talent, it isn't unreasonable to have them in for an audition to make sure that their movement style matches your needs. Many times you can negotiate a test day with your chosen mocap facility as a final due diligence step before signing a contract, so this can also be a good day to have your talent audition.

When the day of the shoot arrives, your animation director will most likely be the best person to direct the talent and get the motions you need. In the case of working with a Hollywood production, it's not unusual for them to assign a director to direct primary talent, especially if you are on a union stage. It's always a wise idea to hire an experienced Hollywood assistant director to keep the day moving and the call lists organized. Your primary director will be concerned about getting the shots they need, so they'll need help with the other director responsibilities like call sheets and making sure everyone gets back from the catering truck after lunch on time.

MOTION CAPTURE CHECKLIST

Creating a checklist of what tasks must be completed for the voiceover session can be helpful. Figure 11.3 is an example that can be used.

MOTION CAPTURE CHECKLIST	Y/N	NOTES
PRE-PRODUCTION		
Is initial animation list design completed?		
Are animations to motion capture identified?		
Is initial motion capture schedule completed?		
Is initial motion capture budget completed?		
Is file naming convention established?		
Is file management system established?		
Are file delivery formats defined?		
Have bid packages been sent to motion capture studios?		
PRODUCTION		
Is motion capture studio selected?		
Have dates been tentatively booked with the motion capture studio?		
Is initial motion capture list prepared?		
Are final actor selections completed? Are they available for the tentative dates?		
RECORDING SESSION		
Are dates finalized and booked with the actors?		
Is the motion capture list final?		
Is game footage available to show the actors?		
Is director booked for the session?		
Are all final takes selected?		
POST-PRODUCTION		
Has motion capture studio edited the final takes of animation files?		
Are files delivered in correct format? Are uncompressed versions available?		
Has the raw data from the recording session been delivered?		

FIGURE 11.3 Motion capture checklist.

SUMMARY

As technology improves, game characters will start to look more realistic, and the character motion is a big contributor to this. Motion capture is something to consider if you want natural and realistic motions in your game. This is the best way to capture all the little movements that occur when someone is walking, running, jumping, or picking something up. Motion capture shoots can be complex, but if you have a knowledgeable animator and lead artist, the producer's involvement is mainly finding the vendor and organizing the shoot. This chapter discussed what to look for in a motion capture studio and how to prepare for the actual shoot.

12 Marketing and Public Relations

In This Chapter

- Working with Marketing
- Packaging
- Demos
- Marketing Assets
- Game Builds
- Strategy Guides
- Working with Public Relations
- Asset Deliverable Checklist

INTRODUCTION

The marketing department works closely with production to coordinate the ship dates and marketing campaigns for the games. It is their job to create a good marketing campaign that will be instrumental in generating game sales, so it is necessary to work closely with them to ensure that key information about the game is accurately communicated. Marketing can, however, be a source of frustration during development because they might make last-minute asset or feature requests, but remember marketing wants the same thing as everyone else—a quality game that sells well. This chapter discusses how to make the most of the relationship between the marketing department and development team.

WORKING WITH MARKETING

Developers must get marketing involved early in the development process, because marketing has an endless supply of information that is useful to developers, including competitive analyses, information gleaned from focus groups, sales figures, upcoming trends, and a host of other things. The game's hook is also usually determined in the concept phase, so marketing can provide useful feedback on what this hook should be.

When working with marketing, establish a communication chain in which a single point of contact on the development team is designated for the marketing department. If marketing starts asking one person about the status of the game code, another person about the status of the demo code, and yet another person about the status of the manual assets, things get confusing. It also causes misunderstandings about what features the product includes, which are then mistakenly communicated to the public, and as we all know, it is not good for the game's Web site to post an incorrect feature set. However this communication pipeline is set up, try to enforce and maintain it throughout the duration of the development process.

Some of the key assets the development team needs to provide marketing are the manual text, screenshots, demos, and builds of the game. The amount of assets requested from the development team can be overwhelming, especially if the team does not know what the expectations are. However, if the developers work closely with their marketing contact, they can be prepared for the majority of marketing requests.

Development Milestone Schedule

Ideally, marketing requests should be planned around the development schedule to avoid delivering assets around critical development dates. This way, the marketing contact will know when the team is crunching to meet key milestones. The development schedule should include a general overview that shows the marketing contact what these key dates are:

- Alpha
- Beta
- Console submission
- Code release
- Ship date

Figure 12.1 is a schedule with the key development milestones and general timeline information that marketing will want.

Milestone	General Timeline	Deadline
Alpha	~6–8 months before ship date	March 15, 2007
Beta	~1–2 months before ship date	August 15, 2007
Console Submission	~4–6 weeks before ship date	September 15, 2007
Code Release	~2–4 weeks before ship date	October 1, 2007
Ship	ship date	October 15, 2007

FIGURE 12.1 Key development milestones.

Game Documentation

In order to create a strong marketing campaign, marketing needs general information about the game, including characters, story, and gameplay mechanics. If different assets or features will be included in different versions of the game, such as a unique character that is exclusive to the game on a particular gaming platform, this must be communicated as well. Marketing may also request that each version of the game have something special that can be targeted to fans of each platform. So be sure to send the following game documentation to the marketing department to ensure that they fully understand the game:

Feature list: This lists all the major features in the game, such as the number of levels, the characters, key gameplay mechanisms, and game genre. This list also details any unique features or gameplay elements that are exclusive to a particular gaming platform.

Story: This contains the overall story elements and how they fit into the game as a whole. Elements from the story can be built into the marketing campaign.

Control scheme: Whether a computer or a console game, the user needs to understand how the controller works. The control scheme gives a quick overview of how to navigate the game world.

Core gameplay rules: Any documents that detail how the core gameplay works. The marketing contact needs to understand the game mechanics, so he can accurately communicate this to potential buyers. In some instances, this might be too much documentation to send, especially if there is a complex design. In cases like this, a brief overview of the main points should be provided and sent instead.

Character descriptions: The character descriptions give details on the physical look of the character, the character's tone of voice, and the character's personality and general demeanor. The characters are great marketing tools for the game. If using celebrity voiceovers, indicate who is being used on these descriptions as well.

Cheats and walkthroughs: To demo the game to journalists and buyers, cheats and walkthroughs should be provided to make sure that the gameplay experience is represented positively. If the person demonstrating the game is nervous or not a good player, it will be frustrating for the people watching the game if the main character keeps dying or cannot find key objectives quickly. The person demonstrating the game should be fully prepared and knowledgeable of the level he is demonstrating.

Focus Groups

At some point in pre-production, marketing might want to set up a focus group to get feedback on game concepts, features, storylines, characters, or numerous other things about the game. Marketing will coordinate with an external vendor in order to set up the focus group with the desired set of people.

Most likely, marketing will contact the game's producer to see whether there is certain information the development team wants to ask about in the focus group. Developers find it helpful to get feedback directly from the targeted consumer, especially if a new feature is being designed or a major feature of a successful franchise is being altered. These types of questions can be submitted to the person setting up the focus group. If the producer attends the focus group, he can gain firsthand knowledge about the group's reaction is to any particular item.

In some instances, formal focus groups cannot be arranged, so the developer might decide to set up an information focus group with friends and family. If this is the case, the developer will still want the participants to sign non-disclosure agreements (NDAs). Please see Chapter 4, "Legal Information," for more information on NDAs.

If setting up an informal focus group, define exactly what the objectives are going to be. If feedback is needed about the current control scheme, make sure there is a stable build of the game to play, that there is enough hardware to accommodate all the participants, and that some method is used to gather the desired information—either a questionnaire the participants fill in or observations from members of the development team.

PACKAGING

The developer also needs to provide marketing with all of the necessary assets and information for creating the manual, box, and any reference cards or inserts; therefore it is important to include deadlines for providing these assets in your development schedule. This way, the release of the game is not delayed because the manual is not completed. Small developers might need to create and lay out the packaging and manual and get it to the printer themselves, but usually larger companies have a creative services department that is responsible for actually producing the packaging. However, they still need the developer to supply the necessary assets, such as manual text, screenshots, and controller information.

Manuals

As the producer, you will work closely with marketing to create the manual. Marketing will rely on you and your development team to provide the final draft of the manual text. It is important to determine a deadline early on for completing the final draft, because marketing will need time to edit, layout, proofread, and print the manual before the game's ship date. Because of the time needed to do all these things, marketing might request a final manual draft before all the game features are implemented and working correctly in the game. So you will need to provide the most accurate information you can and keep the manual writer updated on any major changes in the game. Also, the international marketing team might need a final draft of the English manual before their U.S. counterparts, so there is enough time to get it translated and laid out in numerous languages.

A general rule of thumb for PC games is that marketing will need the final manual text about six to eight weeks before the project ship date. This should allow enough time for them to do all the necessary work and get the manual printed and delivered for replication.

However, this timeframe changes for console versions, because the packaging will need to be approved by the console manufacturer before it is approved for replication. Because of this, it is especially important that you work closely with marketing to ensure all the packaging assets are received in a timely fashion. It is not unheard of for a game to miss its initial ship date because the packaging was not ready for approval. To prevent this, double-check your packaging submission dates with the appropriate third-party account managers to ensure these dates are met.

You also need to determine a process for providing accurate updates and corrections to the manual text early in the process. After the final version of the manual is delivered to marketing, critical issues will be discovered that need to be addressed. For example, a feature might get cut at the last minute, or a new section might be added based on urgent feedback from QA and tech support.

A simple way to give updates is to provide a first draft of the manual that is 95 to 99 percent complete on the requested due date and then allow time in the schedule for an additional round of updates and revisions. These updates and revisions should be scheduled to happen as late as possible in the manual creation process. And, don't forget to communicate these changes to the people responsible for creating the localized versions of the manual.

When you first discuss the manual needs with marketing, find out whether there are word restrictions, and, if so, make sure that the manual writer stays within these limits. In some cases, localized manuals might have a more restrictive word count than the U.S. version, so you might have to create an abridged version of the English manual. That way, the international marketing departments do not have to edit the manual themselves and risk omitting key gameplay information.

Another manual asset to be delivered is screenshots. Often, screenshots appear in the manual to explain the UI elements more clearly to the user, and if you're creating localized manuals, they will need localized screenshots. The localized product does not need to be the final version in order to take these screenshots; the important thing is that the screenshots are clean.

An additional marketing request for PC versions might be to include an electronic version of the manual on the gold master. This is sometimes requested to save on manual printing costs, especially on budget-priced game. Electronic manuals are also useful if several languages are included in a single game or if the game is released as part of a hardware bundle.

If an electronic version of the manual is needed for the gold master, make sure that the deadline for getting the final electronic manual from marketing is clearly communicated. A placeholder manual file can be used during development and then replaced with the final version when it is ready. However, if the final version is not ready, the team will need to quickly disable any Start menu shortcuts or any in-game shortcuts that point to the manual. To avoid this, some developers do not include any shortcuts to the manual and just place the manual at the root of the game disc, where it is easy for users to locate.

Box Art

Marketing staff usually create the packaging and decide on the final layout for the box. Providing assets for the boxes is not usually as involved as providing assets for the manual, because the box text is usually written by the marketing department. The developer only needs to read the text and provide corrections and suggestions. Generally, the main assets to provide for the boxes are exciting screenshots of the game.

Just remember to work closely with your marketing contact to ensure that everything needed to print the box is delivered on time. As always, pay special attention to the packaging deadlines for console SKUs, since the boxes have to be approved by a third party before they can be printed.

Keyboard Reference Cards

Keyboard reference cards list the keyboard layout and commands for PC games, which can be an extra asset deliverable separate from the manual or included as a foldout from the manual cover. If a keyboard reference card is going to be included with the game, you should note this on the development schedule so QA will have time to check the game functionality against the keyboard reference card. International keyboard layouts also need to be taken into consideration when creating this packaging deliverable, as a separate keyboard layout card will need to be created and tested for each language.

DEMOS

Demos are popular marketing tools that create hype for the game by letting the consumers try the game before buying it. There are many ways to supply demos to players—over the Internet, as a stand-alone disc, or as part of a magazine's demo disc. Depending on the development schedule, demos are sometimes created after the main game version has been code released. Although creating a demo during the production of the main game is not the ideal situation, it may be necessary in order to release the demo close to the game's release date. For example, offering a demo on a magazine disc that is on newsstands the same month the game ships can really create a buzz and have a positive impact on sales.

Planning for a Demo

If a demo is needed and budgeted for, it should be planned for months in advance. Even if marketing decides during pre-production that a demo is not needed, plan for one anyway. It is inevitable that a demo will be needed for something—a trade show, as a incentive to pre-order the game, or a way to increase the game's hype. Planning for one does not cost any extra resources and ensures that dealing with a last-minute demo request will be easy to handle.

Your demo plan doesn't need to be detailed, and it can be formulated during pre-production and updated as production progresses. For example the demo plan can outline:

Content: Work with marketing to determine the specific demo content. Which level is featured? Which characters are available? Which new features will be included? What game modes will be represented? Will multiplayer be available? The content should be enough to give players a good feel for the game, but not so much that they feel that they have seen everything the game has to offer. The content will depend on how marketing wants to position the game.

Preliminary production schedule: After content has been decided, the team will know which assets and features need to be working for the demo. If there is a particular game level that's featured in the demo, this level can be the first one polished and ready to ship. This can all be worked into the production schedule, so the necessary demo features can be planned for up front. If a feature is cut, the demo schedule can be updated at the same time as the main game production schedule.

Testing schedule: If the QA department knows far enough in advance when a demo will be ready for testing, they can schedule time appropriately. They might need to pull testers off the main game for a few days, especially if the demo is being created during the game's production cycle. They can also plan to hire more testers during that time period so there are enough testers for the demo and main game.

Key magazine deadlines: Ideally, marketing likes to get a demo before the release of the main game. If the demo is to be featured on a magazine disc, there are specific magazine deadlines for each monthly issue. For example, if the demo will be featured on the magazine's March issue, the developers will need to submit the final version of the demo weeks and maybe months ahead of time. Print magazines have long lead times and will need a completed demo months in advance for inclusion on a disc. For example, if a demo was going to be featured in the October version of the magazine, you might need to supply a demo to them as early as July.

Technical guidelines: If the demo is part of a magazine's disc, the demo needs to adhere to certain technical guidelines. Check with the magazine on whether the demo will have a size limitation. If working on a console demo, the demo will need to function with the magazine's demo launcher. Check with the magazines to get the necessary files and information before submitting a demo for inclusion on their demo disc.

If marketing decides they don't need a consumer demo, which is highly unlikely, this plan can be used to create a strong and polished version of the game that can be featured at trade shows, conferences, and press events. This build can also highlight key new features of the game.

Console Demos

If console demos are being created, there are additional factors to consider:

Are PAL and NTSC versions required? If creating a console demo for international markets, regardless of whether it is localized, PAL and NTSC versions might be needed. If this is the case, work with the engineers to make sure that the game is playable in both of these modes.

Does the demo need to be submitted to a third party for approval? Console demos must be submitted to third parties for approval before they are released.

The approval time can vary, depending on the publisher and how many other games or demo the publisher is trying to approve. Allow at least two weeks in the development schedule to get a demo approved by a third party. This includes time to resubmit a demo, if an issue is found during the first submission.

Has the demo fulfilled the technical requirements?   Sony, Microsoft, and Nintendo all have specific technical requirements for demos. Check with the third-party account manager for specifics on these requirements.

If these things are kept in mind when planning for demos, your development process will go more smoothly. So make sure that everyone on the development team is aware of the deadline for finishing the demo and create a detailed schedule so there is enough time to develop, test, and submit it.

Localized Demos

If a localized demo is being developed, there are several other factors to consider:

How many languages will be in the demo?   If the demo is being localized into several languages, time is needed to organize the assets for translation, get the translations, integrate the assets, and test the localized versions. A few weeks will be necessary to complete these tasks. The marketing department should inform the team well in advance about which languages will be required for the demo. If development time is short, or marketing is asking for the demo mid-project, ask whether an English-only version will be acceptable. Creating a localized demo mid-project can have a substantial impact on the development schedule because it will affect the tasks of several people.

Will the demo be multilingual?   Multilingual demos mean that a delay in one language can put the release of the other languages at risk. The translation, integration, and testing of each language also need to be carefully scheduled so that all the translated assets can be integrated and tested at the same time.

How will language selection be handled?   If a multilingual demo is created, the team must know how the demo will select which language to display. This language selection can be stored in a configuration file so language selection is remembered the next time the player launches the demo.

MARKETING ASSETS

In addition to packaging and demos, the marketing department will require other assets, such as high-resolution artwork and gameplay footage. To prepare for delivering these additional assets, work with the marketing department to establish an asset-deliverable schedule during pre-production.

Screenshots

As mentioned, the marketing department will request screenshots throughout the development process for various purposes. Some of these screenshots are sent to gaming Web sites or magazines in order to show players what the game looks like. Most developers are very choosy about the screenshots delivered to marketing, because they want to show the game looking its very best.

When you take screenshots, turn off all the in-game UI elements in order to showcase the game instead of the UI. Gamers are generally more interested in seeing the actual game instead. In addition, the UI will probably go through many changes during the development phase, and if it is not shown, the screenshots don't look dated.

Before taking your screenshots, find out the preferred format and resolution of the images from the marketing contact. Generally, the resolution for screenshots appearing in print should be at least 300 dpi (dots per inch), and the desired resolution for screenshots appearing only electronically is at least 75 dpi. Screenshots can be delivered in most common graphic formats, such as .bmp, .tiff, .tga, and .jpg.

Gameplay Movies

Another common marketing request is raw gameplay footage of the game. The developer can tape the raw footage and deliver it electronically to the marketing department, where it can be edited as necessary. The raw footage is useful for creating Web site promos, showcasing game features, or for creating a teaser trailer or cinematic. If the same gameplay footage is used to promote localized versions of the game, turn off the UI elements to avoid showing any assets that are language specific.

High-Resolution Artwork

High-resolution artwork is necessary for magazine covers, magazine ads, and posters. You will you need to get specifics from marketing on the type of images needed. For example, marketing may request the main character be poised a certain way so that it utilizes a magazine cover image effectively, or they might want certain game elements featured.

Specifications on image size, resolution, and file format are also important. As an example, marketing might request a layered .psd file at 300 dpi that can be scaled up to 20 by 30 inches or scaled down to 8 by 10 inches. The file will need to be layered so the characters are on one layer and the background location is on another. Layering allows the character to be used alone, if necessary, for a magazine cover or feature story.

Demos from Other Games

Demos from other games might also be included on the game's gold master, so the deadline for delivering the final demos to the development team should be clearly communicated to marketing. Demos that have a higher age rating than the main game should not be included, as it is likely that the rating of the main game will increase as well. If a console game is being developed, any additional demos featured with your game will need to be approved by the appropriate third-party manufacturer before they can be included.

In addition, when working on PC demos, find out whether these demos require a Start menu or in-game shortcuts. If so, take precautions so that these shortcuts can be quickly disabled if the demo is not delivered on time. Finally, make sure that marketing realizes that the gold master cannot be delayed if another game's demo is not ready.

GAME BUILDS

During development, marketing will want builds of the game that can be shown to journalists, buyers for retail outlets, and other key people to build buzz and anticipation for the game. The press and buyers are used to looking at games still in development, so they will not expect to see a polished version of the game until it is code released. In fact, they are excited to see games in development, since it gives them a good idea what to look forward to in the final game.

Any time builds are sent to marketing or external people, you will want to include a document detailing which features are implemented, any known bugs, installation instructions, and any other information that will be useful. Since the members of the development team cannot personally demonstrate the game to all the journalists and buyers, this document should include all the information and caveats that need to be disclosed when showing a game that is still in production. Make the document easy to read and provide developer contact information in case someone needs assistance with the build or has questions about it. Also, write a demo brief that details the best way to demo the game, so that someone unfamiliar with the product can learn how to demo it effectively.

It is a good idea to fingerprint any builds sent to people outside of the development team. This entails creating a unique marker on every single build that is sent to anyone external to the team. A master list is maintained of all the marked builds and of who received each build. If an unauthorized build is posted on the Internet, the unique marker can be checked against the master build list to reveal which build was leaked. Both commercial software programs and proprietary solutions are available for software fingerprinting.

Trade Show Builds

Another item marketing will want is versions of the game that they can demo at tradeshows. The biggest games tradeshow in the United States is Electronic Entertainment Expo (E3), held each May, so always plan to show the game at this venue and other international tradeshows, depending on the marketing needs. Special builds of the game might be needed to highlight specific features and to restrict access to the full version of the game. Unless the game is about to launch, it is unlikely the whole game will be polished enough to show to press and buyers.

Preview and Review Builds

Preview builds are usually beta versions of the game that are sent to press contacts two to three months before the game ships. Preview builds allow journalists to play an early version of the game and write a brief impression of the game for a magazine or Web site. The press understands that these builds are not final versions and, thus, will have bugs and incomplete features, but preview builds are invaluable for generating early buzz around the game. Preview builds are different from demos: demos are final and polished and geared toward consumers who will eventually buy the game; whereas preview builds are unpolished and sent exclusively to journalists so they can write about the game for their magazine.

Review builds are sent to journalists just before the game ships and are final versions created from the gold master. This build should be sent as soon as possible to journalists, so that the reviews are printed as close as possible to the game's ship date. Some gamers wait to read game reviews before buying the game.

Other Builds

Marketing might want current builds of the game delivered on a regular basis so they can keep up with the progress of the game. They will also use the build to take screenshots or capture game footage for publicity purposes. An alpha build should be the first build delivered, since that is the point at which the game will start looking like a game. After that, builds can be sent on a monthly basis. It should be stressed that any regular builds sent to marketing are for internal use only; only the builds specifically prepared and tested for external use should be shown to journalists.

Additionally, marketing will need builds to submit to the ratings board, such as the Entertainment Software Rating Board (ESRB) in the United States. Other countries also have ratings boards that will review the localized version of the game and assign a rating for that specific country. Ratings boards have different standards and guidelines, so the different localized versions of the game will receive different ratings. Refer to Chapter 19, "Software Ratings," for more information on software ratings boards.

STRATEGY GUIDES

Marketing will work with strategy guide publishers to license out the rights for a game strategy guide. Because these guides provide the player hints and assistance on how to complete the game, they are usually published simultaneously with the game's launch. The book publishers will hire a freelancer to play the game and write the guide. If a strategy guide is written, the development team will be expected to provide game assets so the writer can do his job. Marketing usually coordinates this transfer of assets between the team and the author of the guide.

The most requested assets will be as follows:

Current build: The author needs the current version of the game in order to write the guide. He will usually start working on the guide around beta to ensure that he is working on a fully playable build with all the features and assets locked in. Of course, he might need to get multiple versions if the game content is not locked down. In many cases, there is not enough time to wait for the game to be code released before work begins on the strategy guide, so don't be too frustrated if the guide is based on a nonfinal version.

Game artwork: The guides usually feature screenshots, character renders, and concept art from the game. These assets are used to create a look and feel for the guide that will complement the look and feel of the game packaging.

Cheats and walkthroughs: The author will need cheats and walkthroughs to ensure that he covers all areas of the game. If there are special cheats to unlock game extras, those might be printed in the guide.

After the guide is written, the author might send a draft of the manuscript to the development team for review to make sure the correct features are included and so on. There might be a lot of small errors in the guide, especially if the author was not using the code-released version of the game, so make sure that the development team does not spend days picking apart the guide and writing up the mistakes. They will not have time for this, especially if they are in the process of finishing up the game for code release.

WORKING WITH PUBLIC RELATIONS

Public relations (PR) is responsible for interfacing with journalists and other media members in order to generate publicity for the game. PR will set up interviews, press tours, and also provide advice on what key elements of the game should be communicated. They will also provide assistance on the best way to communicate these elements. The PR contact works with the producer, especially as the game gets closer to release, to coordinate which team members are available for interviews and press tours. The team members who are well spoken and don't get nervous talking in front of others make excellent PR resources.

Press Tours

Press tours are a popular way to promote high-profile titles and involve national and international travel. If working on a high-profile title, confirm the dates for any press tours as soon as possible. It is not advisable to have members of the development team traveling during a critical milestone push. As a side note, make sure that team members who are slated for international press tours have valid passports; sometimes, press tours are cancelled or delayed for this reason. Also, plan for any builds that will be shown on the press tour. As with tradeshow builds, certain parts of the game that are more polished might be showcased and access restricted to the full version of the game.

If people from the development team are too busy to travel for a press tour, marketing might want to compromise by having a small contingent of press people visit the development studio. Journalists can fly in for a few days to get a hands-on presentation of the game and play some multiplayer games against the developers. If an on-site press tour is organized, the PR representatives from the game's publisher will accompany the journalists to assist the development team in presenting the game.

Interviews

Throughout the development process, journalists will want to conduct interviews with members of the development team. Most of these interviews can be handled via email and do not have to be planned in advance. When an email interview is sent to the team, it is important to know the specific deadline for responding to it. International journalists might have to get the answers translated before the interview is printed in the magazine.

Developer Diaries

Developer diaries are other assets generated by the development team specifically for PR and marketing purposes. Developer diaries are written by the developer to describe what work they are doing on the game, thoughts on game development, or any other information the players are interested in hearing about. There is usually a dedicated space on the game's Web site where these diaries are posted on a regular basis.

Tradeshows

As mentioned earlier in this chapter, tradeshows are a critical way to garner publicity for a game. For some of the larger tradeshows such as E3, or the Games Convention in Germany, members of the development team might be required to attend and demo the game. Having members of the development team present at these tradeshows is a big draw for journalists. They enjoy speaking directly to the developers of the game, in order to get firsthand information about the game and some of the new features that are available.

If members of the development team are showing the game at a tradeshow, they need to practice playing the game in front of other people so they don't get flustered. Additionally, they should be very familiar with the game and all the features it has and will have in the final version. It is helpful to write up a demo speech with which they can become familiar, so they are not at a loss for words. Do not send people to demo games at the tradeshows who are uncomfortable talking in front of others.

ASSET DELIVERABLE CHECKLIST

Figure 12.2 is a sample asset deliverable checklist. The first column describes the asset deliverable; the second column is the date that marketing wants the assets; and the third column gives a general timeframe about when the asset will be needed. Some projects have an accelerated development schedule, which means that the asset deliverables are also on an accelerated schedule. Some projects might have a much larger asset deliverable schedule, depending on the scope of the marketing and PR campaign. This sample schedule gives a good overview of the types of assets usually requested and time estimates for planning purposes.

Product Title	Marketing Requested Date	Notes
Localizations: French, German, Spanish, Italian		
PRODUCTION		
PC VERSION:		
Alpha		generally 8-10 months before ship date
Beta		generally 3-4 months before ship date
Gold master (US)		generally 4-6 weeks before ship date
Ship date (US)		
Gold master (French/German)		varies, depending on targeted ship date
Gold master (Spanish)		varies, depending on targeted ship date
Gold master (Italian)		varies, depending on targeted ship date
		(continued)

FIGURE 12.2 Sample asset deliverable checklist.

Product Title	Marketing Requested Date	Notes
Ship date (French/German)		
Ship date (Spanish)		
Ship date (Italian)		
CONSOLE VERSIONS:		
Alpha		generally 8-10 months before submission date
Beta		generally 3-4 months before submission date
Pre-submit to Sony, Nintendo, or Microsoft (US)		after beta, generally 2-3 months before submission date
Final submit to Sony, Nintendo, or Microsoft (US)		generally 2 months before ship date
Ship date (US)		
Final submit to Sony, Nintendo, or Microsoft (French/German)		varies, but should be after US version is approved
Final submit to Sony, Nintendo, or Microsoft (Spanish)		varies, but should be after US version is approved
Final submit to Sony, Nintendo, or Microsoft (Italian)		varies, but should be after US version is approved
Ship date (French/German)		
Ship date (Spanish)		
Ship date (Italian)		
BOX AND DOCS		
First draft of manual (US and Europe)		generally 10 weeks before US submission or ship date
Final draft of manual (US and Europe)		generally 6-8 weeks before US submission or ship date
Final box and manual screenshots (US)		generally 6-8 weeks before US submission or ship date
Box and manual layout for developer approval (US)		generally 4-6 weeks before US submission or ship date
Updates to manual text (Europe)		generally 6-8 weeks before Europe submission or ship date
Final manual and box screenshots (Europe)		generally 6-8 weeks before Europe submission or ship date
Box and manual layout to developer approval (Europe)		generally 4-6 weeks before Europe submission or ship date
MARKETING		
BUILDS:		
Alpha build		generally 8-10 months before ship date
Preview build for print magazines (US)		generally 3-4 months before ship date
Build for ratings boards (US and International)		generally 3-4 months before ship date
Beta build		generally 3-4 months before ship date
Preview build for online press (US)		generally 2-3 months before ship date
Review build (US)		as soon as US version is code released
Review build (Localized)		as soon as localized version is code released
Demos of other games for gold master (Marketing)		generally 2 months before game is code released
Demo (US)		ideally 3-4 weeks after code release of US version
Demo (Localized)		ideally 3-4 weeks after code release of localized versions
ASSETS:		
Production milestone schedule		generally 8-10 months before ship date

(continued)

FIGURE 12.2   Sample asset deliverable checklist.

Product Title	Marketing Requested Date	Notes
Design summary		generally 8-10 months before ship date
Feature list		generally 8-10 months before ship date
Assets for magazine cover pitches		generally 6-8 months before ship date
Game assets for Web site (sound, art)		generally 6-8 months before ship date
Developer's concept sketches		generally 6-8 months before ship date
High resolution images (for magazine covers)		generally 6-8 months before ship date, varies depending on need
Character art and personality summaries		generally 6-8 months before ship date
Video footage of game for teaser trailer		generally 4-6 months before ship date
Video footage of game for E3 video		generally 6 weeks before E3 date
AVI footage of game for Web movies		generally 4-6 months before ship date
Cheat codes and walkthrough		generally 4-6 months before ship date
Tips and hints for Web site and magazines		generally 2 months before ship date
Weekly screenshots		weekly deliveries, determine number in advance
Monthly developer diaries		monthly deliveries
E-mail interviews		varies, depending on need
Dates for US press tour		varies, depending on need
Dates for international press tour		varies, depending on need

FIGURE 12.2 Sample asset deliverable checklist.

SUMMARY

As the producer, it is important that you manage the relationship between development and marketing in order for them to work together to promote the game in the best way possible. While the developer is busy actually making the game, time needs to be added to the development schedule to accommodate key marketing deliverables. If the developer does not provide useful assets to marketing in a timely fashion, the game's publicity will suffer. This chapter presented a general overview of the types of assets needed by marketing and general deadlines for when these assets are required.

Part

V

Pre-Production

P re-production is the first phase of game development and is arguably the most critical one. During pre-production, the goals of the game are defined and agreed upon by the team, management, and the publisher. At the end of pre-production, a full game plan is created, which details what work needs to be done, who is going to do it, and when it needs to be completed.

This section of the book focuses on the key tasks to complete during pre-production. Information is presented on defining and approving the concept, analyzing risks, and prototyping and creating budgets, schedules, and staffing plans. Topics include the following:

- Defining a Concept
- Risk Analysis
- Defining Game Requirements
- Schedules
- Budgets

13 Concept

INTRODUCTION

Pre-production starts with defining the game's concept. After all, you can't start working on a game until you have some idea of what the game's goal is and what the final game will look like when it is completed. Initial concept starts with a broad idea—what would it be like to race concept cars against each other—and then more details are added to narrow the concept and create a vision for the game. Elements such as the hardware platform, genre, and key features are defined, along with more specifics on what the game world is like, the character designs, and the game-play mechanics. After all this is defined, anyone presented with the game information should understand the goals of the game's concept.

Rarely does only the producer determine the initial game concept and the general game design, unless he is funding a game development team and has final authority over all game design decisions. In reality, game design is a collaborative process, and the producer's main role is to manage the development process and make sure that all the key elements of the design are completed. A lead designer or creative director usually manages the creative process to ensure that all the game's elements support the initial concept. In some cases, if you try to manage both the creative and production processes, you can find yourself in a dilemma when you have an idea for a cool feature but need to cut it for production reasons. Additionally, if you assume some of the lead design responsibilities without strictly defining this in your role as producer, the other team members—particularly the lead designer—might be frustrated if they do not understand the reasoning behind your creative authority on the project.

Of course, there are instances where the producer is also the main creative leader, and this can be a successful way to structure a team, as long as everyone understands what your role as producer-director entails. The key is to define the creative and production management responsibilities clearly on the project, so that people are assured that both aspects of these areas are being expertly handled in the game development cycle. After the roles are clearly defined for pre-production tasks, you can start working on the game's concept.

Remember that when a team collaborates on a creative project, people are never in 100 percent agreement. If you spend your time trying to get everyone to agree on everything about the game, then little progress is made. People can spend too much time disagreeing with decisions and so no final decisions are made. If people are in disagreement on how a certain element functions in the game, don't waste time trying to convince the dissenter that the idea is good. Instead, spend the time prototyping the idea, get some actual gameplay feedback on the fun factor, and make adjustments or change the functionality based on this information.

This chapter presents an overview of what game elements are defined in the concept phase. In order to demonstrate some of the key points, a sample game will be used throughout this chapter and subsequent chapters discussing the game development process.

BEGINNING THE PROCESS

At the beginning of the game development process, the team will likely consist of a producer, lead designer, lead engineer, and lead artist. This core team is responsible for taking a concept and turning it into a game design. This means determining the concept, platform, genre, gameplay mechanics, character designs, and any other key game elements.

If you are working for a publisher-owned developer, the publisher will likely assign your team specific games to work on, including the platform, genre, and initial concept. With this basic information, the core team needs to define all the other elements of the game. If you are working for an independent developer, your core team will come up with the initial concept and further define it. Regardless of where the initial concept originates, there is still plenty of creative work for the team to do.

The work on the initial concept should not take more then a few weeks. Any longer than that, and you will lose valuable pre-production time and any creative momentum the team has built up in anticipation of working on a new project. One of the first things the team will participate in is a brainstorming session.

Brainstorming

Brainstorming sessions are an opportunity to involve the team in generating a large number of ideas about the game. You can brainstorm about the initial game concept, the basic gameplay mechanics, the game's setting, or what the characters will look like in the game. Well-managed brainstorming sessions are also a great team-building exercise because they allow everyone to offer their opinions about what makes a fun game. The core team is involved in the brainstorming session, or you can open it up to other people within the studio; it depends on how many ideas you want to generate in the sessions.

Before organizing a brainstorming session, familiarize yourself with guidelines for how to effectively manage one. If the session is not managed properly, it will not yield useful information, and the participants might feel frustrated by their experience. Some common complaints of an unsuccessful brainstorming session are as follows:

- The session lost focus and did not provide useful information.
- Participants' ideas were not listened to.
- No new ideas were generated.
- Participants felt used when the final decisions had no relationship to their initial input.

These mistakes can be avoided if a few guidelines are followed when setting up and conducting the session. Prepare for the session beforehand:

Clearly define the purpose of the session: If the purpose is to think of names for the game's main character, make sure that everyone involved in the session knows this. Also, define who's running the session and who's taking notes.

Get the right group of people involved in the session: In some cases, it isn't conducive to have 50 people involved. You might need to have several smaller sessions on different topics or be selective about who is invited. For example, if you are brainstorming on what graphics features to include in the game, you will need to have more artists and engineers and fewer designers.

Have everyone prepare for the session beforehand: Let people know what topic they will be discussing so they can do some preliminary research. They might want to find out what the competition did, what technologies are available, or sketch out some ideas. This way, everyone is already thinking about the topic before the session, which makes the time spent brainstorming more productive.

During the actual session, establish a set of norms to follow during the session. The purpose of these norms is to create an environment in which people feel comfortable throwing out their ideas. Some basic norms are as follows:

Do not criticize anyone or his idea during the session: When someone throws out an idea, don't start picking it apart right away. The purpose of the session is to generate information, not to eliminate it.

Do not start discussing an idea during the session: Write each idea on the board and then move on to the next one. The session will quickly lose focus after people start discussing an idea in detail, and you will miss opportunities to generate other great ideas.

When ideas stop flowing, be prepared to generate more: If people start running out of ideas in the session, look at the ideas already generated and start expanding on them or prepare some thought-provoking questions to ask to get the conversation started again. For example, what does our competition do that we aren't doing? How can we avoid the problem of _____?

After the ideas are generated, spend some time with the team grouping them together into like-minded ideas and then prioritize them. From this, generate a report of the results of the brainstorming session and add it to the meeting notes. The higher priority ideas are assigned to specific people for follow up and research. Be very clear about the action items generated in each brainstorming session and include these in the meeting notes. If you don't follow up on any of the ideas generated, people will feel that their participation was a waste of time. Some of the topics to be brainstormed might include the genre, platform, and initial game concept.

Schedule the brainstorming session as one of the first tasks for pre-production, so you can get everyone's ideas out in the open. Try to get as many brainstorming sessions completed and documented as possible in the first week of the project. The longer you put off the brainstorming session, the longer it will take to determine the game's initial concept. Ideally, each brainstorming session is managed by someone who has a neutral stance on the topic addressed. This way, his attention can be focused on running the session effectively and taking notes. When each session is completed, publish the notes within 24 hours. Also, each action item generated should take no more than a few days for the assigned person to complete.

Initial Concept

The initial concept can be generated by anyone—the publisher, the producer, the lead designer, or any other team member. The initial concept does not need to be detailed but does need to present a compelling goal for the game to achieve. This is also sometimes referred to as the game's *hook*. This hook provides the basis for all game decisions and is something the marketing department can communicate easily to the target audience when the time comes.

Initial concepts usually start off as a question to be answered—what if zombies existed and were living in outer space? What if animals had humans as pets? After the initial concept is determined, decisions are made that shape what the final version of the game will be like.

Here is an example of the initial concept for a game called *Justice Unit:*

Can a group of misfits come together as the Justice Unit, and save the world from super villains?

Genre

Genre refers to the type of game, such as fighting, role-playing, or first-person shooter. By categorizing games into genres, developers and publishers have a better understanding of what the gameplay is like. For example, the genre of first-person shooters (FPS), involves a first-person perspective where the player shoots things in the game world and is positioned behind the weapon, seeing only his weapon and his avatar's hand. *Doom* and *Half-life* are examples of classic first-person shooters. Other game genres include fighting, sports, simulations, role-playing, strategy, and third-person shooters.

The genre affects the design of the game. Here is an example of how the genre shapes the game, using *The Justice Unit* as an example:

Fighting game: If *Justice Unit* were a two-player fighting game, it might feature a roster of superheroes and villains from which to choose. Selling points could include unlockable characters, combination moves, and possibly a crossover with a licensed property, such as an existing comic book hero.

Real-time strategy: As an RTS, the game would feature an army of superheroes fighting against waves of alien invaders.

Role-playing game: As a first-person RPG, the player takes on the role of a single character, fighting evil in a superhero universe of masked villains and crime fighters.

At some point during the concept phase, the game genre will be defined. The designer might combine several genres, improve on an existing genre, or even try to create new genre. Also, ideas for genre are something that be discussed in the brainstorming session.

Platform

Platform refers to what hardware is used to play the game, such as a PC, Microsoft Xbox 360, Nintendo DS, or a cell phone handset. The platform difference, such as controller configurations and technical limitations, influence the game design. For example, a game designed for a cell phone will not feature cutting-edge graphics or technology. Cell phone games are less complex and easy to complete when the player only has a few minutes to spare. A PC game has cutting-edge graphics and a more complex controller scheme. Gameplay requires a much longer time commitment.

When games are released on multiple platforms, consider what game design elements work best with each platform and tailor the design accordingly. With next-generation consoles, players expect a game that caters to their platform of choice, instead of playing a game designed for a PC that's been ported to an Xbox 360, and vice versa. Here's an example of how the design for *Justice Unit* would change for different platforms:

> **PC:**   A PC-based version of *Justice Unit* would feature customizability as a primary feature, enabling the player to create new enemies, maps, and mission types.
>
> **Nintendo Double Screen:**   As a DS game, *Justice Unit* would be a simple, easy-to-learn FPS with a layout similar to *Metroid Prime.* The player would progress through several levels, fighting bank robbers and super villains.
>
> **Xbox 360:**   As an Xbox 360 game, *Justice Unit* is an explosive action title featuring fast-paced action sequences and team-based multiplayer. Key selling points include the immersive first-person perspective, dozens of multiplayer modes, and a story-driven single-player campaign.

Competitive Analysis

A competitive analysis identifies the strengths and weaknesses of your game's competition, market opportunities for your game, and any threats that might impact the game's success in the market. This analysis is sometimes referred to as a SWOT analysis, which stands for *Strengths, Weaknesses, Opportunities,* and *Threats.*

Begin by identifying which games are current and potential competition. This can include games with similar genres or gameplay features, games that appeal to your target audience, or games based on similar licenses. After you've determined who the competition is, analyze their strengths and weakness. Use this information to compare your game's strengths and weaknesses against the competition's. When you can clearly define what your game's strengths and weaknesses are, you are able to figure out ways to exploit or neutralize them accordingly. This information contributes to a solid game design and provides the basis for the game's marketing strategy.

Threats and opportunities identify external influences on the project. For example, if Microsoft is coming out with a new console platform at the same time your game is scheduled to launch on another platform, this constitutes a threat to your game's success. Conversely, if you are scheduled to launch a title for Microsoft's new console, this is an opportunity for your game to take advantage of a market that is not crowded with competition.

Figure 13.1 is a form that can be used to conduct a SWOT analysis. The SWOT analysis will become part of the game plan and is updated throughout production as more decisions are made about the game and more information is available about the competition. Based on your market research, you might decide to change or modify some of the game's features to either differentiate it from the competition or make improvements on what the competition is doing.

INTERNAL FACTORS		EXTERNAL FACTORS	
Our Strengths	How to Exploit	Our Opportunities	How to Exploit
INTERNAL FACTORS		EXTERNAL FACTORS	
Our Weaknesses	How to Neutralize	Our Threats	How to Neutralize

FIGURE 13.1   SWOT analysis form.

The SWOT analysis should be completed during the first few weeks of preproduction so everyone on the team has a full understanding of the competition, as this will affect the choices made on the game they are developing. Appoint one person to head up this analysis, such as an associate producer, or even the producer. This person needs to get input from the development team and the marketing department.

A basic competitive analysis for *Justice Unit* is as follows:

The primary competition for *Justice Unit* is PostMortal, a first-person shooter set in a superhero universe.

Strengths: Compared against rival *PostMortal, Justice Unit* features a strong multiplayer experience, including a customizable multiplayer avatar, dozens of gameplay types, and several maps.

Weaknesses: *Justice Unit* features a free-roaming, nonlinear single-player experience, which will not deliver the same thrills as the linear, heavily scripted *PostMortal.*

Opportunities: *Justice Unit* will be a next-gen launch title and will benefit from the early adopter rush.

Threats: *PostMortal* is based on a popular comic book, and the strong crossover appeal will help sales. *Justice Unit* is an original IP and has no built-in fan base.

Approval

After the basic concept information is defined and a SWOT analysis is conducted, put together a summary document and present it to all interested parties for approval. If the publisher likes the direction you are going, they might make a few minor suggestions and let you continue working. However, if the concept is veering away from what the publisher envisioned, they might request major changes and ask you to present to them again. If you are working on a two-year development cycle, plan to schedule this initial approval meeting about two–three weeks after starting pre-production. If working on a six-month project, try to have this meeting about one week after starting pre-production.

Getting approval at this stage is important, as it can save you a lot of work. If you continue to define the concept and write up design documents, you might find that your team spent months putting all this information together, only to find that it is not what the publisher or studio management envisioned. And since they are footing the bill for game development, it is best to make sure the team is delivering the type of game they want.

Schedule a meeting for all the stakeholders and present what information you have so far. Involve other key members of the team in this meeting so they are on hand to answer any questions, and so they can hear the feedback firsthand. Be sure to take accurate notes at the meeting, post them for the team to review, and follow up on any action items.

INTERVIEW

Clint Hocking, Creative Director, Ubisoft

The best constraint to take into account when creating a concept and initial design is to *not think about features and content*. You need to define what your game is *about*, not how many levels you have or how many guns you have and what their alt-fire is. You need to know what your game is *about* in the broadest strokes, and you need to be able to represent that with some kind of simple system diagram. (I don't mean what it's about in terms of its *story* I mean what it's about in terms of its *systems*.) That concept needs to be beautiful and elegant, because it is the foundation of your entire game. When you are confident that your high-level concept is strong, then you can start to think about the mechanics and dynamics that support the high-level concept. Your features and content should then flow naturally out of those mechanics and dynamics. If you do it this way, I strongly suspect that you will not have problems limiting your content and features to a meaningful set. Ideas are cheap, but harmony among ideas is really hard to achieve. If you start with a random collection of good ideas and try to build a concept from the bottom up, you will not have a harmonious whole. If you start with a vision of the whole and then support it robustly with the systems that it requires, then you probably will not have to worry about limiting yourself for schedule or resources.

On *Chaos Theory* I worked very closely with our marketing manager to understand the needs of the audience and to communicate my vision of the game. There was a definite synthesis of ideas that took place there. The concept of *Chaos Theory*—of small actions having potentially large repercussions—as well as the *Closer Than Ever* system in the game and the systems that support them came about through lengthy discussions between design and marketing (and others). They arose from both the need to have expressive, unified, and robust systems, as well as from the need to differentiate the title from the competition and strengthen the franchise and the brand where it was weak. The game's marketing bullet points are concepts like tension, freedom, cinematic quality, and meaningful choices. These come from that initial collaboration between marketing and design. Some people take shots at that idea and say that makes me a marketing-driven designer and that designers who design for the market are simply rehashing the same old proven designs and not bringing anything new. I would suggest those people compare the bullet points I mention above with the more standard bullet points of "20 different weapons," "3 playable races," "5 different alien worlds." Design needs to work closely with marketing, if only to make sure that marketing understands what your game is actually about so they can communicate about it and help create the need for more meaningful, less derivative games.

DEFINE THE CONCEPT

After the stakeholders have approved the initial direction of the concept, your core team continues to define the concept. During this phase, the team starts detailing more specifics about the game mechanics, setting, characters, storyline, and major features. Technical limitations should be loosely considered, but don't censor any ideas on perceived limitations at this point. Instead, focus on creating and proto-typing a fun game. When these elements are ready for review, the engineers can fully assess the technical limitations. Although they might not be able to implement what was originally designed, they can take a look at what was intended and come up with some alternative ways to do this within the technical constraints.

During the concept definition phase, the lead designer and lead artist need to produce several deliverables. They will most likely create these deliverables them-selves, especially if there are not other resources available. The types of information defined during this phase include the following:

- Mission statement
- Game setting
- Gameplay mechanics
- Story synopsis
- Concept art
- Audio elements

On a two-year development cycle, plan to spend about one month to two months defining the initial concept. On a six-month cycle, plan to spend about one to two weeks on this.

Mission Statement

The mission statement defines the major goals of the project. Jim Lewis, author of *Project Planning Scheduling and Control,* believes that a mission statement answers these two questions:

- What is going to be done?
- Who is it being done for?

If you can't clearly answer these two questions, it will be difficult to formulate a mission statement that concisely sums up the essence of the game. Good mission statements act as the measuring stick for all the ideas considered for the game. If the idea enhances the mission statement, it is likely a good fit for the game. If the idea goes against any aspect of the mission statement, it should not be in the final vision of the game. After a mission statement is defined, publicly post it for the team, stu-dio management, and the publisher.

Involve the core team in a brainstorming session to determine what the mission statement is. Spend a few hours brainstorming and try to finalize the mission statement by the next day. After it is determined, each team member has a better idea of what direction to take for his pre-production deliverables.

For example, the mission statement for *Justice Unit* is

Justice Unit is a mass-market superhero game with streamlined controls. It is intended for fans of comic books and superhero movies who want to experience the larger-than-life adventure of their four-color heroes.

Game Setting

The game setting influences the look and feel of the game, such as the environment, objects, location, character designs, and any other elements that are part of the game universe. The game can have settings such as science fiction (*Halo*), real-world (*Ghost Recon 2*), fantasy (*Final Fantasy Series*), and historical (*Call of Duty*).

The lead designer has some ideas on what settings work well with the initial concept and can work with the lead artist to determine the look and feel of the setting. The lead designer can write up a description of the setting, and the lead artist can create concept art to show what the setting looks like. This might take a few days or weeks to complete, depending on what other assets these resources are generating as well. The setting might evolve based on other decisions made about the story, characters, and gameplay mechanics.

The setting for *Justice Unit* is as follows.

The game is set in a classic world of fiendish villains and gun-toting thugs. The player's team consists of oddball heroes with super powers. In a universe full of straight-faced heroes and villains, the Justice Unit are a group of bizarre misfits with strange powers and wacky personalities. Justice Unit *is part parody and part tribute of the classic superhero-teams of the sixties, complete with improbable origin stories and larger-than-life villains.*

Gameplay Mechanics

Gameplay mechanics encompass many of the actions the player does or experiences in the game. The mechanics comprise the bulk of the design documentation as the functionality of the different gameplay systems is detailed. Some of the systems that fall under this category are as follows:

- Challenges for the player (such as end-level bosses and puzzles)
- Player rewards (such as points, extra weapons, or special items)
- Learning curve (How fast can the player learn the basics and start having a fun experience?)
- Control scheme (How will the player use the controller or keyboard?)
- Player actions (such as running, jumping, and casting spells)
- Multiplayer elements

This doesn't list all the necessary gaming systems for any one game but is a good starting point for determining which areas of the game need more details. The systems are defined before pitching the game to the publisher.

The lead designer will take the lead on generating the bulk of the design documentation. He works with the other leads and producer to make sure that all the necessary elements are defined and work with the approved concept. At this stage in production, the documents will outline a vision for how each of the gameplay systems might work, without providing minute details. The functionality requirements will be worked out after the overall gameplay mechanics are approved. If working on a two-year development cycle, it might take the lead designer two–four weeks to produce these game play documents.

For example, the multiplayer game mechanics for *Justice Unit* are

Justice Unit features two multiplayer modes. In Justification, two teams of up to eight players (16 total) square off against each other in objective-driven battles. In Vindication, up to 16 players can play in every-man-for-himself free-for-all battles.

Story Synopsis

Story is becoming increasingly important in games. Not only do players want compelling game play, they also want a compelling story. A good story is the difference between a good game and a great game, because the story helps to immerse the player further in the game world. The details of the story don't need to be fully defined in the concept phase; this is something the writer can work on while the designer finalizes the design documents. However, the synopsis must present a storyline that integrates the game setting, gameplay mechanics, and characters into a cohesive entertainment experience for the player.

The story synopsis for *Justice Unit* is

When marketing executive Mark Ferrier was struck by lightning during a presentation, he developed astonishing powers. At first, he kept these to himself, but after witnessing the Justice Unit *in a pitched battle with the villainous Wire Hanger, he joined in their defense. The Unit recruited Ferrier, who chose the name Bulletpoint. Along with Montezuma, Ice Queen, Major Malfunction, and The Caribou, he fights crime and those who commit it.*

Concept Art

As the saying goes, a picture is worth a thousand words. Concept art shows what the visual elements of the game will look like before any art assets are produced for the game. Concept art can be appreciated by anyone, from studio management down to the team, and since everyone is looking at the same thing, it is a useful tool for communicating the game's vision. Any core pre-production team must include a concept artist who can start sketching out some of the team's ideas. The concept artist will work mainly with the lead artist and lead designer on what the characters, levels, and objects look like in the game. There should be a process in place, managed by the lead artist, for the team to give feedback. Concept art can take several weeks to produce, depending how much needs to be generated and how detailed it is.

Figure 13.2 is an example of character concept art for *Justice Unit*.

FIGURE 13.2   Character concept art for *Justice Unit.* © 2005 Richard Case. Reprinted with permission.

INTERVIEW

Carey Chico, Art Director, Pandemic Studios

In the past, game development teams were not very big, and technology was a limiting factor to creating realistic-looking game worlds. Now that teams have gotten larger, and we can create huge, believable worlds, game developers have taken on a concept art paradigm that's derivative of the film industry—we concept out all the assets before creating them for the game.

The main reasons concept art is important and will become more important when creating assets for next-generation technology are as follows:

→

■ It helps the artistic vision to be carried all the way through to the final assets that appear in the game.

■ The artists can work and rework assets on paper, when the cost is much lower, and then only create the actual assets when everyone agrees on what will appear in the game.

■ Outsourcing art assets will become more common as the volume of assets needed for next-generation titles increases, so clearly defined concept art will ensure that the assets look consistent with the game, no matter where they are created.

Audio Elements

Audio is a critical part of the game, as it helps immerse the player into the game world. Think about the *Silent Hill* series of games—would they be as creepy if you played with the sound and music turned down? The lead designer might want to work with a sound designer for a few days to come up with an initial plan for voiceover, sound effects, and music. The sound designer can advise on what audio elements work best with the proposed setting, story, and gameplay mechanics.

The audio overview answers questions such as the following:

■ Will each character have a unique voice?
■ How do the characters' voice cues function in the game (for example, help for the player, comic relief, or character development)?
■ What types of music work best with the game (such as licensed heavy metal songs, an original orchestral score, or instrumental techno music)?
■ Where in the game will the music play (for example, only in the UI shell or real-time in gameplay during climatic battles)?
■ What types of sound effects will work best in the game?

PROTOTYPING

Some gameplay elements can be prototyped during the concept phase, and the team should plan to prototype as much as possible. Prototyping game elements helps the team determine the strengths and weaknesses of any idea, before time is spent generating assets and coding a feature into the game. If you can't see a feature working in the game until beta, there is not much time left for tweaking or re-design if the feature is not functioning as anticipated.

If you don't have a functioning game engine, use a commercially available editor, such as UNREAL, in order to create playable spaces and test out different gameplay mechanics. Paper prototyping can also be effective. If possible, create a playable prototype that shows off the first five minutes of gameplay. If a playable prototype is not doable, write up a description that evokes what the player experiences when he first starts playing the game. The prototyping phase is on-going during pre-production and is headed up by the lead designer, or possibly the producer.

INTERVIEW

Tracy Fullerton, University of Southern California

One of the most important things a game prototype gives you is the ability to understand the player's experience immediately. A prototype also makes an idea tangible and, therefore, creates something that is much easier for team members to speak about and work on from their own perspective. People tend to butt their heads together most when they are speaking in the abstract, so you will see designers and programmers butting heads, and they might actually be saying the same thing, but because they don't have a prototype or something concrete to reference, they don't even realize it.

I am personally a strong believer in paper prototyping, and I don't like students to write up any game specifications until they have some form of prototype. From the moment you come up with an idea, you can begin to model the core mechanics and the underlying structures. Those early paper models—and you might have to build two or three to understand all the systems—will be used to build digital prototypes. After these are created, people can start defining specs.

I think that truly innovative design comes from asking wild and impertinent questions and spending small amounts of time and money on proving whether these questions will provide interesting and provocative answers. This is why I am so focused on paper prototyping. This is something a dedicated designer can do on their own time. A designer can usually complete a prototype, enlist play testers, and make changes, all in a short amount of time. It's a fantastic experimental method for asking these kind of interesting questions. For example, right now I'm working on a game where the central question we're trying to understand is "how can you make a game about the journey of spiritual enlightenment?"

I think it is very important that the technology team be a part of the creative team; but it is equally important that technology doesn't drive the experience design. This means the designer has to understand and respect the technical limits of the platform with which they are working, but creatively they don't have to live within those limits the same way that technologists do. Designers need to understand the technical limitations well enough to work around them or to use them as a springboard

$\rightarrow$

for some type of creative twist that doesn't restrict the game but actually makes the game better. One of the best ways to do this is to have the technologists play the paper prototypes. Again, when the idea is tangible, people can talk about it, and out of the discussion comes the true essence of what the designer was trying to do with that feature or technique. This means the technologists don't have to just blindly implement the feature; they are actually part of the process of discovering what the feature is really about. Being part of the process makes it easier for the technologists to implement the essence of the feature.

RISK ANALYSIS

Risk assessment is an ongoing process, and the producer must be constantly aware of what the biggest risks are for the game, even after production begins. Doing an initial risk assessment in pre-production, involving all the project stakeholders, is a good way to identify and start preparing for risks.

Risks are things that *could* go wrong on a project, such as a key team member leaving mid-project, not getting the graphics pipeline completed in time to begin production, or an external vendor missing his final deliverable date. When the risks are identified, prioritize them and plan mitigation strategies. Keep in mind that all risks are not equal. Although some risks might have a higher probability of occurring, the impact may not be as severe as a risk that has a low probability of occurring.

Steve McConnell's book, *Rapid Development*, contains an excellent chapter on risk management and is recommended reading for anyone who wants to learn more about this. As he points out in his book, a project utilizing risk management is not as exciting to work on because there is little need for people to run around putting out fires. Instead, everyone can focus on getting the game done, because risks have already been identified and planned for in the schedule.

His approach is divided into two parts: risk assessment and risk control. During risk assessment, the core team needs to do the following:

- Identify risks that could impact the project.
- Analyze each risk's likelihood of occurring and the impact it has on the project.
- Prioritize each risk beginning with the ones with the most impact.

There are numerous potential risks on any given game that can affect the ship date, the quality of work, the scope of features, and the cost. When doing the risk assessment, brainstorm as many risks as possible and then prioritize them accordingly. Your biggest risks are the ones that have a high probability of occurring and will have the biggest impact on the project. Figure 13.3 is a basic classification grid for four levels of risk. More risks levels can be added as appropriate for your project. Risks that fall into categories 1 and 2 are considered critical risks and must have solutions in place to manage them if they occur.

The second part of McConnell's risk management strategy involves risk control. After the risks are identified and prioritized, the team needs to do the following:

■   Create a management plan for neutralizing or removing the most critical risks. Make sure the plans for each risk are consistent with the overall project plan.
■   Implement the proposed plans to resolve the risks.
■   Monitor the progress toward resolving the known risks.

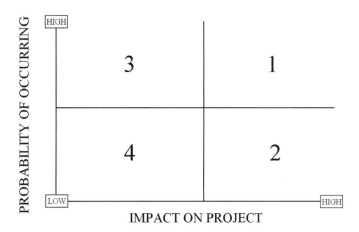

FIGURE 13.3   Risk classification grid.

In addition, any new risks must be identified and controlled throughout development by using the same process of risk assessment and risk control discussed previously.

Risk management is the responsibility of everyone on the team, although the producer should spearhead the effort to identify risks and solutions. The initial in-depth risk assessment meeting should happen after some of the major game elements have been defined. This way, there is a better idea of what elements are risky. Spend one day defining the risks with the team, one or two days creating a risks resolution plan, and then publish this plan to the team.

PITCH IDEA

After the concept documents, prototypes, and risk analysis are complete, the producer schedules a pitch meeting with the publisher and studio management. Be prepared to present all aspects of the game to them, including the risk analysis. The project leads should attend as well, so they can answer any questions within their areas of expertise.

The pitch meeting might last two–three hours. Plan an agenda and include a break in the middle so that people have chance to take a break and refresh themselves (you don't want people falling asleep in the meeting). Make sure that all presenters are enthusiastic about the game and can communicate this enthusiasm to the meeting attendees. People who are poor public speakers should not be presenting in the pitch meeting. Make sure that someone is taking notes during the meeting so that all the feedback is accounted for.

After the presentation, the publisher and studio management might love exactly what you've showed them and will give you the green light to continue with those ideas in pre-production. It is more likely they will have feedback on certain elements of the game and will want this feedback incorporated before they greenlight your project for the next phase of pre-production. In any situation, this is a positive outcome for all the hard work the team has done so far. In extreme cases, they might decide to shelve the project or ask you to go back and re-conceptualize it. If this happens, be sure that you understand exactly what they didn't like about the pitch and what areas need major changes.

PROJECT KICK-OFF

When the idea is approved by all the stakeholders, schedule a formal project kick-off. The kick-off is a great team-building exercise because it provides an opportunity for all the team members to come together and talk about the project. It is also a great way to welcome any new team members who might be added at this phase in development. Consider having a team lunch or a group outing as part of the kick-off, so that people can also casually socialize with each other and get to know their teammates.

Additionally, if you are working on a console title, you will need to submit this initial concept to the console manufacturer for approval. They might request changes to the concept as well. If they reject the concept entirely, you might be able to revamp it and resubmit for approval. However, there is a small chance they could reject the concept and not allow you to resubmit a revised concept, but this does not normally happen.

CONCEPT OUTLINE

Figure 13.4 is a summary of each step that must be completed in the concept phase. This is based on a two-year development cycle.

Initial Concept	Resources	General Timeline	Tasks
Brainstorming	Producer runs sessions, team participates.	1 week	Brainstorm initial concepts for game, including genre and platform.
Initial Concept	Lead Designer	1 week	Review brainstorming notes. Define initial concept, genre, and platform. Incorporate feedback from team.
Competitive Analysis	Producer, Marketing	2 weeks	Review current and potential competition, complete SWOT analysis based on initial concept.
Approve Initial Concept	Producer runs meeting, leads attend.	2–3 weeks after pre-production begins	Present intial concept, with genre and platform, for approval. Initial competitive analysis completed. Incorporate management feedback.
Define Concept	**Resources**	**General Timeline**	**Tasks**
Mission Statement	Producer runs sessions, team participates.	1–2 days	Define mission statement for the game.
Game Setting	Lead Designer, Lead Artist	3–5 days	Define game setting, including look and feel.
Game Play Mechanics	Lead Designer	2–4 weeks	Create general overview of how major game elements will function: challenges, rewards, learning curve, control scheme, audio elements, multiplayer.
Story Synopsis	Lead Designer, Writer	3–5 days	Create game's back story, character biographies, general outline of how story unfolds in the game.
Concept Art	Lead Artist, Concept Artist	3–5 weeks	Create concept art for game setting, characters, and objects.
Audio Elements	Lead Designer, Sound Designer	2–4 days	Create general overview of how voiceover, sound effects, and music will be presented in the game.
Prototyping	Lead Designer, Producer	4–6 weeks	Prototype major game elements.
Risk Analysis	Producer runs sessions, team participates.	2–3 days	Assess risks on project, determine resolution strategy, publish to the team.
Pitch Idea	Producer, Leads	1.5–2 months after approval of initial concept	Present all major game play elements to management for approval, incorporate their feedback.
Project Kick-off	Producer	After management approves pitch.	Meet with team to celebrate the concept approval. If working on console title, submit game concept to console manfacturer for approval.

FIGURE 13.4 Outline of concept phase.

SUMMARY

The importance of the concept phase in pre-production cannot be underestimated. This concept is the foundation the game is built on, and if the concept is weak or is not fully defined before beginning the next phase, there might be major elements missing from the game that are not discovered until the team is well into production. This chapter discusses some of the major areas that must be defined and approved by the project stakeholders before pre-production continues. These areas include the initial concept, game-play mechanics, setting, characters, and audio elements. Information is also presented on prototyping and risk analysis, which are an integral part of the process as well.

After the concept is firmly established, the next phase of pre-production, determining game requirements, begins. The next chapter discusses the deliverables that are generated during this phase, such as a core feature set, milestones, and design documentation.

14 Game Requirements

In This Chapter

- Define Game Features
- Define Milestones and Deliverables
- Evaluate Technology
- Define Tools and Pipeline
- Documentation
- Risk Analysis
- Approval
- Game Requirements Outline

INTRODUCTION

When the initial concept deliverables are completed and approved, the team needs to determine the game's requirements. The requirements detail how the concept will be turned into a real game. Decisions are made about the main project goals, the core feature set, and the milestone deliverables. In addition, the core technology and production pipeline must be established. Finally, all documentation needs to be written and finalized. After these items are completed, you have a clear idea of what needs to be done to create the game. These items are then used to further determine the budgeting, scheduling, and staffing needs for the game.

DEFINE GAME FEATURES

During pre-production, everyone has an idea about what cool features can be included in the game. Obviously, you can't include every single feature request: some won't fit with the game's vision; the team won't have enough time to get everything in; or the technology cannot support the functionality. Therefore, you need to prioritize the features into different tiers for implementation. For example, tier one features are the core features of the game; tier two features add value to the core features; and tier three designates features that would be nice to include. Ideally all the tier one features are included, and you might find time to add many (or all) of the tier two features. Usually, the tier three features are considered for the next version of the project and will not make it into the final game.

To begin with, involve the team in a brainstorming session as to what features should be included in the game. Conduct these sessions over the course of two–three days. Brainstorm about multiplayer features, single-player features, gameplay mechanics, sound, and any other aspects of the game. Gather all the feature ideas in a single list and then categorize them by type. Doing this will help the producer and leads to better prioritization of the features. Some categories to consider are as follows:

Process: These features revolve around improving the development processes. This includes improving the formats of the design documentation, establishing an approval process for multiplayer levels, and setting up mini-tutorials to teach people how to use the development tools.

Production: These features involve improvements to the tools and technology used to make the game. For example, adding cut-and-paste functionality to the scripting tool, improving how destructible objects function in the game, and adding enhanced lighting functionality to the art tools.

Gameplay: These features consist of gameplay elements that will directly impact the player's experience and be visible to the player. This includes the ability of the player to control vehicles, functionality for changing options on-the-fly, and the ability for the player to customize his avatar.

You could also create categories around specific gameplay elements, or by discipline, or any other grouping that will help you get a better handle on the types of features being requested. Figure 14.1 is an example of what this categorized master feature list looks like.

After this list is generated and categorized, the producer sends the list to the leads and asks them to each assign a priority to every feature on the list. The leads

Category	Feature
Gameplay	dynamic missions objectives
Process	mission review process should also include multiplayer levels
Process	establish a system for circulating design documents and updates to documents to the team
Gameplay	easy to understand user interface
Gameplay	replayable missions
Production	improve physics so explosions look more realistic
Gameplay	ability for player to customize character appearance
Production	support cut-and-past functionality in scripting tool

FIGURE 14.1   Categorized master feature list.

should base their priorities on the known project constraints. For example, if the game is a *time to market* game, the final code release deadline is the main constraint, and all of the core features must be doable within the limited time on the project. If the game is a sequel to a best-selling franchise, the constraint is to create a game that lives up to its predecessor, so more time might be added to the schedule to ensure that the game has all the key features.

The leads also need to consider the overall art, engineering, design, and testing concerns when assigning priorities. For example, the lead artist might be tempted to assign the highest priority to all the art feature requests and a lower priority to all the design feature requests. However, if the lead artist does not fairly consider the overall game needs, the game might end up with stunning graphics but so-so gameplay. Experienced leads will know how to strike a balance among the art, design, engineering, and gameplay needs on a project.

After each lead has assigned a ranking to the features (with 3 being highest priority and 1 being lowest priority), collect all of the data and add it to the master feature list. Include a column for each person's rankings and make the last column an average for the rankings. After calculating the average ranking, use this value to sort the entire list. Figure 14.2 is an example of what the feature ranking spreadsheet will look like after sorting it by the average ranking.

After this is completed, schedule a meeting with the leads to discuss the results. This meeting might last a few hours as you will need to go through each feature, assess its overall ranking, and finalize whether it is a "must have," "like to have," or "nice to have" feature. Even though everyone might not be in 100 percent agreement about the rank for each feature on the list, this exercise provides a good way to garner consensus on what features are most important for the game. When the meeting is over, publish the final ranked feature list to the team. This feature list will provide the basis for defining the milestones and deliverables.

Category	Feature	Prod.	Art	Design	Eng.	QA	Average
Gameplay	dynamic missions objectives	3	3	3	3	3	3
Process	establish a system for circulating design documents and updates to documents to the team	3	3	3	3	3	3
Gameplay	easy to understand user interface	3	3	3	3	3	3
Process	mission review process should also include multiplayer levels	3	3	3	2	3	2.8
Production	improve physics so explosions look more realistic	2	3	1	3	1	2
Gameplay	replayable missions	2	2	2	1	2	1.8
Gameplay	ability for player to customize character appearance	1	2	3	1	1	1.6
Production	support cut-and-paste functionality in scripting tool	1	1	3	1	1	1.4
3 = MUST HAVE **2 = LIKE TO HAVE** **1 = NICE TO HAVE**							

FIGURE 14.2 Feature ranking spreadsheet sorted by average ranking.

INTERVIEW

Clint Hocking, Creative Director, Ubisoft

Part of the problem is that features are not discrete—basically any new feature could be called an improvement or a bug fix for an existing feature, so there can be no rigid definition of when the rule has been broken. My feeling is that if you design correctly, this should not be a problem. If you start with a concept for the entire game and then you specify the mechanics and dynamics that support that concept, you won't be in a feature-hunt. You won't be looking to copy random sexy features from other games because your game won't be a random collection of features, it will be a unified whole. That's pretty idealized, and there's no way any game development is going to work like that, but it's a good place to start. Limit your scope to what is *meaningful* under the creative concept of the game. Anything outside that (even if it's awesome) is feature creep.

DEFINE MILESTONES AND DELIVERABLES

After the core features are determined, the producer can put together initial documentation on the milestones and deliverables. Milestones mark a major event during game development and are used to track the project's progress. They provide the team smaller, more manageable goals to work toward and can be easily defined by listing what deliverables are expected for each milestone.

Each development team will have a different set of milestones to mark the game's progress. Some teams establish monthly milestones, and other teams work toward bigger milestones every few months. When working on a two-year development cycle, a common set of milestones is as follows:

First playable: This is the first major milestone for the game. It contains representative gameplay and assets. Often, it is based on the prototype that was created in pre-production. This milestone is usually scheduled to occur 12–18 months before code release.

Alpha: At this milestone, key gameplay functionality is implemented, assets are 40–50 percent final (the rest are placeholder), the game runs on the correct hardware platform in debug mode, and there is enough working that you can start to get a feel for the game. Features might undergo major adjustments at this point, based on play testing results and other feedback. Alpha occurs 8–10 months before code release.

Code freeze: At this point, the game is code complete, and the engineers are only fixing bugs from this point forward. No additional features are added so that the code has time to stabilize, and the critical bugs can be identified and fixed. This milestone happens about 3–4 months before code release.

Beta: By beta, the game is code and asset complete. Art, design, and engineering only focus on fixing bugs that are listed in the bug database. No new assets are generated; no new features are coded; and no changes are made to existing features and functionality unless it is identified as a bug. Beta occurs about 2–3 months before code release.

Code release candidate: At this milestone, all the bugs have been addressed, and the developers are confident that the build is ready to be shipped or submitted to the console manufacturer for approval. The code release candidate is tested against the QA test plan, and any crash bugs or other critical issues are fixed as necessary. The team is not actively making any fixes. The first code release candidate should be ready for QA testing about three–four weeks before the code release date.

Figure 14.3 is a table with more details about each of these development milestones.

	First Playable	Alpha	Code Freeze	Beta	Code Release
Time Frame	12–18 months before code release	8–10 months before code release	3–4 months before code release	2–3 months before code release	First code release candidate available to QA 3 weeks before final code release deadline.
Engineering	Basic functionality for a few key features are in to demonstrate very basic game play.	Key game play functionaltiy is in for all game features. Features work as designed, but may be adjusted and changed based on feedback. Game runs on target hardware platform.	Code complete for all features. Only bug-fixing from this point forward. No new features are added, unless approved by senior management.	Code complete, only bug fixing from this point forward.	Full code freeze. During this phase only crash bugs can be fixed. Critical bugs can be fixed with approval.
Art	Two to three key art assets are created and viewable in the build. The assets demonstrate the look and feel of the final version of the game.	Assets are 40–50% final, with placeholder assets for the rest of the game.	Assets are 80–90% final, with placeholder assets for the rest of the game.	All art assets are final and working in game. Only major bug-fixes from this point forward.	Full art freeze. No art fixes, unless it is to fix a crash bug.
Design	Basic features are defined, key game play mechanics have basic documentation and a playable prototype if possible.	All design documen-tation is completed. Feature implemen-tation is in progress. 40–50% of design production tasks are completed. Major areas of game are playable as designed.	Game is 80–90% playable. Playtesting feedback is being incorporated.	All design assets are final and working in the game. Only major bug fixes from this point forward. Minor game play tweaks can be done, based on playtest feedback.	Full design freeze. No design fixes, unless it is to fix a crash bug.
Sound	The sound of the game is determined, including voiceover, music, sound effects. Samples are available to communicate the sound vision of the game.	40–50% of sound effects are in a working. Voiceover design is in progress, placeholder VO files are recorded. Music in process of being composed.	Final voiceover is recorded and in-game. Final music is in-game. Sound effects are 80–90 % implemented.	All final sound assets are in and working in the game.	Full sound freeze.
Production	Basic game require-ments and game plan are completed.	Full production has begun. The game requirments and game plan are fully completed and approved. If working with licenses, all licenses are secured and an approval process is in place.	Localizations have started. Manual is in process of being written. Marketing assets are being generated.	Localizations are complete, only bug fixes from this point forward. Manual is complete. External vendors are finished with work. All approvals for licenses are secured. Devel-opment team can start rolling off project.	All production tasks are completed. If submitting game to console manufac-turer, the submission forms are filled in and ready to go.
QA	Can test game against the first playable mile-stone deliverables defined in the game requirements phase.	Game is now playable as a full game, although there are some rough edges and holes in some of the function-altiy. Playtesting can begin. Can test against the alpha deliverables expected for this milestone.	Test plan is 100% complete. Full game functionality can be tested and bugged. Play testing continues. Can test against the code freeze milestone deliverable list.	All aspects of game can be fully tested and bugged. Some playtesting continues in order for design to put the final polish on the game.	Test code release candidates for any crash bugs that will prevent the game from shipping.

FIGURE 14.3   Common development milestones.

After you have determined which milestones to include in the production schedule, define in as much detail as possible what the expected deliverables are for each one. Doing this is important so that there is a clear way for the team to determine whether the milestone is completed. If nothing is defined, how will the team know whether the milestone is completed? This list is also useful for the QA department, since they know exactly what parts of the game need to be checked for functionality. These lists are also a great way to track the game's progress to ensure that nothing important is omitted.

A simple way to define the milestones is to establish a list of deliverables for each one. These lists can be started in pre-production and updated as information about the game is defined. Include information about what is completed and ready for testing on each aspect of the game. If an asset or feature is not 100 percent complete, state what should be completed and viewable in the game for each milestone delivery, as some items are so large they might span several milestones before they are fully complete. Use categories such as the following:

- Characters, objects, levels
- Cinematics
- Gameplay features
- Engineering features
- UI
- Sound
- Localization
- Scripting
- General

You might not be able to fill in a lot of information at the beginning of the project, as there are many decisions still to be made, but fill in what you can. After the initial lists are established, send them to the leads for review so they can check that the goals for each milestones are attainable. Publish these lists to the team so they clearly understand the expectations for each milestone. Also, get into the habit of checking the lists for updates on a regular basis. However, don't make changes to a set of milestone deliverables that are due in a few days—that is, don't add things to the alpha deliverable list one week before the milestone is due. Figure 14.4 is an example of a partial deliverable list for the *Justice Unit* alpha milestone.

```
JUSTICE UNIT
Alpha Deliverable for March 30, 2007
Last Updated February 10, 2007

Levels
—The following levels are asset complete, with game play scripting:
            *Justice Hall
            *Villain's Lair
—The following levels are have basic geometry and are viewable in game, but have no game play scripted:
            *City Hall
            *Office Complex

Characters
—The following characters are asset complete:
            *Bulletpoint
            *Montezuma
—The following characters are viewable in game, but don't have final textures
            *Caribou

UI
—UI color scheme and font are final and approved
—UI flow is prototyped in Macromedia Flash
—Basic UI screens are implemented and functioning:
            *Start screen
            *Profile screen
            *Options screen
—In-game UI has placeholder art with basic functionality for:
            *Health bar
            *Inventory

Sound
—Placeholder VO cues and sound designs are implemented for the following levels:
            *Justice Hall
            *Villain's Lair
—Sound designs completed for remaining levels in the game

Engineering
—Scripting tools completed and functioning
—Art tools completed and functioning
—Networking APIs are implemented
—Build process finalized and in place
```

FIGURE 14.4   Partial alpha deliverable list for *Justice Unit*.

EVALUATE TECHNOLOGY

During the game requirements phase, the lead engineer is evaluating the technology needs of the project. Decisions must be made on what game engine, art tools, scripting tools, AI systems, physics systems, and other technical elements are needed to provide the desired game functionality. The technology used will depend on the schedule, the resources, the desired features, and the quality of these features. For example, if the main goal of the game is to have cutting-edge graphics, the lead engineer will spend some time evaluating what graphics technology is necessary.

The lead engineer must also research how this technology will be obtained: will it be coded by in-house engineers, or will an existing software package be licensed and modified for use in the game? There are pros and cons of each choice, and larger games will probably use a combination of in-house technology and licensed technology.

The benefits of creating the technology in-house are that it is owned by the studio and, therefore, has no licensing fee; in-house experts are readily available to bug-fix and add feature enhancements; and the technology can be specifically tailored to the game. One con is that the engineers have to spend valuable development time re-inventing the wheel for basic technical functionality (such as physics, AI, and animation), meaning that they have less time to focus on game specific functionality. Also, using a team of in-house engineers to code basic functionality, such as a physics system, might be more expensive in the long run instead of licensing a middleware solution, such as Havok.

The main benefit of licensing an existing technology is that it provides a basic framework for common technologies, meaning the engineers can focus on game-specific functionality. The drawbacks can be costs (especially if the budget is small), limited technical support from the vendor, and the need to alter the code to fit the game's functionality. However, these drawbacks might be worth the trouble if licensing saves time and/or money during the development process.

After the lead engineer has researched the available technologies, he will make a recommendation to the producer. The producer can use this information when creating the budget and schedule and will work closely with the lead engineer to determine the best technology solutions for the game.

DEFINE TOOLS AND PIPELINE

In addition to evaluating which technologies will be used for the game, the lead engineer will work with the other leads to define the production pipeline. The production pipeline refers to the series of steps that are needed to get code and assets working in a playable version of the game. It must smoothly incorporate the tools, assets, and production needs of the game. It is very rare that an asset can be created and be instantly useable in the game; the asset might need to be converted to a specific file format or compiled into the code. The game is not instantly playable with the new updates and assets; the engineers have to compile the code and build a new executable first. Key things to consider when defining the pipeline are the following:

> **What tools and software are needed?**   Software tools are needed to convert the file formats, and source control software must be used to check assets in and out of the build. Decisions must also be made on which compilers and coding languages are used.

Can the pipeline support two-way functionality? The pipeline should support functionality for assets to be converted for game use and the ability to convert game assets back into their original source assets. This allows asset changes to be made more readily.

What is the critical path? Are there any bottlenecks? Make sure that no one person has a disproportional amount of work in the pipeline and becomes a bottleneck for getting assets converted. Also, limit the number of steps in the pipeline; assets should be viewable and playable in a build as quickly as possible.

When does the system need to be fully functioning? In order to create a playable build of the game with the correct assets, the pipeline must be functioning. Partial functionality is useable for a few months, as long it is does not prevent people from creating assets and seeing them in the game.

How are assets managed and tracked in the system? Decide which source control software to use, so that people can check out assets before working on them. Everything should be kept under version control to prevent multiple versions of a file from causing confusion in the pipeline.

Which areas of the system can be automated? Automate as much of the pipeline as possible in order to reduce time and human error.

After these questions are answered, the leads can determine what pipeline will best work for the game. *The Game Asset Pipeline* by Ben Carter is an excellent resource for more details about setting up a production pipeline. For example, the production pipeline for *Justice Unit* requires the artists to create their character models in Autodesk® 3ds Max®, convert them to a proprietary file format, and check them into the build. The build is set up so the artist can copy over the model to a build of the game on his personal development kit and instantly see how it looks in the game. However, in order for the character model to be fully viewable in an official build, the engineers must create a new build and publish it to the team.

INTERVIEW

Carey Chico, Art Director, Pandemic Studios

One of the necessities of game development is a solid tools strategy. You must have a core group of engineers who are dedicated to tools programming on your team. They can enhance the proprietary tools that are part of your pipeline by upgrading features, fixing bugs, and adding new features based on the game development needs.

→

This is important because a lot of what we battle during game development is tools not working or being too slow. Because efficient game production depends on creating assets quickly, the developers are constantly thinking of ways to use tools to speed up the asset production pipeline—especially if the same type of asset is being created over and over. The longer it takes an artist to get an asset from source art to an asset that can be seen in game, the less they want to deal with the process, and the lower the quality.

The art director and technical director can work together to create an efficient production pipeline for the art assets. There are several things to consider when defining how the pipeline should work. For one thing, make sure that the pipeline is not bottlenecked by a single component in the process. For example, if the process is heavily dependent on Autodesk 3ds Max, the pipeline is frontloaded for art, and everyone will have to go through an artist to see something working in the game. All pertinent people on the team must be able to access, manipulate, modify, and change the content in the game simultaneously or equally. This spreads development risk and provides multiple pipelines to complete the job.

Make sure that the number of steps in the pipeline are as few and bug-free as possible. Don't have nontechnical artists doing lots of technical things in the pipeline in order to get their assets working in the game. The artists are likely to make mistakes and will need to go back and re-do the assets. This slows them down. The pipeline should be focused on speeding up the development environment.

Make sure that the data going through the pipeline is manageable in a fast and efficient way. If the pipeline begins with a nodule of data that has information added to it as it progresses in the pipeline, figure out how mistakes can be corrected along the way, instead of having to start the process from scratch. It also helps to limit the tools used in the pipeline. For instance, don't mix Autodesk 3ds Max and Maya®, pick one. Additionally, keep the number of data conversions to a minimum.

Another key thing is a two-way pipeline. Anyone should be able to easily convert from one set of data to another. For example, if an artist needs to create a cinematic of two people walking around in a scene, he exports all the necessary art assets into AfterEffects, creates the scene, and then re-exports this back into the game.

Finally, automate communication of when steps are completed in the pipeline. It might seem very simple to remember to tell the person waiting on your data that you are finished with it and they can start working on it. However, communication will break down because people are not effective at maintaining it. People get busy and completely forget that someone else is waiting to be told the asset is ready for them. Therefore, the more ways this communication can be automated, the more efficient the pipeline is. If an artist checks something into SourceSafe, an email can automatically be sent to the appropriate person that states what was completed.

DOCUMENTATION

As pre-production comes to a close, documentation must be completed for all major elements of the game. This includes art, design, and technical documentation. If the documentation is not clearly written or doesn't provide the desired information to the target audience, people might not read it. If this happens on your project, it is your responsibility as the producer to work with the documentation writers to create something that is useful for the team. If the team is not reading the documents because of some other reason—they don't have time, or they think they already understand how a feature works—you need to set aside a time for everyone to meet and read through the documentation together.

Each development team will have a different format for design, art, and technical documentation. The key is to have a format that is easy to read and provides clear information about how the game works. There are several books on game design that discuss how to format design documents in detail. These same lessons can be carried over to art and technical documents. *Game Design Workshop: Designing, Prototyping, and Playtesting Games* by Tracy Fullerton, Chris Swain, and Steve Hoffman is a good resource to consult about writing effective documentation.

Consider having different document formats for different audiences. The documentation needed by the development team must include all the details of each gameplay feature. The idea is that any member of the development team can consult the documentation for clear directions on how a feature is supposed to work in the game. The design documentation is the definitive resource for any game design questions, so if a feature design changes, update the documentation to reflect this. Documentation for studio management should focus on the overall gameplay mechanics, key features, and how these all fit together to provide the overall gameplay experience to the player.

Even if the feature has a working prototype, some type of documentation is needed as a written record of how the feature works. For one thing, not everyone will have access to the prototype or be able to get it working correctly, and if there is documentation, they can read through it to understand how the feature works. Additionally, the QA department usually uses design documentation when writing the test plan. For example, if an artist creates a working prototype of the game's shell and does not document the functionality, it will be difficult for QA to write an accurate test plan to check that all the buttons, boxes, and screens are working correctly in the game. You cannot expect QA to load up the UI prototype on a computer and then play through the game and compare the actual game UI screens with the screens in the prototype. This creates a lot of additional work for them, work that they don't really have time for; they might miss a large chunk of functionality if they forget to click on a button.

Design

The design documentation details how all the features will function in the game including the following:

- UI
- Multiplayer
- Character backgrounds and dialogue
- Scoring
- Mission designs
- Control scheme
- Player actions
- Storyline
- AI
- Weapons, special objects, power-ups
- Voice recognition

The documents need to provide enough detail that an engineer, artist, QA tester, or another designer can read them and understand how to implement the feature as designed. After the feature is implemented according to the specs in the documentation, it can be play tested and adjusted as necessary. The documentation must be updated with any changes, as it is the central written resource for the game design.

It is useful to create a comprehensive list of all the documentation and prototypes that must be generated for the game. This list can be used as the basis for the design tasks for the production schedule. Please refer to Chapter 15, "Game Plan," for more information on creating a schedule.

INTERVIEW

Clint Hocking, Creative Director, Ubisoft

The best practice for writing useful design documents is to keep them short, precise, and technical, like this sentence. Additionally, all design documentation should follow the exact same standards and formats. This should be rigidly enforced. There is a time and place for your artists and designers to be creative—within documentation is *not* one of those places. You have a cover page, a table of contents, and three double-spaced pages . . . every page beyond that halves the number of people who will read the document. If people are not reading documentation, a producer or associate should first enforce document formatting to make sure that the documents are short,

→

precise, and technical. If they are, and documents are still not being read, they should gather people together into meeting rooms and read the documents out loud to them. They will learn to read them on their own very quickly. Finally, as far as getting people to understand what's in a document . . . if it is short, precise, and technical, and it has been read, then the designer and the implementer need to communicate. Simple as that.

Art

Art documentation is also necessary during pre-production. The types of art documentation created by the lead artist and/or art director are as follows:

- Style guide
- Asset list
- Tool instructions

The style guide details the look and feel of the universe, the objects, and characters that are portrayed in the game. It includes concept art, color palettes, and other visual examples of what the finished game will look like.

The asset list is a comprehensive list of every art asset that must be created for the game. This includes character models, levels, cinematics, textures, and any other visual elements in the game. As with features, prioritizing the art assets into three tiers ensures that the most critical art assets are completed first, and then additional assets are added as time allows. The art asset list can also be used as the basis for the art production schedule.

Tool instructions are technical documents that provide information on how to use the art tools in the production pipeline, such as the lighting tool, the level-building tool, or cinematics conversion tool. This documentation should be written in conjunction with the engineers who are programming the tools.

INTERVIEW

Carey Chico, Art Director, Pandemic Studios

The pre-production is a time when *everyone* can discuss the game design and artistic vision and make compromises—many ideas can be explored and considered for concept art and prototyping. There are also several art tasks that must be completed

→

before full asset production can begin. The core art team should be comprised of an art director, concept artist, and asset artist. The goal is for the art director to envision what the game will look like and then have the concept and asset artists create different sets of assets to support the vision. From these assets, the final look and feel can be determined, and work can begin on the art bible.

The *art bible* details concept art and other references for the art assets in the game. It demonstrates to the team and the publisher what the game is going to look like. While the art bible is being created, art assets can be prototyped, added to the engine, and viewed in the game. This process allows the art director to get a clear idea of what works and what doesn't work in the game. A large part of creating this bible is research; if the game is set in World War II, the art team will want to research locations, weapons, uniforms, and anything else that will evoke that time period.

The art director works closely with the lead designer to determine how to develop the art direction around the story content. The story content will have a direct effect on what the art director's final artistic vision of the game will be.

Also during pre-production, the art director works with the lead engineer on what features are needed for the art asset production pipeline. This includes making decisions on what shaders will be used, what the polygon limits are, what type of environments the engine will support, and so on.

Technical

Technical documentation is written by the lead engineer and discusses things such as the following:

- Coding standards
- Technical design
- Tools instructions

Documentation on the coding standards includes specifics on coding conventions, hardware and software specifications, naming conventions, technologies used (includes middleware), file types, data layout, and any other technical information that is necessary for developing the game. The documentation should also provide an overview of what all the functions and data do and how they interact with each other.

Technical design documentation is the counterpart to design documentation. The engineers will read through the design documents and provide technical information on how the features will be coded for the game. This documentation is disseminated to the appropriate engineers on the team for implementation.

Tools instructions provide information on how to use the tools. For example, an engineer and designer will work together to document how the scripting tools work. These tools instructions must be updated when any changes are made to the tool functionality; otherwise, the documentation will quickly become unhelpful and even obsolete.

INTERVIEW

Tobi Saulnier, President, 1st Playable

Part of the lead engineer's responsibility on a project is to put together a technical design document (TDD) that describes the software systems that are needed to produce the game, both existing systems and systems that need to be developed. They are usually working on this document in parallel with the game design documents (GDD) being written by designers.

A detailed GDD is extremely useful for the engineers when they start working on the TDD, as it assists them in identifying the list of in-game features and the needs of the art and design pipelines required to develop those assets and integrate into the game. If some areas are missing from the GDD, this can cause problems for engineering, either resulting in an important feature not being included in the upfront software planning or the engineers not fully understanding how a feature is expected to work. For example, if one of the bosses (the enemy at the end of a level or mission) does not have a detailed description of his expected behavior, the engineers will not know how much time to plan for implementing his AI, or the boss once implemented will not behave as the designer envisioned.

Detailed examples and mock-ups should be included in all documentation, as words alone often can't fully define what the desired functionality is. Use of references from other games is extremely helpful, especially for complex concepts like camera behavior and art style. For example, if you are describing how the camera will move in the game, include reference examples of the desired and undesired camera movements. It is also useful to mock-up a reference movie of how the character will move through the game world.

A final note is that the TDD should be user-friendly, which in this case means easily reviewed by art and design, not just other software engineers. Writing the GDD and TDD is usually an iterative process, which means the information from each affects the other. For instance, the memory planning in the TDD will impact things like the number of levels or the number of unique AI. Having all disciplines involved in reviewing each document will help catch anything that is forgotten and more quickly synch up the game design with the technical restrictions.

RISK ANALYSIS

After you have defined the project requirements, conduct another in-depth risk analysis with the team. You will find new risks to be aware of as production starts, and other risks identified earlier can be neutralized or removed. Please refer to Chapter 13, "Concept," for detailed information on how to conduct a risk analysis.

INTERVIEW

Stuart Roch, Executive Producer, Treyarch

If I can get onto a project early enough I'm a big fan of proactively identifying any game features or new technology that pose a scheduling risk. Once I've identified these particular risks I set lifeboat milestones to launch if things start running behind schedule. The idea is to have your plan A and plan B worked out ahead of time so you don't have to scramble and make reactive decisions if things go wrong. After you identify your at-risk features and set your plan B milestones, it's important to follow up regularly to help the at-risk features along and identify the warning signs if things aren't going as planned. If handled correctly, this method will help keep the risky features on everyone's radar, thus maximizing their chances of success and in a worst-case scenario, reducing the impact of the feature cuts if the original goals aren't met.

APPROVAL

After the game requirements are defined, present them to the stakeholders for approval. As with the concept phase, the stakeholders might have feedback they want implemented before they sign off on the requirements.

You don't need to wait for all the requirements to be defined before seeking approval. Instead, schedule regular meetings to present completed required deliverables for approval. This allows you to stagger out the deliverables. If there is feedback to include, you can take a few days to implement it and then re-submit it for approval. This keeps the process going during pre-production, and bottlenecks are not created in the process while waiting for management approval. Refer to Chapter 17, "Production Techniques," for information on how to set up an efficient approval process.

GAME REQUIREMENTS OUTLINE

Figure 14.5 is a summary of each step that must be completed in the game requirements phase. This is based on a two-year development cycle.

Step	Resources	General Timeline	Tasks
Brainstorming	Producer runs sessions, team participates.	1 week	Brainstorm initial concepts for game, including genre and platform
Define game features	Lead Designer	1–1.5 weeks	Core features are defined. Secondary and tertiary features also defined.
Define milestone deliverables	Producer		Define the main project milestones and what the deliverables are for each milestone.
Evaluate technology	Lead Engineer	4–6 weeks	Evaulate the technology needs for the game and make a recomendation.
Define tools and pipeline	Lead Engineer works with other leads.	2–3 weeks	Define the production pipeline that will produce a playable build with updated assets.
Design documentation	Lead Designer	6–8 weeks	Document the key features in the game, include prototypes where possible.
Art documentation	Lead Artist	6–8 weeks	Document the artistic look and feel of the game, generate asset lists, and write up instructions on how to use the art tools.
Technical documentation	Lead Engineer	6–8 weeks	Document the coding standards, technical design, and tools instructions for the game.
Risk Analysis	Producer	Ongoing during requirements phase	Assess risks on project, determine resolution strategy, publish to the team.
Approval	Studio management, publisher	2–3 months after requirements phase begins.	Present all major game play elements to management for approval, incorporate their feedback.

FIGURE 14.5 Outline of game requirements phase.

SUMMARY

On a two-year development cycle, the game requirements phase will take about two–three months to complete. However, this phase will not have a hard start and end date; you might need to design an additional feature during production, revamp the pipeline, or start production on some aspects of the game while completing pre-production on other aspects.

The goal of the game requirements phase is to more fully flesh out the design, art, and technical needs of the game. This includes writing the documentation; making decisions about the tools, pipeline, and milestone deliverables; and conducting a risk analysis. All of this information will be used to create the game plan in which all of these tasks are scheduled and a budget is created. The next chapter presents details on what tasks to complete during the game plan phase.

15 ■ Game Plan

INTRODUCTION

After the game requirements are determined, the game plan is created. The game plan defines the following:

■ What work must be done
■ What order the work is done
■ Who will do the work
■ When the work must be completed

All the information generated during the requirements phase is needed in order to make an accurate game plan. There are many useful project management books that provide detailed information on creating project plans. Most of these techniques are applicable to game development, although some modifications might be necessary. *Project Planning Scheduling and Control, Third Edition* by Jim Lewis is recommended reading, as it provides practical and easy-to-understand information about creating project plans and managing projects.

Keep in mind that the game requirements might change after the initial game plan is completed. For example, the plan might show that the game will be too expensive to make, and some of the requirements will need to be adjusted to lower the cost. After the initial game plan is completed, expect to make changes to it during production. In order to create a solid game plan, it is important to understand the dependencies of the schedule, budget, and staffing plan.

DEPENDENCIES

If the budget, schedule, and staffing needs are not planned during pre-production, you cannot manage these elements efficiently during the development process. In some cases, the feature set of the game might need to change in order to accommodate a change in schedule, such as a request by the publisher to accelerate the release date. Therefore, factoring in the allotted time (schedule), available staff and budget (resources), the feature set of the game (features), and what quality is expected, such as next-generation graphics (quality), is extremely important when putting together your game plan.

Figure 15.1 illustrates this dependency between the schedule, resources, features, and quality. If one of these factors changes, it will affect the other three factors. If all of these factors are constantly changing during the development cycle, the project is never stable and is always at risk. One of the producer's biggest challenges while managing the game development process is striking a balance between the schedule, resources, features, and quality. As stated throughout this book, all development teams are different and never have the exact same processes in place or risks to mitigate, but the producer's ultimate goal is still releasing a quality game on time and on (or under) budget. If the producer carefully controls the balance among the schedule, budget, and staffing, there is a much higher chance this goal can be achieved.

When working on schedules, budgets, and staffing plans, you must keep these dependencies in mind at all times so your game plan is accurate. The schedule is a good starting point, because a lot of information is generated during pre-production that can easily translate into a robust schedule.

FIGURE 15.1 Dependencies among budget, schedule, features, and quality.

SCHEDULES

A schedule lists each task to be completed, estimates of the task duration, who is doing the task, and what tasks are dependent on the given tasks. Consider using some type of scheduling software as this makes tracking the tasks easier. Scheduling software enables the user to plug in new tasks and dates to see how changes affect the overall schedule. Microsoft Project is a popular scheduling software that is useful in creating detailed schedules. Even if dates and deliverables are shifting, the schedule's basic task list will essentially stay the same unless the feature is cut from the game. For example, the level-building section of the schedule outlines each task needed to build a level. It might include creating a concept, prototyping, building basic geometry, creating textures, polishing the assets, and bug-fixing. The important thing to note is that even though dates may change, the same tasks need to be completed.

Game development schedules can be extremely frustrating to create and track. For one thing, feature creep runs rampant in game development, which makes it difficult to create an initial schedule and use it throughout the game development process. On a two-year development cycle, feature creep has a huge impact; people will see a feature functioning in the game and figure there is plenty of time to change or add functionality to make it better. This is why it is helpful to schedule small milestones along the way, so you can keep better control of the features being implemented and additional feature requests.

When creating the game development schedule, there might be a tendency to be overwhelmed by the thought of scheduling six months to two years worth of work at the beginning of the project. How can anyone know all of the tasks that need to be done? However, don't let this prevent you from creating a useful schedule as early in the development process as possible. Even if the schedule changes, which it will, it is much better to have an initial baseline schedule of the estimated work, than to have nothing to compare against the actual schedule changes. For example, if there is no schedule and the publisher tells you the game has to ship three months earlier, how will you know which tasks need to be cut from the schedule or how many people need to be added to the team to accomplish this goal?

Involve the entire team in creating the schedule. Generally, if people are just told to complete all their work by a specific deadline, with no explanation on how this date was determined or why this date is important to the project, they are less likely to take the date seriously. Because they don't have full knowledge of what the impact is when they miss their deadlines, they might treat the due date as more of a guideline than a deadline. When this happens, the schedule can quickly get out of control.

If the team is involved in creating the schedule, they have more ownership over their tasks and treat the deadlines more seriously. Also, each person best understands how much work he can accomplish in a day and can better inform you how long it will take them to complete each of their assigned tasks. They are also able to point out areas where critical tasks are missing and identify high, medium, and low risk areas on the schedule.

Creating a Schedule

Creating a schedule will take some time, especially during pre-production when many game elements are not final. The producer can expect to spend several days or even weeks putting together a complete schedule and will continue to update it throughout production. Although time-consuming, a schedule is not too difficult to put together as long as you stay focused on the actual tasks to be completed. Avoid creating a schedule based on what you *think* needs to be done, instead of what *actually* needs to be done.

One way to properly determine which tasks to complete is to determine exit criteria. Exit criteria are a pre-defined set of conditions that must be fulfilled before a task is deemed completed. Exit criteria mainly consist of tangible assets that are easily defined. For example, the exit criteria for the concept phase include the following:

- Initial concept
- Competitive analysis
- Pitch presentation
- Risk analysis
- Concept approval
- Project kick-off

When all of these deliverables are completed, the concept phase is fully complete. Involve the team in determining exit criteria for each phase of production, with the final exit criteria being an approved gold master that can be manufactured and shipped to stores.

INTERVIEW

Carey Chico, Art Director, Pandemic Studios

The art director and lead artist will be able to provide estimates for each art task and define what the final deliverables will be for each task. As you create the art schedule, break down the tasks into smaller tasks that can be assigned to individual artists. In addition, it is helpful if you schedule groups of artists to work on similar assets and appoint someone as the point of contact for this group. For example, you could have one group working on all the character and vehicle models on the game and another group working on all the Havok destructible objects in the game.

Initial Schedule

An initial schedule is created in pre-production and communicated to the development team in order to plan for key dates. Start the scheduling process by listing all the major exit criteria for each area of the game: production, approvals, art, engineering, design, audio, localization, QA, external vendors, and marketing. More exit criteria can be added as development progresses.

After these criteria are determined, fill in estimated dates. Figure 15.2 is an example of an initial production schedule. Major exit criteria are listed for each phase of the game, and eventually deadlines are assigned to each one. Currently, only the console manufacturer submission date is estimated, as this title must ship at Christmas. So the overall goal of the game plan is to adjust the other project factors (resources, features, and quality) in order to hit the ship date. From this submission date, you can determine a general timeframe for the first playable, alpha, code freeze, beta, and code release candidate dates, which can help you better gauge the work to be completed for each milestone.

Justice Unit	Estimated Date	Notes
Languages: English, German, French, Italian, Spanish		
Production		
Concept Phase Completed		
Requirements Phase Completed		
Initial Game Plan Completed		
First Playable		
Alpha		
Code Freeze		
Beta		
Pre-Cert Submission to Microsoft		
Code Release Candidate		
Certification Submission to Microsoft		10/15/07
Approvals		
Concept Approval		
Requirements Approval		
Game Plan Approval		
License Approval		
Console Manufacturer Approval		
Design		
Deliverables Completed for Concept Phase		
Deliverables Completed for Requirements Phase		
Detailed Documentation Completed for Game Features		
Character and Story Documents Completed		
Voiceover Scripts Completed		
Mission and Scenarios Designed		
Mission Prototypes Scripted		
Playtesting		
Final Missions Scripted		
Art		
Deliverables Completed for Concept Phase		
Deliverables Completed for Requirements Phase		
Prototypes Completed		
First Playable Level Completed		
Special Effects Completed		
UI Completed		
Cinematics Completed		
Engineering		
Deliverables Completed for Concept Phase		
Deliverables Completed for Requirements Phase		
Art and Design Tools Completed		
Production Pipeline Completed		
Engineering Prototypes Completed		

(continued)

Justice Unit	Estimated Date	Notes
All Major Game Play Features Implemented		
Code Freeze		
Audio		
Sound Designs Completed		
Sound Prototypes Completed		
Placeholder VO Recorded		
Final VO Recorded		
Final Music Implemented in Game		
Localization		
Determine Localization Needs		
Organize Assets for Translation		
Integrate Assets		
Functionality Testing		
Linguistic Testing		
QA		
Test Plan Completed		
First Playable Testing Completed		
Alpha Testing Completed		
Playtesting Completed		
1st Code Release Candidate to QA		
Code Release		
Cinematics (External Vendor)		
Deliver Initial Specs to Vendor		
Storyboard from Vendor		
Animatic from Vendor		
Rough Cut from Vendor		
Final Movie from Vendor (no sound)		
Movie to Sound Designer		
Final Movie Ready for Game		
Marketing		
Demo Build		
E3 Build		
Preview Code for Journalists		
Review Code for Journalists		

FIGURE 15.2   Sample of initial production schedule.

Although the initial production schedules provide a good guideline for the overall development process, a more detailed schedule must be created as information is confirmed. This detailed schedule contains subtasks for all the main tasks listed in the initial schedule. The exit criteria for detailed tasks is based on deliverables from the concept and requirements phases:

- Tiered master feature list
- Milestone deliverable lists
- Art documentation
- Design documentation
- Technical documentation

These deliverables include detailed information on how many levels, characters, and objects must be created, what engineering features will be coded, how much voiceover needs to be recorded, and everything else about the project. In order to best determine all the little things to do, it is helpful to break down these large deliverables and tasks into smaller ones.

Work Breakdown Structure

Work Breakdown Structures (WBS) are useful for breaking down large tasks into smaller ones. By breaking down a large task into specific, incremental tasks, a master task list is created. The WBS process initially involves the producers and leads, with input from the team as needed. Here is a sample WBS process for determining what tasks are necessary to create a shippable level:

1. The producer and leads meet and define the specific tangible steps that are needed to create a level and mission from start to finish. All departments are involved—production, art, design, engineering, and QA.
2. During the meeting, the group brainstorms about every possible task to be completed for a level. Describe tasks in the present tense, with an active verb. For example, "design initial level layout." This helps the group determine the tangible tasks to be done.
3. The tasks are grouped together by department and then placed in rough chronological order.
4. Durations are set for each task by the appropriate lead. (Art lead provides art estimates, and so on.)

Figure 15.3 is an example of a WBS to create one shippable level for *Justice Unit.*

Detailed Schedule

When the WBS is completed, have the team double-check it to ensure that no tasks were forgotten. This task list is then added to the project schedule; dependencies are added; and the actual team members are assigned their tasks. They must assess the original duration estimated by the lead. Each task should be no more than three–five days in duration. Ideally, each task takes one–two days. If the task owner agrees with this estimate, the number stays as is. If the task owner disagrees with the estimate, he

Art Tasks (Villain's Lair)	Duration
Create prototype	5 days
Implement prototype feedback	1 day
Create level geometry	20 days
Add placeholder textures	3 days
Fix first round of bugs	3 days
Create destructible objects	2 days
Add final textures	10 days
Create player reference map	.5 days
Create special effects	2 day
Optimize level for budget constraints	5 days
Polish map	5 days
Fix final round of bugs	3 days
Design Tasks (Villain's Lair)	**Duration**
Design initial level layout	2 days
Design initial mission scripting	2 days
Script prototype	.5 days
Playtest prototype scripting	.5 days
Implement prototype feedback	1 day
Script first pass of mission scripting	5 days
Script first pass of multiplayer scripting	2 days
Review scripting	1 days
Script second pass	5 days
Verify all supporting files are tagged correctly	1 day
Create localization tags for in-game dialog	1 day
Polish scripting	3 days
Fix final round of bugs	2 days
Sound Tasks (Villain's Lair)	**Duration**
Create sound design	3 days
Implement sound design prototype	2 days
Implement prototype feedback	2 days
Complete first pass of sound implementation	3 days
Polish sound	2 days
Fix final round of bugs	1 day
QA Tasks (Villain's Lair)	**Duration**
Playtest prototype	1 day
Test geometry and terrain navigation	7 days
Check textures	2 days
Test initial scripting	1 day
Test second pass scripting	1 day
Final test all level geometry and textures	5 days
Final test for mission scripting	1 day
Approvals (Villain's Lair)	**Duration**
Approve initial layout	1 day
Approve initial art prototype	1 day
Approve initial design prototype	1 day
Approve sound design	1 day
Approve final level, scripting, and sound	1 day

FIGURE 15.3 WBS for completing Villain's Lair level.

provides an updated estimate, which is added to the project schedule. This process gives team members more ownership of their tasks, instead of feeling like they are just assigned an arbitrary deadline that must be achieved no matter what.

If there is some difficulty in determining how long a task will take, the lead should make an educated estimate based on experience. Don't leave the duration for any task blank, as this will not give a true picture of the overall schedule. Accurately estimating tasks is very subjective and improves with experience. It is good to build some extra time in the schedule to accommodate any work that takes longer than originally estimated. Some people like to add this extra time on a per-task basis, although this is not recommended as it does not give an accurate picture of the overall schedule. However, adding some slack at the end of the schedule provides a good padding for accommodating any task overruns.

One technique to use for estimating tasks is called time-boxing. A time-box is a fixed period of time during which someone attempts to complete a well-defined task. The task should have each of its requirements prioritized from highest to lowest, so that the most critical work is completed first. To use this technique, assign start and end dates to a given task, assign someone to work on it, and then measure how much is completed in the allotted time. After the agreed-upon period of time is over and the feature is not fully implemented, assess the work that is completed and determine whether further work should be done, whether the work done already is good enough, or whether the feature should be cut because the effort already put into it indicates the feature will take too long to implement in the given schedule. This method can help you maintain more control over the schedule, instead of just letting a feature continually run over schedule.

For example, if the lead engineer makes an educated estimated of three weeks to implement normal mapping into the graphics pipeline, check with the engineer on a regular basis to check his progress. At the end of three weeks see how much normal mapping functionality is implemented. At this point, the feature might be good enough to ship, or further work might be needed. If you are going to have the engineer invest more time in the feature, determine a new set of feature priorities and define a new time box.

When durations are assigned to the schedule, add in time for sick days, holidays, and vacations. You can't assume that everyone will be in the office every single work day. Also, don't schedule overtime. This is a bad practice and will quickly cause you to have an unhappy and, therefore, unproductive team. Instead, limit the scope of the project so that everything can be completed in a reasonable amount of time. In fact, all the task durations should be based on accomplishing about five–six hours of work during a normal eight-hour work day. The other two–three hours per day account for time people spend checking email, going to meetings, and dealing with general nontask related work.

Keep in mind that task dependencies and assigned resources can dramatically affect a schedule. For example, if it takes several days to get the prototype approved, level production comes to a standstill, valuable time is lost, and a bottleneck is created. Additionally, if someone is overloaded with too many tasks, they cannot keep up the same pace of work as others involved in the level production process and will cause delays. So it is important to make sure that the correct dependencies and resource allocations are included in the schedule. The importance of this is best shown in Figures 15.4, 15.5, 15.6, and 15.7.

	ⓘ	Task Name	Duration	Start	Finish	Predecessors	Resource Names
1		⊟ Villain's Lair Level Production	15 days	Mon 2/19/07	Fri 3/9/07		
2		⊟ Art	15 days	Mon 2/19/07	Fri 3/9/07		
3		Create prototype	5 days	Mon 2/19/07	Fri 2/23/07		
4		Implement prototype feedback	1 day	Mon 2/19/07	Mon 2/19/07		
5		Create level geometry	15 days	Mon 2/19/07	Fri 3/9/07		
6		Add placeholder textures	3 days	Mon 2/19/07	Wed 2/21/07		
7		Fix first round of bugs	3 days	Mon 2/19/07	Wed 2/21/07		
8		Create destructible objects	2 days	Mon 2/19/07	Tue 2/20/07		
9		Add final textures	10 days	Mon 2/19/07	Fri 3/2/07		
10		Create player reference map	1 day	Mon 2/19/07	Mon 2/19/07		
11		Create special effects	3 days	Mon 2/19/07	Wed 2/21/07		
12		Optimize level for budget constraints	10 days	Mon 2/19/07	Fri 3/2/07		
13		Polish map	5 days	Mon 2/19/07	Fri 2/23/07		
14		Fix final round of bugs	5 days	Mon 2/19/07	Fri 2/23/07		
15		⊟ Design	5 days	Mon 2/19/07	Fri 2/23/07		
16		Design initial level layout	2 days	Mon 2/19/07	Tue 2/20/07		
17		Design initial mission scripting	2 days	Mon 2/19/07	Tue 2/20/07		
18		Create initial prototype scripting	2 days	Mon 2/19/07	Tue 2/20/07		
19		Implement prototype feedback	2 days	Mon 2/19/07	Tue 2/20/07		
20		Script first pass of mission scripting	5 days	Mon 2/19/07	Fri 2/23/07		
21		Script first pass of multiplayer scripting	2 days	Mon 2/19/07	Tue 2/20/07		
22		Review scripting	1 day	Mon 2/19/07	Mon 2/19/07		
23		Script second pass	5 days	Mon 2/19/07	Fri 2/23/07		
24		Verify all supporting files are tagged corr	1 day	Mon 2/19/07	Mon 2/19/07		
25		Create localization tags for in-game dialc	1 day	Mon 2/19/07	Mon 2/19/07		
26		Polish scripting	3 days	Mon 2/19/07	Wed 2/21/07		
27		Fix final round of bugs	2 days	Mon 2/19/07	Tue 2/20/07		
28		⊟ Sound	3 days	Mon 2/19/07	Wed 2/21/07		
29		Create sound design	3 days	Mon 2/19/07	Wed 2/21/07		
30		Implement sound design prototype	2 days	Mon 2/19/07	Tue 2/20/07		
31		Implement feedback	2 days	Mon 2/19/07	Tue 2/20/07		
32		Complete first pass of sound implementa	3 days	Mon 2/19/07	Wed 2/21/07		
33		Polish sound	2 days	Mon 2/19/07	Tue 2/20/07		
34		Fix final round of bugs	1 day	Mon 2/19/07	Mon 2/19/07		
35		⊟ QA	7 days	Mon 2/19/07	Tue 2/27/07		
36		Playtest prototype	1 day	Mon 2/19/07	Mon 2/19/07		
37		Test geometry and terrain navigation	7 days	Mon 2/19/07	Tue 2/27/07		
38		Check textures	2 days	Mon 2/19/07	Tue 2/20/07		
39		Test initial scripting	1 day	Mon 2/19/07	Mon 2/19/07		
40		Test second pass scripting	1 day	Mon 2/19/07	Mon 2/19/07		
41		Final test all level geometry and textures	5 days	Mon 2/19/07	Fri 2/23/07		
42		Final test for mission scripting	1 day	Mon 2/19/07	Mon 2/19/07		
43		⊟ Approvals	2 days	Mon 2/19/07	Tue 2/20/07		
44		Approve initial layout	2 days	Mon 2/19/07	Tue 2/20/07		
45		Approve initial art prototype	2 days	Mon 2/19/07	Tue 2/20/07		
46		Approval initial design prototype	2 days	Mon 2/19/07	Tue 2/20/07		
47		Approve sound design	2 days	Mon 2/19/07	Tue 2/20/07		
48		Approve final level, scripting, and sound	2 days	Mon 2/19/07	Tue 2/20/07		

FIGURE 15.4 Level production schedule with no dependencies or assigned resources.

Figure 15.4 is a detailed level production schedule for the *Villain's Lair*. This does not include any task dependencies or assigned resources. Based on this schedule, all the art, design, sound, QA, and approval tasks will take 15 days to complete.

Figure 15.5 is the same level production schedule with assigned resources. Now that resources are assigned, you can see it takes 63 days to complete the work. This increase happened because there is only one artist, one designer, one sound designer, and one tester available to do all the work, and they can only work on one task at a time. If the tasks were assigned to multiple artists and designers, the time could be reduced.

	❶	Task Name	Duration	Start	Finish	Predecessors	Resource Names
1		⊟ **Villain's Lair Level Production**	**63 days**	**Mon 2/19/07**	**Wed 5/16/07**		
2		⊟ **Art**	**63 days**	**Mon 2/19/07**	**Wed 5/16/07**		
3		Create prototype	5 days	Mon 4/9/07	Fri 4/13/07		Artist 1
4		Implement prototype feedback	1 day	Tue 5/15/07	Tue 5/15/07		Artist 1
5		Create level geometry	15 days	Mon 2/19/07	Fri 3/9/07		Artist 1
6		Add placeholder textures	3 days	Mon 4/30/07	Wed 5/2/07		Artist 1
7		Fix first round of bugs	3 days	Thu 5/3/07	Mon 5/7/07		Artist 1
8		Create destructible objects	2 days	Fri 5/11/07	Mon 5/14/07		Artist 1
9		Add final textures	10 days	Mon 3/12/07	Fri 3/23/07		Artist 1
10		Create player reference map	1 day	Wed 5/16/07	Wed 5/16/07		Artist 1
11		Create special effects	3 days	Tue 5/8/07	Thu 5/10/07		Artist 1
12		Optimize level for budget constraints	10 days	Mon 3/26/07	Fri 4/6/07		Artist 1
13		Polish map	5 days	Mon 4/16/07	Fri 4/20/07		Artist 1
14		Fix final round of bugs	5 days	Mon 4/23/07	Fri 4/27/07		Artist 1
15		⊟ **Design**	**28 days**	**Mon 2/19/07**	**Wed 3/28/07**		
16		Design initial level layout	2 days	Thu 3/8/07	Fri 3/9/07		Designer 1
17		Design initial mission scripting	2 days	Mon 3/12/07	Tue 3/13/07		Designer 1
18		Create initial prototype scripting	2 days	Wed 3/14/07	Thu 3/15/07		Designer 1
19		Implement prototype feedback	2 days	Fri 3/16/07	Mon 3/19/07		Designer 1
20		Script first pass of mission scripting	5 days	Mon 2/19/07	Fri 2/23/07		Designer 1
21		Script first pass of multiplayer scripting	2 days	Tue 3/20/07	Wed 3/21/07		Designer 1
22		Review scripting	1 day	Mon 3/26/07	Mon 3/26/07		Designer 1
23		Script second pass	5 days	Mon 2/26/07	Fri 3/2/07		Designer 1
24		Verify all supporting files are tagged corr	1 day	Tue 3/27/07	Tue 3/27/07		Designer 1
25		Create localization tags for in-game dialc	1 day	Wed 3/28/07	Wed 3/28/07		Designer 1
26		Polish scripting	3 days	Mon 3/5/07	Wed 3/7/07		Designer 1
27		Fix final round of bugs	2 days	Thu 3/22/07	Fri 3/23/07		Designer 1
28		⊟ **Sound**	**13 days**	**Mon 2/19/07**	**Wed 3/7/07**		
29		Create sound design	3 days	Mon 2/19/07	Wed 2/21/07		Sound Designer 1
30		Implement sound design prototype	2 days	Tue 2/27/07	Wed 2/28/07		Sound Designer 1
31		Implement feedback	2 days	Thu 3/1/07	Fri 3/2/07		Sound Designer 1
32		Complete first pass of sound implementa	3 days	Thu 2/22/07	Mon 2/26/07		Sound Designer 1
33		Polish sound	2 days	Mon 3/5/07	Tue 3/6/07		Sound Designer 1
34		Fix final round of bugs	1 day	Wed 3/7/07	Wed 3/7/07		Sound Designer 1
35		⊟ **QA**	**18 days**	**Mon 2/19/07**	**Wed 3/14/07**		
36		Playtest prototype	1 day	Fri 3/9/07	Fri 3/9/07		Tester 1
37		Test geometry and terrain navigation	7 days	Mon 2/19/07	Tue 2/27/07		Tester 1
38		Check textures	2 days	Wed 3/7/07	Thu 3/8/07		Tester 1
39		Test initial scripting	1 day	Mon 3/12/07	Mon 3/12/07		Tester 1
40		Test second pass scripting	1 day	Tue 3/13/07	Tue 3/13/07		Tester 1
41		Final test all level geometry and textures	5 days	Wed 2/28/07	Tue 3/6/07		Tester 1
42		Final test for mission scripting	1 day	Wed 3/14/07	Wed 3/14/07		Tester 1
43		⊟ **Approvals**	**10 days**	**Mon 2/19/07**	**Fri 3/2/07**		
44		Approve initial layout	2 days	Mon 2/19/07	Tue 2/20/07		Management
45		Approve initial art prototype	2 days	Wed 2/21/07	Thu 2/22/07		Management
46		Approval initial design prototype	2 days	Fri 2/23/07	Mon 2/26/07		Management
47		Approve sound design	2 days	Tue 2/27/07	Wed 2/28/07		Management
48		Approve final level, scripting, and sound	2 days	Thu 3/1/07	Fri 3/2/07		Management

FIGURE 15.5 Level production schedule with assigned resources.

Figure 15.6 is the same level production schedule with just the task dependencies added. Now the scheduled time has increased to 77 days. This is because there are several tasks that are on hold until another task is completed. For example under the QA section, you can see that QA has more than three weeks of nonproductive time between tasks 36 and 37. In an actual game development environment, several levels would be in production at once, so it is likely that QA would be testing another level during these three weeks.

	ⓘ	Task Name	Duration	Start	Finish	Predecessors	Resource Names
1		⊟ Villain's Lair Level Production	77 days	Mon 2/19/07	Tue 6/5/07		
2		⊟ Art	73 days	Fri 2/23/07	Tue 6/5/07		
3		Create prototype	5 days	Fri 2/23/07	Thu 3/1/07	44	
4		Implement prototype feedback	1 day	Tue 3/6/07	Tue 3/6/07	45	
5		Create level geometry	15 days	Wed 3/7/07	Tue 3/27/07	4	
6		Add placeholder textures	3 days	Wed 3/28/07	Fri 3/30/07	5	
7		Fix first round of bugs	3 days	Wed 4/11/07	Fri 4/13/07	37	
8		Create destructible objects	2 days	Mon 4/16/07	Tue 4/17/07	7	
9		Add final textures	10 days	Wed 4/18/07	Tue 5/1/07	8	
10		Create player reference map	1 day	Wed 4/18/07	Wed 4/18/07	8	
11		Create special effects	3 days	Wed 4/18/07	Fri 4/20/07	8	
12		Optimize level for budget constraints	10 days	Wed 5/2/07	Tue 5/15/07	9,10,11	
13		Polish map	5 days	Wed 5/16/07	Tue 5/22/07	12	
14		Fix final round of bugs	5 days	Wed 5/30/07	Tue 6/5/07	41	
15		⊟ Design	69 days	Mon 2/19/07	Thu 5/24/07		
16		Design initial level layout	2 days	Mon 2/19/07	Tue 2/20/07		
17		Design initial mission scripting	2 days	Mon 2/19/07	Tue 2/20/07		
18		Create initial prototype scripting	2 days	Wed 3/7/07	Thu 3/8/07	17,4	
19		Implement prototype feedback	2 days	Tue 3/13/07	Wed 3/14/07	46,36	
20		Script first pass of mission scripting	5 days	Wed 3/28/07	Tue 4/3/07	5	
21		Script first pass of multiplayer scripting	2 days	Wed 3/28/07	Thu 3/29/07	5	
22		Review scripting	1 day	Wed 4/4/07	Wed 4/4/07	20,21	
23		Script second pass	5 days	Thu 4/5/07	Wed 4/11/07	22,39	
24		Verify all supporting files are tagged corr	1 day	Wed 5/16/07	Wed 5/16/07	12	
25		Create localization tags for in-game dialc	1 day	Wed 5/16/07	Wed 5/16/07	12	
26		Polish scripting	3 days	Thu 5/17/07	Mon 5/21/07	23,24,25	
27		Fix final round of bugs	2 days	Wed 5/23/07	Thu 5/24/07	42	
28		⊟ Sound	29 days	Tue 3/6/07	Fri 4/13/07		
29		Create sound design	3 days	Tue 3/6/07	Thu 3/8/07	45	
30		Implement sound design prototype	2 days	Wed 3/7/07	Thu 3/8/07	4	
31		Implement feedback	2 days	Tue 3/13/07	Wed 3/14/07	47	
32		Complete first pass of sound implementa	3 days	Thu 4/5/07	Mon 4/9/07	22	
33		Polish sound	2 days	Thu 4/12/07	Fri 4/13/07	23	
34		Fix final round of bugs	1 day	Fri 4/13/07	Fri 4/13/07	40	
35		⊟ QA	58 days	Fri 3/9/07	Tue 5/29/07		
36		Playtest prototype	1 day	Fri 3/9/07	Fri 3/9/07	18	
37		Test geometry and terrain navigation	7 days	Mon 4/2/07	Tue 4/10/07	6	
38		Check textures	2 days	Wed 5/2/07	Thu 5/3/07	9	
39		Test initial scripting	1 day	Wed 4/4/07	Wed 4/4/07	20,21	
40		Test second pass scripting	1 day	Thu 4/12/07	Thu 4/12/07	23	
41		Final test all level geometry and textures	5 days	Wed 5/23/07	Tue 5/29/07	13	
42		Final test for mission scripting	1 day	Tue 5/22/07	Tue 5/22/07	26	
43		⊟ Approvals	66 days	Wed 2/21/07	Wed 5/23/07		
44		Approve initial layout	2 days	Wed 2/21/07	Thu 2/22/07	16	
45		Approve initial art prototype	2 days	Fri 3/2/07	Mon 3/5/07	3	
46		Approval initial design prototype	2 days	Fri 3/9/07	Mon 3/12/07	18	
47		Approve sound design	2 days	Fri 3/9/07	Mon 3/12/07	30	
48		Approve final level, scripting, and sound	2 days	Tue 5/22/07	Wed 5/23/07	12,26,33	

FIGURE 15.6 Level production schedule with dependencies.

Figure 15.7 is the same level production schedule with both the assigned resources and task dependencies added. Now the work requires 81 days to complete. This time could be brought in a few days by assigning another artist and designer on the project for a few days.

Work breakdown structures and detailed schedules must be created for every aspect of the project. If the producer and leads commit to making this happen, the schedules can be very useful to everyone on the team. Also, after spending all this time creating the schedule, put an equal amount of effort into tracking and updating it.

	0	Task Name	Duration	Start	Finish	Predecessors	Resource Names
1		⊟ Villain's Lair Level Production	81 days	Mon 2/19/07	Mon 6/11/07		
2		⊟ Art	77 days	Fri 2/23/07	Mon 6/11/07		
3		Create prototype	5 days	Fri 2/23/07	Thu 3/1/07	44	Artist 1
4		Implement prototype feedback	1 day	Tue 3/6/07	Tue 3/6/07	45	Artist 1
5		Create level geometry	15 days	Wed 3/7/07	Tue 3/27/07	4	Artist 1
6		Add placeholder textures	3 days	Wed 3/28/07	Fri 3/30/07	5	Artist 1
7		Fix first round of bugs	3 days	Wed 4/11/07	Fri 4/13/07	37	Artist 1
8		Create destructible objects	2 days	Mon 4/16/07	Tue 4/17/07	7	Artist 1
9		Add final textures	10 days	Wed 4/18/07	Tue 5/1/07	8	Artist 1
10		Create player reference map	1 day	Mon 5/7/07	Mon 5/7/07	8	Artist 1
11		Create special effects	3 days	Wed 5/2/07	Fri 5/4/07	8	Artist 1
12		Optimize level for budget constraints	10 days	Tue 5/8/07	Mon 5/21/07	9,10,11	Artist 1
13		Polish map	5 days	Tue 5/22/07	Mon 5/28/07	12	Artist 1
14		Fix final round of bugs	5 days	Tue 6/5/07	Mon 6/11/07	41	Artist 1
15		⊟ Design	79 days	Mon 2/19/07	Thu 6/7/07		
16		Design initial level layout	2 days	Mon 2/19/07	Tue 2/20/07		Designer 1
17		Design initial mission scripting	2 days	Wed 2/21/07	Thu 2/22/07		Designer 1
18		Create initial prototype scripting	2 days	Wed 3/7/07	Thu 3/8/07	17,4	Designer 1
19		Implement prototype feedback	2 days	Tue 3/13/07	Wed 3/14/07	46,36	Designer 1
20		Script first pass of mission scripting	5 days	Wed 3/28/07	Tue 4/3/07	5	Designer 1
21		Script first pass of multiplayer scripting	2 days	Wed 4/4/07	Thu 4/5/07	5	Designer 1
22		Review scripting	1 day	Fri 4/6/07	Fri 4/6/07	20,21	Designer 1
23		Script second pass	5 days	Thu 4/12/07	Wed 4/18/07	22,39	Designer 1
24		Verify all supporting files are tagged corr	1 day	Tue 5/22/07	Tue 5/22/07	12	Designer 1
25		Create localization tags for in-game dialc	1 day	Wed 5/23/07	Wed 5/23/07	12	Designer 1
26		Polish scripting	3 days	Thu 5/24/07	Mon 5/28/07	23,24,25	Designer 1
27		Fix final round of bugs	2 days	Wed 6/6/07	Thu 6/7/07	42	Designer 1
28		⊟ Sound	35 days	Tue 3/6/07	Mon 4/23/07		
29		Create sound design	3 days	Tue 3/6/07	Mon 3/12/07	45	Sound Designer 1
30		Implement sound design prototype	2 days	Wed 3/7/07	Thu 3/8/07	4	Sound Designer 1
31		Implement feedback	2 days	Thu 3/15/07	Fri 3/16/07	47	Sound Designer 1
32		Complete first pass of sound implementa	3 days	Mon 4/9/07	Wed 4/11/07	22	Sound Designer 1
33		Polish sound	2 days	Thu 4/19/07	Fri 4/20/07	23	Sound Designer 1
34		Fix final round of bugs	1 day	Mon 4/23/07	Mon 4/23/07	40	Sound Designer 1
35		⊟ QA	63 days	Fri 3/9/07	Tue 6/5/07		
36		Playtest prototype	1 day	Fri 3/9/07	Fri 3/9/07	18	Tester 1
37		Test geometry and terrain navigation	7 days	Mon 4/2/07	Tue 4/10/07	6	Tester 1
38		Check textures	2 days	Wed 5/2/07	Thu 5/3/07	9	Tester 1
39		Test initial scripting	1 day	Wed 4/11/07	Wed 4/11/07	20,21	Tester 1
40		Test second pass scripting	1 day	Thu 4/19/07	Thu 4/19/07	23	Tester 1
41		Final test all level geometry and textures	5 days	Tue 5/29/07	Mon 6/4/07	13	Tester 1
42		Final test for mission scripting	1 day	Tue 6/5/07	Tue 6/5/07	26	Tester 1
43		⊟ Approvals	71 days	Wed 2/21/07	Wed 5/30/07		
44		Approve initial layout	2 days	Wed 2/21/07	Thu 2/22/07	16	Management
45		Approve initial art prototype	2 days	Fri 3/2/07	Mon 3/5/07	3	Management
46		Approval initial design prototype	2 days	Fri 3/9/07	Mon 3/12/07	18	Management
47		Approve sound design	2 days	Tue 3/13/07	Wed 3/14/07	30	Management
48		Approve final level, scripting, and sound	2 days	Tue 5/29/07	Wed 5/30/07	12,26,33	Management

FIGURE 15.7 Level production schedule with assigned resources and dependencies.

If you are working on a two-year development cycle, don't try to create a detailed scheduled for the entire two-year process. Instead, concentrate on creating detailed schedules for each project milestone as needed. This gives you more flexibility with the schedule, and adjustments can easily be made when necessary.

INTERVIEW

Clint Hocking, Creative Director, Ubisoft

From a design standpoint, all I can say is that the amount of time you're given for research (if any) is never enough, and the amount of time you're given between the end of any research phase (if you have one) and the beginning of production is too much. I know that the two–three months I spent in research on *Splinter Cell Chaos Theory* was invaluable. I have recently had the opportunity to go back over the documentation and notes that I took during that phase, and I can see very clearly that that is where the game was born. I can also see that we were not quite ready to transition out of that phase and that the things that were still not understood at the end of the research phase would end up adding a lot of risk to the production.

Tracking Tasks

Tracking the schedule is important so that you know whether you are on schedule or in danger of getting off schedule. Keeping the team informed of the schedule progress is also important for the same reasons. If the team is not informed of the schedule progress, it is similar to them working without a schedule at all; they do not know whether things are on track and whether they are hitting the milestone deadlines together as a team.

After the schedule is defined, appoint someone on the team to be the official schedule tracker. There are several ways to track schedules, and each person will have a preferred method for doing this. If you are using Microsoft Project, you can track the actual time against the baseline schedule and make adjustments as needed. If someone delivers an asset earlier or later, Microsoft Project will recalculate the schedule. If you plan to use Microsoft Project to track the schedule, it is worth the investment to train someone to become expert on using this software.

One way to track tasks for simpler or more straightforward schedules is to print the schedule out and post it in the team rooms. As tasks are completed, they are highlighted on the schedule; when the schedule is colored in, the project is completed. This is a strong visual aid to the team of their progress and can be a motivator to get all the tasks colored in a quickly as possible.

Figure 15.8 is an example of a spreadsheet that tracks the progress of the levels produced for the game.

Level Name	Artist	Scripter	Geometry Complete	Art Lockdown	Design Lockdown	Sound Lockdown	QA Status	Notes
Justice Hall	John Doe	Jane Doe	1-Oct	15-Nov	22-Nov	22-Nov	Playtesting completed	
Villain's Lair	Bob Smith	Betty Smith	7-Oct	15-Nov	22-Nov	22-Nov	To be playtested Oct 15	Original geometry complete date Oct 1, pushed to Oct 7 because artist was sick for a few days.
LAST UPDATED: Oct 7, 2007								

FIGURE 15.8 Example of a level production spreadsheet.

This spreadsheet is a distilled version of the information contained in the production schedule. It only presents the key deadlines for completing a map, as opposed to the detail of a typical development schedule, and can be quickly looked at to determine progress. As a milestone is completed, the cell is shaded in. Again, this is a strong visual cue of the progress being made. So even if no one bothers to read the actual dates, they can tell at a glance how much work is completed on each level.

If someone is falling behind on his work for a critical milestone, they need to inform the person tracking the schedule as soon as possible. Most people are aware of when they are behind schedule, but they always think they can catch up to meet a milestone. Although this might be the case in some instances, it is still important to know about any delays ahead of time so contingencies can be prepared. Some delays are critical, meaning the large parts of the development process comes to a standstill. For example, if the scripting tool is not completed by the time the designers need to start scripting the levels, the scripting is on hold until the tool is finished. This puts the design schedule at risk, and it needs to be adjusted to accommodate this delay. In other instances, the delay is less critical; the final art textures for a character model are delayed by a few days.

If you are aware of delays ahead of time, you can have a better chance of coming up with a contingency plan that mitigates the schedule risk. For example, a milestone is coming up, and the game is expected to be feature complete with placeholder content. You find out a week ahead of time that Artist A thinks he might not get his level completed. Since you know ahead of time, you can assign an extra resource to help him get back on track or alter the testing schedule so this map will be checked last in the testing cycle, buying the few extras days that are needed to complete the level. Refer to Chapter 17, "Production Techniques," for more information on how to handle schedule delays.

One thing is for certain—the schedule will not track itself. Someone will have to follow up with each team member on a regular basis and keep the schedule updated with everyone's work. Schedule changes must also be added to the schedule right away; otherwise, the person tracking the schedule will not have an accurate picture of where people are expected to be with their tasks.

The person in charge of tracking the schedule can make the job easier by communicating upcoming deadlines to the team. For example, emails can be sent to remind the team of critical milestones on the project. Keep the emails short and simple. This person should also follow up with each team member on a regular basis (at least once a week) to check progress. If someone is routinely missing deadlines, the schedule tracker should check in with this person on a daily basis and assist him in organizing his work so he can learn to better manage his time.

INTERVIEW

Scheduling for Multiple Platforms, Stuart Roch, Executive Producer, Treyarch

In my experience the best way to handle multiplatform releases is to have 95 percent of the team focused on your lead platform with the remaining 5 percent trailing a couple steps behind the core team working on platform-specific issues. The mistake many developers make is not assigning development talent to the specific platforms, in hopes that some of the superstars on the team can pick up the slack. In practice, this never works out since your superstars are inevitably overloaded, and the secondary platforms get less attention than your lead platform. If you can be sure to devote specific team members to the secondary platforms, they'll champion their assigned platform and give it the love it needs.

Another aspect of a multiplatform release that is often overlooked is investing in a tool chain that supports all of the platforms under development. For example, if you can set up art tools that allow the artists to work at the maximum level of detail supported by your most powerful console platform and then have the tools automatically make adjustments to the art assets to accommodate your weakest platform, you reduce a lot of special case work. A little preplanning can go a long way in reducing the pain of a multiplatform release late in your development cycle.

BUDGETS

After the initial schedule is created, you can start creating the budget. The budget must be within reason for the quality, scope, and schedule, so that the game will make a profit when it is released. The publisher also watches the bottom line closely to ensure that development costs are justified and that they have made a profitable investment in your game. Ultimately, the producer is responsible for managing the costs. If the game development is poorly planned, it will require more time or more personnel, and thus cost more money, resulting in lower profit margins. If the game development is efficiently planned, it is easier to identify areas where there is cost-saving potential.

To determine the likely profitability of the game, the publisher creates a profit-and-loss statement (P&L). A P&L, which measures the overall profit and loss of a game, is a spreadsheet that compares the development, marketing, packaging, and distribution costs for the game against the projected sales. If the projected sales numbers increase, the better chance there is of making a profit. For example, if it is determined that 20,000 copies can be sold, the budget will be smaller than for a game that is predicted to sell 500,000 copies. The P&L is used to run different profitability scenarios to determine a reasonable balance between costs and potential profits.

Because the schedule, budget, and staffing plan are dependent on each other, the budget can change markedly depending on what your schedule and staffing plans are. Therefore, when you create an initial budget, be prepared to make adjustments to it and the other elements as necessary. After the budget is established and approved, manage the cost closely so you don't find yourself grossly over budget.

There will be instances when unexpected costs arise—for example, you need to buy three new computers and three copies of Autodesk 3ds Max so don't panic when this happens. You might be able to reallocate some money in the budget for these items without increasing your overall budget. If that doesn't work, you might be able to reallocate actual computers from another project in the studio and use them temporarily. Just remember to be as cost conscious as possible when these things happen.

Creating a Budget

Budgets consist of all the costs associated with the project, both one-time and recurring costs. One-time costs are things such as hardware, software, and supplies, whereas recurring costs are items such as salaries and taxes. Determine all of these costs up front so there are no surprises during the development process.

When creating the budget, refer to the game requirements and schedule to determine what costs to plan for. These documents provide guidance on how much you need to spend on certain areas of the game. Don't automatically assume that the cheapest item is the best solution, as this will ultimately affect the quality of the game. For instance, if the game needs to be completed in one year and be top-quality, you probably don't want to cut corners on the personnel and hire entry-level people. You probably want to spend money on more experienced people who can work effectively within the tight schedule. However, if you have several years to complete a game, you might want to hire some entry-level people and train them on the job so they can be experienced people for the next project.

These types of decisions are best made by taking all of the game elements into account. By this point, the major goals of the game are approved and the requirements are defined, so you have a good idea of whether the game is a budget title or a AAA one. Additionally, the game requirements indicate which technology is being used, so you have an idea of what the hardware and software needs are. The schedule defines how much time you have and how many people you need. Of course, each project will have a different budget dependent on the game requirements, but there are general things to be planned for in each budget.

Start by creating a list of all the major line items that must be accounted for in the budget—this includes both fixed and recurring costs. Figure 15.9 lists of some of these line items.

Recurring Costs
Art Personnel
Design Personnel
Engineering Personnel
Production Personnel
QA Personnel
Overhead
Fixed Costs
Hardware
Software
Licensing Fees
External Vendors
Food
Shipping
Office Supplies

FIGURE 15.9   Major budget line items.

Next, just as you did with the major tasks in the schedule, break them down into smaller line items. Use the information on the schedule to determine all the personnel needs and the information from the requirements to determine all the hardware and software needs. Figure 15.10 is an example of these the recurring costs broken down into smaller line items.

Art Personnel
Art Director
Lead Artist
Concept Artist
World Builder
Asset Artist
Animator
Technical Artist
Marketing Artist
Design Personnel
Creative Director
Lead Designer
Designer
Writer
Engineering Personnel
Technical Director
Lead Engineer
Networking Engineer
Sound Engineer
Tools Engineer
AI Engineer
Gameplay Engineer
Production Personnel
Executive Producer
Producer
Associate Producer
QA Personnel
Lead QA Analyst
Tester
Overhead
Rent, taxes

FIGURE 15.10 Smaller budget line items.

After determining all of the budget line items, add the costs to each one and create your budget. Figure 15.11 is a sample budget for the recurring costs on a project. In this example, the number of each type of personnel is indicated in the "Number" column, which is then multiplied by the "Monthly Rate" and "Number of Months" needed on a project. All of these costs are added for the grand total.

Figure 15.12 is a sample budget for the fixed costs on a project. In this example, each line item represents a fixed cost. The "Number" column is used to indicate

Art Personnel	Number	Monthly Rate	# of Months	Cost
Lead Artist	1	$8,000	24	$192,000
Concept Artist	1	$6,000	10	$60,000
World Builder	5	$6,000	12	$360,000
Object Artist	3	$6,000	8	$144,000
Animator	2	$6,000	8	$96,000
Design Personnel				
Lead Designer	1	$8,000	24	$192,000
Designer	4	$6,000	18	$432,000
Writer	1	$6,000	6	$36,000
Engineering Personnel				
Lead Engineer	1	$8,000	24	$192,000
Networking Engineer	2	$6,000	16	$192,000
Sound Engineer	1	$6,000	12	$72,000
Tools Engineer	3	$6,000	18	$324,000
AI Engineer	2	$6,000	12	$144,000
Production Personnel				
Producer	1	$8,000	24	$192,000
Associate Producer	1	$6,000	18	$108,000
QA Personnel				
Lead QA Analyst	1	$8,000	24	$192,000
Tester	6	$6,000	10	$360,000
GRAND TOTAL	**36**	**$112,000**	**268**	**$3,288,000**

Based on 24 month development cycle
Monthly rates are for example only, do not reflect actual rates

FIGURE 15.11 Sample budget for recurring costs on a project.

multiple purchases of a given item—for example, 10 computers. The "Number" column is multiplied by the "Rate" column to determine the total "cost" for each line items. These, in turn, are added for the grand total.

After the development budget is determined, it can be added to the publisher's P&L statement to determine whether the title will yield a profit. If not, you will be asked to make adjustments to the budget and schedule until they are satisfactory.

Managing a Budget

As with the schedule, you will need to track your budget during the development process. The same person who is appointed as the schedule tracker is also a good candidate to be the budget tracker. Any budget expenditures should be noted on a weekly, or at least a monthly, basis.

Hardware	Number	Rate	Cost
Computers	36	$3,000	$108,000
Console Development Kits	18	$10,000	$180,000
Graphics Cards	14	$300	$4,200
DVDs	200	$2	$400
Software			
Perforce	36	$750	$27,000
3ds Max	9	$4,000	$36,000
Adobe Photoshop	3	$600	$1,800
Visual C++	9	$3,000	$27,000
Licensing Fees			
Justice Unit Royalty	1	$100,000	$100,000
External Vendors			
Voiceover	1	$60,000	$60,000
Music	1	$20,000	$20,000
Cinematics	1	$100,000	$100,000
Localization	4	$30,000	$120,000
Food			
Snacks	12	$200	$2,400
Late Night Dinners	24	$200	$4,800
Shipping			
International Postage	1	$300	$300
FedEx	1	$500	$50
GRAND TOTAL			**$792,400**
Based on 24 month development cycle Rates are for example only, do not reflect actual rates			

FIGURE 15.12 Sample budget for fixed costs.

The studio or publisher's accounting department will also be involved in watching the budget. They keep records of all the expenditures on the game—salaries, hardware purchases, and costs of external vendors—and will allocate all of these things against your game's budget. They are a good source of information if you need to find out the total amount spent on the game at any given point.

Keep detailed records for any expenditures. Each studio has a different process for paying expenses, so check with the accounting department and studio management on what forms need to be filled out to make purchases, pay a vendor, or hire new team members. For example, if paying an external vendor, you might need to get an invoice and detailed statement of work from the vendor. After receiving this, you might need to fill out a check request form and submit it to accounting for payment. The form probably will ask for general information about the expenditure: was it budgeted and what part of the budget it is applied to. After all the paperwork is received, accounting will cut a check and mail it to the vendor.

If you find that the project is going over budget, don't ignore the problem because it won't go away. Instead, take time to re-asses your game plan and determine whether there are any adjustments that can be made to the schedule, staffing, or scope on the project.

STAFFING

The schedule details what work needs to be done, and the staffing plan determines who will do it. When these elements are combined, and the resources are added to the schedule, it determines when all the work is completed. Therefore, it is important to understand the strong dependencies between the staffing plan and schedule. The staffing plan is also affected by budget; if you need to hire additional people to complete the work, you need to have money in the budget to do this. If you can't afford extra people, you will need to reduce the scope of work so that the people you do have available can complete it on time and at budget.

Your staffing plan is largely based on what tasks must be completed. For example, if the game requires 10 character models and five levels, you are going to need several artists to complete this work. If the game is utilizing brand new technology, you'll want to have enough engineers on the project to prototype, code, and debug it. In the sample schedule illustrated in Figure 15.7, the schedule can be brought in a few days if more artists and designers are added to the project. As you can see, it is helpful to add or subtract people to the schedule to determine the effect this has on the deadlines. After you find a good balance between the tasks to be completed and people needed, you can fully define your staffing plan.

In general, the pre-production phase will include a small group of people that will be on the project until the end. During production, people will roll on and off the project as needed. By beta, the team will again be reduced to a small group of people who will bug-fix and code release the game. All of these staff changes will be reflected in your production schedule. Figure 15.13 is an example of partial staffing list for a game with a two-year development cycle. The information was pulled from the schedule and contains an overview on the amount of time people are needed for the project.

Outsourcing

Outsourcing work to an external vendor is a good way to save time and possibly money on the project. You might want to use an animation house to create the game's introductory movie so that your artists can focus on creating in-game content. Obviously, using an external vendor saves time for the internal development team since they are not responsible for completing a given section of work. Money is saved

Role	Duration	Notes
Lead Artist	24 months	Need for pre-production, production, code release.
Concept Artist	10 months	Need for pre-production and part of production.
World Builder 1	12 months	Need for production.
World Builder 2	12 months	Need for production.
World Builder 3	12 months	Need for production.
Texture Artist 1	8 months	Begin after first round of levels are geometry complete.
Texture Artist 2	8 months	Begin after first round of levels are geometry complete.
Lead Designer	24 months	Need for pre-production, production, code release.
Designer 1	18 months	Need for production.
Scripter 1	8 months	Will start after first round of levels are built and textured.
Scripter 2	8 months	Will start after first round of levels are built and textured.
Producer	24 months	Need for pre-production, production, code release.
Lead Enginer	24 months	Need for pre-production, production, code release.
Engineer - Multiplayer	16 months	Need to start right after pre-production.
Engineer - Tools	18 months	Need to start right after pre-production.
Lead QA Analyst	24 months	Need for pre-production, production, code release.
Tester 1	10 months	Part-time for alpha, full-time at code freeze.
Based on 24 month Development Cycle		

FIGURE 15.13   Example of partial staffing list.

if the vendor can do something more quickly and/or more cheaply than the internal development team, such as voiceover recordings.

There are many types of game development services you can outsource without impacting the quality or schedule of the project. These areas involve design and art assets, as these tend to be discrete sets of tasks that are not dependent on work from several parts of the team. Other things to outsource include the following:

- Cinematics and animation
- Motion capture
- Voiceover
- Music
- Sound effects
- Writing
- Localization

Outsourcing engineering tasks is not recommended, as the engineering tasks are more dependent on each other, and code merges can be time-consuming, making it difficult to test outsourced code on a regular basis. Additionally, an engineering vendor will need access to source code, which is highly confidential, and will need to set up a development environment that exactly matches what the internal engineering team is using.

Before contacting an external vendor, clearly define the scope of work to be outsourced. The earlier work can be scoped out, the more prepared the vendor is to accurately estimate the workload and complete it on time. Also, provide as much information as needed to the vendor about the game, as this will help them plan their work better. For example, if hiring an external vendor to compose music for the game, it is helpful to show them concept art, playable prototypes, the style guide, and anything else that can help them get a good idea of what the game's vision is and what music will best fit with this vision.

As with any project, there are pros and cons to working with external vendors. Overall, using a vendor can save time and resources during the development process, making it more likely for the game to be finished on time. Another benefit is that the team can concentrate solely on their tasks for the game and spend additional time play-balancing features, fixing bugs, and polishing the assets so the game is the best it can be. If you select vendors that are highly specialized in one area, their quality of work will be high and will contribute to the overall quality of the game, leaving the team to concentrate on the areas they do best.

There are a few drawbacks to working with a vendor, such as the extra costs involved. But if the project is large and complex, the cost of an external vendor might be worth the time and resources saved by the internal development efforts. Another drawback is that the developer loses the flexibility to shift project deliverables and internal deadlines around. When working with a vendor, the developer must to be organized and confident in the team's ability to meet key milestone dates. The developer needs to provide the vendor with necessary assets when needed. For example, a cinematics vendor might need to have the final character models to complete the final version of the movies. Providing this information requires the developer to think months ahead in the production cycle in order to give accurate estimates to the vendor.

Another large risk to outsourcing is the vendor might not meet his deadlines. This can severely impact the project if the deadlines are extremely tight. In order to mitigate this risk, be sure to schedule ample time in the schedule for finding a vendor. Additionally, after you get the vendor's schedule, add some padding to it so there is some slack if needed. It is never a good idea to schedule a vendor's deadline at the same time as a major milestone. For example, don't have a vendor deliver final cinematics or music on the beta date; plan to have it delivered at least a week ahead of time.

If the vendor is running behind schedule and all necessary assets and documentation have been provided to him by the development team, this is a problem. In order to avoid this, schedule regular milestones for the vendor as well. He should get into the habit of making deliveries every week or every few days, depending on the work to be done. If he misses any of these deadlines, it is a red flag that he might be in jeopardy of missing the final and most important deadline.

In some cases, the vendor might be good at convincing you everything is fine, and then miss the final deadline by a long shot. If the situation is this bad, you might need to cut your losses and look for another vendor to complete the work, or bring the work in-house and assign someone on the development team to finish it. This is not an ideal situation, as it means people need to work overtime to complete the work.

Communication

After an external vendor is hired, the key to a good relationship is effective communication. If the developer and vendor do not establish the communication pipeline up front, information will fall through the cracks, and key details will be missed. Poor communication might also impact the vendor's ability to meet proposed deadlines, especially if necessary information from the developer is not received on schedule.

Most external vendors will have a project manager who is responsible for managing the vendor's part of the development process from beginning to end and acting as the primary contact for the developer.

It is important to designate a single person from the development team to be the primary contact for the vendor's project manager. These two must communicate on a daily basis, even if it is just to provide a brief status update on what went on that day with the project. If more people are involved in the communication chain, it is likely that confusion will occur. If it is necessary to have a few people from the development team in touch with the vendor, such as the person who is handling all the voiceover for the game, the lines of communication must be clearly delineated so confusion does not exist about team members' responsibilities.

The internal development contact is responsible for delivering all the necessary assets and resources to the vendor and must inform the vendor of any changes to the schedule that affect the vendor's deadlines. If the vendor is not informed of a schedule delay that affects his work, you might find yourself paying extra money to the vendor because he received the assets late, had to work overtime, or hire more people in order to meet the deadline. If the vendor is flexible, unforeseen schedule changes can be accommodated.

INTERVIEW

Stuart Roch, Executive Producer, Treyarch

Many times the best contractors are found through referrals, just as you find the best full-time team members through personal recommendation. I've rarely hired contractors without a personal recommendation, but when this has occurred, the best you can do is to invest some serious time in due diligence. Reviewing past work, demo reels, meeting with the contractors, and checking on their references can mean the difference between a productive contract partner and one whom you cut loose due to creative differences.

   Like most things with production, pre-planning and forward thinking are key. Most developers contract freelancers late in development when they reactively realize that they don't have the resources they need to get the job done. The best producers are proactive and will identify the need for contract resources early in development so that they can find the best people, retain them early enough to be effective, and strike the best possible deal for the company when they aren't under pressure to contract a warm body.

SUMMARY

The game plan is a critical component of pre-production as this pulls together all the requirements and shows how the work is all going to get done on time. The schedule, budget, and staffing plan are the key components, and all of these factors will fluctuate during production. However, if you spend time in pre-production creating an in-depth game plan, you have a better idea of what factors can be adjusted when changes happen during the development process. This chapter discussed the basics of determining the schedule, budget, and staffing plan and ways you can define these for your game plan. After the game plan is completed, you have a clear idea of what to expect during production.

   The next section begins the discussion of what happens during the production phase, such as asset creation, making builds, and testing. If you put together a solid plan during pre-production, hopefully there will be no unexpected surprises during production.

Part VI Production

I f things are properly planned during pre-production, the production phase should present no unexpected surprises. The goal of production is to implement the game plan created during pre-production and get the game shipped to the stores.

Many elements need to be managed during production, especially the relationship between art, design, engineering, and QA. These departments will be working at full capacity during production and must work well with each other to keep the development process running smoothly.

Production is the point at which the game starts to look like a game, and a playable version is functioning. This section of the book presents key information about the production phase. Topics include the following:

- Production Techniques
- Art, Design, and Engineering Production Cycles
- Making Builds
- Software Ratings
- Localization

16 Production Cycle

In This Chapter

- Design Production Cycle
- Art Production Cycle
- Engineering Production Cycle
- Working Together

INTRODUCTION

When pre-production is completed, you will have a clear idea of the game that is being made, how to make it, who is going to do the work, and how much time you have to do it. It is important to note that there is not a definite point where pre-production ends and production begins. The transition will be gradual. For instance, while art and engineering begin working on the features outlined in the core design documentation, design is still busy designing the actual mission scenarios that appear in the game. Also, art will begin production on some assets, while still prototyping others. Engineering begins coding the game but might still be working on technical prototypes for some of the minor features.

What's important about production is that the team can start implementing the plan and watch the game take shape. So even though some small details are still being worked out, production can begin after the major aspects of the game are defined and approved. The main tasks occurring in production are implementing the plan, tracking the game's progress, and finishing the game. It is the producer's responsibility during production to manage these tasks smoothly and deal with any surprises or problems.

Every producer hopes that they have planned for every possible contingency during pre-production, and production is where this plan is put to the test. However, on a game that takes two years to develop, it is a bit optimistic to think that a plan made in January 2007 will be completely valid 18 months later in June 2008. Games change and grow with time, and a plan made more than a year ago might not take into account the hot new graphics feature that marketing wants added to the game. This is why the producer must be constantly vigilant about the game's progress during production, so that high-risk areas are identified and corrected, and that high-priority feature requests can be accommodated when necessary.

During production, the producer's day-to-day tasks will involve interfacing with the leads and team on a daily basis, assessing the game's progress, evaluating gameplay, working with QA, keeping management happy, providing assets to marketing, working with external vendors, approving milestones, filling out paperwork, and a host of other things. Each day will be different; on some days, there may be several fires to put out, and on other days, you can spend your time catching up on work. Whatever a day brings, be prepared to get the production back on track so the game ships on time. Chapter 17, "Production Techniques," discusses some ways for producers to manage the production cycle.

Of course, the art, design, engineering, and QA departments are also busy during production. Each discipline is working hard on their assigned tasks. Individuals can complete some tasks on their own or with help from someone in their discipline, but other tasks will require multiple people and disciplines to complete. If the team is enthusiastic and has high morale, getting them to work well with each other won't be difficult. They will become involved in each other's work, offer feedback, and work together to make the game the best it can be.

INTERVIEW

Jeff Matsushita, Greenlight Czar, Activision

If a project is in trouble, you might not see any tangible evidence, such as missed milestones or personnel burnout, until it is too late. By then the project might be in such a desperate situation that it will take much more time and money to get it back on track than if it was caught early. And, if ample time and money are not available to make these adjustments, and they rarely are, the quality of the game will likely suffer.

→

Producers need to constantly evaluate the game's progress at every level to make sure that things stay on schedule and on budget. This requires the discipline to focus on finishing the project, knowledge of good project planning, and the willingness to stick to a plan. After a plan has been defined, it is essential that everyone make a commitment and stick to it. That is why it is valuable to work with the entire team to help devise these plans. That way, if individuals are not meeting their own self-defined milestones, prodding them back on track before they begin affecting the overall quality of the project will be faced with less resistance. If the team is not meeting deadlines because the plan was not a fair assessment of bandwidth, or conditions have changed to make it obsolete, the plan must be redefined and the process started again. It is common for this to happen several times on a project. Having to redo it might seem like a lot of overhead, but an invalid plan is dangerous because it creates the illusion that the project is better managed than it really is.

One way to evaluate progress is to encourage regular builds of the game. If a team is unable to provide builds as expected, then something is likely to be amiss. It could mean that they are not making adequate progress or that there is a lack of under-standing as to the value of the deliverable. In any event, it is important that the pro-ducer find out what is stopping the build. In order to establish this discipline, producers should consider implementing regular builds early in the development process. Start by getting into the habit of making builds once a month with the fre-quency of the builds increasing as production continues. At alpha, daily builds should be the norm. Any less means that the team might not have the processes and disci-pline in place to be able to iterate quickly and effectively enough to close out the game in time. With frequent builds in hand, the producer will have a tangible work product to evaluate progress over time.

DESIGN PRODUCTION CYCLE

By the time production begins, design has completed documentation for the major parts of the game. They spend their production day implementing gameplay into the build, tweaking existing gameplay features, and providing feedback to the artists and engineers on their work. In addition, a designer might be writing all of the di-alogue for a game and working with the producer to organize the voiceover shoot.

The design production cycle also involves a lot of iteration and feature evolu-tion. After a feature is implemented in the game as originally planned, the designer will continue to tweak and polish the implementation until it is perfect. This in-cludes how the controls work, scoring, dialogue, UI buttons, and anything else that needs to be tweaked when a playable version is evaluated. In some cases, a feature might be redesigned if necessary. A feature redesign is not something to be taken lightly and will need to have approval from the producer and leads before it is done.

INTERVIEW

Clint Hocking, Creative Director, Ubisoft

You can do several things to create useful play tests. First, you need external people to participate in the play tests who can look at the game neutrally. You also need dedicated people to plan, schedule, monitor, record, and report upon these tests. You need to conduct the tests regularly from first playable until you reach the point where you don't have time to implement anything your testing might uncover anyway (which is literally at about the master date). You need to do the testing in small groups of three to six players, and you need to do dozens of different tests. You need to have each group test as much of the game as it is possible for them to test, and the people running the test group need to know exactly what they can and should test for in each test. They need to gather as much data as they can, and they need to know how to construct questionnaires and how to compile the data they gather into useful information. The information you get from 100–200 individual players is absolutely invaluable in terms of improving the overall quality of your title.

Play testing is also a large part of the design cycle. As gameplay mechanics start functioning in the game, the designers conduct play tests to determine whether a feature is fun or whether more work is needed. Ideally, there are people outside of the development team who can be play testers, so that the designer can get unbiased feedback. However, it is a good idea to involve the team when possible, as this builds camaraderie and gives people more ownership over the game. In some instances, publishers will conduct open beta tests in order to get information directly from the target audience about what works and what doesn't work in the game. The feedback is useful to the designers, as they are getting feedback directly from the players and don't have to guess what they want.

INTERVIEW

Erik Louden, Beta Tester

I have participated in more than 70 beta tests (both open and closed) as a beta tester for PC games. I find this to be very rewarding because I get to play games and offer feedback and suggestions for improvement before the game is released to the general public.

→

The beta test process will vary for each game, but in general, the publisher determines which games have beta tests and how many beta testers are needed. They may decide to have a more free-form test where the testers do not follow a test plan or answer a specific set of questions, but rather will go into the game and play it under real-world conditions. In other cases, they might have a questionnaire for us to fill out so they can more accurately track our feedback on the game. When I was a beta tester at Activision, forums were set up for the testers to write comments and to discuss the game. Sometimes, a member of the development team would respond to questions on the forums and would keep us updated on how things were progressing with the game.

Before we were allowed to test anything, we had to be screened and selected for the beta test and then sign an NDA. After we were approved for the test, we would receive a build of the game. A few years ago, before broadband was prevalent, we received builds of the game in the mail. These often included a pre-addressed return envelope so we could return the build when we were finished testing it. Nowadays, we usually download the build directly from the publisher's secure FTP site.

The amount of time we beta test a game also depends on what the publisher's needs are. Sometimes, beta tests start about six months before the game is released; other times as long as a year (alpha testing). Alpha tests usually focus on bits and pieces of the game since the alpha release is not completely functional; feedback is requested on new or experimental features that are added to the game. After the beta test begins, we usually continue testing updated builds of the game until it is almost ready for code release. We are directly responsible for finding and reporting bugs, and sometimes the developers ask that we test the game play and make suggestions about features and playability.

Developers and publishers can do a few things in order to get the most out of their beta tests. First, it is good to have two core teams of testers. One team can do directed play testing, via a test plan, and the other team can do freeform testing. The freeform team will not read the documentation but will jump right into the game and start playing it. Often they will discover things that will cause problems that could be overlooked during a more formalized testing process. For example, I was once beta testing an online game. There was a UI screen where you could select different cities. I decided to find out what happened if I started rapidly clicking all the cities, and ended up crashing the server. The developer called me on the phone, and I re-created the bug for him. In the background, I could hear the QA lead say, "this is why we have beta testers, I would have never thought to have tried that."

Another thing is to make sure that the developers are available, even in a limited capacity, to interact with the beta testers. We are working hard for you, often without pay, and it is good to know we are being listened to and our feedback is taken seriously. This could be as simple as having developers post on the message boards or jumping into an online game and playing a game with us.

$\rightarrow$

Finally, be careful with selecting beta testers. Some people are more interested in playing a free version of the game than in providing useful play test feedback. It is really good to have a trusted core team of beta testers that you know do good work. This core group can work throughout the entire beta testing process and on features that you don't want competitors to learn about. The developer then can have other testers (non-core) focused on less sensitive areas of the game if the situation warrants.

ART PRODUCTION CYCLE

The art production cycle revolves around asset creation—characters, vehicles, objects, weapons, environment, UI art, and cinematics are created during the production phase. Each artist has assigned deliverables to produce by specific deadlines. After the deliverables are completed and working in the build, the feedback starts coming in. As with design, art will then revisit their work, implement feedback, and polish the asset until it is in a shippable state. Because each game has numerous art assets, the lead artist also spends a lot of time tracking the asset creation and making sure the artists are getting feedback in a timely manner.

Prototyping is still being done at this point. Even though the list of assets is defined, concept art and prototyping are necessary for specific assets that are generated. Also, an animator will work with the producer on planning the motion capture shoot if one is necessary.

Art will spend a lot of time working with the engineers to refine the art production pipeline. Usually when art production begins, some of the proprietary art tools are still being coded by the engineers. Usually artists can start creating assets if the pipeline is not ready, especially if the source assets are created in a commercial software package, but they won't be able to view these assets in-game until the pipeline is complete. Be aware that any delays in getting the pipeline up and running has a negative impact on the overall schedule. If these delays drag on for weeks, it is possible that milestones will be missed, or marketing will not have viewable builds of the game for important conferences and tradeshows.

INTERVIEW

Carey Chico, Art Director, Pandemic Studios

Prototyping is extremely important when creating art assets for a game. To this end, the art director and producer must commit to doing everything in their power to get prototypes of levels, models, special effects, and any other key art assets running

→

in-game. One thing you can do, if the game's engine is not up and running, is to use a ready-made engine and level editor (such as UNREAL) to build a temporary world. If this is not possible, create a lot of concept art to convey the mood, feeling, and style of the game. Although concept art will not solve technical challenges, it can help define them when considering what technical art features need to be included in the game.

Prototyping and concept art also gets the team excited about the game. The more the team can see, the more they can share the vision of the game with each other. Completed concept art and prototypes can create a lot of excitement and positive energy on a project.

ENGINEERING PRODUCTION CYCLE

During production, engineering is working hard to get the features coded and debugged in the game. If they are using middleware, they also work with a middleware vendor to get the code up and running. They will work closely with QA to identify crash bugs and test fixes. As with design and art, engineering will also implement any necessary feedback.

Additionally, engineering is responsible for making regular builds of the game and maintaining the production pipeline. If the build is not working, more than likely the lead engineer and his team will need to fix the problem.

Engineers might spend a lot of production time debugging and putting out fires. Technology never works the way it is expected to, so a feature that was originally planned for might need to be cut because the technology can't support it. Sometimes these problems are not realized until engineering begins production and is finally seeing how things will function in the game.

WORKING TOGETHER

INTERVIEW

Carey Chico, Art Director, Pandemic Studios

Giving effective feedback to an artist is not difficult, if you answer two questions: do you like it? and why? *Why* is the cornerstone of useful feedback; if you can't explain why you don't like something, the artist will not understand the feedback and will not know what changes to make.

$\rightarrow$

All feedback on art assets should go through the art director and not directly to the artist who created the asset. This way the art director can filter the feedback, so there is no confusion on what changes must be made. The art director can also rephrase the feedback so that it is diplomatic and provides useful information to the artist. This also prevents the lines of communication from getting crossed, especially in a situation where the lead designer and lead artist might have conflicting feedback.

Establish a good process for tracking all the feedback. For example, *Alienbrain* and *Perforce* force you to add a comment when you check something in, which is a good way to track what changes were made to an asset. You can also track these changes in a change control log or in a designated area on the team Web site.

As discussed in Chapter 7, "Teams," it is important that everyone on the team work together toward a common goal. Art should be talking with design and engineering on a regular basis about the game, and so on. If you have a team in which art, design, engineering, production, and QA don't interact with each other, you might soon find that communication between the departments is rare, and that when it does happen, it's to complain about each other.

Feedback between art, design, engineering, and QA is valuable to the game and the team. If an engineer takes time to play some of the missions the designers has scripted, he might have some suggestions on ways to improve it or discover a minor change he can make to the scripting tool that provides some added scripting functionality to make the missions more fun. Constructive feedback is always welcome if delivered in a tactful and respectful manner.

INTERVIEW

Clint Hocking, Creative Director, Ubisoft

Sadly, everyone is a critic, and because design is something everyone thinks they can do, everyone seems to think they are entitled to give feedback on the design and have that feedback be integrated. I might ask the counter-question… What is the best way for an artist, producer, designer, or manager to give feedback on code? The answer is: go learn how to program, work your way up from intern to lead, and then conduct a thorough code evaluation and present that feedback in writing. Unfortunately, it is true that because design is so ill-defined and because we tend to not be rigorous, we are subject to this kind of input in ways that programmers or producers are not. *This is our fault.* We need to develop and improve our methodologies and

→

work on formalizing our field and developing ourselves and our abilities to the point where some guy off the street who happens to like *Quake* does not have a 50–50 chance of being as good or better than any working designer. Until we reach the level where there is a quantifiable skill-set that is possessed only by designers, until we get past the 'wouldn't it be cool if. . .' approaches to design, we will always be required to integrate feedback from people in other professions. That said, programmers and producers and artists out there have valuable design feedback. This is because they are engaged by design problems; they are analytical; and they know what they are talking about as much as your average designer. The best way for them to give their feedback is simply to be able to analyze and criticize the design in the same vocabulary as the designer. In other words, by coming to speak to me in my own language, you have shown that you understand my field. It's the same with art and programming and production.

It can be a challenge to get engineers, artists, and designers to effectively communicate with each other. We don't yet have a full formalized vocabulary for talking about and, thereby, facilitating design. This is a primary goal for modern game designers. Go read the books, lectures, or papers of Doug Church, Mark Leblanc, Harvey Smith, Chris Crawford, Raph Koster, Ben Cousins, Robin Hunicke,– or basically any designer who is linked off of their Web sites or blogs. Then you will start to understand how to communicate with designers. Then you won't be coming to your designer and saying, 'I think it would be cooler if. . ..' When you can do that, you will find yourself in one of two positions: you'll either find yourself talking to a designer who designs by saying 'wouldn't it be cool if'—in which case your project is probably in trouble—or you will find a designer who can communicate with you, in which case, everyone wins. Designers need to be more thorough, and when they become more thorough, they will expect those who want to discuss design with them to be thorough as well.

During production, it is also important for the team to realize what the task dependencies are and how any delays affect the overall deadlines. People need to work together closely, especially if multiple departments are working on the same feature. Each team member should set aside a few minutes each day to check in with his co-workers about where they are with their work. Also, people should not be afraid to raise red flags or bring any concerns to their lead or the production.

Overall, production is a time filled with a lot of activity, and the team will grow to its maximum size. Things will be happening quickly, so everyone needs to be conscientious about getting their work done in a timely fashion. Production is also when crunch time becomes necessary, so be sure to keep an eye peeled for burnout or other potential personnel issues. Because so much is happening during production, it is also one of the most enjoyable times of the project if you have planned carefully during pre-production.

SUMMARY

Production starts after the game concept and requirements are defined in pre-production. If the game plan is detailed and well-organized, production will go smoothly. During production, art, design, engineering, production, and QA are all focused on the same goal—delivering a high quality and entertaining game. Each discipline will have different priorities for the game: art wants the game to look its best; design wants the game to play its best; and so on. But they all work together to strike a balance between each goal. These goals are influenced by all the play testing and feedback that occur during production. The next chapter presents some ways to keep the production process on track.

17 Production Techniques

In This Chapter

- Getting a Project Back on Track
- Project Reviews
- Critical Stage Analysis
- Weekly Status Reports
- Running Meetings
- Resource Allocation
- Preventing Feature Creep
- Establishing Approval Processes
- Task Forces

INTRODUCTION

As a producer, it is your responsibility to navigate through the various development phases and successfully run a project from concept to completion. This is a big, but not impossible, challenge, especially if you are constantly monitoring the development process to ensure that the game's goals are being met and if you are actively looking for ways to improve the quality and efficiency of the production process. Many production techniques can be used to get a project back on track, monitor progress, and improve efficiency. This chapter discusses a few techniques that are simple, but effective to implement.

GETTING A PROJECT BACK ON TRACK

In order to fully understand how the project variables of schedule, resources, features, and quality fit together and directly impact each other, it is useful to envision a triangle. Figure 17.1 is diagram of this.

FIGURE 17.1 Relationship of project variables to each other.

The sides of the triangle correspond to the resources, the schedule, or the features that are necessary to complete any given project. The area inside the triangle represents the quality of project. If one of these factors changes, it will affect the other factors; one measurement of a triangle cannot change without affecting the others. If all four of these factors are constantly changing during the development cycle, the project will never be stable. This makes it hard to estimate when the game will be completed, how much it will cost, how many features it has, and the quality of the final version.

For example, if the schedule is shortened, either more people are added, features are cut, the quality of the product is lessened, or any combination of these is necessary to get the project completed on time. If head count is reduced, either more time is added, features are cut, or the quality is lessened to compensate for the reduced resources. Jim Lewis explains concepts like these more in depth in his book, *Project Planning Scheduling and Control.*

Striking a balance among the schedule, resources, features, and quality is a challenge for any project. However, when faced with a project that is getting off track, there are four fundamental areas to examine for ways to get the project successfully running again:

Increasing scheduled time: More time is something that teams always request on a project. However, time is not a luxury you have if the game has to be finished in time for the holidays. Adding time to the schedule might seem like an easy solution, but make sure that any time added to the schedule is used effectively. If more time is added and the team slows down their working pace, the extra time will be used up quickly.

Increasing resources: Adding resources can also be a straightforward way to bring a project back in line with the plan, but it is possible to reach a critical mass where adding more resources will actually increase the time to get the tasks completed. When more people are added to a project, you have to account for training time, defining their tasks, setting up their hardware and software, tracking their work, and so on. These items will also take time away from people already working on the project, especially if they are responsible for training.

Cutting features: Nobody ever wants to cut features, because it is perceived as diminishing the value of the game. However, examine the feature set to determine which core features must be preserved that give the game value and focus on cutting the extra features that could be used in a second version of the game. Also, focus on eliminating extra features that will have a positive impact on the most pressing resource and schedule constraints.

Reducing quality: If the people in charge insist that the full feature set must be implemented with the current staff and schedule, then the quality of the project will diminish. If you are put in this position, define specifically where the quality will suffer and explain why to the powers that be. Sometimes, this will convince them that adding more time, money, or resources is important to ensure the game's quality.

If a project is extremely off base—it is way off schedule, or it is costing too much—it may be cancelled, especially if there is no hope of realizing a profit from its eventual release, or there is an opportunity to utilize the time and resources on another project that is more likely to be profitable. Canceling a project is never a pleasant task and is not something that is taken lightly by senior management. Canceling projects means potential layoffs, loss of money and time spent, and is a huge blow to employee morale.

However, this decision can be healthier in the long run, since the developer can focus efforts on improving the quality of another game in production or start working on a new game and use the lessons learned from the previous project. If you are in a position where canceling the project is being seriously considered, make sure that you understand the pros and cons of all the other proposed solutions to ensure that cutting the project is indeed the best thing to do for all concerned.

INTERVIEW

Tobi Saulnier, President, 1st Playable

When a project is in trouble, communication is often one of the first things to go! People are stressed and tired, which in addition to impacting communication, also makes it difficult for them to step back and look at what is happening on the project as a whole.

One technique I use to get a project back on track is to simply create a list of how much work remains to be implemented. When a team is in trouble, they often stop tracking how much is left to do and, therefore, have only a conceptual idea, not a concrete list, of what work needs to be completed. I work with the team to put this list together and make sure that everyone agrees that it is complete. Must-have items are differentiated from wish list items, and high-risk or problem areas are noted. This helps create a shared understanding of the scope or implementation problems at hand, which is necessary for any effective problem solving.

After the list is completed, the team needs to shift process to only work on what's on the list. If a task is forgotten (which is common at this stage), add it to the list to be worked on. This way everyone is working on the same plan.

→

Meanwhile we can take the tasks remaining and start to prioritize and plan the work, with the goal of estimating the time and resources needed to complete the game. If a game is late, we can see where adding more resources will help and identify areas where the work can be scoped back. The list also helps the team to identify situations in which team members might think a task is done, but it still needs work to complete, and so on. In addition, the list provides a way to double-check the specifications of the work that is already in progress and a way to track actual time versus estimated time, so that the estimates can be updated accordingly. This can be an effective and visible tool, since you can post the list in team rooms and cross off items when they are completed.

The most important thing this technique does is to get the team working together on a plan that they believe they can accomplish. It also helps get management, the team, and the customer on the same page. There have been times when I thought a project was in trouble, but the team thought things were fine; and times that I thought a feature requested by the customer could be added, but the team felt they were already overcommitted. The nice thing about putting together a list of remaining tasks is that when everyone is looking at the same data, 99 percent of the time we will come to the same conclusions.

PROJECT REVIEWS

Regular and comprehensive project reviews with management are vital in monitoring the game's development progress. The review requires you to look at the established development plan and compare that with the game's actual development progress. Further, the review presents an opportunity to identify problems and formulate solutions for them, because potential red flags are exposed and can be neutralized before they become problems.

Before starting a review, make sure that everyone is prepared and focused on the goal. Reviews can be can be ineffective and a waste of time for the following reasons:

- Unclear objectives/no focus
- Lack of preparation
- Wrong people involved
- No follow-up

The follow-up is critical, especially if solutions were discussed for potential problems. If the solutions are not followed up on and implemented at the team level, a small problem will quickly grow into a large one.

Conducting a Project Review

Conducting a project review is not difficult. Several project management books discuss the review process more in depth. Please consult Appendix B, "Resources." First, define the review's goals and objectives. If these are not defined beforehand, the proper information will not presented, and the review will not beneficial to the team or anyone else involved. It is important that the correct people attend the review—studio management, project leads, and perhaps someone from the publisher will need to attend. These are the people with the most responsibility on the project and the ones who can authorize changes.

Second, establish a format. The review format is important in establishing the goals of the review. The format must include the following types of information:

Comparisons: Compare the project plan with the current status of the project. This includes such information as the original milestone dates and when they were actually achieved, what content was scheduled to be created versus what content has actually been created, and how much was originally in the budget and how much has actually been spent.

Accomplishments: List any accomplishments since the last review. This shows the concrete progress of the game's development. If there are no accomplishments to list, the project is in trouble. Accomplishments include things like recording all of the voiceover, sending all the assets to be translated, and completing all the character models for the game.

Risks: Identify any potential risks and propose solutions. The risks can be prioritized as high, medium, or low to give a better assessment of the impact they might have on the project.

Roadblocks: Roadblocks are anything that prevents the team from making progress. For example, if the team is still waiting for console development kits, that directly prevents them from running a version of the game on the correct platform. Roadblocks are something that can be identified and quickly removed so that progress does not come to a standstill.

Supporting Documentation: This includes the updated project schedule, deliverable lists, status reports for each area of the game, and anything else that concretely illustrates the progress made on the game.

Resources: Identify any additional resources needed. For example, you might need another engineer for two months to help code a new feature that was approved. An additional artist might be needed for two weeks to create objects for the levels.

Including this information in the format will keep the reviewed focused.

Third, plan sufficient time for the review. The initial review might take several hours, depending on the size the project. After the initial review is completed, the follow-up reviews might not take as long. But don't cut the time short. If you find that you are running short on time and the review is not completed, schedule some time in the next few days to complete it.

Fourth, take notes at the review and publish them everywhere—email them to the team, post them on the Web site, and discuss them during the team meetings. Any decisions made or solutions proposed should be noted in the meeting minutes. Also, be sure to follow up on action items. Please refer to the section later in this chapter that discusses how to run meetings for more information on meeting minutes and action items.

Benefits

Project reviews are beneficial because they keep everyone focused on the big picture of what needs to be completed during each phase of the project. So instead of getting mired down in the little details of how many weapons are going to be in the game, the focus is on when all the weapons have to be finished and who is working on them.

Reviews also keep people honest about the reality of the project. If the project is thoroughly examined on a monthly basis, the problem areas will be exposed and discussed. If you are participating in a monthly project review and are tempted to gloss over the problems, you are not doing the game or your team any favors. Problems can't be fixed unless they are known about and discussed.

A monthly project review keeps the producer in regular contact with the project leads and project's status. Many producers will claim they know what is going on with their projects, but when asked to provide a comprehensive status report, they find they don't know everything and must consult with their leads on the exact status of many items. This does not mean the producer is doing a bad job, it just demonstrates how many people are necessary to keep track of all the tasks on the project.

Although regular project reviews are not a norm in game development, they are becoming more popular as development teams get larger and more risk is attached to a project. If you are working at a studio that does not currently do these reviews on a studio management and publisher level, you can start by working with your team leads on a monthly review. Eventually, you can ease management into the process as well, especially when they see these reviews are providing them with pertinent project information.

CRITICAL STAGE ANALYSIS

Critical Stage Analysis (CSA) is a technique developed by Wolfgang Hamann to provide ongoing improvements in the production process by examining the game's progress at critical stages in the development cycle. This process is described in detail in his article, "Goodbye Post Mortems, Hello Critical Stage Analysis," which is cited in Appendix B, "Resources."

CSA is a simple process that happens on a regular basis (usually monthly) and involves the entire team answering these three questions:

- What are five things that went right during this past development period?
- What are five things that went wrong during this past development period?
- What are five things that can be improved for future development periods?

Each team member writes up his own answers and ranks them according to importance. It does not matter if the producer or leads agree with the items listed or the rankings, because it really is a measure of what each individual thinks about the project at this point in time. Additionally, these questions should be answered within two–three days of completing a critical milestone. What's nice about this technique is that provides a snapshot of what each person thinks about the current standing of the project.

These answers are then turned in to the producer who compiles the information in a master document. The document is emailed to leads and a meeting is scheduled within two days to discuss the findings. Solutions are discussed for the most important findings, and the leads are tasked with implementing solutions for these issues within the next development period.

When this plan is finalized, a team meeting is scheduled, and the findings and solutions are presented to the entire team. During the meeting, all the feedback and proposed solutions are discussed and any questions answered. At subsequent team meetings, status updates are given on where things stand with solving the issues. Hopefully, the top five issues are solved, and the development process has improved as a result. The main goal is to emphasize the positive and to show the team that their feedback is taken seriously.

WEEKLY STATUS REPORTS

Weekly status reports are also a good way to track development process, but they should not be used in lieu of the comprehensive project review. If you are working on a small project that takes less than two months to complete, you might be able to accurately gauge the development progress with a weekly report, but projects that run longer than a couple months need project reviews as well.

Weekly status reports communicate the game's current status to the development team and management. Oftentimes, a producer might forget that the members of the development team are hard at work on their assigned tasks and don't have a chance to keep up with everything being done during production. For example, the engineer coding the animation system might not realize when the cinematics are finished or when the first few missions are ready for play testing. The weekly status report is a chance to tell the team where the project is.

For the Development Team

Weekly reports for the development team are a positive way to show the progress they are making as a team. It's also a good forum to inform the team of critical deadlines, discuss the latest marketing updates, and introduce new team members. The following types of information can be included:

Departmental updates: This is a good way to keep everyone informed on just exactly what the artists, designers, and engineers are doing on the project. If a new game type has been added, include that in the design update. If new characters are working in the build, make sure to add that to the art update. Include anything that gets the team excited about the work they and their teammates are doing.

Marketing and PR information: Include information on tradeshows where the game will be showcased, the latest articles and interviews about the game, upcoming press tours, the current status of the packaging, and anything else that marketing is doing for the game. This section will show the team how hard other parts of the company are working to promote the game.

New employees: As teams get larger, new employees are bound to start mid-production. Introduce these people and give some brief background information to make it easier for other team members to get to know them.

Upcoming deadlines: It is always a good idea to note upcoming deadlines and what main items need to be accomplished in order to meet them. If the team is consistently reminded of any upcoming deadlines, they will plan to be have their work ready on time.

These reports can be emailed, posted on the team Web site, presented verbally during the regular team meeting, or all three. It is good to present the information in as many forms as possible, to ensure that everyone gets it.

For Management

Management usually requires some type of weekly summary of the projects status. They are interested in the progress the game is making, any risks that will impede the progress, and any areas that are not progressing smoothly. The weekly report also serves as a good reminder to the producer of what is going on with the project. The types of information to include in a weekly status report to management should include the following:

Departmental updates: Include information on the progress art, design, and engineering have made in the past week.

Risks: Call out which areas are a risk and don't be shy about it. If management is not aware that something is even slightly at risk, they cannot propose any solutions. Also, if the risk grows into something bigger, management will want to know why they weren't informed of the problem before it got to be serious.

Key deadlines and approvals: Note upcoming milestones and whether there is any risk the milestone will be late. If you are waiting on approvals for any content or features, include this as a line item in the report as well.

Resources: If you need additional resources on the project—hardware, software, or personnel—noting this on the report is a good way to bring this to management's attention.

RUNNING MEETINGS

Since meetings are a big part of game development—producers and leads probably spend half their time in meetings—it is important that they are useful. Also, finding ways to make meetings shorter and more effective increases the time people can actually work on the project. Some simple techniques can be used to make meetings more useful.

Set an Agenda

Before the meeting, define the agenda and clearly state the goals of the meeting. For example, the goal could be to get more information on how the AI will work in the game or deciding on the game controls. If you don't know why you are meeting, cancel. Avoid having meetings that combine information gathering and decision making. Meetings like this are often frustrating because people will spend a lot of time in discussion mode and very little in decision mode, or vice versa.

Assign time limits to each topic of discussion and make sure that all meeting attendees are aware of these limits. For example, if the meeting is 60 minutes and there are 10 items to discuss, each topic will get about 5 minutes of discussion.

Be aware that time is also needed at the beginning to state the meeting goals, and time is needed at the end to state the conclusions and action items. If the topic runs over the allotted time limit, either table the discussion for another meeting, or if the topic is important, table the remaining topics for discussion another time. In either case, just remember to keep the meeting focused and on track.

Appoint a Moderator

Appoint a moderator for each meeting. This person is responsible for keeping the meeting on track. The best moderator is someone with a neutral position on the topic being discussed. They can focus on running the meeting smoothly, because they will not be involved in the meeting discussion, except to redirect discussion. They can also be the time-keepers and inform people when the allotted discussion time for a topic is concluding.

Record Meeting Minutes

Minutes are valuable tools that should required of all meetings, no matter the size. How many times have you attended a meeting where decisions were made, and then nobody remembered what the final decision was or mistakenly remembered the wrong decision? Minutes create a record of the meeting and are readily available for future reference.

The minutes should record who was at the meeting, what the goals of the meeting were, what was discussed, what was decided, and what action items resulted from the meeting. A simple template can be put together and used for all meeting minutes.

Assign a minute taker for each meeting. Like the moderator, this should be someone who is not involved in the meeting discussion. It is too distracting for participants in the meeting to stop the discussion to take notes. The moderator and minute taker can usually be the same person. This role is a good learning experience for a junior person on the team and is a good way to train potential team members for leadership roles on future projects.

Follow Up on Action Items

Action items are a critical by-product of meetings. Often during a meeting, additional tasks need to be done in order to come to a resolution on the meeting topic. Instead of just forgetting these tasks, record them as action items in the meeting minutes. A table can be created at the end of the meeting minutes that states the date the action item was entered, the resource assigned, the deadline, and the current status. Keep this table up to date and follow up with everyone on their action items.

RESOURCE ALLOCATION

From time to time, the game might not have enough personnel to complete critical tasks on time. This could be for a variety of reasons: the work was underestimated; people are out sick or on vacation; more features were requested; and so on. When trying to solve the personnel issues, consider temporarily reallocating resources.

One way is to pull people from noncritical tasks to help out with the critical ones. In order to do this, you, as the producer, must be aware of everyone's skill set. Most team members are not utilizing all of their skills on a given task and are more than happy to pitch in on other tasks when needed and if they have time. For example, a level artist might be familiar with how to use After Effects and can temporarily help out the cinematics team, or a tools engineer might be able to help with coding UI.

When temporarily pulling people from their tasks, you must schedule start and end dates so that they know when they must wrap up their temporary assignment and get back to work on their main tasks. If you reallocate someone, and it turns out that they are needed permanently on the new task, assign someone else to pick up the old tasks.

Another way, if you are working in a large studio with multiple projects in production, is to temporarily pull people from other project teams to help. The other team might be impacted, but if they have more time in their development schedule, they might be able to spare someone temporarily.

Finally, look at hiring external contractors. You do not want them on critical path tasks, but if you have already reallocated internal resources to the critical tasks, the contractors can come in to work on the noncritical tasks. This frees up the internal team members to shift around where needed.

PREVENTING FEATURE CREEP

Feature creep occurs if additional features are added without adjusting the other project variables (time, resources, and quality) to accommodate the additional work. It's something that developers are always fighting against, since feature requests are made on a regular basis by the team, studio management, the publisher, marketing, the fans, and so on. If feature creep is not controlled, the project is put at risk, and you might miss the ship date.

Some feature creep is a good thing, as it makes the final game more enjoyable to play. For example, if the control scheme is implemented as designed, new feature requests to improve the usability might come in after people have had a chance to play with them. Or after the UI is in place, some of the screens and buttons might need to be redesigned to be more intuitive to the player. Because of this, developers must not ignore additional feature requests.

On the other hand, some feature requests can be damaging to the project—either they are completely unreasonable given the other project parameters; they impact a lot of work already done; or they are so small that it is not worth putting the project at risk to include them. When features like this are requested, it is the producer's job to diplomatically explain why this feature cannot be included. This can be difficult to do, especially if you have to explain to a senior vice president why his pet feature can't be in the game.

A good method for explaining why a feature can't be included is to illustrate the impact that adding this feature will have to the game's cost, schedule, and resources. For example, if marketing requests that an online ranking system be added, the producer can research how long the feature will take to design, implement, and test and who is available to do these tasks. Most likely, a feature of this nature will take several weeks and several people to implement, requiring a shift in the schedule and resources, which directly impacts the work already being done on a project. Essentially, if someone asks for a new feature to be added after the game is in production, a feature (or features) must be removed in order to get the game finished without changing the schedule, resources, or quality.

INTERVIEW

Stuart Roch, Executive Producer, Treyarch

Feature creep is difficult to handle for many reasons. When a project is locked down and supposedly content complete, a producer faces many challenges. For one, the people wanting to get the extra features in post-lock are the most influential people on the team. Sometimes the studio head is pushing for a feature he feels passionately about, and others such as the creative director might be lobbying for that one last feature to make the game great.

Outside of the difficulty producers face in saying no to key team members, simply identifying the features can be a trick in itself. What to one producer is a feature being requested late in the project can be a polish tweak or even a bug-fix when defined differently on another team member's plate. Unless the project has been managed well from the start, this is not a black-and-white problem. Some features will inevitably have to be approved post alpha, and some tolerance will have to be allowed. The best

→

defense late in the project is to set up a feature approval pipeline with checks and balances to make sure that anything that gets added or rejected from the game goes through the appropriate parties. The feature request pipeline should include people like the executive producer, project director, and creative director to make sure every feature request is handled with business, schedule, and creative concerns in mind.

Prioritizing Features

If you plan ahead for future feature requests, you might be able to get some additional feature requests added to the game, without removing anything else that is already planned. When someone makes a feature request, evaluate the feature and prioritize it. Refer to Chapter 14, "Game Requirements," for information on prioritizing features. Then, examine the current set of features to determine whether any tier one features can move to tier two, and so on. This way, the new feature request can replace an existing feature that was already planned for, thereby minimizing feature creep.

Change Requests

Formal change requests are another way to monitor and track feature requests. Essentially, when someone requests a feature change or enhancement, they fill out a request form. The form should ask for the following:

- Description of request
- Reason for request
- Impact if feature not added
- Recommended alternatives
- Analysis of how this affects the project schedule, resources, and quality
- What existing feature can potentially be removed to accommodate this request
- Who needs to be notified of the potential change

After the form is filled out, it is sent to the producer for review. The producer will want to double-check the details in the form, particularly the project analysis, to ensure that the correct people have been consulted about the proposed feature and have given accurate estimates on how this affects their work. After the producer reviews the form, he can discuss the request with the necessary people, such as the project leads, studio management, or the publisher.

One person should be the main point of contact for approving or rejecting a feature change. When a final decision has been made, all interested parties must be notified. If the feature is approved, make sure that it is properly documented and added to the project plan.

INTERVIEW

Wade Tinney and Coray Siefert, Large Animal Games

If a project is behind schedule, we usually re-evaluate the design and figure out what features can be scaled back. We might reduce the number of levels or characters, remove a piece of music, or re-use assets from a previous title. This way, we can preserve the core features and have something to add on to the next iteration of the game. For example, on *Rocketbowl,* we originally planned for 10 levels, but we ended up shipping with 7 levels and then offered the final 3 levels as downloadable content.

Game developers have to be proactive about addressing problems on a project. This is especially true for Large Animal because we are a small developer whose projects are typically completed in six to eight months. This means we can't wait a month or even a week to deal with any problems that put the ship date of the project at risk. If we are two days behind schedule on the character art, for example, we need to make up for this time by reducing art time on another aspect of the game.

ESTABLISHING APPROVAL PROCESSES

From studio management on down, many people are involved in the game development process who need to approve certain parts of the game before production begins. For example, they are paying the bill and want a say in how the money is spent, or they are in charge of coding a particular feature and need to make sure that the proposed design is doable with the technology. It is useful to put approval processes in place in order to present everyone with all the necessary information, track the approvals, and record the feedback. These processes will differ based on the project size, how many people have approval rights, and how much information needs approval, but there are three major things in common with any approval process: keeping it simple, defining and publishing, and centralizing the tracking.

Keep it Simple

Keep the process as simple as possible. Eliminate any unnecessary steps and don't involve anyone in the approval process who is not absolutely necessary. More people means more bottlenecks in getting things approved, so the fewer people involved means less time for approval. For example, if the approval process for the mission designs involved the lead artist, the lead engineer, the lead designer, the artist working on the level, the producer, and management it will take weeks to get something approved. Although it is extremely important to get feedback from all of these people, they don't have to actually be involved in approval. Instead, their feedback can be incorporated into the final deliverable that is presented for approval. Instead, their feedback can be incorporated into the final deliverable that is presented for approval. Our mission approval process eventually reduced in scope to include only studio management, a producer, one lead artist, and one lead designer.

Define and Publish

Define and publish the process. This is a step that often gets overlooked, because there is never enough time to write anything down. However, if the process is defined and published, it has a greater chance of working, because everyone involved in the process has a full understanding of what their obligations are. During preproduction one one project, for example, the author defined an initial design document approval process, wrote it down, and published it to the leads. The process evolved as the project went on, but defining the initial process allowed people to see where bottlenecks were likely to happen and to have a better understanding of where each document was in the process.

Centralize the Tracking

Assign one person to track all steps and assets in the approval process. Depending on how many assets there are, this can be a full-time job. Restricting it to a single person creates a single point of reference for the status of all approvals. This also creates a librarian who tracks all the final assets and deliverables needed for the game. For example, confusion can be created if there are several different art asset lists from which people are working, instead of one master list; no one knows for sure which is the correct list. The librarian can create the master asset list and has final work on what assets will be created for the game.

TASK FORCES

Task forces are cross-discipline groups who are put in charge of looking at problems, formulating solutions, and getting them implemented in the game. They are flexible and autonomous, which means they can operate independently within the team. Their decision is considered final. For example, a task force can be set up to determine how the game controls will work, how the AI will function, or how the multiplayer scoring system will be implemented.

Each task force should consist of at least one engineer, one artist, one designer, and maybe one or two other experts in the feature being worked on. One person is designated as the leader and is responsible for facilitating any necessary meetings and research to be done, collecting the data, and summarizing the final decision for the rest of the team. When putting together task forces, assign a specific deadline and follow up with their progress on a regular basis.

Task forces are useful in that they give people a stake in the game. People are empowered to work together as a small team without worrying about the established management hierarchy. Because they are able to work unimpeded and do not need the consensus of the entire team to make a decision, solutions can be implemented quickly. In some cases, the task force's initial decisions will not work, so they need to re-examine the problem and come back with another solution.

SUMMARY

This chapter discussed some production techniques that will improve the production process, communication, or the ability to identify risks. Although these techniques are not cure-alls, they certainly can help a producer solve some common problems encountered during the development process.

18 Making Builds

In This Chapter

- Build Process
- Multilingual Builds
- Build Notes
- Preventing Piracy

INTRODUCTION

It is important to have a process in place for creating builds on a regular basis so that features and assets can be checked in-game. If regular builds are not created, the development team cannot do proper checks of the game's functionality or ensure that the assets are displaying correctly in-game. There is a noticeable visual difference in how art assets for a console game display on a PC and how they display in-game on a television. There are numerous settings on televisions—some with lighter displays and some with darker displays—all of which can affect how something looks in-game. The developer will not see these differences unless he creates a build and looks at the assets directly in-game.

If there is difficulty creating a build, it can also indicate that there are bugs in the game that are preventing the code from compiling. The developers might not realize these bugs are there until they try to create a build. If a long time elapses without creating a build, critical bugs will remain undiscovered in the code and will be more difficult to deal with as development progresses.

BUILD PROCESS

Every development team will have a different build process, which is usually determined by the lead engineer. The important thing is making sure that this process gets defined during pre-production and implemented as soon as assets are available for creating a build. Waiting too long to establish a build process will cause development delays during critical milestones; the engineers will spend precious production time trying to work out kinks in the build process instead of coding features and fixing bugs.

The process must be flexible so that it can be modified to create builds with special requests. For example, marketing might request a stable build they can demo at a conference, which has only a certain area of the game available to play. Access to the other game levels can be prevented by locking out UI functionality or by removing items completely from the game.

The process must also have a way to track what has been added to the build. This is helpful if an artist is waiting for a certain tool to be finished or if a designer is waiting on a level to be finished so he can begin scripting it. One simple way to do this is to set up a "New in Build" mailing list for what's been added to the build. This way, if an engineer checks in updated vehicle AI code, he sends an email to this list stating what new code he just checked in. An artist would send an email to the "New in Build" list every time an art asset was checked into the build, and so on. This helps the team as a whole track what's being added to the build, and it also gives QA a better idea of what to expect in each build that is delivered to them for testing. The "New in Build" emails also provide a good foundation for creating build notes, which are discussed later in this chapter.

Although a primary person will oversee the build process, several people need to know how the process works. This is useful if an unplanned build needs to be created, and the primary person is not available to do it.

Build Schedule

After production starts, the initial build must be made as soon as possible—well before a first playable build. This provides a benchmark for measuring the progress of future builds. It provides proof of concept and technology to the development team and studio management. By the time the game is at a first playable stage, builds should be made two to three times a week. By alpha, it is ideal to be in the habit of making daily builds.

At the point when daily builds are being made, the QA department will work with the team to decide how often builds will be submitted for testing. It is counter-productive to give QA a new build to test every day. They need to spend several days with a single build to make sure they have tested all aspects of the game thoroughly. QA will probably only want to look at a new build every three to four days during alpha. The frequency of builds submitted to the QA department will increase as the game gets closer to code release. The build schedule will keep production progressing on the game. People can check in their assets and know when the build will be ready and submitted to QA.

Build Checklist

Creating a build checklist is helpful for remembering all the steps that are necessary when creating builds. Figure 18.1 is a build checklist for creating builds of *Shanghai: Second Dynasty*. This game was a PC/Macintosh hybrid and had several technical steps in the build process. In addition, several other steps were required to ensure that the correct set of assets was used and that any assets not included in the build were removed, such as development cheats and saved game files.

The checklist also tracked which version of the build was being made and what files had changed since the last build. The build steps for *Shanghai: Second Dynasty* are difficult to understand out of context, but the checklist gives a good idea of complexities involved in making a build. This build checklist can also be given to QA so they can double-check the modifications during the code release process. Refer to Chapter 22, "Code Releasing," for more information code releasing builds.

Automated Builds

An automated build process is usually simple to set up and saves a lot of development time. If the process is automated, the person responsible for making the build does not have to take time to manually complete all the steps in the build checklist. If the build process for *Shanghai: Second Dynasty* were automated, the build would take less time, and fewer mistakes would be made. The checklist can provide the framework for what tasks can be automated.

All of these tasks can be automated by setting up a separate "build" machine, which has programming script that will instruct the machine to pull out all the updated code and assets from the version control system and compile them. When compiled, it will generate the latest build and copy it to an appropriate place on the computer network. This programming script can be set to run on a regular basis. For example, the build script can be set to run at midnight each night, so there is a new build waiting for the team in the morning.

Build Checklist– SD2 GM v.1103.1	COMPLETED
BEFORE STARTING TOAST:	
Delete old build from network	
Copy latest version of installer to network	
Confirm that e-reg.exe is removed	
Confirm that Earthlink folder is removed	
Confirm that correct localized assets are being used	
Check that .ldl files are all encrypted	
Delete setup (debug).exe from build	
Make sure "TEXT" file is included in setup folder	
Make sure "TEXT" file is hidden	
Test installer to make sure it is working properly from network	
Place updated files from QSI in build on my hard drive	
Change version number for Crash Logger in anet.inf file	
Change QA version number in anet.inf file	
Update tln.dat file, get latest version by making one from latest CD	
Encrypt tln.dat file	
Test encrypted tln.dat file	
Make sure sendcrsh.exe included	
Confirm that SAVED GAMES folder is empty	
Confirm that development cheat files are deleted	
Test build to confirm it is working properly	
Uncheck read only box, so that you can do MAC file-typing	
Copy game files to Builds folder (setup/data) on network	
Put .exe in correct folder (setup/HighResExe, setup/LowResExe)	
Make sure readme is at root of CD	
Make sure readme is in setup folder	
Make sure MAC applications are in proper folders	
Include most updated version of MAC readme	
Include most updated version of MAC installer	
Test Mac Installer	
File type PAT for MAC	
File type HTML text for MAC	
File type HTML JPEG for MAC	
File type BMP for MAC	
File type CRD for MAC	
File type TEXT for MAC	
File type DATA for MAC	
Copy build to Burner hard drive. Make sure build copied to correct partition	
Change MAC installer icon	
Change MAC CD icon	
Arrange icons in user friendly way in MAC window	
Restart MAC computer	
Empty Trash	
	(continued)

Build Checklist– SD2 GM v.1103.1	COMPLETED
LOCALIZED VERSIONS:	
Confirm that e-reg.exe is removed	
Confirm that Earthlink folder is removed	
Confirm that correct localized assets are being used	
Confirm "TEXT" file is include in setup folder	
Confirm "TEXT file is hidden	
Confirm version number for Crash Logger in anet.inf file	
Confirm sendcrsh.exe included	
Confirm that SAVED GAMES folder is empty	
Confirm that development cheat files are deleted	
Confirm readme is at root of CD and in "setup" folder	
Confirm most updated version of MAC readme is included	
Confirm correct MAC Installer and CD icon	
AFTER STARTING TOAST:	
Select MAC/ISO hybrid with Audio Tracks	
Select MAC button and highlight the correct partition	
Select PC button and drag over correct PC files	
Rename PC CD label	
Make sure file settings are set to JOLIET	
Remove MAC only files	
Add music tracks in AIF format	
Put 80 minute CD in drive	
Start burn	
Files that got updated since last build:	

FIGURE 18.1   Sample build checklist.

The automation process can be taken a step further in reducing time in other areas of development. For example, on certain days the build script could be instructed to copy the latest build to all the QA machines, so that when the QA testers reported to work in the morning, the latest build was ready for testing. The process can also include scripts that check the build for errors, such as misnamed files, missing assets, or incorrect file formatting. The error log can be automatically emailed to the team so that people can begin fixing the errors before the next build is created. The lead engineer can work with the development team to set up the best way to automate the build process.

A publicly visible indicator can be added to show when the build is not working. Clinton Keith of High Moon Studios has integrated lava lamps into the build process: "when an asset is checked into the game, there is an automated test suite that tests everything that is committed art- and code-wise to pipeline. If the tests determine that an asset has produced a fault, a red lava lamp is triggered to indicate that the build is broken. If the tests determine the asset is working correctly, a green lava lamp is triggered. The lamp is visible to the whole team and is a fun way to remind people to double-check the correctness of their work before checking it into the build."

MULTILINGUAL BUILDS

Multilingual masters save money on the replication process and are easier for operations to track. If a single disc contains English, French, and Italian versions of the game, there is only one master to keep track of, instead of three. Ultimately, this saves money, because a great number of copies can be made from the single multilingual master that can be distributed in three countries. If planning to make multilingual masters, consider the following issues:

Is there enough room on the disc to store multiple sets of language assets? As games get more robust, disc space becomes limited. Check to see how much storage space the full version of the game needs, and then calculate how much is needed for the localized assets. Even though DVDs contain a lot of storage space, they can quickly fill up with prerendered cinematics, art assets, audio assets, and demos from other games.

Is the release schedule flexible enough to accommodate a delay for multiple languages? If working on a multilingual master that contains English, French, and Spanish, the other versions will be at risk if one of the localizations is running behind schedule. When creating the schedule, consider this issue and include additional time to the overall schedule to account for delays. If the delay is severe, the language causing the delay might need to be removed from the multilingual disc and released as a stand-alone version instead.

How will the appropriate language be selected when loading the game? The game needs to know which language to install. The user can select the appropriate language at the beginning of the installation process, or the game can automatically display the appropriate language based on the hardware's language settings.

BUILD NOTES

Build notes should accompany any build that is submitted to QA or sent to someone outside the team. Build notes describe pertinent information about the build, such as what is working, what isn't working, and what bugs have been addressed since the last build.

Depending on who the audience is, the build notes will be different. All the build notes must provide basic details on the date the build was made and the version number of the build so they can be matched to the correct build. As development progresses, not everyone will receive every build, so noting the date and version number will allow people to see how long it has been since they last saw a working build.

For the Development Team

Build notes for the development team should focus on what is new in the build. This includes any crash bug fixes, any new features implemented, any changes to existing features, and any art assets that have been added or changed.

This type of information is especially useful to the QA department, because it lets them know which bugs have been fixed. They can regress these bugs by confirming these fixes in the current build and marking them closed in the bug-tracking database. If QA does not receive build notes, they might spend time regressing bugs that have not been fixed by the development team.

For Management

Build notes for management do not need to detail the specific bug numbers addressed since the last build reviewed, as they are more interested in seeing the progression of the game.

Instead, focus on what features are implemented, what features aren't implemented, and any feature changes that have occurred since the last build they reviewed. Also note why the change was made: was this a specific request from management, or was it something that the team changed? If the feature change was requested by management, it is good to note this because it might affect future milestone deliverables, especially if another feature was dropped to accommodate this request. Build notes can provide a good record of all the project milestones and can track the history of the game's progress.

If an independent developer is working with a publisher, the publisher might have a specific format for the build notes, which might be based on the milestone definitions defined in schedule. This makes it easier for the publisher to check the accuracy and completeness of the deliverable.

Other important information to include in the management build notes are instructions on how to install and run the build. This is especially important during the development process, as the PC builds will not have installers, and the console builds will need to be copied to a development kit in order to be properly viewed. This information should be basic and written in layman's terms so that anyone can copy the build and get it to work. If special software is needed in addition to the build, this needs to be included in the build, along with instructions on how to install it.

For Marketing and PR

Build notes for marketing and PR should definitely not mention specific bug numbers that have been addressed. Instead, the notes should focus on what key features are working and what percentage complete they are. These notes will be sent directly to journalists, along with preview and review builds, so make sure that the wording is positive, even when discussing visible bugs that appear in the game.

Include specific instructions for installing and running the game. Also include basic gameplay information—the controller scheme, the main gameplay mechanics, the goal of the missions, and so on. This is a good chance for the development team to communicate what areas of the game look good and are really fun to play. If there is time, hints and tips for playing the game can also be included.

Journalists often play builds that are still in development, so they will forgive anything that is listed in the build notes as being incomplete or having a bug. If the game only has 5 levels out of 10 that are playable, list which levels should be looked at in the build notes. Make sure to note which levels are not yet finished and the major things that are still being worked on in the level. Any placeholder assets also should also be mentioned in the notes.

PREVENTING PIRACY

Piracy, the act of selling illegal copies of game software, is an ongoing problem for game publishers, and they are always looking for ways to minimize the impact on the profitability of a game. According to the Entertainment Software Association (ESA), piracy costs the U.S. entertainment software industry several billion dollars each year. This number increases when adding the losses for the games distributed in international markets.

Piracy includes acts such as making and selling illegal copies of the game and offering the game for free download on the Internet (often referred to as "warez"). In some cases, the games made available through these illegal channels are not even the final versions.

Although these games are copyrighted and the copyright is enforceable under law, it is fairly easy for software pirates to create and sell copies of the game. Since piracy is an ongoing problem, software developers and publishers are taking steps to make this practice more difficult. The most common methods for deterring this behavior are copy protection schemes and lock-out schemes.

Copy Protection Schemes

A copy protection scheme prevents the user from making an illegal copy of the software. Such schemes include the following:

Writing unique data on a disc that must be verified before the game will launch: Macrovision® uses technology that places unique data on a disc that will not be transferred if a copy is made of the game. When the game launches, it checks for this unique piece of data, and if the data is unavailable, the game will not launch.

Serial numbers that must be verified before the product can be installed: Unique serial numbers, also referred to as *CD keys*, ship with each disc and are usually located on the back of the disc case or in the manual. When installing the game, the user is asked to supply this serial number. If unavailable or incorrect, the game will not install.

Dongles: A dongle is a piece of hardware that ships with the software and must be plugged into the computer before the program will run. It is an expensive method of protection and not usually used for games. It is more commonly found with high-end software development packages that cost thousands of dollars, such as MotionBuilder®.

Proprietary copy protection schemes: Some publishers are developing their own proprietary protection schemes. This allows some degree of protection because details on how the copy protection works are not readily available to the public, making it harder for software pirates to figure out ways to disable it.

These types of copy protection schemes are effective in preventing the casual user from making a copy or two of a game and giving it to a friend, but are not as effective against professionals. Piracy networks have the tools to crack these protection schemes and create massive numbers of software copies that are then sold on the black market. As a whole, the software industry is still finding ways to fight against this practice.

Lock-Out Schemes

Lock-out schemes are also used by publishers on PC games to cut down on gray market imports. Gray market imports are official versions of the game that are "unofficially" available in territories where the product was not distributed. The full

U.S. version of a game in the original packaging will often show up for sale in Korea, China, or other countries. One way to cut down on this practice is to lock out certain operating systems (OSs). For example, the U.S. version can lock out Korean, Chinese, or any other non-U.S. OS in the installer. The installer will check the OS before installing the game to make sure that it is a valid OS for the game. If not, the game will not install. These schemes are easy for hackers to work around, but they do provide a small level of security and will deter a casual user.

SUMMARY

A well-organized build process makes game development go more smoothly, and it is not difficult to set up an automated process that is even more effective. This chapter discussed how to set up and automate the build process and why this is important. It also includes a brief discussion of various copy protection schemes that help prevent piracy.

19 Software Ratings

In This Chapter

- Software Age Ratings
- Banned Games

INTRODUCTION

Most countries have an established board that assigns an age rating to entertainment software, similar to assigning a rating to a movie. The producer must be aware of what rating is desired when developing a game. For example, if the game's target market includes children 13 or older, the game content should stay within the appropriate rating guidelines for young teens. If a game depicts graphic violence, drug use, or sexuality, it will run the risk of being banned in certain countries—which is definitely not good for sales. This chapter discusses the international software ratings boards and the various guidelines they have for rating games.

SOFTWARE AGE RATINGS

Games are presented to the regulatory boards for review and are then assigned an age rating appropriate to the content of the game. In some countries, such as Germany, a game is required by law to receive a rating before it can be released for sale. In other countries, a game is not legally required to be submitted for a rating, but some of the bigger retail chains, such as Wal-Mart®, will not stock unrated games.

As a system, the ratings boards can be difficult to navigate internationally since there are several software ratings boards throughout the world. If a game is going to be published internationally, it needs to be reviewed by the ratings board for each country in which it is released. For example, the Entertainment Software Rating Board (ESRB) rates games that are released in the United States; Pan European Game Information (PEGI) rates games distributed in most of Europe; and the Office of Film & Literature Classification rates games released in Australia.

The ratings boards do not have a standardized ratings system; instead, each board sets its own guidelines for what is acceptable. Since these guidelines are subjective, it is difficult to determine exactly what types of content will place the game in which category. For example, the ESRB does not have specific rules on what constitutes a teen or mature rating. The publishers have to submit their game to find out the final rating, and if it is not the desired rating, they will need to make edits to the game or accept the assigned rating. When in pre-production, developers need to consider which rating they prefer and then develop the game within acceptable guidelines.

As a whole, the ratings boards are mainly concerned with the behaviors depicted in the game, not whether the gameplay is challenging and fun. They also do not want games with suggestive content to be readily available to young children or teenagers. The main areas of concern are as follows:

- Violence
- Adult themes
- Sex and nudity
- Language
- Drug use

The ratings boards are not opposed to games containing these elements; they just prefer that when these themes are depicted in the game, they are age-appropriate to the rating. For example, PEGI distinguishes between games with violence against realistic humans and games with violence against nonrealistic humans. Games that depict strong violence against realistic human characters can receive an automatic 18+ age rating. Games that depict strong violence against nonrealistic humans, such as aliens or fantastical characters, usually receive a 16+ age rating.

The boards are also concerned with games that include detailed depictions of how to commit criminal acts or how to use drug paraphernalia. In addition, the boards consider the overall themes in the game and will give a mature rating to games containing strong adult themes and situations. As a general rule of thumb, any strong or graphic depictions of the themes listed previously will likely get a rating that restricts sales of the game to people over the age of 18. Anything with a moderate depiction of the taboo themes will likely get a rating that restricts sales of the game to people over the age of 16.

Another component of the ratings systems is the content descriptors. These descriptors are used in conjunction with the age ratings to give more details on what specific aspects of the game might be considered mature material. For example, the ESRB has a list of more than 30 descriptors that cover a wide range of levels concerning violence, sexuality, and drugs. Some of these descriptors include "Blood," "Blood and Gore," "Language," "Simulated Gambling," "Tobacco Reference," "Tobacco," and "Comic Mischief." As a contrast, PEGI has only six content descriptors: "Violence," "Sex," "Drugs," "Fear," "Discrimination," and "Bad Language." Icons for each of these categories are presented next to the ratings logo.

If the developer is working for an international publisher, it is likely the publisher has someone devoted to tracking the requirements for all the ratings boards and making sure that the game is submitted for ratings at all the appropriate ones. If the developer is working with a smaller publisher, the developer might be responsible for submitting the game directly to these boards.

In addition to the ratings boards, there are some country-specific requirements that developers should be aware of when creating international content. Keep in mind that rating content is very subjective, and people have differing opinions about what they consider "extreme violence." When the game is designed, the developer should decide on the target age group and stay within the boundaries of what is considered acceptable content for this group.

ESRB (United States)

The ESRB, established by publishers of entertainment software, is a voluntary age ratings board for games distributed in the United States. Games are not required to be rated by the ESRB, but most mainstream retail outlets will not stock unrated games, which can be bad for game sales. The system consists of the following ratings:

Early Childhood (EC): Suitable for persons aged three and older. The game does not contain anything parents consider unsuitable for young children.

Everyone (E): Suitable for persons aged six and older. The game contains comic mischief, minimal violence, or infrequent use of mild language.

Everyone Ten and Older (E10+):   Suitable for persons 10 and older. The game contains comic mischief, mild violence, and mild language.

Teen (T):   Suitable for persons aged 13 and older. The game contains moderate violence, strong language, or suggestive themes.

Mature (M):   Suitable for persons aged 17 and older. The game contains strong violence, strong language, and/or mature themes.

Adults Only (AO):   Suitable for persons over the age of 18. The game contains graphic depictions of sex and violence.

Rating Pending (RP):   Game is waiting a final rating from the ESRB. Games cannot be published without getting a final rating.

In addition, more than 30 content descriptors can be used to supplement the age rating.

Other game components also affected by ESRB guidelines include the following:

Demos: The ESRB considers anything that is a playable or nonplayable sample of gameplay to be a demo. Demos must display the appropriate ESRB rating icon at the start of the demo, before the user sees the game.

Trailers: Trailers present the game's central thread or story, usually with a voiceover, and are nonplayable. Trailers must display the appropriate ESRB rating icon either at the beginning or end of the trailer and be accompanied by a voiceover.

Online components: If a game allows users to have unrestricted communication with other players over the Internet, it is required to display a notice that states: "ESRB Notice: Game Experience May Change During Online Play."

Expansion packs: Expansion packs that require the main game to run will have the same rating as the main game. Content offered in an expansion pack must remain within the guidelines for the age rating of the main game. For example, an "M" rated expansion pack cannot be created for a "T" rated game.

Downloadable content: As with expansion packs, downloadable content must remain within the guidelines for the main game's age rating.

Bonus content: Bonus content includes such things as interviews, strategy guides, and "making-of" videos. The bonus content is not required to be submitted for review, unless it contains extreme footage. If the bonus content is more extreme than the actual game, the game's overall rating might be higher. For example, a "T" rated game might end up with an "M" rating if some of the bonus content contains graphic violence.

Developers can check with the ESRB directly if they have any questions about the ratings and requirements. The ESRB works closely with developers to make sure that a game and its other components are properly rated.

INTERVIEW

Patricia Vance, President, Entertainment Software Rating Board

What materials must be submitted to the ESRB when applying for a rating?
In order to have a game certified with an ESRB rating, software publishers must fill out a detailed questionnaire explaining exactly what content is in the game. This questionnaire is submitted to ESRB along with actual videotaped footage of the game and relevant supplementary materials (for example, soundtracks, cheat codes, scripts, and so on). The video footage must not only accurately represent the final product as a whole, but it must also show the most extreme content of the game.

How does the rating system and process work?
The rating system includes two equal parts. The first part is the rating symbol, found on the front of the game packaging, which suggests age appropriateness. The second part contains content descriptors, found on the back of the game packaging, clearly stating why a game received a particular rating or indicating content that might be of interest or concern.

After a game submission is received and checked for completeness, a minimum of three raters independently view video footage of each game and, for every scene, as well as the overall product, recommend a rating and content descriptors they deem most appropriate. In rating a game, raters must consider a wide range of content elements including, but not limited to, violence, sex, humor, language, and the use of controlled substances. They also must weigh other factors such as player control, realism, reward system, frequency, context, and overall intensity.

ESRB compares the raters' independent recommendations to make sure that there is consensus. Usually, the raters agree on an overall age rating, and their recommendation becomes final. However, when the raters recommend different ratings, additional raters will review the game in order to reach a consensus. After consensus on a rating is reached, ESRB issues an official rating certificate to the game's publisher. If a publisher is not satisfied with the rating issued, it may resubmit the game with changes, and the process starts anew.

It is critical to note that ESRB raters have no ties to the industry and are specially trained to rate computer and video games. Most ESRB raters have prior experience with children, either as parents, caretakers, or through prior work and education. They are part-time employees of the ESRB and typically attend one three-hour rater session per week. The ESRB strives to recruit raters who are demographically diverse by age (must be over 18), marital status, sex, race, and cultural backgrounds to reflect the U.S. population overall.

$\rightarrow$

Finally, after a product ships to retail, ESRB randomly tests games to ensure complete content disclosure during the submission process. In the event that the ESRB discovers undisclosed content that would have affected a rating assignment, enforcement measures are taken, involving the imposition of significant fines and/or corrective actions (for example, restickering or recalling product).

How long does it take for the ESRB to evaluate a game and assign a rating?
When submission materials are complete, it takes an average of five business days to evaluate a game and assign a rating.

At what point in the development process should a game be submitted for a rating?
A game should be submitted when all of the pertinent content is complete, including graphics, sound effects, music, and dialogue. Often the product is submitted prior to testing, which is one of the major reasons why ESRB requires content be submitted on videotape.

Is a rating required from the ESRB in order to distribute entertainment software in the United States?
The ESRB rating system is voluntary, although virtually all games that are sold at retail in the United States and Canada are rated by the ESRB. This is thanks in part to the commitment of major retailers not to carry games that have not been rated by the ESRB. The video game industry created the ESRB in 1994 as its self-regulatory body to ensure that parents and other consumers have accurate and reliable information about game content prior to purchase.

If developers are looking to achieve a particular rating, can the ESRB advise them on what needs to change in order to achieve this rating?
After the ESRB informs the submitting company of the rating assignment, reflecting the consensus of the independent raters, the submitting company has three choices:

1. Accept the rating assignment.
2. Consider making changes to the game and resubmitting materials to possibly receive a different rating assignment.
3. Formally appeal a rating assignment before an industry-appointed appeals board.

The submitting company might request a copy of the original rater consensus report to understand what content in the game resulted in a specific rating assignment, and any changes it should decide to make to the resubmitted product will be at its sole discretion.

$\rightarrow$

Are there specific ESRB guidelines on exactly what differentiates a "T" or an "M" rating?

There are general guidelines and a sense of parity about how certain types of content relate to various rating categories, such as intense and prolonged scenes of violence, nudity, sexual content, language, use of controlled substances, real gambling, and so on. Beyond those obvious types of content, there are few hard and fast rules when it comes to rating games. The manner in which a particular act is depicted, the context in which it occurs, the intensity of the image itself, the reward system, and the degree of player control all can greatly affect which rating category and content descriptors are ultimately assigned to the game. And raters must use their own judgment as to what content they feel is most relevant and important to inform consumers about.

It is worth noting that, according to a survey regularly conducted by Peter D. Hart Research Associates commissioned by the ESRB, parents overwhelmingly agree with the ratings assigned by the ESRB. In 2004, parents agreed with ESRB ratings 83 percent of the time, and 5 percent of the time parents thought they were too strict. This level of agreement tells us that the ratings provide an accurate indication of game content and reflect the tastes and values of mainstream America, most importantly those parents who use the system to help determine which games are appropriate for their children.

PEGI (Europe)

PEGI was established in 2003 and is a single rating system that replaces the country-specific ratings systems for most of the European countries. The PEGI system is currently applicable to games released in Austria, Belgium, Denmark, Finland, France, Greece, Ireland, Italy, Luxembourg, Netherlands, Norway, Portugal, Spain, Sweden, Switzerland, and the UK. Germany is not represented by this system, as they are rated by the Unterhaltungssoftware SelbstKontrolle (USK), their own national ratings system.

The PEGI system consists of the following ratings:

3+:   Suitable for ages three and older. The product does not contain anything that parents would find unsuitable for young children.

7+:   Suitable for ages seven and older. The product contains things that might be stressful or scary for young children, occasional violence against fantasy characters, or nudity in a nonsexual context.

12+: Suitable for ages 12 and older. The product contains graphic violence against fantasy characters, nongraphic violence against realistic humans or animals, moderate sexuality, or mild profanity.

16+: Suitable for ages 16 and older. The product contains graphic violence against unrealistic humans or animals, strong sexual content, illegal drug use, or the glamorization of crime.

18+: Suitable for ages 18 and older. The product contains graphic depictions of violence against realistic humans or animals, graphic depictions of sexual acts, glamorization of drug use, racism, or detailed information on how to commit criminal acts.

They also have six content descriptors: "Violence," "Sex," "Drugs," "Fear," "Discrimination," and "Bad Language."

Their rating process is more self-regulatory than the ESRB's. The developer fills out a form, and the rating is automatically generated based on the answers to the questions. The form contains a series of "yes" and "no" questions that are divided into sections based on the amount of mature content a game contains. For example, the first group of questions is concerned with graphic depictions of sex, drugs, violence, and racial hatred, particularly in relation to realistic humans or animals. If the answer is "yes" to any of these questions, the rating is automatically 18+. The second set of questions is concerned with strong depictions of sexual themes, violence, drugs, and the glamorization of crime, particularly in relation to nonrealistic humans and animals. If the answer is "yes" to any of these, the rating is automatically 16+, and so on.

After the rating has been generated, the Netherlands Institute for the Classification of Audiovisual Media (NICAM) reviews and approves the rating. NICAM has been contracted to administer the PEGI system and must check all ratings for accuracy. When the rating is approved, the publisher is provided with the appropriate ratings logo and content descriptor logos for their packaging.

Although the goal of the PEGI system is to create a single rating system for Europe, some exceptions must be noted for the UK and Germany.

VSC and BBFC (United Kingdom)

Although the United Kingdom uses the PEGI system, its ratings are administered by the Video Standards Council (VSC), not NICAM (who administers the PEGI system for all the other countries). Additionally, the VSC determines whether a game needs to be legally submitted to the British Board of Film Classification (BBFC) for further classification. Some games with strong adult content must be classified by the BBFC before they can be legally distributed in the UK. Most games are exempt from this submission. If a game required to be submitted to the BBFC is released without the classification, the publishers and any retail stores carrying the game could be criminally prosecuted.

When a game is submitted to the BBFC, the publisher must provide a copy of the game, along with flow charts and other documentation, so that the evaluators can walk through the game to assess it. The classifications applicable to games are as follows:

U: This is an advisory only rating. The product is suitable for young children ages four and up to play unsupervised.

PG: This is an advisory only rating. The product is suitable for young children ages eight and up.

12:    This is an age restriction. No one under the age of 12 will be allowed to buy a "12" rated product.

15:    This is an age restriction. No one under the age of 15 will be allowed to buy this product.

18:    This is an age restriction. No one under the age of 18 will be allowed to buy this product.

USK (Germany)

Germany has very strict age ratings that are assigned and regulated by its national ratings board, Unterhaltungssoftware SelbstKontrolle (USK). It is a legal requirement for all games to be submitted for ratings. Software companies will be prosecuted if they do not comply. Their age restrictions are as follows:

No age restriction: Games that are fine for all ages and contain nothing offensive or questionable.

Suitable for ages 6 and over: Games that have an element of competition and are clearly perceived by young children as unrealistic.

Suitable for ages 12 and over: Games have an overt competitive element and require the player to understand complex concepts. Players can differentiate between fantasy and reality.

Suitable for ages 16 and over: Games in this category require the player to have a more developed degree of maturity and social conscience. The games can have strong adult themes but should not dwell on them.

Not suitable for persons under the age of 18:   Games in this category are deemed to have an unbalanced component of violence that is depicted in detail. In some cases, games in this category are banned in Germany, even after they are rated.

Germany is known for having more restrictive age ratings than other countries, and these age rating guidelines do not offer much insight into what's allowed and what's not. Developers should err on the side of caution if they are planning to release a game in Germany. In general, if a game is going to be released in Germany, it should follow these guidelines to ensure that it is not banned or given an 18+ rating:

Minimize blood and gore in the game: In the past, games released in Germany could not have any blood or gore in the game. This requirement has been relaxed in recent years, provided the game does not contain graphic and gratuitous violence. If erring on the side of caution, blood can be removed from the game completely or changed to a different color. Gratuitous gore must be removed: do not show parts of dead bodies blowing off, or parts of bodies lying around the game world; the parts must disappear along with the dead bodies.

Avoid the use of profanity: Profane language is another area that is closely watched in Germany. Dialogue might have to be revised for the German version if it contains a lot of profanity.

Don't use symbols associated with racial hatred: Germany is tough on hate symbols, particularly those associated with Nazis. Swastikas and other references to Nazi involvement are generally not allowed, unless they are in a historical context, such as a realistic game during the World II era. Even then, the symbols are closely regulated, and the developer might be required to remove them before releasing the game in Germany.

The submission process is more complex than with some of the other ratings boards. Since a rating is required, the self-regulatory aspect of the PEGI and ESRB systems is removed. A valid game submission to the USK includes game code, packaging, manual, cheat codes, walkthroughs, and the submission form with all the required game information. After these materials are received, the USK examines them closely and determines whether the game is violating any laws or contains material that will cause the game to be banned. If the game is suitable for distribution, the board will assign a rating to it and issue a ratings certificate. In most cases, a final version of the game is required before final approval is granted.

OFLC (Australia)

The Office of Film & Literature Classification (OFLC) is the entity that classifies games for release in Australia. This board is regulated by the Australian government, and all games are required to be classified before being released in Australia. Their classifications are as follows:

G: Advisory rating that means the product is suitable for all ages. Very mild violence, discreetly implied sexuality, mild language, and discreet drug references are allowed as long as they are justified by context. No sexual violence is permitted.

G8+: Advisory rating that means the product is suitable for children ages 8 and up. Parental guidance is suggested for anyone under the age of 15. Mild depictions of violence, drug use, language, and sexuality are permitted as long as they are justified by context. No sexual violence is permitted.

M15+: Advisory rating that means the product is not suitable for children under the age of 15. Moderate violence, drug, use, language, and sexuality are allowed as long as they are justified by context. Sexual violence should be infrequent and justified by context.

MA15+: Age restriction that means children under the age of 15 cannot view or buy the product unless in the company of a parent or guardian. Strong themes and depictions of violence, drug use, sexuality, and language are allowed as long as justified by context.

RC: This means the product has been refused classification. Any game that exceeds the guidelines for an MA15+ rating will be refused classification and cannot be distributed for sale in Australia.

The submission process is straightforward. The developer sends the OFLC a copy of the game, an application, information on how to play the game, and any statement disclosing contentious material in the game and instructions on how to access this material. Additionally, a video of the material in question can also been sent. The board sends these materials to an independent evaluator and assigns a classification based on their recommendation.

CERO (Japan)

The Computer Entertainment Rating Organization (CERO) is the organization that classifies games for release in Japan. Their rating categories are as follows:

- All ages
- Ages 12 and up
- Ages 15 and up
- Ages 18 and up

They judge each submission on the degree of sex, violence, language, and socially unacceptable behaviors and assign an age division category. In addition, they have nine content descriptors used in conjunction with these ratings for "romance," "sex," "violence," "horror," "gambling," "crime," "alcohol/tobacco," "drugs," and "language."

The submission process requires the developer or publisher to submit a copy of the game, along with documentation on how to play the game, and a videotape of anything that might be considered questionable or excessive. These materials are reviewed by the board, and a rating is assigned.

KMRB (Korea)

The Korea Media Rating Board (KMRB) rates games for release in South Korea. Their ratings categories are as follows:

- All
- 18+

According to their Web site (*www.kmrb.or.kr*), they are concerned with content that might be undesirable for the following reasons:

- Violating the constitutional and democratic order and damaging the national honor
- Containing graphic depictions of violence or other taboo areas that are harmful to public morals and might disturb the social order
- Damaging to the diplomatic relationships and national identity and, thereby, adversely affecting the national interests

Games will be banned in South Korea if the board considers the content to be offensive. In 2004, *Tom Clancy's Ghost Recon 2* was refused a rating by the KMRB and subsequently banned. The storyline involved a rogue North Korean general who was trying to consolidate his power in North Korea. The ratings board found this story to be too extreme and sensitive for the Korean market.

RECOMMENDED RESOURCES

If you have any questions about how your game's content might be received in another country, you will find the following resources on software ratings and classifications to be useful.

$\rightarrow$

Software Ratings Boards

Entertainment Software Rating Board (ESRB) —*www.esrb.org*
Pan European Game Information (PEGI) —*www.pegi.info*
Unterhaltungssoftware SelbstKontrolle (USK)—*www.usk.de*
Office of Film & Literature Classification (OFLC)—*www.oflc.gov.au*
Computer Entertainment Rating Organization (CERO)—*www.cero.gr.jp*
Korean Media Rating Board (KMRB)—*www.kmrb.or.kr*

Classification Boards

Video Standards Council (VSC)—*www.videostandards.org.uk*
British Board of Film Classification (BBFC)—*www.bbfc.co.uk*
Netherlands Institute for the Classification of Audiovisual Media (NICAM)—*www. nicam.cc*

Software Publishing Associations

Entertainment Software Association (ESA)—*www.theesa.com*
Interactive Software Federation of Europe (ISFE)—*http://www.isfe-eu.org*
The Entertainment and Leisure Software Publishers Association (ELSPA)—*www. elspa.com*
Syndicate des Editeurs de Logiciels de Loisirs (SELL)—*www.sell.fr*
Asociación Española de Distribuidores y Editores de Software de Entretenimiento (ADESE)—*www.adese.es*

BANNED GAMES

In general, most countries shy away from games with graphic depictions of violence, sexuality, and drug use, as there is concern about the effect these depictions of sex and violence might have on young people. Lauren Gonzalez, the author of an excellent article published on the Gamespot Web site titled "When Two Tribes Go to War: A History of Videogame Controversy," discusses several key controversies surrounding games and their depictions of sex and violence.

Her general premise is that there are three main areas:

- Games deemed so violent or controversial that governments and legal bodies intervene
- Games controversial enough that retailers pull them from store shelves
- Games that solicit a negative response from specific groups who feel maligned by the game's message or mission

For more detailed information about these controversies, this article is recommended reading. It goes into thorough detail that is beyond the scope of what can be covered in this book.

As a response to these controversies, countries are likely to ban games if they are deemed to have unsuitable content that depicts graphic violence, sex, or drug use. Additionally, the games may be banned if they provide detailed information on how to commit violent and criminal acts or use drugs.

These ratings are taken seriously, and if a game does not meet the classification standards, it runs the risk of being banned from the country. For example, in 2001, Australia's Office of Film and Literature Classification (OFLC) refused a classification for *Grand Theft Auto III*, and the game was subsequently banned in Australia. The developer was allowed to edit the game to make it suitable for sale in Australia.

SUMMARY

Software age ratings ensure that the game content is appropriate for the target audience. Extremely violent or controversial games should be available only to adults, and the content in children's games should not contain inappropriate topics or realistic violence. This chapter discussed the process for submitting a game for a rating and presented information on what type of content is appropriate for each rating.

20 Localization

In This Chapter

- Creating International Content
- Localization-Friendly Code
- Level of Localization
- Localization Plan
- Organizing Assets for Translation
- Integrating Translated Assets
- Testing
- Console Submission
- Localization Checklist

INTRODUCTION

Localization is often the last thing on people's minds and the last thing that is completed in the game development cycle. However, if localizations are planned in advance, they can be completed in a timely fashion and can get the game more exposure in international markets. Currently, most publishers automatically plan to localize their games into French, German, Spanish, and Italian. Korean, Japanese, and Chinese localizations are becoming more common, and publishers continue to add more languages to their game catalogs on a continual basis. Because of this, developers need to think about how to create game content that is easily localized and has universal appeal to players in different countries.

This chapter presents an overview of the main issues to consider and ways to plan a successful localization. The topic of localization is quite large, and it is beyond the scope of this book to delve into specific details. For more information on localizations, please refer to *The Game Localization Handbook* by Heather Maxwell Chandler. Full reference information on this book is available in Appendix B, "Resources."

CREATING INTERNATIONAL CONTENT

For starters, think about how the game's name and content will sell in other countries. Will a *Route 66* adventure game sell many copies in Japan if no one there has any idea what Route 66 is? How about trying to market a real-time strategy game called *Third World* in Mexico, where connotations of this phrase are completely different than in the United States? Will a cricket game sell very well in the United States? Creating special hooks or exclusive content to appeal to international markets helps the game garner more regional publicity. It also give the marketing department a strong feature to build into a country-specific marketing campaign. If making a car-racing game, include a special French car that is available exclusively in the French version. If designing a skateboarding game, include a skate park from Japan or Italy. The same goes for music. If licensing music from well-known American bands, replace one of the tracks with the hottest band in Germany.

Avoid making specific references to culturally-specific situations, such as "speed dating," unless it is necessary for game design. Also don't use slang like, "Keep it on the D.L." and "That is whack!" This will prevent your game from appearing too dated. This also makes it easier to translate the game for distribution in other countries.

Be aware of how the age ratings are defined in other countries. For example, Germany has strict censorship guidelines, particularly in regards to blood and violence. Adhering to Germany's guidelines might require a separate German master with the blood and violence minimized. Refer to Chapter 19, "Software Ratings," for detailed information on international age ratings.

LOCALIZATION-FRIENDLY CODE

Localization-friendly code is easy to localize. When developing localization-friendly code, asset organization, asset integration, and linguistic testing are taken into account, along with international alphabets, user-interface (UI) design, and compatibility between languages. Even if a developer is working on a game that does not have localized versions currently planned, they might be needed after the original game has shipped. Developing localization-friendly code is a good practice for all game developers, as this saves many localization headaches in the long run.

Many factors are considered when planning for localization-friendly code. Some main areas to consider are the following:

- How will the language assets be organized in the game?
- What type of fonts and special characters are supported?
- Will localized keyboard inputs be supported?
- What platform-specific areas need to be considered?
- Will the game support subtitles or lip-syncing?

If these issues and others are planned for in the pre-production phase, localization-friendly code is easily created.

Trying to retrofit code so that it is localization-friendly is not recommended; it is time consuming, challenging, and introduces a number of bugs. It can be done, but the time and risk must be carefully considered before attempting a code change of this magnitude.

Language Assets

The organization of the game assets has a great impact on the ease of localization. Organizing the language-specific text, art, and audio assets in a centrally located place in the game code is a simple solution. By placing the assets into a separate language-specific directory within the game, the development team knows exactly where all the necessary language assets are located.

One way to organize the assets is to place them in a language-specific directory that is labeled with the appropriate language; for example, "English." Figure 20.1 is an example of how this directory structure looks. In each of the English, French, and German folders are subdirectories for "Audio," "Cinematics," and "Text." A directory called "Art" could be added if there were art assets to localize. If multiple languages are not supported in the game, the directory for all the language assets can be labeled "Language," and the appropriate set of language assets can be stored here.

FIGURE 20.1 Directory structure for organizing language assets.

Easily integrating the localized assets is another benefit of having the assets organized in a centralized directory structure. The developer knows exactly where the integrated files belong in the game, and in an ideal situation, is able to drop the assets into the appropriate directory and have a fully localized game.

Text Assets

Store the game text in a format that is easy to access and integrate. Since a majority of the developer's localization time can be spent organizing the text for translation and integrating it back into the files, a lot of time is saved in the process if the text is logically organized. Some ways to make text assets more localization friendly include the following:

Do not hard-code text: Basically, this means don't include any game text within the code files. This makes it difficult to organize the text for translation, because the developer will have to search through a lot of game code to locate the text to be translated.

Store text in easily accessible files: Game text available in separate files is easy to organize, integrate, and test because the developer knows exactly which files must be localized.

Art Assets

Art assets can be difficult to localize because specific software, such as Adobe Photoshop, is required to manipulate them, along with someone who knows how to use the application. However, if a process is set up so that an artist is not required to localize graphic files, the process is more efficient. A few ways to make art assets more localization friendly include the following:

Put the text in a separate layer in the image file: If the text is embedded in the image, an artist will spend extra time integrating translated text. If doing multiple languages, the time quickly adds up. If the text is located in a separate layer in the image file, the text can be quickly replaced.

Use game code to display the text in the images: If the engineer can program this capability into the game engine, there will be fewer art assets to localize. The game engine pulls the appropriate text from the text files and displays it in the images.

Voiceover Assets

The process for localizing VO files closely mirrors the process for recording the original files in the source language and is just as time consuming. Ways to make voiceover assets more localization-friendly include the following:

Use an established naming convention: The VO files must be named according to an established naming convention. This naming convention includes the rules for indicating a VO file's language. For example, all the French VO files could end with "_f" and the German files could end with "_g." These naming conventions prevent the developer from having to open a file to figure out what language it is.

Cinematic dialogue, music, and special effects should be on separate audio tracks: If the dialogue used in prerendered cinematics is on a separate audio track, it is easy to integrate the localized VO. The developer can swap in the localized VO file to replace the original VO.

International Characters and Fonts

The engine needs to be able to handle both uppercase and lowercase versions of special linguistic characters, such as ä, Õ, and Ç. Currently, Unicode is the standard for representing text characters, since it provides a unique number for every character regardless of the platform, software program, or programming language. This gives the game code the capability to display more than 65,000 unique characters, including Asian alphabets and Cyrillic. Keep in mind that if the language uses an Asian alphabet or Cyrillic font, the engine must be double-byte enabled and capable of displaying bidirectional text.

Choose a font that is easily read on televisions and computer monitors. Televisions display at a lower resolution, so don't choose fonts that will be difficult to read when they are displaying international characters. Keep in mind that some languages, such as Japanese, display better in larger fonts. However, make sure that the font size is not too large. If it is too large, there will be issues with overlap when displaying other languages.

User Interface

The User Interface (UI) has many localization challenges. The text usually overlaps or is cut off, forcing the translator to come up with an abbreviation or an alternative translation that will fit the space better. Keep these things in mind when designing a localization-friendly UI:

Leave extra room in the UI for localized text: As a general rule of thumb, plan for localized text being about 25 to 30 percent longer than English text. Extra space must be designed in the UI to accommodate the longer words.

Use scalable UI elements when possible: If the UI buttons, drop-down menus, text boxes, and other elements can scale depending on the size of the text, localized text can be accommodated more easily. For example, if paragraphs of text are going to be displayed in a text box, don't put a hard limit on the amount of text that can fit in the box. Instead, program the text box to display a scroll bar or arrows so that the user can scroll up or down in the text as necessary.

Use icons whenever possible: Using icons is a useful way to avoid localized text. Use icons that will be recognized universally. For example, use the silhouette of a single person to indicate "Single player" and the silhouettes of two people to indicate "Multiplayer."

Avoid cluttered UI screens: If the UI is cluttered with a lot of text and information, the screens might need to be redesigned for the larger text strings in localized versions.

Support international date and currency formats: If the game will include dates and currencies, the UI should display the information in a format appropriate to the country.

Keyboard Input

For PC games, determine how the keyboard commands are mapped to the keyboard. If the keyboard commands are mapped by location (that is, the far left key on the bottom row will reload a weapon), make sure this key functions the same way on all international keyboards. Also, the manual writer for each language will want to make a note of the exact key when writing the manual, since the name of the key will be different in each country. If the keyboard commands are mapped directly to the keys (that is, ~ will switch the weapon the player is using), make sure that all versions of the keyboards have this key available. If not, it is necessary to pick a different key to map the command to for that language.

PAL versus NTSC

If console games are being developed, it is important that the game engine supports both the NTSC and PAL video standards. NTSC is the video display standard for the United States and Japan. In this format, the video image delivers 525 lines of resolution at 60 half-frames per second. PAL is the video display standard for Europe, and the video image delivers 625 lines at 50 half-frames per second.

If the game does not support PAL standards, it will display incorrectly on PAL video monitors. If an NTSC image is displayed on a PAL video monitor, the image will appear to have black bars at the top and bottom of the screen, because NTSC has 100 fewer lines of resolution. In addition, the image will flicker because a game running at 60 half-frames per second is being displayed on a monitor that can only support a refresh rate of 50 half-frames per second.

Additionally, the console developers Sony®, Microsoft®, and Nintendo® each have specific technical requirements, as their game standards differ in Asia, Europe, and the United States. These requirements must be addressed in all international versions.

Other Technical Considerations

You must consider several other technical things when creating localization-friendly code:

Subtitles: Will the game have subtitling functionality? If so, the publisher might choose to subtitle the voiceover files for the localized versions, instead of fully translating them.

Lip-syncing: How will lip-syncing be handled in-game and for prerendered cinematics? The common way is dubbing, in which the localized dialogue replaces the original source dialogue, and the animator attempts to match up the character's mouth movements as best as he can.

Compatibility between languages: If there is an online component to the game, users from different countries can usually play against each other. If this is the case, the different localized versions must be able to play with each other.

LEVEL OF LOCALIZATION

The extent to which game assets are localized can vary from project to project, depending on how many resources are available to invest in the localization and the likely return on the investment. The localization process is scaled according to the needs and expectations of the game. There are three main levels for localizing games:

Packaging and manual localization: Localizing the game's packaging and manual, commonly referred to as "box and docs," is one level of localization. The game code and language are unchanged from the original version, but the manual, packaging, and other supporting documentation are localized into the target language. The developer might have to assist the translator with understanding the game-specific terms to be translated for the packaging. Additionally, on PC versions, the developer might have to double-check the functionality of international keyboards to ensure that the English keyboard commands are carried over correctly to international keyboards.

Partial localization: A partial localization means that only the in-game text is translated, and none of the voiceover files are translated. This method is cost effective, since time and money are not spent to translate the extra voiceover text, set up recording sessions, hire actors, process the sound files, and complete other tasks necessary to localize voiceovers. In some cases, the voiceover files can be subtitled, but only if the code supports this feature.

Full localization: A full localization includes translating the text, voiceover, manual, and packaging. Often, a small team within the main development team will be charged with the completion of the localizations. This team works closely with the main team to organize the assets for translation, integrate the assets into the game, and coordinate the localization testing. This can be costly and challenging if the game code is not localization-friendly and the assets are not well organized within the code.

LOCALIZATION PLAN

Before localizing a game, work with sales to determine whether the projected sales point to a profitable localization. Start by figuring out how many assets need to be localized, how much the translations will cost, and how much development time is needed. This information is also necessary for any external vendors who want to bid on producing the localizations.

If an external vendor is going to do the localization work, a lot of burden is removed from the development team. Using an external source to develop the localized versions is a smart way to go if the team needs to be focused on the main game. In some cases, an external vendor will be used for translation and testing, while the team is responsible for organizing the assets for translation and integrating the localized assets into the game. However the work is divided, it needs to be accounted for in the localization plan.

Figure 20.2 illustrates an asset overview form that is used to estimate the number of assets to translate. The developer fills in the requested information and then sends it to the translator for cost estimates. This form is a good starting point for collecting all the necessary information about the localizations. Since this form provides a general overview of the project and is filled out before the game assets are final, estimates will have to suffice.

Title	Platform	US Code Release Date	Foreign Languages	Localization Contact
TEXT ASSETS IN-GAME	**quantity**	**delivered format**	**final received format**	**Comments**
number of words as in-game text strings				
number of text files to be modified				
ART ASSETS	**quantity**	**delivered format**	**final received format**	**Comments**
number of words in images				
number of art files to be modified				
AUDIO ASSETS IN-GAME	**quantity**	**delivered format**	**final received format**	**Comments**
number of words in script				
number of audio files to be modified				
number of main speakers				
number of supporting speakers				
Total time of voice-overs (min:sec)				
CINEMATICS ASSETS	**quantity**	**delivered format**	**final received format**	**Comments**
number of words in script				
number of movies to be modified				
number of main speakers				
number of supporting speakers				
seconds performed as lip-synch				
Total time of cut-scenes (min:sec)				
PRINTED MATERIALS	**quantity**	**delivered format**	**final received format**	**Comments**
Manual—number of words				
Manual—number of graphics to be modified				
Box—number of words				
Box—number of graphics to modify				
Keyboard ref. card—number of words				
Any other printed materials?				

FIGURE 20.2 Asset overview form.

Simultaneous Release

Ideally, localized versions of the game are released simultaneously with the primary version or as closely as possible. This is very difficult to do, especially if no advanced planning has been done. The main obstacles to achieving simultaneous code release are working with assets that are not final and starting the asset integration process too late. Schedule deadlines for finalizing batches of assets that can be sent off for translation in order to mitigate these obstacles.

The disadvantage of not working with final code means that the QA department will take longer to test since they will be finding a lot more bugs, and these bugs will be duplicated across all the versions. One last deterrent for trying to release all versions simultaneously is the increase in manpower and workload. If the development team has to complete the localized versions at the same time as the primary version, they split their already limited time between the U.S. and localized versions.

Instead of trying to release the localized versions simultaneously, some developers prefer to wait until the game's primary version is completely finished before beginning work on localized builds. The advantages to this are as follows:

Code is final: If the code is localization-friendly, the code base probably will not change. Therefore, most of the team can be off-loaded to work on other projects. About two–three core people are needed to integrate the assets and create builds. The other advantage is that the QA department will not find as many code-related bugs.

Source assets are final: If the source assets are final, tracking localized assets will be much easier. The translator will not receive constant updates from the development team on text or VO changes, greatly simplifying the asset tracking, translation, and integration process.

Schedule

Create a rough schedule of all the tasks needed to complete the localization. The duration of the tasks depends on how many assets need to be localized and tested. When planning a schedule, include task breakdowns and time estimates for these major areas:

Organizing assets for translations: Make sure that the all the assets are organized so that the text and context are very clear for all the translations needed. This includes such things as creating a glossary, adding time codes to the VO script, and creating a master sheet with all the in-game text.

Translations: Get estimates from the translator for how long it will take to have everything translated. If doing voiceover, include time for translating the script, casting actors, recording the voiceover, adding special effects, and converting to the necessary audio format.

Integrating translated assets: Schedule time for things such as integrating text files, modifying art files, adding localized VO, and compiling the build.

Testing localized builds: This can be one of the most time-consuming aspects of localizations. All the translations need to be checked in the game to make sure no bugs were introduced when the localized assets were added. Also, check to make sure that the translations are displaying correctly in the game. Allow for several rounds of testing and bug fixing.

Of course, each localized project will have a different schedule, but if localizations are planned for in advance and run according to schedule, expect to spend on average two–three months in production on the localized versions. Figure 20.3 is an example of an initial localization schedule with general estimates. This schedule is created in pre-production and communicated to the localization team in order to plan for key dates. As the project moves forward into production, a detailed schedule is created to reflect the specific languages being localized, the level of localization, and the exact release dates.

Task	Languages	Task Resource	Task Start Duration	Task End Date	Date
Asset freeze for English VO assets	German	Development Team	1 day	July 5, 2006	July 5, 2006
Asset freeze for English text assets	German	Development Team	1 day	July 26, 2006	July 26, 2006
VO assets organized for translation	German	Development Team	3 days	July 6, 2006	July 9, 2006
Text assets organized for translation	German	Development Team	3 days	July 27, 2006	July 30, 2006
Translate in-game text	German	Translator	2 weeks	July 30, 2006	August 13, 2006
Translate VO script	German	Translator	2 weeks	July 9, 2006	July 23, 2006
Cast actors for localized VO recordings	German	Sound Studio	1 week	July 9, 2006	July 23, 2006
Record and process localized VO files	German	Sound Studio	3 weeks	July 23, 2006	August 13, 2006
Integrating localized text files	German	Development Team	1 week	August 13, 2006	August 20, 2006
Integrating localized VO files	German	Development Team	1 week	August 13, 2006	August 20, 2006
Linguistic Testing	German	Linguistic Testers	4 weeks	August 27, 2006	September 17, 2006
Functionality Testing	German	Functionality Testers	3 weeks	August 20, 2006	September 17, 2006
Approval process for third party publisher	German	Third Party Publisher	6 weeks	September 17, 2006	October 29, 2006
Ship Date	German	n/a	1 day	October 29, 2006	October 29, 2006

FIGURE 20.3   Initial localization schedule

Budget

After the schedule and the asset overview form is completed, costs can be calculated. The translator provides costs for translations, and the development team provides development and testing costs. Figure 20.4 is a form to determine the development and testing costs. Fill in the daily rate of the people doing the work and then multiply it by the amount of time they spend on the project. This is just an estimate, so be sure to track the actual time spent on the project to see how close it comes to the original estimate. This information can be used to estimate future localizations.

Translating	Resource Name	Task	Daily Rate	Est. Days	Cost
	Engineer	Extract text for localization	$0.00	00000	$0.00
	Associate Producer	Organize assets for translation	$0.00	00000	$0.00
Integrating	**Resource Name**	**Task**	**Daily Rate**	**Est. Days**	**Cost**
	Engineer	Asset integration, making builds for 4 languages	$0.00	00000	$0.00
	2D Artist	Update 2D art (if necessary)	$0.00	00000	$0.00
	3D Artist	Localize Cinematics	$0.00	00000	$0.00
	Associate Producer	Assist with asset integration for 4 languages	$0.00	00000	$0.00
Testing	**Resource Name**	**Task**	**Daily Rate**	**Est. Days**	**Cost**
	QC Manager	Copyprotect GMs (4 languages)	$0.00	00000	$0.00
	Asst. System Admin	Set up localized machines (4 languages)	$0.00	00000	$0.00
	QA Analyst	Test game (2 rounds of testing, GM certification)	$0.00	00000	$0.00
	Tester (German)	Test game (2 rounds of testing, GM certification)	$0.00	00000	$0.00
	Tester (French)	Test game (2 rounds of testing, GM certification)	$0.00	00000	$0.00
	Tester (Italian)	Test game (2 rounds of testing, GM certification)	$0.00	00000	$0.00
	Tester (Spanish)	Test game (2 rounds of testing, GM certification)	$0.00	00000	$0.00
	Engineer	Fix bugs, make builds	$0.00	00000	$0.00
	Associate Producer	Fix Bugs	$0.00	00000	$0.00
			Grand Total	**00000**	**$0.00**

FIGURE 20.4   Estimate for development costs.

Staff

One person on the development team, usually an associate producer, must be in charge of managing all aspects of the localization process. This person is the main point of contact for all localization issues. If one person is in charge of managing all the languages and tasks, he can delegate the responsibilities to other members on the team and still keep close track of the overall localization. Any type of delay caused by miscommunication can add time and cost to the schedule, so if one person in the development team is responsible for all communication, these delays can be avoided.

Other development team resources will also be needed. Plan to include at least one engineer to help with integrating assets, creating builds, and debugging code. If there are art assets to localize, a part-time artist is needed. Testers are needed to check the functional aspects of the each localized version.

If working with a localization coordinator provided by the publisher or an external vendor, this person is the main point of contact for the translators and linguistic testers. This simplifies the communications pipeline, since the associate producer does not interface directly with the translators.

ORGANIZING ASSETS FOR TRANSLATION

The assets sent to the translator must be organized so that the translator can easily work with the files. The developer can't just send the game source files and expect the translator to pick through all the assets and translate any text they find. Additionally, the translator will need to know detailed information about the game's setting, characters, and gameplay mechanics in order to provide translations in the correct context.

If the localizations will be produced after the primary version is released, a localization kit can be created and sent to the translator. Refer to Chapter 24, "Closing Kits," for more information on this.

If the localizations are planned to ship simultaneously with the primary version, assets need to be sent during production, before everything in the game is finalized. If working in this manner, schedule dates to lock down areas of the game assets and get these assets sent to the translator. After assets have been sent off for translation, restrict access to the source assets so that changes cannot be made without first notifying the person managing the localizations.

If things are disorganized or the assets aren't finalized, a lot of time is spent sending different versions of the assets back and forth to the translator. Doing this is a sure way to lose track of the current assets and create additional bugs in the game.

Documentation

Send game-specific documents in order to make the context of the game clear to the translators. Having these resources makes it much easier for the translator to translate within the correct context. Send these resources to the translator as soon as they are available, before actual production begins on the localized versions:

Build of game: Provide an up-to-date version of the game. The translator can become familiar with the game and be better prepared to provide exact translations.

Design documents: Provide all the design documents so the translator knows exactly what features are included in the game and which areas need special attention from a localization standpoint. These documents can also clarify any questions the translator might have while playing through the game.

Cheats/walkthroughs: In order to check the translations quickly in the game, cheats and walkthroughs must be provided so the translator can quickly jump to different levels, screens, characters, and so on. They need access to all areas of the game that are going to be localized.

Voiceover casting notes: In order to maintain audio quality standards, provide detailed casting notes of the major and minor voiceovers in the game. The translators need information like gender, voice pitch, character description, and how this character fits into the game. This makes it easier to direct the VO session so that the localized VO files maintain the same overall emotion and context as the English VO files.

Glossary: This is useful for describing common and technical terms specific to your game, such as mission names, character names, and slang phrases that appear in the game.

Technical overview: This includes detailed information on file delivery formats, video editing requirements, and any post-production or integration work required to create the localized assets. If an external vendor is integrating localized VO into the game cinematics, also include information on any compression tools used.

Text Assets

Organizing the text assets for translation can be very easy or very hard, depending on how the text assets are laid out in the game. If all the text is located in a single text file, the text to be translated can be added to a spreadsheet, with notes about context, and sent to be translated. If the text is located in various files throughout the game, the developer needs to track down all text to be localized and organize it into a table that is easy for the translator to work with. As seen in Figure 20.5, this table should list the filename, context, and text to be translated. This table can be modified based on the translator's needs.

Text Filename	Context	Text to be translated	Translation
Prision.rsf	This appears in game when a player tries to access a locked door.	You cannot use this door; find a different path.	
Prision.rsf	Appears in game when your team is in control of the enemy base.	You have captured the enemy base!	

FIGURE 20.5 Spreadsheet for text translation.

Art Assets

If layered art assets have been created with text on a separate layer, the developer can use a spreadsheet similar to the one shown in Figure 20.5. The text to be translated is organized into a spreadsheet and sent off to be localized. The developer can then import the translated text into the text layer of the image, or the translator can do this if they have the technical expertise. If the translator does it, make sure they have the necessary software to modify the files, like Adobe Photoshop and any necessary or proprietary plug-ins.

If the text is embedded in the images, collect all the art files to be localized in a central area. Create a checklist that details the name of the art asset to be localized and the text that needs translated. The text can be placed into the appropriate spreadsheet and sent to the translator. The artist integrating the text into the art files can use the checklist to track his progress on the text integration. Figure 20.6 is an example of this checklist. The translations are put in the appropriate column, and the artist can indicate which languages are completed in the last column.

Art Asset	Context	Text to be translated	German	French	Italian	Spanish	Completed
sign.jpg	Sign appearing outside of a local department store.	Closed for the day. Gone fishing.					G,F,I

FIGURE 20.6 Checklist for localized art assets.

Voiceover Assets

Organizing audio files is more involved since you have to cast actors and record in a studio. Additionally, you must be very clear about the format you need the localized files delivered in, since there are many technical variations of audio files. The delivery format should be included in the original asset overview (see Figure 20.1) and the technical overview that the developer gives to the translator.

The translators and international recording studios will need the exact same information that was organized for the original voiceover shoot. Please refer to Chapter 9, "Voiceover," for complete details on how to organize this information.

If the game has lip-syncing, provide additional information such as the length of the voiceover in minutes and seconds. The actors will need to know this so they can properly match the length of the original voiceover line during the recording session. This way, the audio files will not be longer or shorter than the character's mouth animation, and the dialogue will be more closely in sync with the mouth movements. Figure 20.7 contains an example of a VO spreadsheet with information about timed dialogue; the last column indicates what the time constraints are.

Audio Filename	Length	Character	Context	Text to be translated	Comments
Medic.wav	1.2 sec	Sammy	A teammate has been wounded and Sammy is calling for medical help.	We need a medic here, stat!	Time sync. Max length = 2 secs

FIGURE 20.7 Example of voiceover sheet with timed dialogue.

As discussed earlier in this chapter, if there is enough time and resources are available, it's possible to re-do the lip-syncing for each language. However, this is very time-consuming, and the cost is rarely justified. Additionally, a time-coded Betacam tape (for live video action) or digital files of the cinematics and in-game characters should be provided to ensure accuracy with lip-syncing in the localized versions. The actors and sound engineer can use the movies to more accurately time the dubbing.

Provide the original English audio files to the translator. This will ensure that the translators, director, and actors have a good reference for the voiceovers and that the voice inflections in the localized files correspond to their English equivalents.

Other Assets

In addition to the actual in-game assets, other game-specific things are localized. Be sure to include these in the game's budget and schedule. Examples include the following:

- Manuals and box text
- Screenshots for manual and box
- Keyboard reference card
- Customer support information
- Readme file
- End user licensing agreement
- Installer

INTEGRATING TRANSLATED ASSETS

Integrating localized assets is time-consuming work since it involves a lot of file modification and file replacement. Development teams are always looking for more efficient ways to create the actual localized assets.

The ease of integration is affected by how the assets are laid out in the game. If the text is hard-coded, replacing all the text with localized text is risky. There is a high chance that bugs will be introduced in the code if someone is trying to cut and paste text within the code file. This is also very time consuming to do and can't be automated very easily.

If the assets to be localized are separated out in a language-specific folder within the game code, the text is more easily replaced with translations. This method also allows for easy automation of this process. Finding ways to automate text integration, either by writing a proprietary tool or by using existing software, will reduce the number of linguistic bugs.

Basically, there are two major development processes for asset integration. One process is for the developers to handle the asset integration themselves. They rely on the translators only for the translated text. The benefits of this process are that technical difficulties can easily be addressed; the integrity of the assets is maintained so they can easily be placed in the build without introducing any additional crash bugs; and the developer has more control over the schedule and resources.

The drawbacks are that the developer needs to allocate production time for this task, and this might take away time spent on polishing the game. Also, time is spent waiting for the translators to provide corrections to linguistic bugs. If the time to wait gets to be too long, the developer will fight the urge to find translations elsewhere, which might not be very reliable. Furthermore, the developer often has to rely on a third party (usually international marketing) to approve the final versions. This can be very time-consuming as the third party might go back and forth on minor bugs and hold up the release of the game.

The other integration process is to contract a localization house to do the integration along with the linguistic testing. The benefit is that the developer does not have to spend additional time creating localized software. The developer just needs to provide the vendor a localization kit (discussed in Chapter 24, "Closing Kits"). One drawback is that some localization houses might not have the technical expertise to independently localize a game, resulting in the developer getting involved to fix a problem created by a translator's error. Also, this can be expensive, depending on the scope of the game and work requested.

After creating the initial set of translated assets, check them into a version control system so they can be easily tracked during the bug-fixing phase. Additionally, if working on multiple languages at one time, version control will prevent the language assets from getting mixed up, resulting in German assets in the French version.

After the assets are integrated, plan for an increase in file size, since localized assets are at least 10–15 percent larger then their English counterparts. Make sure that there is enough room on the game disc to accommodate this size increase. If there is enough room, you might decide to include several languages on one CD.

Finally, make sure that each localized version has the correct set of game assets. In some cases, the localized versions will need to have some game assets that were originally intended for the U.S. market removed or changed. Following are some of these assets:

- Software registration information
- Tech support information
- Third-party software (such as Internet Service Providers)
- Demos from other games

TESTING

This is time-consuming because both functionality and linguistic testing have to be done for each language version. Additionally, all the versions need to be tested for compatibility between languages when playing multiplayer games. Time can be saved in the testing schedule if there are two teams to do concurrent linguistic and functionality testing.

Functionality Testing

Functionality testing checks for any bugs created by the localized assets that require a code change to fix. Ideally, if doing a straight asset swap, there should not be any functionality bugs introduced. However, special characters and increased text length were not planned for; code changes might be needed to accommodate the localized assets. Functionality testing can be done by the same QA team that did the primary version of the game, since they are familiar with the game and the functionality test plan. They can log bugs in the same bug reporting format used for the main game. A unique bug field should be included for each language, so the database can be sorted by language if necessary.

Functionality bugs in the localized versions should be entered in the bug database for the primary game. This is because the game engineers will be needed to address any code fixes to accommodate localized assets.

On PC titles, remember to have the QA team check keyboard input of all the special characters and the keyboard commands. In addition PC testing will require multiple copies of each language's operating system and the appropriate keyboard for each language. When testing console titles, debug kits will be needed from Sony, Microsoft, or Nintendo.

Linguistic Testing

Linguistic testing checks all the language assets in the game to make sure text is not overlapping, truncated, misspelled, or grammatically incorrect. It also checks that all the localized VO files play correctly. Linguistic testing should be done by a native speaker of the language being tested. If working with a large publisher, they might already have arrangements with an in-country translation house to provide this service.

In some cases, particularly for more complex localizations, the linguistic testers can be on-site with the development team. This speeds up the linguistic testing and bug-fixing process immensely since the linguistic testers can provide corrected translations right away. Advance planning needs to be done if linguistic testers will be traveling and working on-site with the development team for a few weeks. If this is not well-organized, the most cannot be made of the testers' time.

Linguistic testers will need to familiarize themselves with the game before they begin testing. The game's functionality test plan can also help them become familiar with the game and all its features.

They will need a localization test plan to show them where to check all the translations. One way to do this is to have them check the text in the game against the text translation spreadsheet they already completed. A column can be added to indicate where to look for the text in the game. Figure 20.8 is an example of this.

ocation	English	French	Notes
AI(M01)	A police officer is down! Mission Failed.	Un officier de police a été abattu. Echec de la mission.	Failure condition that appears as pop-up message in game
M01	1. Disarm the security system	1. Désactivez le système de sécurité	Appears in loading screen, set up screen, and in-game start menu
Install	Would you like a shortcut placed on the desktop that can be used to launch the game?	Souhaitez-vous créer un raccourci pour pouvoir lancer le jeu à partir du bureau?	Appears during installation
Uninstall	Do you wish to clean up the entire game folder? This will delete the folder the game was installed to and everything in it.	Souhaitez-vous effacer complètement le dossier du jeu ? Cela détruira l'ensemble du dossier dans lequel le jeu a été installé et les éléments qu'il contenait.	Appears during installation
Equip	The primary weapon assigned is the M4, with a 9 mm pistol as a secondary. Flashbangs are provided to suppress enemies, and a heartbeat sensor should help in locating them.	Les armes assignées sont le M4, comme arme principale, et le pistolet 9mm, comme arme secondaire. Les grenades aveuglantes sont fournies pour éliminer les ennemis. Le détecteur cardiaque devrait vous aider à les localiser.	Appears on the help screen for equipment selection
IFF(M03)	a Guard	un garde	Appears when you place reticle over a character

FIGURE 20.8   Sample localization test plan.

Determine in advance how linguistic bugs will be reported. If the developer does not provide a bug report form, the linguistic testers may not give enough information about the bug and how to fix it. This is especially true when fixes are being made by people who don't speak the language. Figure 20.9 is a sample bug report template for linguistic bugs. It includes information on where to find the bug, what the current (incorrect) translation is, and what the correct translation should be.

Bug#	Language	Location in Game	Description/ Comment	Original Localized Text	Corrected Text	Status
3	Italian	Mission 4—Briefing	Please use lower case letter.	...Come forse sapere, il colpo di Stato ad Addis Abeba...	...Come forse sapere, il colpo di stato ad Addis Abeba...	FIXED
9	Italian	After Action Screen (single player)	Text not translated.	Originals Only	Solo originali	CLOSED

FIGURE 20.9 Linguistic bug report template.

CONSOLE SUBMISSION

When working on console titles, the localized versions of a game must be submitted to the Microsoft, Sony, or Nintendo for approval. All of these publishers have European and Asian offices that must approve the game before it is released in their respective countries. In most cases the developer will submit versions to the European, Asian, and U.S. offices of these publishers at the same time, in anticipation of a worldwide release of the game. However, this does not guarantee that the submission approvals will occur at the same time; a game could be approved for release in Europe before it is approved for release in the United States.

In order for the submission process to go smoothly for localized versions, keep the following in mind:

Technical requirements: Overall, the technical requirements for the localized version will be the same as the U.S. versions. There might be specific requirements regarding PAL and NTSC signals, but nothing too major. However, if there are specific requirements about how text displays on the UI, the developer will want to check localized words in the UI to ensure that it is compliant with the requirements.

Terminology: Sony, Microsoft, and Nintendo all have specific terminology for their hardware and peripherals that are used in the game. This terminology list is checked during the compliance check, and if the correct term is not used in the game or packaging, it must be fixed and the game resubmitted. Each publisher has an approved list of terminology that includes the approved translated terms for any localized versions. Forward these terms to the linguistic testers so they can check for correct terms during linguistic testing.

Error messages: Third-party publishers will also verify all the error messages in the game to ensure that they are compliant with the required wording. Error messages can be difficult for linguistic testers to check, since they will not see most of them or know what steps are needed to get a specific error message.

Print out the localized error messages and send them to the linguistic testers before they start testing the game. They can verify the content of the message and ensure that they are compliant and linguistically correct.

LOCALIZATION CHECKLIST

Figure 20.10 is a localization checklist that lists major tasks to address during the pre-production, production, and wrap-up phases of localizations. This checklist can provide a good starting point for formulating a localization plan from start to finish. For more detailed information on localizations, please refer to *The Game Localization Handbook.*

PRE-PRODUCTION	Y/N	NOTES
TECHNICAL CONSIDERATIONS		
Does game support unicode?		
Are all language assets in an easily accessible directory in the game?		
Will subtitling functionality be needed?		
Are localized keyboards supported for player input?		
Will several languages ship on a single CD-ROM?		
Will localized versions be multiplayer compatible?		
Do boxes in UI scale to accommodate different size text strings?		
Is any additional software needed to aid in localization?		
Are international currency and date/time formats supported?		
Has a version control system been decided on for the localizations?		
Has the localization pipeline been decided on?		
OTHER CONSIDERATIONS		
Will the localized versions ship simultaneously with the English version?		
Has the asset overview form been filled in and sent to the translator?		
Have the languages been been determined?		
Will external vendors be producing the localizations?		
If so, are the bid packages prepared?		
Has the budget been completed and approved?		
Has the level of localization been determined for each langauge?		
Has the overall schedule been completed and finalized?		
Are there development resources available for the localizations?		
Has a method for integrating text assets been determined?		
Has a method for integrating VO assets been determined?		
Has a pipeline been determined for fixing bugs?		

(continued)

FIGURE 20.10 Sample localization checklist.

PRE-PRODUCTION CHECKLIST	Y/N	NOTES
Have the appropriate measures been taken to comply with all of the international ratings boards?		
Have the third party publishers been contacted about the localized versions?		
Will PAL support be necessary for console versions?		
Is there enough hardware for functionality and linguistic testing?		
PRODUCTION		
Has a detailed schedule been completed and communicated to the team?		
Has the localization overview document been sent to the localization coordinator or translators?		
Has all the pre-production game documentations been sent to the localization coordinator or translators?		
Has the latest English build of the game been sent to the translators?		
Have the text assets been organized for translation and sent to the localization coordinator?		
Have the voiceover script and character casting notes been sent to the localization coordinator?		
Have the final English voiceover files been sent to the localization coordinator?		
Have all the art assets to be localized been sent to the localization coordinator?		
Have all the cinematic assets and time codes been organized and sent to the translator?		
Are the translations for the text assets completed?		
Have the localized voiceover files been recorded and processed?		
Have the text and voiceover files been integrated?		
Have the cinematics been localized?		
Have the localized versions been sent to the appropriate ratings board for approval?		
Does the master contain demos from other games that were requested by marketing?		
Is functionality testing completed?		
Are all functionality bugs fixed and has the game been code released?		
Is linguistic testing completed?		
Are all linguistic bugs fixed and has final linguistic approval been given?		
Have the localized versions been sent to the replicator (PC) or submitted to the third party publisher (consoles and cell phones?)		
WRAP-UP		
Have the manual and box text been sent for translations?		
Does a localized demo need to be produced?		
Have localized screenshots been taken for the manual and box?		
Has a closing kit been created for all the localized versions?		
If necessary, have all patches been localized and made available?		

FIGURE 20.10   Sample localization checklist.

SUMMARY

Quality localizations are becoming an expectation in today's international markets. Gamers want to feel that they are playing a game made for them, not just some hastily translated game that has poor voice acting and typos in the translations. If developers plan ahead for localizations at the beginning of the production process, it is possible to create high-quality localizations that ship at the same time as the primary version of the game. This chapter gave a general overview on how to plan for and execute localizations. Organizing assets for translation, integrating assets, and testing the localized versions were all discussed in this chapter. Additionally, information was presented on submitting localized games to third-party publishers for approval.

Part
VII   Testing

Testing will begin at some point in the production cycle, usually around alpha. At this point in development, several elements in the game need to be checked for defects and crash bugs. Testing is an integral part of game development, so it is important not to short change the testing schedule as the production phase comes to a close.

The QA testers provide a valuable service throughout the production cycle, and the lead QA tester must be included in all high level decisions about the game. After testing begins, time is spent checking for defects and then making sure that they are corrected before the game ships. This section of the book presents key information about the testing phase. Topics include the following:

- Writing Test Plans
- Testing Cycle
- Code Release Process
- Console Submission Process

21 Testing

In This Chapter

- Testing Schedule
- Test Plans
- Testing Pipeline
- Testing Cycle

INTRODUCTION

To many people outside of the game industry, testing seems like a glamorous job. After all, you get to play games all day! However, if you talk to anyone who has tested games for a living, you know that it is anything but glamorous. In reality, testing is an extremely stressful and difficult job. Most testers spend at least five to eight months testing the same game day in and day out, looking for defects, confirming bug fixes, and playing testing missions. This becomes pretty tedious after a few weeks, no matter how fun the game is. Oftentimes, because testers are looking for specific issues with the game, they don't even have a chance to actually just play and enjoy the game.

Another thing that adds to the stress of testing is that most game development schedules never allot ample time to test everything thoroughly, which means the testers are often working massive overtime (late nights, weekends, and holidays) to get the game tested and ready for code release. One reason this happens is because testing is the last thing to happen in the production cycle. So if things are running off schedule for art, engineering, or design, these delays are amplified by the time testing begins. Testing time is often the first thing cut when extra time production time is needed.

The producer must work closely with the lead QA analyst to alleviate as many of the testing problems as possible. The lead QA analyst is responsible for testing the game, closing bugs, and determining whether a game is ready to be code released. Involve the QA analyst in pre-production so he can comment on any features that will propose testing challenges. For example, if there are plans to include 200 options in the character creation system, the QA analyst can comment on how much testing time it will take to test each option and the different combinations. The testing time alone is probably reason enough to drastically limit the options for this feature. Things like this will help create a tighter loop between the development team and the testing team, which will hopefully translate into more manageable testing schedules.

TESTING SCHEDULE

Since testing time is often cut short to accommodate other schedule slips, create a solid testing schedule during pre-production. This ensures that everyone on the team has a clear understanding of the testing schedule and what the expectations are. If the team understands how their delays negatively impact testing, they will be more conscientious about meeting their deadlines in a timely fashion. Refer to Chapter 15, "Game Plan," for detailed information on creating a schedule.

Build the testing schedule directly into the production schedule and show the testing dependencies so that delays affecting the test cycle can be immediately seen and mitigated. Also, add in testing time for each major milestone of the game so the testing department can spend a few days with a single build to evaluate the game's progress against the milestone deliverables. Refer to Chapter 14, "Game Requirements," for details on milestone deliverables.

Other things to include in the testing schedule are as follows:

Play testing: During production, make sure to schedule time for QA to play test the game and offer feedback to the developers. Ideally, conduct these play tests with people who haven't already spent months playing the game, so the feedback is based mainly on the fun factor of the game.

Demo: Marketing will want a demo, and it will need to be tested. If the demo is already in the schedule, everyone will be prepared to fulfill this request when marketing makes it.

Marketing builds: If marketing is sending development builds out during production, schedule time for the testing department to check them before they leave the building. Even though journalists expect to see bugs and unfinished work in these builds, there might be critical errors uncovered in testing that must be added to the build notes.

Code release candidates: After beta, the development team's main goal is to get the bugs fixed as quickly as possible and create a suitable code release candidate. Schedule a few weeks at the end of the testing cycle for the QA department to thoroughly check each code release candidate against the test plan. If things go well, the first code release candidate will pass with flying colors, but more than likely, several code release candidates will need to be submitted and tested.

During pre-production, the testing team is mainly used as a resource for play testing the prototype and offering feedback on proposed features. At this point in the testing schedule, the QA analyst can be on the project part-time, as long as he can provide feedback on all the deliverables being generated at this time. If there are prototype or playable builds to check, he can arrange to have a few testers available for a few days at a time to test these deliverables during pre-production.

Production is where the bulk of testing takes place. The QA analyst will be on the project full-time after production starts—working on the test plan, testing gameplay features, and working with leads on managing the production pipeline. A few testers will be needed for a few weeks here and there between alpha. However, if the game is very large and complex, there might be plenty to test before the game reaches alpha. Remember that the sooner something can be tested, the sooner bugs are uncovered and fixed. In some cases, a difficult bug to fix found later in the development cycle was an easy bug to fix earlier in the cycle.

At alpha, the QA analyst will put together a group of full-time testers who can test the features as they are implemented. At this point, it is likely the testing team will not have reached full capacity, as the full game is not completed. After code freeze happens, about three to four months before the game is scheduled to code release, expect to have a full group of testers looking at the game until it is finished. If the game is especially content heavy, the full group of testers might begin looking at the game before code freeze.

TEST PLANS

A test plan is a road map the QA department uses to thoroughly check all areas of the game. The test plan is written by the QA analyst and details all aspects of UI functionality, gameplay, art, AI behavior, and so on. It is usually presented in some type of checklist or pass/fail format that is easily understood by the tester. The tester can take this plan and compare it against what is seen in the game. If the game functionality does not match the test plan, the tester knows to enter a bug in the database. The test plan ensures that all areas of the game are functioning as designed.

In order for the QA analyst to write a thorough test plan, he will need complete design documentation for each of the game features. If some of the documentation is missing or is unclear, the feature will not be recorded properly in the test plan, which will cause problems later. For one thing, features not included in the design documentation won't be added to the test plan and, therefore, won't be tested. Features that are unclear in the documentation might not be listed correctly in the test plan, and the game will be released with a feature that is not functioning as intended.

Figure 21.1 is an example of a test plan for a localized demo. This test plan lists information on the expected functionality of the UI in the Main Menu Screen and Briefing Screen. Since this is a demo, some of the choices are dimmed out and not available, but they will be available in the full version of the game. The tester will take this plan and verify that the correct buttons are nonfunctional and the correct buttons are functional. Additionally, this test plans checks that the appropriate localized assets appear when the game is run on different operating systems.

The test plan for the entire game will be hundreds of pages, since every UI screen, every mission script, and all other features of the game need to be detailed so they can be fully tested for proper functionality. Because the test plan is so large, don't expect the testing department to test each build they receive against the entire plan. At best, they can complete certain sections of the test plan, based on what new features were implemented and what areas need to be re-tested. Milestone builds and code release candidates are usually the only builds that are thoroughly checked against the entire test plan.

Verify:
Dimmed = displays dimmed and not selectable.
Available = can be highlighted and selected and works as expected.
Functional = can be selected and all functions need to be tested and work as expected.

Results	Main Menu Screen	
P F	Attract Mode (Stand alone only)	Plays
P F	Training	Dimmed
P F	Campaign	Dimmed
P F	Quick Mission	Available
P F	Multiplayer	Available
P F	Options	Available
P F	Dossier (Stand alone only)	Dimmed
P F	Exit (demolette launcher)	Functional
P F	Main Menu Trigger Help	Available
P F	"Forced" Dossier	Available
Results	**Briefing Screen**	
P F	Briefing Text—scrollable	Functional
P F	Voice over matches— Text	Functional
P F	Objectives Display	Functional
P F	Correct Objective images	Functional
P F	Proceed	Available
P F	Briefing START menu	Available
P F	Trigger Help	Available

Load in each language and verify that the correct language is displayed.

English
German
French
Spanish
Italian

FIGURE 21.1   Sample test plan for localized demo.

TESTING PIPELINE

Before testing begins, the testers and the development team need to determine the pipeline for tracking and reporting bugs. If this is not established, there will be confusion about how the testers are reporting bugs and which bugs are most critical for the development team to address first. In addition, everyone needs to understand how to access and use the bug tracking database.

Bug Tracking Database

In order to efficiently track bugs, a centralized bug tracking database is critical. Don't rely on emails as a reliable form of bug-tracking. Instead, set up a bug-tracking database such as Seapine's TestTrack or Bugzilla. Both of these programs offer robust bug-tracking functionality for writing and closing bugs.

After the database is set up, the QA analyst can conduct a tutorial to train the team on using it. The team must understand how to use the database correctly so they can enter bugs, comment bugs, change the status on bugs, and basically understand what they must do to address their bugs in the database. During the tutorial, the QA analyst can also discuss bug definitions, so that everyone has a common understanding of the differences between crash bugs, critical bugs, minor bugs, and feature requests.

Bug Definitions

When bugs are added to the database, make sure the correct bug definitions are used so that the bugs can be fixed in the most efficient order. For instance, crash bugs should be fixed well before any minor bugs or feature requests are even considered. If the bug is not properly defined in the database, crash bugs might not be addressed for a while and will ultimately become more difficult to fix as production continues. Additionally, if feature requests are defined incorrectly as bugs, feature creep will sneak up on you before you know it. Common bug definitions are as follows:

Crash bug: A crash bug is extremely seriously as it prevents the player from progressing in the game. Crash bugs can freeze the game, or in the worst cases kick the player out of the game and display an error message. The "blue screen of death" sometimes seen in Microsoft Windows is a crash bug.

Critical bug: A critical bug is a major functionality problem with the game, but it does not prevent the player from progressing in the game. A critical bug is a level missing all of is textures, or a major gameplay feature not functioning as designed.

Minor bug: A minor bug is one that is noticeable by the player but does not detract greatly from the overall game experience. Stretched textures and typos can be considered minor bugs.

Feature request: A feature request is not a bug, so be sure everyone entering bugs in the database clearly understands the difference. A feature request is additional functionality that would be nice to add but that is not part of the defined feature set. For example, someone might request an option to turn the in-game Heads-up-display (HUD) off and on, but if this feature was not an original part of the design scope, it is considered a feature request and not a bug. If the user is supposed to have the ability to toggle the HUD on and off, and this is not working in the game, then this is a bug.

When writing the bug, there is usually a section for including information on the type of bug it is. Please refer to the "Writing Bugs" section later in this chapter for detailed information on writing bugs.

TESTING CYCLE

The testing cycle for a build begins when the development team officially submits a build for testing. As discussed in Chapter 18, "Making Builds," even though builds will be available on a daily basis around alpha, it is not useful for QA to test each and every build, as they would never make it through the entire game before a new build was ready. Instead, if the build is stable, the QA department can spend a few days or a week with a single build and test as much as possible.

As development progresses, and the game becomes more robust, the QA analyst will test different sections of the game on different builds. For example, when a level artist checks in a new level, the testers will do a thorough pass on the geometry and textures and submit any bugs to the database. This level will not be tested again until the artist has fixed all the bugs and resubmitted the level for testing, which could be several weeks. Meanwhile, the testers will concentrate on testing other levels and features in subsequent builds as they wait for things to be fixed. Work with the QA analyst to schedule certain sections of the game for testing. If it is indicated in the schedule when certain parts of the game are supposed to be ready for the testing, the development team is better able to plan their work so they can accommodate the testing schedule.

After the build is in testing, the testing cycle is fairly straightforward. The testers will run through the test plan, find bugs, and enter them in the database. When the bugs are in the database, they are assigned to the appropriate person for fixing. This person fixes the bug and resubmits his work for verification in a future build. The tester will then check the fix in the build and indicate that is it is ready to be closed out of the database.

Writing Bugs

Bugs need to contain enough information so the development team can identify and fix them. Anyone can write up a bug and enter it into the database, even members of the development team. Encouraging everyone to use the bug database as a central tracking system for all the bugs and feature requests is good practice. After production is in full swing, it is good to have all the information in a central place, instead of relying on emails which list bugs and feature requests.

How often have you played your game during production and seen a problem—a logo is incorrect; there is a typo; or the wrong character model is used? Did you verbally tell someone about the problem and expect it to be fixed? If so, it is highly likely that the person you told will forget to fix it, unless it is listed in the database. During code freeze, most engineers will not fix anything unless it is officially entered into the bug database, as this makes it much easier for them to track any changes made from this point forward.

A typical functionality bug report would contain the following fields of information:

Code version: Indicates the version of the code in which the bug was found.

Type: Indicates where the bug was found. For example, it could be an art, engineering, or design bug.

Component in game: This section offers further categories for classifying the type of bug. For example, art components could include geometry, texture, or interface bugs.

Summary of bug: A brief one-sentence summary of the bug. General information about the location of the bug should be listed here as well. For example, "Mission 3: Can't complete the last mission objective."

Description of bug: More details on the bug so it can be located, fixed, and verified. For example, "The last objective in mission 3 did not appear after completing the previous objective."

Severity: This indicates whether a bug is a crash, critical, minor, or a feature request. High-severity bugs are addressed first.

Steps to reproduce: The exact steps for reproducing the bug. This is especially important for critical crash bugs or bugs that show up during specific circumstances. The steps should be written clearly enough so that anyone can follow them and successfully reproduce the bug. Include information about how often the bug was reproduced: is it reproducible 100 percent of the time, or was it a one-time crash bug?

Screenshots: A screenshot is immensely helpful in pinpointing the location and nature of the bug.

Crash log files: Log files that are generated by the game when it crashes in a debug version of the game. When the game crashes, the tester can attach the log file that was generated to the bug report. Engineering can then look at this report for more information on what caused the bug.

Figure 21.2 shows a sample bug reporting form in Test Track Pro®. After the bug is written, it must be assigned to someone to be fixed.

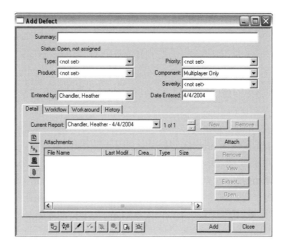

FIGURE 21.2 Bug reporting form in Test Track Pro.

Assigning and Closing Bugs

Assigning bugs is a large part of the testing cycle, because the bug has to get to the right person in order to be fixed and verified. The process for assigning bugs should be clearly defined and presented to the team during the testing tutorial conducted by the QA analyst. The goal of assigning bugs is to get bugs addressed as quickly as possible.

A simple process for assigning bugs involves the tester, the QA analyst, and the lead:

1. The tester finds a bug in the game, writes it up, and submits it to the database.
2. The bug is automatically assigned to the QA analyst who will check the bug to ensure that it is indeed a bug and not a duplicate. He will also check the information in the bug to make sure that the problem is clearly written.
3. The QA analyst will assign the bug to the appropriate lead. The art lead receives all the art bugs and so on.
4. The lead will review the bug, verify that it is assigned to the appropriate discipline, and assign it to the appropriate person on the team. In some cases a bug appears to be one type (such as art) and is really another type (such as engineering), which is why it is helpful for the lead to review the bugs. If the bug is a crash bug, the lead might request that the person address the bug right away so it can be fixed for the next build.

5. After someone is assigned to fix the bug, he will implement a fix and assign it back to the QA analyst for verification. If the bug can't be fixed for one reason or another, the person should add a comment to the bug, explaining why, and assign it back to his lead for verification.
6. After the analyst is assigned a bug for verification, he will assign it to a tester to check in the next build to make sure that it is fixed. If the bug is not fixed, the tester will add a comment to the bug, and the process will begin again. If the bug is fixed, it is closed by the analyst.

As the game gets closer to code release, you will find that it will be impossible to fix every single bug in the game. This isn't anything to be concerned with, as many games ship with bugs. Every project has some bugs that are designated "will not fix" at the end of the project. These are usually minor bugs that will not impede the gameplay or the player's enjoyment of the game. There is a variety of reasons for not fixing a bug. One is that the risk is not warranted by the severity of the bug: you don't want to risk touching a lot of code just to fix one minor bug that doesn't impede gameplay.

Another reason why bugs do not get fixed is because the time required to make the fix for a minor bug would impact the ship date. In some instances, these bugs are put on a list to be fixed if the code is opened up again for a critical bug fix. Each developer has different ways of determining which bugs will not be fixed, so be sure to work with the studio management to determine a process for designating which bugs will not be fixed. Of course, as many bugs as possible are fixed in the scheduled time so that the user can have a relatively bug-free game experience.

Checking TCRs

As discussed in Chapter 5, "Developer and Publisher Relationships," each console manufacturer has a predefined set of technical requirements to which each game must adhere. The console manufacturer will provide a complete checklist of each requirement the game must follow, and in some instances will provide tools to assist in checking the title for compliance with the appropriate requirements. Non-compliance with these requirements puts your game at risk of not being approved. Therefore, testing for compliance to the requirements is extremely important. Please refer to Chapter 22, "Code Releasing," for more information on the console submission process.

Appoint someone on the QA team, either the lead analyst or an experienced tester, to be in charge of testing the build for compliance with these technical requirements. They should have access to the most current set of requirements from each console manufacturer and keep it updated throughout the development process. In addition, they must be knowledgeable of how to check for compliance with these requirements in the game. Ideally, the requirements are accounted for in the design and technical documentation, so the lead designer or lead engineer knows that the requirements are fulfilled and the manner in which the game fulfills them.

Any bugs found that indicate a violation of requirements are considered high priority and need to be addressed immediately. Although non-compliance is not the equivalent of a crash bug, it is still considered an extremely critical bug because your title could fail to be ready if the requirement is not addressed, putting the game's ship date in jeopardy.

SUMMARY

Testing is a time-consuming and stressful aspect of game development. As you are trying to get the game out the door, the tester might find a crash bug that was not uncovered earlier in development. If this happens, tensions run high as the developers scramble to prepare another code release candidate as quickly as possible. This scenario is bound to happen on some game development teams, but if the producer, leads, and team are constantly keeping the QA needs in mind during production, some of these instances can be avoided. This chapter discussed general information on how to work effectively with the QA department from pre-production to code release. Topics included the testing schedule, the testing cycle, and closing bugs.

22 Code Releasing

INTRODUCTION

Code release is when the game code is finalized and ready to be replicated and packaged for shipment to stores. Normally, the QA department, in conjunction with the developer, determines when a game can be code released. The QA department is heavily involved because they are responsible for finding the bugs and verifying the fixes. They have the best idea of the general stability of the game and will be aware of all the crash bugs and whether these bugs have been addressed in a satisfactory fashion.

Toward the end of the project, the QA department and the developer will usually have daily meetings to discuss the status of the bugs: which ones require fixes and which ones are minor enough to be left as they are. Most games have bugs in them that were deemed too minor to fix; the bugs will not be noticed by the consumer or there was not enough time in the schedule to warrant putting the ship date in jeopardy.

DETERMINING CODE RELEASE

A code release process must be defined so that it is very clear to QA and the development team when the game is finished. The purpose of the code release process is to take some time with the actual code release candidate to ensure that it is ready to be shipped.

A code release candidate is a version of the game that has addressed all the bugs, has all the final assets, and is deemed ready to ship by the development team. When QA receives this candidate, they will make a final run through the test plan, make sure that all bugs are addressed, all game content is correct, everything is functioning properly, and that any technical requirements are fulfilled.

Build the code release process into the development schedule. Plan on five to seven days for checking each code release candidate, depending on the size of the game. The code release process is handled differently at every company and is modified depending on which platform is being released. PC games are less complicated to release, since they do not have to be submitted to a third party for approval and can be patched later if a problem is discovered.

Gold masters for console games must be submitted to a third party for approval. Each third-party manufacturer has a different set of technical requirements that the game must meet before it can be approved for replication. More information on this process is discussed later in this chapter.

Linguistic Approval

Linguistic approval simply means that all the localized versions of the game have been tested by qualified native speakers and are deemed ready for code release. Linguistic approval can happen before the game is ready to be code released, since this approval affects only the actual localized assets and not the game code itself.

Since additional people are involved in creating and testing the localized versions, more people have a say in when the build is approved for code release. Remember to include time in the schedule for the linguistic approval process.

CODE RELEASE CHECKLIST

It is helpful to create a code release checklist that is easily modified for each game. This ensures that everyone involved in the code release process has a clear understanding of the requirements. Figure 22.1 is a sample code release checklist that can be used. This sample provides only a basic overview for what should be double-checked before a game is code released.

CODE RELEASE CHECKLIST	Y/N	NOTES
Are all the bugs closed?		
Are all the "Will Not Fix" bugs approved to leave as is?		
Can game be played from the beginning to end without any crashes?		
Have all necessary cheat codes been disabled or removed?		
Is all debug software disabled or removed?		
Has the game passed all areas of the test plan?		
PC Only - Has it been verified that product works with all major hardware (sound cards, video cards, and PCs)?		
If some hardware is not supported, is this noted in the documentation?		
Has the customer support manager signed off on the documentation and customer support information?		
Has the QA department approved this for submission to Sony, Microsoft, or Nintendo?		
Does game display the correct ratings information and disclaimers?		
THIRD PARTY SUBMISSION		
Microsoft		
Has product passed internal checks on Microsoft's TCR Checklist?		
Sony		
Has product passed internal checks on Sony's TCR checklist?		
Nintendo		
Has product passed internal checks on Nintendo's TCR checklist?		
LOCALIZED VERSIONS		
Has the game properly edited out violence for the necessary versions?		
Is the correct customer service information listed for the localized versions?		
Is the in-game text displaying in the proper language?		
Is the audio in the proper language?		
Are the packaging and manual in the correct language?		
Have localized versions been tested for compatibility between all the languages?		
Have the linguistic testers tested and approved all language assets in the game?		
Is the correct legal text being used for the localized versions?		
PC only - are the keyboards mapped correctly for each language?		
PC only - are the appropriate operating systems locked out from the installer?		
PC Only - is the electronic registration for the appropriate country being displayed?		
PC only - is the appropriate localized version of third party software on the disk? (ex. Earthlink)		
INSTALLERS (PC Only)		
Does the installer check for meeting the minimum system requirements and give a warning if the customer's system does not?		
Does the installer check for adequate hard drive space to install and give a warning if there is not enough room?		
Does the game uninstall properly and clear all files from the user's hard drive?		
		(continued)

FIGURE 22.1   Code release checklist.

CODE RELEASE CHECKLIST	Y/N	NOTES
LEGAL		
Is the proper legal text being displayed in the game and on the packaging?		
Have all rights to third party software been cleared for use?		
Has all licensed content appearing the game been cleared for use?		
Is the correct end user license agreement (EULA) included?		
Is the correct warranty information listed?		
Has all packaging, including box and reference cards, been finalized and approved?		
Is the manual finalized and approved?		
GOLD MASTERS		
Have the gold masters been burned, virus scanned, and determined to be virus-free?		
Have the gold masters been compared to the code release candidate and found to be identicial?		
Have the gold masters been installed and/or played briefly to ensure that the CD is not defective.		
Have the gold masters been properly labeled with the product name, gold master date, and language(s)?		

FIGURE 22.1 Code release checklist.

The following areas of the game should be double-checked before code releasing them:

Legal text: Confirm with the legal department that the correct copyright text is used and that the correct software license agreement is included. If working with any type of license, make sure the contracts are finalized and all approvals have been obtained—for example, if music has been licensed from a band.

Contact information: If including technical support or customer support information in the game or documentation, make sure the correct information is listed. Check that all Web site addresses are correct as well. International versions will have different contact information and possibly different Web site addresses.

Localized assets: Make sure that the game contains the correct localized text and audio assets. The manuals for each language need to be double-checked as well to ensure that they are translated and contain the correct localized screenshots.

Third-party software: Some PC games are bundled with third-party software such as AOL or Earthlink. Make sure these are the correct versions, and all contracts are finalized.

Demos: If demos for other games are included on the gold master, make sure that they have been approved by the appropriate ratings board and are allowed to ship in the international territories.

Software ratings information: Make sure that the game has been submitted to the appropriate software ratings board and that any required ratings icons or disclaimers are included in the game.

Console submission requirements: Internal checks must be made to ensure that the game complies with all of the console submission requirements. The console manufacturers might have some tools available to the developers to automate some of these checks.

Depending on the game, there might be other areas to check as well. If the game assets are especially complex, you might want to add the items from the build checklist illustrated in Figure 18.1 in Chapter 18, "Making Builds," to the code release checklist. After a game is code released, the gold masters will either be sent to the replication house so the game discs can be manufactured and packaged or submitted to a third-party manufacturer for approval. Before getting to the final stage of the code release, find out exactly where to send the masters.

PC GOLD MASTERS

PC gold masters are handled differently at every company. Some publishers might designate a single person to handle all masters and ship them to the correct replication house. That person could be based in the United States or Europe, and be in charge of all gold masters, regardless of which versions.

Before getting to the code release phase of the project, find out exactly who these people are, where they are based, and how to get in touch with them. They must be informed of the code release schedule so the gold master can be handled in a timely fashion.

When getting to the end of the project, keep everyone informed of any changes in the code release date, even if it is only one day. One day can make the difference of getting a gold master to replication on a Friday or Monday. The replication vendor can work on the weekends, but this incurs additional costs and should be avoided.

Another way the gold master process can be organized is to have the producer interface directly with the replication vendor. The producer will be in direct contact with the vendor and be responsible for sending them the gold masters. This method works well for smaller developers who are not affiliated with large publishers.

CONSOLE GOLD MASTERS

Before a console gold master can be deemed official, it must be submitted for final approval to the appropriate third-party manufacturer, which includes Sony, Microsoft, and Nintendo. In order to expedite this process, each manufacturer assigns an account manager to work with the developers and to help them navigate the submission process. This person is the first point of contact if there are any questions about the process or the publishers' expectations. The account manager presents the developer with the most recent set of technical requirements and helps determine what submission dates are necessary in order for the product to ship on time.

If the game has a hard ship date, work with your account manager to schedule the submission dates in advance. This way, the submission dates can easily be built into the schedule, and the development team can schedule their work accordingly. For example, if the ship date is October 15, 2007, the submission date would be around August 15, 2007, which means the developers must internally code release the game in mid-August to be prepared to submit the game on time.

Don't forget to include time in the development schedule for submitting the packaging and manual for approval. Usually, these items must be submitted for approval several weeks before the final code so that the console manufacturer has enough time to print and manufacture the packaging to get ready to assemble the final product. If the printed materials are not submitted for approval in a timely manner, the game's ship date might be put in jeopardy, even if the code is submitted on time.

Likewise, console submissions are handled differently at each company. Some companies designate the producer as the main contact for the submission process, and others have a central person in charge of all submissions. The submission procedures can be quite involved, since the code, supporting documentation (such as cheats codes and walkthroughs), and submission forms need to be provided to the third party. The act of submitting the code itself can be complex as well, since it usually requires a specific way for the code to be packaged and presented for approval.

The producer might be directly involved with the submission procedure, since he is responsible for addressing any issues that come up during the approval process. He is the one most familiar with how to package the code for submission. In addition, since he has been working closely with third-party contacts for the duration of the development, he is familiar with how to get through procedures quickly.

Larger publishers might have a single person, separate from the development team, who is designated to handle all the third-party submissions. In this case, the producer works directly with this person and not with the contact at the third-party publisher. This process can be effective as well, since there is one person who has experience with submitting to third-party publishers and getting the code approved in a timely fashion.

Microsoft Approval Process

Microsoft's current approval process requires a pre-certification (pre-cert) at least four to eight weeks before the final submission. During pre-cert, Microsoft checks the game against all Technical Certification Requirements (TCRs) and issues a report to the developer on which TCRs are in violation. The developer then can fix these issues before the final submission.

If the developer creates localized versions of the game that are the same as the U.S version, except for the language assets, the localized versions do not need to go through the pre-cert process. Instead, the U.S. version is submitted for pre-cert, and the final pre-cert report is forwarded to the European and Japanese offices in preparation for the final submission.

The final submission is usually scheduled about eight weeks before the ship date. This gives Microsoft plenty of time for the approval and manufacturing process. It also gives the developer time to fix any issues that are found in the final submission. Ideally, the game will get approved on the first submission, but sometimes, bugs or TCR violations are found that must be fixed. When this happens, the developer makes the necessary changes and resubmits the game for approval. If the developer allows eight weeks for the approval process, this should give him time to resubmit the game at least once, if there are bugs to be fixed.

Each version of the game must be submitted to the appropriate subsidiary for final submission. All U.S. versions of the game are submitted to Microsoft U.S., the European versions are submitted to Microsoft Europe, and the Japanese versions are submitted to Microsoft Japan. Each of these subsidiaries conducts independent checks of the game to ensure TCR compliance for their countries. If a TCR violation is found in one of the localized versions, but the English version was approved, the developer might be able to negotiate with the appropriate subsidiary on the violation, but only if it does not cause serious gameplay issues.

The packaging and manual must also be submitted for approval. Because of the turnaround time required to print and manufacture manuals, these submission deadlines are earlier. The final packaging, including localized versions, is submitted about four weeks before the final game code. This gives Microsoft time to review the contents and helps the evaluators better understand what to expect from the game.

The developer must check with their Microsoft account manager for the latest version of the TCRs and any changes to the approval process. The TCRs are updated regularly, and the developer must be aware of these changes so they can be included in the game. The approval process does not change that often, but double-check with the account manager on the requirements before submitting materials for approval.

Nintendo Approval Process

Nintendo's current approval process is slightly different. Developers have the option to submit their games to Nintendo for different evaluation services before the final approval. This is not a requirement, but it is a service Nintendo offers. The developers can submit their games for the following:

Concept evaluation: The developer submits a detailed design document of the game for feedback. Nintendo will provide information on what areas of the design need to be improved, what areas look fun, and so on.

Interim ROM evaluation (IROM): The developer submits a partially playable build for feedback. Nintendo will give feedback on the current state of the product and offer suggestions for changes. Allow two weeks in the schedule for this.

Final ROM evaluation: The developer submits the final version of the game for feedback. This is a good resource if the developer wants to achieve a final level of polish and play-balancing in the game. Allow one to two weeks in the schedule for this.

1st impression testing: The developer provides a near-complete build of the game, and Nintendo will report back on what the player's impression of the game is likely to be after a few hours of playing. This information can be used to further play-balance and polish the game. Allow one to two weeks in the schedule for this.

If there is time in the schedule, these services should be used when possible. This also gives the developer an opportunity for feedback on how audiences will react to the game as a whole.

Although the previous services are optional, the final version of the game must be separately submitted to each of Nintendo's subsidiaries for final approval or *lot check*. This is a check on the game to ensure that it is hardware compliant and that the game does not crash. Nintendo of America approves the U.S. version; Nintendo of Europe approves the European versions; and Nintendo of Japan approves the Japanese versions. The estimated turnaround time for lot check varies but will take some time. Schedule the submission date well in advance, so there is time for Nintendo to approve, manufacture, and ship the game. As always, the developer must check with the account manager to ensure the most up-to-date procedures are being followed.

Sony Approval Process

Sony's current approval process does not involve submitting the title for any type of evaluation before the final submission. The developer is responsible for testing the game, fixing all the bugs, and mastering the final versions. These final versions are then sent to Sony, along with required forms and other game resources, for approval. Each game must fulfill all the requirements on Sony's Technical Requirements Checklist (TRC) before they are approved for manufacturing.

Sony estimates that it takes two weeks to do a full approval cycle. At the end of the process, the game is either approved, tagged for resubmission, or not approved. If the title is not approved, it cannot be resubmitted without substantial changes. If the game has to be resubmitted, the developer will make the necessary changes and begin the approval process all over again. Submit titles for approval about six to eight weeks before the manufacturing date in order to have additional time for resubmissions. After a title is approved for manufacture, it takes about four to six weeks to press the discs, package the games, and ship them to retailers.

Each title must be separately submitted to Sony of America, Sony of Europe, or Sony of Japan. The companies are all independent entities and will evaluate the games without input from the other offices. It is not unheard of for a title to be approved for distribution in Europe and not approved for distribution in the United States.

Cell Phone Companies

Cell phone games must also be submitted to their publishers for approval. There are a variety of phone carriers, each with different game requirements. When working on games for cell phones, the developer should be in close contact with his account manager to get the latest information on the approval process and the technical requirements. After this information is received, the key deadlines must be added to the production schedule. If creating localized versions, the developer must talk to the correct company representative for the appropriate game version. As with console publishers, the developer might have to submit different versions of the game to different entities in the same company for approval.

SENDING THE CODE

Getting the gold masters to the desired destinations can be difficult. If working with a tight deadline in which every hour counts, plan carefully for the time it takes the master to get to the destination. It is common for gold masters to be delivered to the replication house on a disc, which means the logistics of physically getting the disc there on time must be accounted for in the schedule. In extreme situations, especially when trying to make a holiday ship date, it might be faster to hand deliver the gold. These decisions are usually made at the very last minute, when all other avenues for sending the master have been exhausted. This is obviously the most expensive way to get the masters to the proper destination. The advantage of having someone from the company personally deliver the master to its destination is that there is more assurance that it will get there in time. The downside is cost and finding someone who is able to drop everything and travel at the last minute.

One thing to be careful of when sending masters it to make sure that the correct masters are sent to the correct destination. By the time the game is wrapping up and the masters are ready to be sent, everyone on the development team is probably pretty frazzled. It is easy to mix up the packages and send the German masters to Australia and the French masters to Japan.

Recently, replication houses have started accepting electronic submissions, which reduce the amount of shipping time for the gold master code. When the files are received, the replication house can download the code, burn a master, and verify its functionality. Many third-party publishers and phone carriers now accept electronic submissions as well. This has cut down on the stress of trying to get hard copies of the code sent in a timely fashion. Check with the publisher or account manager to find out whether electronic submission is an option.

SUMMARY

The code release process is one of the most critical steps in developing a game. This is the point at which the developer and publisher agree that the game has been thoroughly tested and is ready to be sent to the manufacturer for replication and shipped to store shelves. If a game is code released too soon, there is a risk that a crash bug will be discovered after the game ships, which will have a negative impact on the game's sales. This chapter discussed a process for code releasing builds to make sure that all the details are accounted for and the game is really ready to go.

Part

VIII

Post-Production

The game development process does not end when the game is code released and on store shelves, although this is when many development teams consider a project to be completed. However, important steps still must be taken in order to officially wrap production on the game. A closing kit must be created, which archives the game code and assets for future use, and a postmortem needs to be conducted with the team.

This section discusses the tasks to complete before officially ending the game development cycle. Topics include the following:

- Completing a Postmortem
- Creating Closing Kits

23 Postmortems

In This Chapter

- Purpose of a Postmortem
- Conducting a Postmortem
- Lessons Learned Document

INTRODUCTION

Usually, postmortems are conducted at the end of the game development cycle, because they provide closure to the entire development cycle. They are an opportunity for you and your team to discuss the ups and downs of the project and how this knowledge can be applied to improving future projects. It's also an opportunity for the team to celebrate the game's completion with each other. The postmortem must involve feedback from the entire team in order to be useful. After the actual postmortem meetings are completed, the information from these discussions is distilled into a Lessons Learned document that outlines a plan for implementing some changes in the process for the next round of games. This chapter provides information on why a postmortem is important and how to successfully conduct one, write up an action plan, and implement changes.

PURPOSE OF A POSTMORTEM

The main purpose of a postmortem is to learn what methods worked and what didn't work during game development. These items are usually focused more on the production process—scheduling, planning, implementing features, and so on—instead of on the actual design features of the game. Although successes and failures in the game are discussed in postmortems, they are usually tied to something that was done correctly or incorrectly in the production process. For example, if the game is not play-balanced correctly, it could be that time was not scheduled to do this, or if the character models are getting rave reviews, it could be that the production process included some validation steps that allowed the characters artists to get the most out of the tools and technology when creating assets. Also, a postmortem is different from the project reviews and critical stage analysis discussed in Chapter 17, "Production Techniques," because they are focused on how the game development process operated, rather then the actual content of the game.

Postmortems tend to be overlooked in the development process for a variety of reasons, such as there is not enough time; it's not a high priority; or people are not interested in improving the process (after all, the game got done, didn't it?). However, postmortems are a vital way to learn from mistakes and validate new ideas that improved the process. By not doing one, developers are overlooking the greatest source of concrete information they have on making things more efficient, less costly, and better on future projects.

In order to extract this knowledge from the team, postmortems should focus on answering these questions:

Did we achieve the goals of the game? In order to document the answers to this question, you will need to prepare a project overview of what the original goals were and what the goals the game actually fulfilled. For example, the original goals might have included four character classes for the player to choose from, and the game actually only has three. The purpose of this question is not to highlight where the team fell short of the goal, but rather to evaluate why the goal wasn't achieved, such as changing scope, shifting priorities, or limited time. Solutions to these impediments can be examined and implemented to prevent this on the next game.

Were the project's schedule, resources, feature set, and quality expectations realistic for achieving the set goals? When discussing this question, you will want to bring up concrete examples of where these areas were properly planned for and areas where they weren't. This is not an opportunity for the team to personally attack others about their shortcomings. Instead, this question should focus on the facts of what happened to impede to goals of the project. For example, people could say something like the schedule did not account for bug-fixing the levels, therefore three levels were cut from the game in order to get the rest of the levels finished, or the approval process took too long and impacted the amount of time available to implement a feature.

What went right? What went wrong?   This is an opportunity for the team to relay personal experiences of what worked and didn't work on the project. By discussing both the positive and the negative, the team can carry over expertise to other projects of which procedures to implement and which ones to avoid. Additionally, if a procedure did not work, solutions can be discussed for ways to make something different work on the next project with the same desired results.

What are the lessons we learned?   The team examines all the information gathered from the previous questions asked and determines the core lessons learned during development. These lessons should focus on big picture items, and less on small details. The details can be used as methods for implementing the lesson learned on the next project. For example, "communicate deadlines clearly to the team" might be one lesson learned, whereas the methods for communicating these deadlines (email, status reports, weekly meetings) provide the details on how to accomplish this. The regular postmortems featured in *Game Developer* magazine provide some great examples of lessons learned.

If working on a project that takes more then a year to develop, try to schedule a mini postmortem after each major phase of the project: pre-production, alpha, beta, and code release. This way, you can continually improve the production process, instead of waiting until the next project to make improvements. If you are working on a project that takes a year or less, you can schedule a single postmortem at the end. Additionally, encourage people to take notes during the development process of things to discuss in the postmortem. This will ensure that the details are not forgotten and can be used to formulate solutions for the Lessons Learned document.

CONDUCTING A POSTMORTEM

Preparing for and conducting a postmortem might initially seem like a lot of work, but the benefits outweigh any inconveniences, especially if the lessons learned are taken seriously and implemented on the next round of projects. If you are currently working at a place where postmortems are not done, or they are done but nothing ever changes, you might want to meet with studio management to find out why this is. You can work together to add this valuable tool to the development process.

There are several different ways of doing a postmortem. Some are fairly simple and take little time; others can be more involved and time-consuming. Which method you use depends on how much time there is to do one, how in depth the lessons learned are expected to be, and what the overall goals are. For example, if you are working someplace where a postmortem has never been done, start off with something uncomplicated so that people can get familiar with the process. They might be overwhelmed if you try to have a postmortem that covers every single aspect of the project and takes a few days to complete. However, a simple postmortem will still help them uncover some basic lessons that can be applied to the development process. On the other hand, if you are working someplace that does postmortems on a regular basis and successfully implements lessons learned, you might want to focus on a more robust postmortem process, as it is likely that your team will benefit from a process that helps improve more than just the basics.

Several project management books are available that discuss how to conduct a postmortem. Please consult Appendix B, "Resources," for a full list. Additionally, *www.projectreview.net*, a Web site maintained by Bonnie Collier, offers a detailed process for conducting a thorough postmortem. Regardless of how you choose to run your game's postmortem, there are a few basics to follow.

Involve the Entire Team

The entire team must be involved in the process—QA testers, production personnel, artists, designers, and engineers. If the team is especially large (more than 20 people), you might want to first set up departmental postmortems and then schedule a final postmortem where the entire team gets together. The benefit of having departmental postmortems before the main one is that people can discuss the positives and negatives of their part of the project, formulate some new department procedures (such as a format for writing more useful design documents), and be better prepared to participate in the team postmortem. This will also prevent the team postmortem from getting bogged down with design, engineering, and art specific issues, since these issues will have been already covered. If the team is smaller, you probably don't need to schedule these departmental postmortems beforehand.

Prepare for the Postmortem

As with project reviews (discussed in Chapter 17, "Production Techniques,"), proper preparation is essential for getting the most out of the postmortem. Before scheduling the meeting, gather all the pertinent project information such as the original project goals, the actual project goals, deliverable lists, schedules, meeting minutes, change request forms, crunch time data, and anything else that provides the facts on what happened during the project. Share this information with the entire team and have them go through it before the meeting.

Establish a postmortem outline and send this to the team a few weeks before the meeting. They can take notes on what information they can contribute to the postmortem and be better prepared for the discussion. The outline does not need to be extremely detailed but should cover the high-level topics that will be discussed:

- Did we achieve the goals of the game?
- Were the project's schedule, resources, feature set, and quality expectations realistic for achieving the set goals?
- What went right? What went wrong?
- What are the lessons we learned?

Add sample questions under these topics to aid the team members in making notes on what they can contribute.

These sample questions should personalize the development experience for the team members, as they will make better contributions if they are speaking directly from personal experience. For example, ask questions such as the following:

- Were your game features completed? What aided or prevented this?
- Were your tasks appropriately scheduled during the course of the project?
- Did you understand your role on the project?
- Were the production pipelines useful to you? How can they be improved?
- Were you satisfied with your contribution to the game?
- What process worked the best for you? The worst?
- What will you do differently on the next project?

Finally, before confirming the time for the meeting (or meetings, if you are doing departmental postmortems), decide on an appropriate location. If the postmortem is going to take more than two hours, you might want to consider having it offsite. This will probably be more comfortable for people, especially if the team is large, and will prevent them from getting distracted by their work. Additionally, if the project was especially grueling, an offsite location will provide a neutral meeting place, and people might feel more comfortable discussing their positive and negative experiences.

Maintain Focus

When you actually sit down to have the postmortem meeting, keep the team focused on the goals by establishing the meeting norms discussed in Chapter 17, "Production Techniques:"

- Set an agenda
- Appoint a moderator
- Record minutes
- Follow up on action items

The agenda can be based on the outline sent to the team beforehand. The moderator should be someone neutral, ideally someone not involved in the project. If you are doing a thorough postmortem or do not have an experienced moderator, you might want to consider hiring an external one. The benefit is that this person knows how to properly facilitate discussion in this forum and can keep the meeting focused and running efficiently. The minutes should be recorded and published to everyone, but these do not take place of the Lessons Learned document that is produced as the final deliverable.

Although it is inevitable that many negatives will be discussed during the postmortem, the overall experience should be a positive one for everyone involved. Establish some participation guidelines in order to keep the mood positive and the criticism constructive. Some basic guidelines are as follows:

- Be professional at all times and don't make personal comments about other team members.
- Don't censor or criticize other people's comments.
- Maintain a positive attitude geared toward improving things for the future.
- Take the opportunity to show appreciation for the work you did together as a team.

Other guidelines can be added as necessary, and it is useful to post these in a prominent place in the meeting room.

After the goals are reinforced and people are reminded of the participation guidelines, you are ready to begin the actual meeting. Follow the agenda for each discussion point and be sure to get everyone to participate. Some team members are naturally more outspoken than others, and if not controlled, these people will end up dominating the meeting and deterring the less vocal people from fully participating. The moderator can control the information flow by calling on people to speak and gently cutting off people who have gotten off topic. If the group is small enough, you can start with the first question on the agenda and get feedback from everyone by calling on them individually. If the team is larger, be aware of who has already spoken a lot and who has not said anything. Overall, keep the meeting focused on the agenda and the set goals.

LESSONS LEARNED DOCUMENT

In addition to the postmortem meeting minutes, the Lessons Learned document is a written deliverable of the postmortem process. As discussed earlier in this chapter, the lessons learned focus on big picture items that can be applied to future projects. Ultimately, the Lessons Learned document will be published to the team, the studio, and perhaps even the publisher so that everyone can benefit from your team's experiences.

Writing the Lessons Learned document should not take too much time, especially if the notes from the postmortem are detailed and accurate. The lessons that will be included in the document will have been determined in the postmortem meeting. The author of the document can be a single person, like the producer, or several authors, such as the leads, can contribute to each section to speed up the writing process.

Limit the number of lessons learned in the document to five. Anything more than that is daunting to implement, thereby reducing the effectiveness of publishing the lessons in the first place. Focus on lessons that have the highest probability of being implemented. For example, one lesson might be "schedule time for risk assessment after each phase of the project." This is something that can be implemented fairly easily and does not require any upfront monetary investment. Conversely, a lesson that states, "Send everyone on team for training in Team Software Process," might not actually have a chance of being implemented due to schedule and budget constraints. However, lessons like these can be implemented if the company is committed to it, so gear each Lessons Learned document toward what the company can willingly commit to implement.

Provide an example of why the lessons learned are important. This is where the team's personal experience really helps define why change in a certain area is necessary. If scheduling time for risk assessment is a lesson, include the example that makes this important. For example, if a risk assessment had been done after the pre-production phase, the team would have realized that the personnel needed to implement the graphics features would not be available until later in the project, putting the level production at a huge risk for missing the beta deadline.

When the document is written, have it reviewed by the team, make any necessary corrections, and then publish it to the rest of the studio. You can publish it by posting it on the company Web site, emailing it to everyone, or sharing it in a specified place on the network. If your studio has multiple postmortems, centralize their location so they are readily accessible to everyone.

In order to ensure that lessons are being implemented, follow up with the team on what changes they've made. For example, before beginning production on the next project, sit down with the core team, review the lessons learned from the last project, and formulate an action plan to implement them. This action plan can become one of the pre-production project deliverables.

SUMMARY

When the team has worked hard to complete a project over the course of six months or three years, a postmortem is necessary to provide closure to the development process. A postmortem is an opportunity for the team to gather one final time to congratulate each other on a job well done and to learn from mistakes.

A successful postmortem does not need to pick apart every little thing that went wrong on a game, but rather should focus on things that went well and things that can be improved for future projects. This chapter discussed how to run a successful postmortem and determine lessons that can be applied to other projects.

24 Closing Kits

In This Chapter

- Defining Closing Kits
- Creating Closing Kits
- Contents of Closing Kits
- Organizing Content Effectively
- Finalizing Closing Kits
- Closing Kit Checklist

INTRODUCTION

When game production is complete, all the assets and code must be organized into a closing kit and archived. Without these archives, it is impossible to go back and rebuild the game for product re-releases, develop ports for different gaming platforms, and create localized versions. Additionally, these archived assets are used to create specialized versions of the game for Original Equipment Manufacturers (OEM), which can be preinstalled on computers or bundled with other hardware, such as video cards. These archives are also used to create any necessary game patches, and the patches themselves should be added to the archives after they are completed.

DEFINING CLOSING KITS

These closing kits can be organized in three ways: a full closing kit, a localization kit, and a translation kit. These kits are interrelated, and the type of kit necessary depends on how it is going to be used.

Full Closing Kit

A full closing kit contains all the final assets, source assets, documentation, and source code necessary to create a working version of the game, without assistance from the original development team. In some cases, the original development team is needed to clarify the documentation, offer expertise to fix a bug, or provide additional assets and code that were not included in the original archives. However, this is a rare occurrence, if all the information has been included in the kit.

This kit can be used to completely rebuild the game, modify the existing game, or create a patch for the game. A full closing kit is sent to people who are working on ports or are updating the current game with new functionality. A full closing kit needs to be completed for every game title to ensure that all the appropriate files are archived for future use.

Localization Kit

A localization kit is a subset of the full closing kit and contains only the assets that are necessary to create a localized version of the game. If the game has localization-friendly code, it is unlikely the source code will be needed to create the localized versions. This kit is smaller than the full closing kit and can be used by localization vendors to get the assets translated, integrated, and tested in the game without assistance from the development team.

A localization kit is easier for a localization vendor to work with since it contains only the assets and documentation needed to create localized versions. If the vendors receive a full closing kit, they will have to search through a lot of code, assets, and documentation just to pull out the items they need. With a localization kit, the vendor can avoid this and focus entirely on the localization. However, if the code is not localization-friendly, the localization vendor might need a full closing kit to modify the code. For example, if an external vendor is creating a Japanese version of the game and the game code is not double-byte enabled, the vendor will need game source code so this functionality can be added.

When an external vendor is working on localized versions that are releasing simultaneously with the primary game, a localization kit will be needed before the primary version is code released. This is not an ideal situation—assets and code included in the kit are not guaranteed to be final. If the vendor is working from a localization kit that is not final, designate a contact on the development team who can provide the vendor with regular asset updates. If this happens, the developer will need to create a proper localization kit after the project is released for future localizations.

Translation Kit

A translation kit is a subset of the localization kit. The translation kit contains only the assets and text that need to be translated. It does not contain all the files that are necessary to actually create the localized versions. A translator can get the translation kit, translate all the necessary text, and send this to the development team so they can integrate, test, and release the localized versions.

CREATING CLOSING KITS

Closing kits are created after the game is code released. This enables the developers to create an accurate archive of the source code and assets used to create the main version of the game and the localized versions. This archive must be created for every major commercially released iteration of the game.

Patches or other game content might be created after the game's initial release. The assets for this content need to be added to the closing kit as well. For example, the Xbox version of *Tom Clancy's Ghost Recon 2* released additional downloadable content after the main game shipped. An initial closing kit was created immediately after the game's original release date, and the assets for the downloadable content were added to the kit a few months later.

When content is added later, it can be organized as a mini closing kit that is added to the main closing kit. This mini kit would have its own set of assets, tools, documentation, and code and would be treated as a supplement to the main kit. This method is the easiest because the initial closing kit does not have to be reorganized to include the updated assets. Clearly label the mini closing with the name of the main game and the type of content it contains.

When the content update is more complex, such as adding a new character class or updating the game code to a different version, a new closing kit should be created with the updated information. Archive the previous version of the closing kit, but be sure this older version is not inadvertently sent in place of the newer version.

CONTENTS OF CLOSING KITS

A closing kit contains several items: assets, documentation, tools, and code. If one of these areas is neglected or does not contain enough information, the closing kit will be difficult to use. When the closing kit is not adequate, time is taken away from the original development team to answer questions and provide any missing information or assets. This can be a risk, especially if the team has moved on to another project, or certain team members are not at the company anymore.

Assets

All of the game's text, art, and audio assets must be included in the closing kit. It must contain the original source files of these assets, so that changes can be made to them and used in the game. For example, if creating a console port of a PC game, the development team might need to reduce the amount of memory used in the level geometry. If the source files for the level geometry are included in the closing kit, the console developers can use these as the basis for making the changes, instead of rebuilding the entire level from scratch. Additionally, if there are art assets to be localized, the developer will have the source files readily available for localization and will not need to re-do the entire asset.

The closing kit also needs the final format of all the assets used to create the game. This includes the source code, cinematics, logos, and so on. This is useful in two ways. First, all of the assets are available in a single place for creating new versions of the game. For example, if creating a console port, some of the final assets can be re-used. Second, the development team working on new content has concrete examples of what the final assets in the game should look like. When new assets are created and converted into the appropriate in-game format, the developer can double-check his work against assets that have already shipped with the main game.

Text Assets

Text assets contain any text, especially text that needs to be translated for localized versions. Be sure to include the following text assets in the closing kit:

- In-game text assets in all languages
- Help files and readme files
- Installer strings
- Error messages

A complete checklist of all the text assets to be modified should be created by the developer. This checklist will be immensely helpful to any external people who need to create localized versions of the game. They can look at the checklist and have an immediate idea of how many files need to be localized and where these files are located in the game. Figure 24.1 is a sample checklist. The first column lists the text filename, the second column provides details on the context of the text included in the file, the third column provides an estimated word count of what

needs to be localized, the fourth column show where this asset is located in the game, and the fifth column is for any additional notes.

Text Filename	Context	Est. Word Count	Game Location	Notes
Rewards.txt	These text strings appear in the game whenever the player wins a reward. They will appear on the screen momentarily after the player wins a reward.	100	\\Localization\French\Text\Ingame	
Level01.txt	These text strings are specific to level one. They tell the player the objectives for the level and contain all the conversations that the non-player characters have with each other.	600	\\Localization\French\Text\Ingame	
Button.txt	This is all the text used for the buttons in the UI shell. The text string limit for these words is about 25 characters.	550	\\Localization\French\Text\UI	

FIGURE 24.1 Checklist for text assets to be localized.

Voiceover Assets

Voiceover assets are another component of the closing kit. Several VO items need to be included in the closing kit:

- Uncompressed versions of all in-game VO files in all languages
- Voiceover scripts
- Casting notes
- Voiceover technical specifications
- Master voiceover sheet

Art Assets

All art files are included in the closing kit. This makes it easy for art assets to be modified for different versions of the game. Following are art assets included in the closing kit:

- Final art assets
- Unconverted source art assets used to create final art assets
- Logo art

As with the text assets, it is helpful to include a checklist of all the art assets that need to be localized. Figure 24.2 is a sample checklist that can be used for tracking the localized art assets. This is based on the checklist presented in Figure 24.1 and includes similar information.

Text Filename	Context	Est. Word Count	Game Location	Notes
PlayerWin.art	This image shows up when the player wins a game round.	3	\\Localization\French\Art	Localize the text layer in the Playerwin.bmp file use the ART tool to convert to .art format.
PlayerLose.art	This image shows up when the player loses a game round	3	\\Localization\French\Art	EMBEDDED TEXT. Need to alter the PlayerLose.bmp file and use the ART tool to conver to .art format.

FIGURE 24.2   Checklist for art assets to be localized.

Cinematic Assets

Include the final version of the cinematics in the closing kit, along with any source files. If the game contains a lot of cinematics, this will likely be many gigs of data. However, if these source files are not archived, no changes can be made to the cinematics without re-creating the entire thing from scratch. The main cinematic assets to include are as follows:

- Final cinematics with final sound mix
- Codecs and movie viewers
- Uncompressed cinematics
- Separate and uncompressed versions of music, sound effects, and VO tracks

Also include a checklist of all areas of the cinematics that would need to be localized. Figure 24.3 is an example.

Intro Cinematic

Asset	Status
Subtitles	
Voiceover	
Text quote at beginning of movie	
Text indicating date, time, location	
Game Logos	

FIGURE 24.3   Checklist for localized cinematics.

Localization Assets

If localized versions of the game have been created before the localization kit is finalized, all the localization assets that were created should be included as well. These assets include the following:

■ Translated text
■ Translated voiceover files
■ Glossaries defining game-specific terms

Box and Docs

Include any box and docs that are created for the original version of the game. Although the vendor might change the layout of the packaging to better suit the version he is creating, he needs to make sure that all the appropriate content is included. The types of box and docs assets are as follows:

Packaging: This is a .pdf file of the box layout and text and can usually be obtained from the marketing or creative services department.

Manual: A .pdf of the manual layout can be obtained from the marketing or creative services department. Additionally, if there is a final draft of the manual text in Microsoft Word form (that is, not a .pdf or Quark file), this should also be included in the kit.

Screenshots: Include screenshots used for the box and manual separately from the manual and box layouts files. Some of the screenshots used in the manual might have text overlays to call out specific parts of the image. For example, UI elements in the screenshot could be labeled on the image and then defined in the manual text. In this case, a labeled and unlabeled version of the screenshot should be included.

Electronic manuals: If an electronic version of the manual is created in .pdf or .html format, all the source assets are needed.

Tools

Tools refer to any proprietary tools or plug-ins that are used to create the final game assets. For example, if a specific text editor is needed to open and edit the text files, it should be included. Any proprietary program needed to convert art files into the graphic file format used by the game should also be included. Additionally, the kit should include any proprietary tools created by the development team to create game content, such as a design scripting tool or level editor. If these tools are not included, people working with the closing kit will not have ways to create new scripting for the game.

If specific commercial software is needed to create any of the game assets, the information and the correct version must be noted. For example, if the game code requires a specific version of Autodesk 3ds Max to create the levels, include this information. If someone is using the incorrect version, they will not be able to create and import new content into the game. The types of tools to include are as follows:

Plug-ins: A plug-in is software that augments the feature set of a larger software system. For example, a plug-in might be used in Photoshop to display a particular graphic file format.

Proprietary tools: These are tools created by the developer to handle the game assets. For example, the developer might create a proprietary scripting tool to create game play on the levels.

Text editor: A text editor opens text files and allows the user to edit the files. If a specific text editor is needed to work with the game's text assets, it should be included in the localization kit. If a specific text editor is not required, this should be noted in the kit documentation.

Localization integration tools: A developer might create proprietary tools that streamline the asset integration for the localized assets. If any localization-specific tools are available, include them in the kit.

Game Code

The game's source code is one of the most important components of the closing kit. If this is not included, the game cannot be rebuilt or modified in any way. The following types of code must be included in the closing kit:

Gold masters: Any gold masters that were created with the assets archived in the closing should be included. This includes masters for the primary version of the game and any localized versions.

Game source code: The game's source code must be included, along with documentation on how to compile and run the source code.

Tools source code: If proprietary tools have been developed, include the source code. This allows other developers to fix any bugs that occur when using the tool. For example, since Korean requires double-byte enabled code, the vendor might find that a tool for converting text files has trouble reading some of the Korean characters. Consequently, the assets do not get properly converted, and the text displays incorrectly in the game. If the source code is available for this tool, the vendor can fix the issue without asking the original development team for help.

Installer files: When working on PC games, the installer files must be included in the kit. If using a commercially available installer, include all the proper files so the vendor can open it and make any necessary changes.

Documentation

Documentation encompasses design documents, technical guidelines, tools information, and general information about the game. This will be the first place people will look when they are trying to use the closing kit. Make sure that the documentation is up-to-date and clearly written. The documentation can quickly explain what the game is, how the assets are organized, and any technical issues the developer will encounter when working with the assets.

When adding documentation to the closing kit, use descriptive filenames to make it easier to locate the correct information. For example, a document should be called "Using the RSB Editor," instead of "RSB." Additionally, provide a brief overview of each document or groups of documentation in the table of contents for the kit.

Table of Contents for Closing Kit

Include a table of contents for the closing kit on the first disc that completely details everything in the closing kit. At a minimum it should include descriptions of each main folder in the closing kit, and ideally it should include descriptions for all the subfolders as well. Figure 24.4 is a sample table of contents that has been started for a localization kit.

Contents of Localization Closing Kit
Kit created: December 15, 2005

1. Documentation—this folder contains all documentation for the closing kit. It includes:
   • Game documentation—Any documentation that pertains to the game itself, such as design documents, controller schemes, and box and docs.
   • Tools documentation—Any documentation that describes how to use the tools included in this closing kit.
   • Code Documentation—Any documentation that describes how to compile the source code to create a build of the game.

2. Assets—this folder contains all the assets that will need to be localized in the game. It includes:
   • Text assets
   • Art assets
   • Cinematic assets
   • Voiceover assets

FIGURE 24.4   Sample table of contents for localization kit.

Game Documentation

Include game documentation in the closing kit. This is useful for people creating ports of the game or creating new content for the game. It is also useful when creating special versions of the game for OEM distribution. The types of game documentation to include are as follows:

- Core design docs
- UI flow chart
- Cheats
- Mission walkthroughs
- Test plans and test scripts

Technical Guidelines

Technical guidelines provide information on how to integrate the assets, convert assets to the game-specific file formats, and hardware/software specifications. These technical guidelines should be clearly written and geared toward someone not on the original development team. The types of technical guidelines to include are as follows:

Production pipeline overview: This document provides information on the overall production pipeline. It should detail how each type of game asset gets created and converted into the final game format. It should also provide details on how to organize a source control system.

Localization pipeline overview: This document includes specific instructions on how to create localized versions of the game. Information on which assets to localize, what tools are necessary to integrate the translations into the assets, and how to convert the assets to the file format used should be included.

Build instructions: Build instructions detail how to set up the development environment to compile and build the game.

Software specifications: These specifications refer to any commercial or proprietary software that is needed for the game. If commercial software is used, include which version of the software is required for the game. If proprietary software is used, be sure to note any hardware specifications that are needed to run the software.

Hardware specifications: These specifications refer to any specific hardware that is needed for the game, such as console development kits or computers that meet certain minimum requirements. If using console development kits, include the contact information for the third-party publisher, so that developers can contact them for additional hardware.

Tools instructions: Any tools that are included in the closing kit need to have specific instructions on how to use them. Information on hardware specifications, how to install and run the tool, how to open and edit files, and how to convert file formats should be included. The instructions for the tools should be clearly written and geared toward someone who is not familiar with how to use the tools.

General Product Information

The general production information should also be included in the closing kit. The contact information is especially important, so that someone knows whom to ask if there are problems with or questions about the closing kit. Figure 24.5 is a form that can be used to list the general product information.

General game information: This gives the vendor specifics on which version of the game is included in the kit. General information about the game's original release date, the version, and the platform should be provided.

Contact information: This should be someone who can be contacted with any questions about the closing kit or the game. This contact acts as the liaison between an external developer and the original development team.

Known bugs: If there are known issues or bugs that are not being addressed for the game, these should be included in the kit. For example, if there is a known bug in the final version of the game code about the capitalized versions of accented letters displaying incorrectly, include this information in the kit.

Project Name	
Internal Contact	
Email	
Phone	
Mailing Address	
Platform	Xbox
Source Language	English
Target Language(s)	French, German, Spanish
English Code release date	September 1, 2004
Version Number	1.00
Multilingual CD-ROM	Italian, Spanish will be on one CD
Number of CD-ROMs	3

FIGURE 24.5 Form to list general product information.

ORGANIZING CONTENT EFFECTIVELY

It is important that the closing kit is well organized and contains thorough documentation. The kit must be useful to someone who has not worked on the game before. Although each kit will be organized differently, there are a few general rules to follow when organizing the localization kit.

Organize the game assets, documentation, code, and tools into separate folders. Figure 24.6 is an example of this basic directory structure. The "Kit_Contents" document is a detailed table of contents for the localization kit. Each main folder is further broken down into subfolders that are logically organized, see the "Game Assets" folder in Figure 24.6 for an example of this.

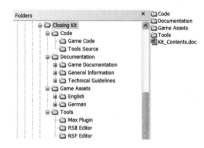

FIGURE 24.6 Directory structure for localization kit.

If putting the kit on multiple discs, the documentation and table of contents file should be located on the first disc for easy reference. If possible, include the documentation and tools on one disc, and the game assets and game code on a second disc.

Documentation

The detailed table of contents is always at the root of the first disc in the closing kit. Next, create a folder called "Documentation" with subfolders labeled "Game Documentation," "Technical Guidelines," and "General Product Information." The directory structure then gets more detailed within these folders. For example, the "Game Documentation" folder contains subfolders for "Core Design Documents," "Cheats," and "UI Flow." Refer to Figure 24.6 for examples of the subfolders to create for the "Technical Gidelines" and "General Information" folders.

Tools

Create a "Tools" folder and include a subfolder for each tool. The subfolders should be labeled with the name of the tool. In Figure 24.6, the tools subfolders are called

"Max Plugin," "RSB Editor," and "RSF Editor." Each folder contains all the files to run the designated tool, along with directions on how to set up and use the tool.

Code

Create a "Code" folder and include subfolders for game code and tools source code. The game code folder should contain all the files that are used to create a master of the game. The tools source code folder should include a subfolder for each tool that has source code. In Figure 24.6, the tools source code folder will contain directories for "RSB Editor" and the other tools. Also include compiling instructions with each set of source code.

Assets

The "Game Assets" folder contains all the source art, source audio, source cinematic files, packaging, and source text assets. A separate folder can be created for each language. In Figure 24.6, "English" and "German" folders are created. This disc can also be used as the basis for a localization kit, because it contains all the assets needed to create the localized game assets.

The structure of the "assets" directory for each type of asset in the kit should mimic how the assets are stored on the game directory structure. Figure 24.7 is a an example of a game asset directory structure. In this example, the audio files are not all located in a single folder; they are organized by character and mission.

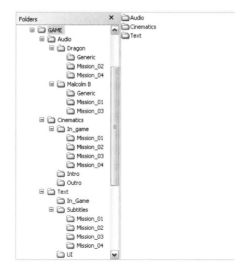

FIGURE 24.7 Directory structure for game assets.

The same is true for text files. If the text files are organized a certain way in the game directory, they should be organized in a similar way in the closing kit. If the assets are organized in this manner, someone unfamiliar with the game can quickly see where all the assets are located in the game. This makes it easier to alter the assets if necessary and correctly replace them.

FINALIZING CLOSING KITS

After everything has been collected and organized into a closing kit, do a final check to ensure that all the proper assets and instructions have been included. Then give the complete kit to a developer who was not on the original development team and ask him to create a sample gold master. While doing this, he is checking the kit for accuracy of contents and clarity of directions. This important step should not be skipped. If the contents of the kit are not verified by a third party before sending it out, the kit might be missing key tools and information that are necessary for creating the game builds.

When the contents have been verified, there are a few more other checks to do before the kit is finalized. First, check all the files to make sure that they are not corrupted. Second, virus scan all the files to make sure that they are all virus-free. Third, verify that no extra files are included and that no files are missing. Fourth, verify that all the files are the most current. After these checks have been made and the contents confirmed, the kit can be considered final.

Storing and Maintaining Localization Kits

Usually, a copy of the closing kit is stored with the original developer; another copy of the kit is sent to the publisher's archives; and another copy of the kit is stored offsite with other closing kits. Multiple storages areas ensure that the correct data will always be available, even if one kit is lost or missing information.

Each disc should be clearly labeled with the following:

- Game name
- Version number
- Platform
- Date the kit was created
- Disc number, out of total number of discs
- General description of contents (documentation, tools, and so on)

This information is useful if there are several discs in the localization kit or if there have been updates to the kit. This information also lets the vendor know which disc will contain the information he is looking for.

If the closing kit is updated to include patches or additional content created after the game was released, create a mini closing kit with the critical assets stored on a separate set of discs. The table of contents should state that this kit is an addendum to the main kit, and include information on how this mini kit should be used in relation to the main closing kit.

CLOSING KIT CHECKLIST

Figure 24.8 is a sample checklist of all the items to include in a closing kit. The first section lists all the assets to include in the kit. The following sections list the code, tools, and documentation to include in the kit. The last section is a list of questions to answer before the closing kit is finalized.

ASSETS	Y/N	NOTES
TEXT ASSETS		
Source text assets (in-game, UI, installer, help files, error messages, etc.) for all languages		
Checklist for all text assets in the game		
VOICEOVER ASSETS		
Source vo files for all languages		
Voiceover script		
Casting notes		
Voiceover technical specifications		
Master voiceover sheet		
ART ASSETS		
Source art assets (to be coverted to game file format) for all langauges		
Logo art		
Checklist for all art assets to be localized		
CINEMATICS		
Final compressed cinematics		
Codecs and movie player needed for cinematics		
Uncompressed cinematics		
Sound mix components (music, sound effects, and voiceover on separate tracks—uncompressed)		
Final sound mix		
Checklist for localized cinematics		
LOCALIZATION ASSETS		
Localization glossaries		
Text translation spreadsheet		
		(continued)

FIGURE 24.8 Closing kit checklist.

ASSETS	Y/N	NOTES
BOX AND DOCS		
Packaging layout		
Manual layout		
Final version of manual in Word document		
Screenshots		
Assets for electronic manual		
Checklist for box and docs to be localized		
TOOLS		
Plug-ins (software specs included)		
Proprietary tools (software and hardware specs included)		
Text editors		
Localization tools		
CODE		
Gold masters of each language		
Game source code		
Tools source code		
Installer files		
DOCUMENTATION		
Contents of closing kit (at root of first CD in closing kit)		
Game Documentation		
UI flow chart		
Core design documents		
Cheats		
Mission walkthroughs		
Test plans and test scripts		
Technical Guidelines		
Production pipeline overview		
Localization pipeline overview		
Build instructions		
Software specifications		
Hardware specifications		
Tools instructions		
General Product Information		
General game information		
Contact information		
Known bugs		
QUESTIONS TO ANSWER		
Is the closing kit table of contents clearly written and contained at the root of the first CD?		
Are assets grouped by kind in separate folders?		
Are assets grouped within the game's directory structure so they can be easily dropped into the game code?		
		(continued)

FIGURE 24.8 Closing kit checklist.

ASSETS	Y/N	NOTES
Have files in kit all be checked to make sure they are not corrupted or contain any viruses?		
Are any files missing?		
Are any extra files included?		
Are all assets finalized and the most current versions?		
Is each disc clearly labeled with game name, version number, platform, date, and disc number?		
Has kit been tested by someone outside the development team to ensure that is properly creates localized versions?		
Are directions clear and easy to understand?		
Has data on closing kit been protected for sending to external vendors?		
Has one copy of kit been sent to offsite storage?		
Is one copy of kit archived on site?		

FIGURE 24.8   Closing kit checklist.

SUMMARY

Organizing a closing kit is an important step in the production process. This kit enables external vendors or other development teams to create additional versions of the game. This chapter provided detailed information on what to include in the closing kit, along with advice on how to organize, finalize, and store the kit most effectively. The chapter concluded with a checklist for what needs to be included in a closing kit.

Appendix

A Glossary

AFTRA Abbreviation for American Federation of Television and Radio Artists. This is a union representing journalists and other artists working in the entertainment and news media.

AI Abbreviation for Artificial Intelligence.

API Abbreviation for Application Programming Interface. APIs are sets of protocols and tools for programming software. Software that uses a common API will have a similar user interface.

ASCII An acronym for the American Standard Code for Information Interchange. This is a standardized code for representing letters and symbols as numbers so data can be easily transferred from one computer to another. ASCII, which is limited to using 7 or 8 bits for each character, defines 256 unique characters numbered from 0 to 255. For example, the ASCII code for "$" is "36." This code is suitable for representing any English language characters but is not suitable for displaying Japanese, Chinese, or Greek characters.

asset pack Another term for *closing kit*. An asset pack or closing kit contains all the necessary assets, documentation, and source code to rebuild a game from scratch without assistance from the original developer. Different types of asset packs and closing kits are available. A full closing kit contains all the necessary assets to rebuild the entire game. A localization closing kit is a subset of the full closing kit and contains only the necessary assets to create localized versions of the game. A translation kit is a subset of the localization kit and contains only the assets that need to be translated for localized versions; it does not contain the items necessary to create the localized build.

bidirectional text The ability to read and input text that can be read either left to right or right to left. Most European languages are traditionally read from left to right. Other languages, such as Hebrew and Arabic, are read from right to left. If an engine supports bidirectional text, both ways of reading and inputting text are supported in the game engine.

box and docs   A game industry term referring to all supporting packaging, such as the manual, box, and keyboard layout card, that ships with the game code.

cinematics   Prerendered or in-game movies that are part of the gameplay experience. They are used to further the game's story during gameplay.

closing kit   See **asset pack.**

code release   A term describing a product that has been fully tested, bug-fixed, and deemed ready to ship by the publisher.

codec   Software technology that compresses and decompresses data. Specific codecs are used for doing this. Some movie players, such as QuickTime®, already have common codecs installed and can view any data compressed with these codecs. Some codecs are not included automatically in the movie player and need to be downloaded and installed.

concatenation   A method whereby different text string files or voiceover files are pulled from the engine, spliced together, and displayed to the player. An example of this is "[Player Name] is now winning," where the appropriate player name is pulled from the string file and displayed alongside the phrase "is now winning."

developer producer (DP)   A producer who heads up an internal development team comprised of artists, engineers, and designers.

double-byte   A character code format that allows Asian characters to be displayed in a game. Most European characters are single-byte, meaning it only takes one byte, or 8 bits, to display them. ASCII is a single-byte character code format. Most Asian languages are double-byte, which means it takes two bytes, or 16 bits, to display them. Because most Asian languages use a very symbol-heavy language system, the extra byte is necessary in order to have enough codes to represent all the unique characters. Unicode is a double-byte character code format.

dubbed   When localized dialogue is substituted for the original dialogue in a cinematic and the character's mouth movements are not resynced to match this localized dialogue.

ESRB   Acronym for Entertainment Software Ratings Board, the entity in the United States that assigns age ratings to games.

EULA   Abbreviation for End User License Agreement, a legal agreement between the game publisher and the game purchaser.

FIGS   An acronym commonly referring to localizing a game into French, Italian, German, and Spanish.

fingerprinting   The process of marking a game build with a unique identifier. This allows developers to track down the source of any unauthorized builds that are replicated or posted on the Internet.

full localization   A game where everything, including all the text, voiceover files, graphics, and documentation, is fully translated into another language.

functionality testing   QA testing that concentrates on finding bugs in the game code.

gold master   The final version of the game code that is code released and sent to manufacturing.

HUD   Acronym for Heads Up Display, common user interface elements in an interactive game. These elements usually indicate the player character's statistics, such as health, time elapsed, weapon status, and so on.

intellectual property (IP)   Ideas that are protected under federal law, including copyrightable works, ideas, discoveries, and inventions.

internationalization   The process of creating a product that can be easily localized without changing the design of the product. For example, international date formats are accounted for in the product design.

lip-syncing   When spoken dialog in a cinematic is synced up to the movement of the character's mouth.

localization   The process of adapting a game to a specific country. This includes the translation, integration, and testing of localized assets.

localization-friendly   Game code that has been developed with the idea of creating efficient and easy-to-do localizations. All considerations have been made in order to best internationalize the game code, which include things such as enabling double-byte functionality in the engine and using icons in the user interface.

NDA   Acronym for Non-Disclosure Agreement, a legal document used to protect proprietary information.

NTSC   An acronym for National Television System Committee. U.S. televisions adhere to NTSC video display standards, which means that the video image delivers 525 lines of resolution at 60 half-frames per second. U.S. console games are developed according to these standards so that they will display on NTSC televisions and other NTSC-compatible video monitors.

OEM   Acronym for Original Equipment Manufacturers. They manufacture hardware add-ons for computers, such as video cards, headsets, and joysticks.

operating system (OS)   The operating system performs basic tasks for the computer, such as recognizing input from the mouse, displaying output to the monitor, and providing a base for running applications. It also manages peripheral devices such as printers and scanners. The OS is language specific and can detect which languages to display when running applications. The application needs to have this capability programmed into the code before the OS will detect the correct language setting.

P&L A profit-and-loss statement generated by the publisher to determine whether a product will be profitable. Production, marketing, and distribution costs are compared against the money made from a projected sale of the game.

PAL An acronym for Phase Alternating Line. European televisions adhere to PAL video display standards, which means that the video image delivers 625 lines of resolution at 50 half-frames per second. European console games are developed according to these standards so that they will display on PAL televisions and other PAL-compatible video monitors.

partial localization A game that only has the in-game text and documentation translated. The voiceover is either subtitled or not translated at all.

patch A piece of game code created to deal with existing bugs in an already shipped product. The patch will modify game files on the user's hard drive to fix any critical bugs that inadvertently shipped with the game. The patch is usually offered for download on the Internet.

PEGI Abbreviation for Pan European Game Information, the entity in Europe that assigns age ratings to interactive games.

platform The type of hardware that is required to run a game. Some examples are PC, Nintendo DS, Sony PSP, and Xbox.

proprietary software Software that is created and owned by the developer. The software is not authorized for public use, and the source code is not available publicly. For example, the developer can write proprietary software to convert .bmp files to a graphic file format that is recognized by the game.

publisher producer (PP) A producer who works for the publisher and interfaces with external development teams.

SAG Abbreviation for Screen Actors Guild. This is a union representing actors working in the entertainment media.

SDK Abbreviation for Software Development Kit. An SDK is a programming package that can be used to develop software. An SDK usually includes APIs, tools, and documentation. If you are working with middleware, the vendor will provide you with an SDK with all the pertinent information.

sim-ship The practice of shipping the localized and English versions simultaneously.

timecodes Refers to copying the start time and end times in a cinematic so the character's dialogue can be synced as closely as possible to his mouth movements.

Unicode An internationally standardized code for representing letters and symbols as numbers so data can be easily transferred from one computer to another. Unicode, which uses 16 bits for each character, represents more then 65,000 unique characters, including Japanese, Chinese, and Greek characters. A

Unicode-enabled application allows characters from all languages to be handled simultaneously by an application, assuming the application has the necessary fonts available to display the characters. Unicode is supplanting ASCII as the standard character-coding format.

user interface (UI)   Areas of the game where the user can input or receive information. For example, the user can select a character from a list of choices or get information about his character's health from a health bar indicator.

work breakdown structure (WBS)   A project management process in which large tasks are broken down into smaller tasks.

Appendix

B Resources

BOOKS

Bennis, Warren, *On Becoming a Leader*, Addison-Wesley Publishing Company, 1989.

Bethke, Erik, *Game Development and Production*, Wordware Publishing, Inc., 2003.

Brooks, Frederick P., Jr., *The Mythical Man-Month, Anniversary Edition*, Addison-Wesley Publishing Company, 1995.

Buckingham, Marcus and Curt Coffman, *First Break All the Rules: What the World's Greatest Managers Do Differently*, Simon and Schuster, 1999.

Carter, Ben, *The Game Asset Pipeline*, Charles River Media, 2004.

Chandler, Heather Maxwell, *The Game Localization Handbook*, Charles River Media, 2004.

Covey, Stephen R., *The 7 Habits of Highly Effective People*, Free Press, 1989.

DeCarlo, Doug, *Extreme Project Management*, Jossey-Bass, 2004.

DeMarco, Tom and Timothy Lister, *Peopleware: Productive Projects and Teams*, Second Edition, Dorset House Publishing Co., 1999.

Drucker, Peter F., *The Essential Drucker*, Harper Business, Division of Harper Collins, 2003.

Esselink, Bert, *A Practical Guide to Localization*, John Benjamins Publishing Company, Microsoft Press, 2000.

Festinger, Jon, *Video Game Law*, LexusNexus Canada, 2005.

Kano, Nadine, *Developing International Software for Windows® 95 and Windows NT™*, Microsoft Press, 1995.

Koster, Raph, *A Theory of Fun for Game Design*, Paraglyph Press, 2005.

Kouzes, James M. and Barry Z. Posner, *The Leadership Challenge*, Jossey-Bass Publishers, 1997.

Kroeger, Otto with Janet M. Thuesen, *Type Talk at Work*, Dell Publishing, 1992.

Landsberg, Max, *The Tao of Coaching*, Harper Collins, 1996.

Laramee, Francois Dominic, editor, *Secrets of the Game Business,* Second Edition, Charles River Media, 2005.

Lewis, James P., *Mastering Project Management*, McGraw-Hill, 1998.

———, *Project Leadership*, McGraw-Hill, 2003.

———, *Project Planning Scheduling and Control*, Third Edition, McGraw-Hill, 2001.

———, *Team-Based Project Management*, American Management Association, 1998.

Litwak, Mark, *Litwak's Multimedia Producer's Handbook*, Silman-James Press, 1998.

Liverman, Matt, *The Animator's Motion Capture Guide: Organizing, Managing, and Editing*, Charles River Media, 2004.

McConnell, Steve, *Rapid Development*, Microsoft Press, 1996.

Mencher, Marc, *Get in the Game: Careers in the Game Industry*, New Riders Publishing, 2003.

Michael, David, *The Indie Game Development Survival Guide*, Charles River Media, 2003.

Schwaber, Ken and Mike Beedle, *"Agile Software Development with SCRUM,"* Prentice Hall, 2001.

Schuh, Peter, *Integrating Agile Development in the Real World,* Charles River Media, 2005.

Wysocki, Robert K., *Effective Project Management,* Third Edition, Wiley Publishing, Inc., 2003.

ARTICLES

Ahearn, Luke, "Budgeting and Scheduling Your Game," available online at *http://www.gamasutra.com/features/20010504/ahearn_01.htm*, May 2001.

Buscaglia, Thomas H., Esq., "Completing Your Contract Arsenal—NDAs, Employee, and Consultant Agreements," available online at *http://gamedevkit.com/gamearticle3.html*, 2005.

———, *"Initial Legal Issues,"* available online at *gamedevkit.com/gamearticle1.html*, 2005.

———, "Just What are These Games Made Of . . . Legally Speaking?," available online at *gamedevkit.com/gamearticle2.html*, 2005.

Dowling, Patrick, "Localizing for Lands Beyond the Wild Frontier," available online at *www.gamasutra.com/features/production/19980828/localization_01.htm*, 1998.

Gonzalez, Lauren, "When Two Tribes Go to War: A History of Videogame Controversy," available online at *www.gamespot.com/features/6090892/index.html*, 2004.

Hamann, Wolfgang, "Goodbye Post Mortems, Hello Critical Stage Analysis," available online at *www.gamasutra.com/resource_guide/20030714/hamann_01.shtml*, 2003.

Hefter, Laurence R. and Robert D. Litowiz, "What is Intellectual Property?," available online at *http://usinfo.state.gov/products/pubs/intelprp/*, 1999.

International Game Developers Association, "Quality of Life in the Game Industry: Challenges and Best Practices," available online at *http://www.igda.org/qol/whitepaper.php*, 2004.

Käpyaho, Jere, "Internationalisation in Operating Systems for Handheld Devices," available online at *http://www.cs.uta.fi/research/theses/masters/Kapyaho_Jere.pdf*, Master's Thesis, 2001.

Jassin, Lloyd J., "Working with Freelancers: What Every Publisher Should Know About the 'Work for Hire' Doctrine," available online at *http://copylaw.com/new_articles/wfh.html*.

Marcus, Aaron and Emilie W. Gould, "Cultual Dimensions and Global Web Design: What? So What? Now What?," available online at *http://www.amanda.com/resources/hfweb2000/AMA_CultDim.pdf*, 2001.

Meltzer, Max, "Managing an International Remote Development Team," available online at h*ttp://www.gamasutra.com/resource_guide/20030714/meltzer_01.shtml*, 2003.

Pavlina, Steve, "Conducting a Project Postmortem," available online at *http://www.gamedev.net/reference/articles/article977.asp*, 2000.

Puha, Thomas "Eurospeak: Localizing Games for the European Market," available online at *www.gamasutra.com/features/20010403/puha.htm, 2001*.

U.S. Copyright Office, "Circular 9: Works Made for Hire Under the 1976 Copyright Act," Library of Congress, available online at: *http://www.copyright.gov/circs/circ9.html*, 2004.

WEB SITES

Academy of Interactive Arts and Sciences (AIAS)—*www.interactive.org*

Agile Game Development—*www.agilegamedevelopment.com*

American Federation of Television and Radio Artists (AFTRA)—*www.aftra.org*

Blues News—*www.bluesnews.com*

Consumer Electronics Show (CES)—*www.cesweb.org*

Develop—*www.developmag.com*

Electronic Entertainment Expo—*www.e3expo.com*
The Escapist—*www.escapistmagazine.com*
Gamasutra—*www.gamasutra.com*
GameDev.net—*www.gamedev.net*
Game Developers Conference—*www.gdconf.com*
Game Development Search Engine—*www.gdse.com*
Game Developer Magazine—*www.gdmag.com*
Game Rankings—*www.gamerankings.com*
International Game Developers Association (IGDA)—*www.igda.org*
Metacritic—*www.metacritic.com*
Moby Games—*www.mobygames.com*
Next-generation—*www.next-gen.biz*
Personal Software Process (PSP)—*www.sei.cmu.edu/tsp/psp.html*
Project Review—*www.projectreview.net*
Screen Actors Guild—*www.sag.com*
Scrum—*www.controlchaos.com*
SIGGRAPH—*www.siggraph.org*
Tom Sloper—*www.sloperama.com*

The following people were interviewed for this book. Their knowledge of and insight into the game industry provides useful information featured throughout the book.

TOM BUSCAGLIA

Tom Buscaglia, the Game Attorney, practices law around the world from his offices in Miami, Florida (*www.gameattorney.com*). Tom is dedicated to the computer and video game industry, assisting developers in all aspects of their legal and business needs, and has been representing game developers since 1991. Tom is a member of the Board of Directors, as well as the Coordinator of the South Florida Chapter, of the International Game Developers Association (*www.igda.org*). He has published numerous articles to help those wishing to start their own game development studios and recently launched *www.GameDevKit.com* to further assist start-up game developers. Tom is a perennial presenter at the annual Game Developer's Conference, the Indie Games Com, and numerous other game-related conferences. He is also the executive director of the Interactive Entertainment Institute, the presenters of the G.A.M.E.S. Synergy Summit (*www.SynergySummit.com*) and of Games Florida (*www.Games-Florida.org*). As FaTe[F8S] Tom plays online on a regular basis with FaTe's Minions and has a gamer's appreciation and understanding of the game industry (*www.f8s.com*).

MELANIE CAMBRON

Since 1997 Melanie Cambron has been recruiting for game industry leaders such as THQ, Ubisoft, and Turbine. Featured in such books as *Game Design: Secrets of the Sages, Game Creation and Careers, The Fat Man on Game Audio, Get in the Game!*

Careers in the Game Industry, and *Secrets of the Game Business* for her game industry knowledge, she also wrote the foreword to the successful book, *Game Programming with Direct X 7.0* and its follow-up. Melanie is a popular guest speaker at universities and high schools and is frequently interviewed by media such as the Dallas Morning News, GIGnews, and Salon.com for her industry expertise. She has been a moderator and panelist at e3 and GDC. She also has several game credits as a PR/marketing consultant.

CAREY CHICO

Carey Chico has been working in the game industry since 1996, after graduating from UCLA with a Bachelor's degree in Design. His foray into the game industry began when he started at Activision Studios as an animator on *Planetfall*. From there, he rose through the ranks as lead artist on *Battlezone* and then as a founding member of Pandemic Studios where he completed *Battlezone 2* as art director. After working again as art director on *Star Wars: The Clone Wars*, he stepped up as studio art director to oversee more global and long-term art interests. Some of the most recent titles under his supervision are *Full Spectrum Warrior*, *Battlefront*, *Mercenaries*, and *Destroy All Humans*.

STEPHANIE O'MALLEY DEMING

Stephanie is a software development producer, consultant, and operations executive with more than 10 years experience in worldwide award-winning educational and entertainment products for companies including Activision, Compton's NewMedia, MGM, The Learning Company, and Roaring Mouse. She specializes in localizations and has successful sim-shipped many language versions of high-profile titles on multiple platforms including *Call of Duty: Finest Hour*, *Vampire: Bloodlines*, *Empires: Dawn of the Modern World*, *Civilization: Call to Power*, *Call to Power 2*, and *Dark Reign 2*. Stephanie founded XLOC (*www.xloc.com*), a company that offers Web-based applications for easy localization management, and works as a consultant for interactive game companies. She holds degrees in both psychology and sociology from the University of California, Santa Barbara.

JAMIE FRISTROM

Jamie has a long history with the industry dating back to 1991, when he graduated from UCSD with a degree in psychology. His first job was at MindCraft working on the *Magic Candle* series. Recently, he was a lead programmer and a designer on *Spider-Man 2*. Currently, he is one of the creative directors on *Spider-Man 3*. Other titles he has worked on include *Die By The Sword* and *Draconus*. He has also ported a couple of games from the *Tony Hawk* franchise to the Dreamcast. He's been blogging about game development since 2002. His current blog is at *www.gamedevblog. com*. He also writes a column for *Gamasutra* titled "Manager in a Strange Land," which discusses aspects of managing game development.

TRACY FULLERTON

Tracy Fullerton is a game designer, educator, and writer with more than a decade of professional experience. She is currently an assistant professor in the Interactive Media Division of the USC School of Cinema-Television where she serves as co-director of the new Electronic Arts Game Innovation Lab. Tracy is also the author of *Game Design Workshop: Designing, Prototyping and Playtesting Games*, a design textbook in use at game programs worldwide.

Prior to joining the USC faculty, she was president of the interactive television game developer, Spiderdance, Inc. Spiderdance's games included NBC's *Weakest Link*, MTV's *webRIOT*, The WB's *No Boundaries*, History Channel's *History IQ*, Sony Game Show Network's *Inquizition,* and TBS's *Cyber Bond*. Before starting Spiderdance, Tracy was a founding member of the New York design firm R/GA Interactive. As a producer and creative director, she created games and interactive products for clients including Sony, Intel, Microsoft, AdAge, Ticketmaster, Compaq, and Warner Bros. among many others. Notable projects include Sony's multiplayer *Jeopardy!* and multiplayer *Wheel of Fortune* and MSN's *NetWits*, the first multiplayer online game show.

Tracy's work has received numerous industry honors including best Family/ Board Game from the Academy of Interactive Arts & Sciences, *ID Magazine's* Interactive Design Review, Communication Arts Interactive Design Annual, several New Media Invision awards, iMix Best of Show, the Digital Coast Innovation Award, IBC's Nombre D'Or, and *Time Magazine's* Best of the Web. In December 2001, she was featured in the *Hollywood Reporter's* "Women in Entertainment Power 100" issue.

RAYMOND HERRERA

Los Angeles-based drummer and producer Raymond Herrera has spent the last 14 years writing, recording, and touring with his bands Fear Factory, Brujeria, and Kush. Raymond is a co-founder of 3volution Productions and Kool Arrow Records. He has produced and acted as a music supervisor on many videogame and movie soundtracks. He has earned three gold records, one platinum record, and the California Music Award for Best Hard Rock Act.

CLINT HOCKING

Clint has an MFA in creative writing from the University of British Columbia, where he completed his thesis at the same time as working on *Splinter Cell* and *Splinter Cell: Chaos Theory*. Along with writer J.T. Petty, Clint was honored for his work on the first *Splinter Cell* with the first-ever Game Developers' Choice Award for Excellence in Scriptwriting at GDC 2003. Clint is on Montreal's IGDA advisory board and also sits on the Advisory Board for the Electronic Game & Interactive Development degree program at Champlain College in Vermont. He is currently working as a creative director at Ubisoft in Montreal, where he lives happily with his fiancée Anne-Marie and their dog.

LEE JACOBSON

Lee never quite grew up as a kid, programming his first video game at the age of 16 on his Atari 400 computer (he couldn't afford the 800 model) between all-night sessions hacking away at Ultima and Wizardry. In 1988, he co-founded one of the first interactive media-based advertising companies in Dallas, Texas, which was acquired in 1990.

He then headed west to manage business development at Virgin Interactive Entertainment/Viacom in Irvine, California, and later joined Midway Games, Inc. in 1998 where he serves as Vice President of Business Development and Acquisitions. Lee's career spans more than 15 years in the entertainment industry and includes managing product/business development, acquisitions, domestic/international licensing, and strategic planning for Midway.

CLINTON KEITH

Clinton Keith came from the defense industry to the game industry in the early 90s as a tools programmer for Angel Studios. There he eventually led the teams that developed the first generation of Angel driving games (*Midtown Madness*, *Midnight Club*, and *Smugglers Run*) and eventually directed all product development. For the past three years, he has been at High Moon Studios (formerly Sammy Studios), first leading the Engine and Tools team and currently as the CTO.

ERIK LOUDEN

Erik Louden has more than 10 years of professional video game testing experience under his belt. Erik has beta-tested almost 50 games, including titles such as *Bad Mojo, Wizards & Warriors, Fighter Squadron: The Screaming Demons over Europe, M.A.X.X, Planet Side, Shadow Bane, Vampire: The Masquerade, Ever Quest,* and *Ultima On-Line* among others. He was an original member of Activision's Visioneers, an external beta-testing program, and he is currently a member of the Atari testing group.

JEFF MATSUSHITA

Jeff Matsushita is a ten-year veteran of the videogame business. After gaining production experience through careers in film, video, IT, and the then-emerging Internet, he joined Activision in Tokyo where he helped localize US titles for the Japanese market. He moved back to the United States where he continued working for Activision as an associate producer in development. As the industry transitioned to separate publishing and development, he decided to bring his experience to bear on the publishing side of the business where he oversaw several externally developed titles as both a producer and a senior producer. Jeff currently works as Activision's Greenlight Czar where he helps ensure the health of all titles in development.

STUART ROCH

Stuart Roch has been a member of the interactive industry for the past nine years working in quality assurance, design, and production capacities. While at Shiny Entertainment, Stuart acted in design and production roles on *Wild 9, R/C Stunt Copter, Messiah,* and the critically acclaimed *Sacrifice.* Stuart led the Shiny team in production of *Enter the Matrix,* which shipped in 2003, eventually going on to sell more than six million units worldwide on all major platforms. Currently an executive producer at Treyarch, Stuart is working on the *Spider-Man* franchise. He is also an active member of the IGDA. Most notably, Stuart is the founder and chairperson for the IGDA Production Special Interest Group, which strives to demystify the production process, promote solutions for both internal and external production management, and increase the professional viability of the games industry via improved educational and organization strategies.

TOBI SAULNIER

Tobi Saulnier is CEO of 1st Playable Productions, an independent game studio located in Troy, NY, which specializes in creating fun games for entertainment and learning. Previously, in her five years as Vice President of Product Development for Vicarious Visions, Tobi was responsible for the delivery of more than 60 game titles ranging from *Blues Clues GBC* to *Doom III Xbox*, with teams ranging from four people to more than sixty and project schedules from two months to two years. She also served as producer and contributed to the design on a number of these titles, with a particular interest in games for nontraditional demographics. Before joining the game industry, Tobi managed R&D in embedded and distributed systems at GE R&D. Tobi holds a Ph.D., M.S., and B.S. in electrical engineering from Rensselaer Polytechnic Institute.

CORAY SEIFERT

Coray Seifert is an associate producer, designer, and writer at Large Animal Games, an independent game development studio in New York City. Coray has developed games as a level designer, voiceover director, and writer for companies like Blade Edge Software, Stottler Henke Associates, and the U.S. Department of Defense. He works with the local game development community as a coordinator for the International Game Developers Association's New Jersey chapter and as the industry representative for the New Jersey Game Developers' Initiative. He contributes to the international game development community as a member of the IGDA's Writing and Production Special Interest Groups and as a guest lecturer at Gameversity. Coray also teaches game design at the New Jersey Institute of Technology, is a guest lecturer at the Parsons School of Design and the New York School of Visual Arts, and has appeared as a panelist, lecturer, or host at numerous IGDA and game industry events.

TOM SLOPER

Tom Sloper has been in the game business since 1979. He's produced, designed, or otherwise contributed to the completion of 120 products, winning six awards. His games have been on a wide variety of video game and computer platforms, from the Atari 2600 on up to the Nintendo DS, not to mention games for watches and calculators and the classic Vectrex system. Tom has worked for Sega Enterprises (game designer), Atari Corporation (director of product development), and Activision (senior producer, executive producer, and creative director). Tom has produced games with developers all over the world and is an international mah-jongg player.

Doing business as Sloperama Productions, Tom is currently consulting, writing, and speaking on game topics.

WADE TINNEY

Wade co-founded Large Animal Games (*www.largeanimal.com*) with partner Josh Welber in 2001. Since then, Large Animal has developed more than 45 games for a variety of platforms, including the Web, mobile devices, and PCs. They've created Web-based promotional games for clients such as LEGO, MTV, Cartoon Network, and Mattel, and their original downloadable game titles are distributed through the leading casual game portals. Large Animal's puzzle game *AlphaQUEUE* was a finalist in the 2004 Independent Games Festival (IGF), and *RocketBowl* was a 2005 IGF Award winner. Wade is an active member of the International Game Developers Association, a regular contributor to their annual Web and Downloadable Games Whitepaper, and the founding editor of the IGDA *Online Games Quarterly*. He also teaches game design at Parsons School of Design and New York University.

PATRICIA VANCE

Patricia Vance was appointed president of the Entertainment Software Rating Board (ESRB) in November 2002. As president, she is responsible for overseeing and enforcing the computer and video game industry's self-regulatory practices. This includes ensuring that video game consumers have effective tools with which to make educated purchase decisions.

Before joining the ESRB, Patricia established herself as a true interactive media veteran and industry leader. She spent 18 years at Disney/ABC, with responsibility for leveraging ABC properties in the development and management of a broad range of new media and market initiatives. These initiatives included the Internet (ABC.com, ABCNEWS.com, Oscar.com, Oprah.com), CD-ROM publishing (Creative Wonders, ABC Interactive), educational film and video distribution (including ABC News Interactive), direct response videocassette marketing, in-flight entertainment, home video, and cable television.

Prior to ABC, Patricia was responsible for planning movie acquisitions for The Movie Channel. She has also held senior management positions with *The Princeton Review* as Executive Vice President & General Manager of Admissions Services and before that as President and CEO of HalfthePlanet.com, an online resource network for people with disabilities.

Patricia holds a B.A. in International Relations/Russian from Washington University in St. Louis.

WIL WHEATON

Wil Wheaton is an actor who is well-known for his roles as Gordie in *Stand By Me* and as Wesley Crusher on *Star Trek: The Next Generation.* He is also an accomplished voiceover actor whose work has appeared in *Grand Theft Auto: San Andreas, Tom Clancy's Ghost Recon 2, Everquest,* and *Tom Clancy's Rainbow Six Lockdown.*

Index